PELICAN BOOKS

A CONCISE HISTORY OF AUSTRALIA

ROBERT LACOUR-GAYET was born in Paris into a family of teachers and scholars. His father was the well-known biographer of Talleyrand. After advanced studies in history and law, he entered the French Ministry of Finances, where he became Financial Attaché to the French Embassy in Washington and then Director of Economic Studies at the Bank of France. Later he became a professor and a writer. For several years he was Head of the History Department of St John's University, New York, and a lecturer at New York University and the Fletcher School of Law and Diplomacy.

His writing has been prolific, and several of his books have been awarded prizes by the French Academy. His *Concise History of Australia* was preceded by a *History of Canada* and a *History of South Africa*. The first volume of a *History of the United States* was published in 1976.

Robert Lacour-Gayet is married and lives in Paris.

JAMES GRIEVE is Senior Lecturer in the Department of Romance Languages at the Australian National University in Canberra.

Robert Lacour-Gayet

A Concise
History of Australia

Translated by James Grieve

Penguin Books

Penguin Books Ltd,
Harmondsworth, Middlesex, England
Penguin Books Australia Ltd,
Ringwood, Victoria, Australia
Penguin Books Inc.,
7110 Ambassador Road, Baltimore, Maryland 21207, U.S.A.
Penguin Books Canada Ltd,
41 Steelcase Road West, Markham, Ontario, Canada
Penguin Books (N.Z.) Ltd,
182–190 Wairau Road, Auckland 10, New Zealand

First published by Penguin Books 1976
Copyright © Robert Lacour-Gayet, 1973
This translation copyright © Penguin Books, 1976
Foreword copyright © Geoffrey Blainey, 1976

Made and printed in Australia at
The Dominion Press, Blackburn, Victoria
Set in Monophoto Ehrhardt

The cover shows a hand-coloured aquatint by Major
James Taylor, d.1829, 'Sidney et Port Jackson'
from the Rex Nan Kivell collection in the National
Library of Australia

CIP

National Library of Australia
Cataloguing in Publication data

Lacour-Gayet, Robert.
(Histoire de l'Australie. English).
A concise history of Australia.

(Pelican books).
Index.
Bibliography.
ISBN 0 14 021995 1.

1. Australia – History. I. Grieve, James, tr.
II. Title. III. Title : Histoire de l'Australie.
English. (Series).

Australian history is full of surprises
and adventures, and incongruities, and
contradictions, and incredibilities,
but they are all true, they all happened.

MARK TWAIN

Contents

Foreword

A French scientist once said that Australia was so unusual that it resembled the fragment of another planet which had landed here by chance. Now, in this new history, another Frenchman shows some of the same sense of wonder.

Robert Lacour-Gayet, in investigating our history, has culled observations so enlightening and simple that one wonders why they had not been made before. He has the insight of the outsider. Perhaps because he spent a comparatively short time in Australia, and perhaps because he did not allow himself to be buried in the warehouse of recent research, he has retained a freshness and a sense of perspective.

His is a comprehensive history of Australia. Unlike many of us Robert Lacour-Gayet does not date the history of Australia from the raising of the English flag ; the first part of his book describes the nomadic ways and culture of the original Australians. Nor does he read back into the colonial history of this land a political and economic unity which belongs more to the twentieth century. He sees the Australian colonies in the last century as six competitors which stood not shoulder to shoulder but elbow to elbow. 'Metternich', writes Lacour-Gayet, 'was fond of saying that Italy was nothing but a geographical expression'; and this saying would 'have fitted Australia much better than Italy in the middle of the nineteenth century.' The book continues with an examination of Australia until the ascension of the Whitlam government in the early 1970s. Indeed the pages on post-war history are amongst the most arresting in the book.

A Frenchman usually has disadvantages in studying the history of Australia. Recent works on Australian history are not found with ease in London, let alone in Paris; and in places this book reveals ignorance of important sources which have long been available. On the other hand a Frenchman has advantages in writing the history of a land which is usually interpreted more through the traditions and assumptions of the English-speaking world. French bias is a useful antidote to Australian or English bias. Moreover, as this book makes clear, France has had a long and varied influence on Australia. An expanse of the south-west Pacific and part of the southern coast of Australia were explored by French navigators. We forget that at one time French map-makers had justification for inscribing the name 'Napoleon's Land' on that long strip of coast from Wilson's Promontory to the arch of the Great Australian Bight ; and we forget that the coast was peppered with the names of Frenchmen before the English maps took over. It was touch and go whether France would create bases on strategic parts of the coast of Australia early in the nineteenth century. And when France annexed New Caledonia in 1853 and eventually sent convicts there, the French escapees influenced the sprouting Australian nationalism.

An obvious advantage of a French interpretation of Australian history is the angle from which the author can view the fluctuating relations between Australia and England. The relations between motherland and overseas empire resemble a long rope that safeguards and strangles. To examine that rope is not easy ; but Lacour-Gayet teases, tugs, and measures it with skill. Occasionally he expresses strong views on Britain's fickleness. Thus when R.G. Menzies went as prime minister to London in 1940 to seek help for Australia's frail defences he received, we are told, the ' sort of lavish, patronizing welcome that the British are so good at ' ; Menzies came home, empty handed. The author also observes that Australia, in proportion to her population, made much heavier sacrifices of fighting men than did Britain in the First World War.

Every decade or so there appears a history of Australia which quietly opens the eyes of readers, even if they disagree. This concise history is likely to have a similar impact on the curiosity of readers as did C. Hartley Grattan's *Introducing Australia* in the 1940s or of Manning Clark's *Short History of Australia* in the 1960s, or of other books which shine a torch on events which previously were seen dimly or in a different light.

GEOFFREY BLAINEY
Melbourne, 1976

Preface

This book goes back twelve years, to the time when the Paris publishing house of Fayard suggested I undertake a 'History of Canada'. It turned out that this was to be only the first of a series on three great member nations of the British Empire. The book on Canada was followed by one on South Africa, and eventually by this one on Australia.

I must admit that to begin with I knew next to nothing about my new subject. But it very soon came to fascinate me. I had to delve into prehistory, so as to do some sort of justice to the extraordinary race of men who were the original inhabitants of the Australian continent. And then I found myself immersed in the legends that the centuries had built round the great *terra incognita*. 'Unknown' was the word that used to be applied to the Great Southland, and 'unique' should be another. The explorers and conquerors were taken aback by the Aborigines, and the flora and fauna. I was scarcely into the historical period when I realized that this latest subject was quite unlike the other two. Great Britain had taken Canada from France, and South Africa from Holland. But in the case of Australia, nobody had governed the country before the British took possession. This meant that the links between the home country and the Australian colonies were always closer than those with the other colonies.

The British in Australia were undisputed masters of a land the size of the U.S.A. in which the only obstacles were those made by nature. The Aboriginal resistance could hardly be compared with that of the Red Indians, let alone with the Zulus. There had been no blood-baths to hold up the progress of colonization. There had been no revolution either, Australia being, in the apt words of one historian, 'the quiet continent'. Quiet as it no doubt was, this did not mean it was easy to colonize. With its deserts and lack of water and the rigours of its climate, much energy and ingenuity were needed to tame it.

The very origins of Australia make its rise all the more amazing. When one remembers that less than two hundred years have elapsed since that first handful of convicts landed at Botany Bay, one cannot help admiring the sheer tenacity that in such a short time has given Australia the place she occupies in the world today and the great future she is bound to have.

I see this book as a token of the gratitude I feel towards the many friends I made in Australia. I wish I could tell each of them individually that I have a pleasant memory of their hospitality and courtesy, and that their help and counsel were invaluable to me. I am glad to dedicate my book to Australia's historians and librarians, without whose assistance it simply could not have been written.

Mr A.P. Renouf, who was then Australian Ambassador in Paris, had been interested to learn of the plan for the first detailed history of his country in the French language. At his suggestion, the Australian government invited me to spend two months in the country, for which I am exceedingly grateful. I am also indebted to the Australian Department of Foreign Affairs, which organized my trip. Last, but not least, I am happy to express my thanks to the Banque Nationale de Paris, which by enabling me to carry out the project gave yet another proof of its continuing interest in Australia.

ROBERT LACOUR-GAYET
Paris, 1975

Prologue

Australia is a vast country, roughly equal in area to the U.S.A., stretching 3,800 kilometres from east to west and 3,200 kilometres from north to south. It is a harsh country, more than a third of its area being desert. It is a weird country, with flora and fauna the like of which are found nowhere else on the planet.

There is something mind-boggling in the calculations of geologists. The continent of Australia was probably formed, they tell us, in three stages. The north-eastern shelf is one of the oldest parts of the world, dating from 1,600 million years ago. The inland plains are no older than the Secondary era. The third stage in the making of the continent probably took place towards the end of the Tertiary, when the eastern plateau was lifted into mountainous folds, and subsidences gave the face of the country its definitive features and individuality. Throughout this whole development the sea must have covered most of the continent, except for the most ancient part, and uncovered it again, several times. If one looks back to a time when figures lose all meaning, Tasmania and New Guinea were part of the continental mainland. Even today the straits that separate these islands from the mainland are quite shallow, Torres Strait being only some fifteen metres deep and Bass Strait probably fifty metres at its deepest point. It is believed that in prehistoric times New Zealand must also have belonged to the great southern continent which for centuries was to hold such fascination for Europeans.

Some of this is of necessity hypothetical. But what the geographers can tell us is undeniable. They find Australia, compared with Europe, to have a rough-hewn, massive quality, like a large untrimmed block. The continent, although indented, has not been sculpted. Deep indentations are indeed rare along Australia's

18,000 kilometres of coastline, apart from the Gulf of Carpentaria in the north which reaches 700 kilometres inland, and the two southern gulfs near Adelaide, St Vincent and Spencer. Elsewhere the coast, usually fringed with islands, curves in long, broad sweeps separated by spacious bays, the most notable of which is Sydney Harbour. There is nothing like Australia's east coast anywhere else in the world. The Great Barrier Reef, stretching along the coast for a distance of 2,000 kilometres, which was once the terror of sailors, is now the joy of zoologists. The Reef is actually composed of a sequence of different smaller reefs, some of them contiguous and some separated from each other, forming a continuous rampart against the open ocean swell which is for ever breaking over them. Some parts of the Barrier Reef must have emerged 4,000 years ago. All the reefs are made of coral and they are the habitat of molluscs, shellfish and turtles. Weird and brightly coloured fish swim about by the million. At certain times of the year, hundreds of thousands of seabirds can be seen flying in from their winter quarters somewhere out in the Pacific to roost on the atolls above this underwater paradise.

Australia's average altitude, at a little over 200 metres, is well below the averages of the other continents.* There are three clear zones on the surface of the land. The first of these is a mountainous region, running down the east side of the continent and fringed by the coastal plains which are at times very narrow. This is the Great Dividing Range, stretching from Cape York in the north to Wilson's Promontory in the south. Some of the highest peaks in the range are in the Blue Mountains, west of Sydney, and the Australian Alps, east of Melbourne. The highest peak, at 2,230 metres, is Mount Kosciusko, which is surrounded by lesser peaks, all of them covered by snow for part of the year. The range continues southward into Tasmania, which is a very mountainous region, adding support to the theory that Bass Strait used to be a land link between the island and the mainland.

The second zone, to the west of these ranges, is composed of vast plains stretching westward for more than 1,000 kilometres. They turned out to be ideal for stock raising and agriculture and some parts of them even moved their discoverers to flights of

---

* Europe, 350 metres ; America, 650 metres ; Africa, 660 metres ; Asia, 1,010 metres.

lyricism (see page 131). These promising horizons are bounded, again to the west, by the third zone. This is the desert. Part of it is called Gibson's Desert, part of it the Great Victoria Desert, part of it the Great Sandy Desert, but whatever its name it is the dead heart of the continent. One geographer, in that decorative prose that used to be one of the charms of his discipline, says:

The whole western part of Australia looks as though it has reached the stage of senility, or even perhaps decrepitude. It has been worn down, levelled and buried under the debris from its own slow disintegration . . . The heart of the country has long since stopped living. Like the astraeas* one comes across on the shores of her warm tropical seas, which are pieces of coral covered in living jelly, Australia has a heart of stone surrounded by intensely alive outer parts.

To put it more prosaically, this zone is composed of alternating sandstone and sand dunes, each as dispiriting as the other. In some places sandstone pillars are found by the hundred. The most famous of these is Chambers' Pillar,† south of Alice Springs, which is nearly forty metres high and seven metres across. It rises from a hill of sedimentary rocks, which is all that remains of a mountain that used to stand there. The reddish summit of the pillar gives off odd glints from the sub-tropical sun. At other places the dunes run on for 600 kilometres, in parallel rows, perfectly regular in shape, brick-red in colour, devoid of grass, stretching as far as the eye can see under the dazzling glare.

The Great Western Plateau is the geographers' name for this 2,000-kilometre stretch of barren country, bisected by the Tropic of Capricorn, which seems to protect the continent from western invaders. It rises to 1,000 metres in the north, declining gradually farther south. It is separated from the sea by coastal strips of varying widths. To the south lies the Nullarbor Plain, crossed in a straight line by the transcontinental railway which runs for 450 kilometres without a single bend. On the Nullarbor there is no vegetation, only granite and shale, covered by a chalky deposit left by the sea at its last invasion. To the west, abutting the Indian

---

* A type of stony polyp with a starry surface.

† The Aborigines call it Idracourza or Etikaura. It was discovered in 1860 by John McDouall Stuart (see page 133), who called it after one of the subscribers to his expedition.

Ocean, are three artesian basins: one round Perth; another, called the North-West Basin, stretching beyond Carnarvon; and the third, called the Desert Basin, stretching much farther inland, behind Broome.

It has been said that Australia's climate is written on the face of the land. There are no high mountains to delay passing cloud, and hardly any forests to retain moisture in the soil. The river system is quite unlike those of the other continents. Only one large river, the Murray, reaches the sea. Rising in the Australian Alps and reinforced by the waters of the Murrumbidgee, the Lachlan and the Darling, it boasts a basin of more than a million square kilometres, which is greater than the Danube basin or the Saint Lawrence basin. But the reality is much less impressive – many other rivers peter out before being able to join up with the Murray; and the Murray itself flows sluggishly over very shallow slopes and through countless meanders. Its average rate of flow, about 350 cubic metres per second, is in fact less than that of a river like the Seine.

Nevertheless, the Murray is a giant compared with all other Australian rivers. The eastward-running rivers flow rapidly off the mountains, the impermeability of the rocks giving them a relatively abundant yield. But because of the narrowness of the coastal strip they soon disappear in the sea. Along the southern coast there is a stretch of 1,500 kilometres without one river mouth on it. The northern rivers are hardly worthy of the name; with their semi-stagnant waters, they are more like strings of drying-out marshes. But if a storm blows up, they can suddenly become fearsome torrents filling their whole valley, after which they very soon disappear again without trace. Cooper's Creek is perhaps the epitome of these incredible streams. It rises in south-west Queensland and runs (sometimes) into the north-east corner of South Australia, covering a distance of more than 2,000 kilometres. It eventually disappears below sea level into Lake Eyre. This, the largest lake in the whole continent, is usually hard mud covered by a layer of salt stretching over an area of almost 8,000 square kilometres.

Lake Eyre, which to the Aborigines was a sacred place, is not the only lake. In fact, Australia's lack of rivers is to some extent compensated for by the number of lakes. Some of them are veritable inland seas, stretching as far as the eye can see, without islands or visible shores; others are slimy places, shimmering with mirages, or full of clay and covered with salt. In some places, for example in the western parts of Victoria, they have formed in the deep craters of extinct volcanoes.

This extraordinary hydrography is explained by the extreme disparities in rainfall figures. Climatologically, the continent spans two broad zones, the tropical zone, north of the Tropic of Capricorn, and the sub-tropical or temperate zone to the south. In general the country has a more moderate climate than the corresponding regions in the northern hemisphere, as can be corroborated by any European who has seen certain dazzling days in Sydney or Melbourne. The summers are hot, and especially humid in Victoria, but the winters are reminiscent of the French Riviera at its best. Inland, the extremes and the contrasts are appalling. The all-time highest temperature of 53°C was recorded in north west Queensland in January 1889. In the deserts, the temperature can range between $-9°C$ and $50°C$. These extremes of temperature are matched by the unpredictability of the barometer. On the east coast, rainfall is abundant at all times, with the maximum in summer and autumn. In the north, which lies within the tropical rain zone, falls of twelve centimetres in one day have been recorded. The lowest rainfalls are recorded in the centre and the west. For instance, round Lake Eyre a reading of two centimetres per year is an event. It frequently happens that several months pass without any rain at all, and when there does happen to be a shower, the water is soaked up so quickly that its effects are more or less negligible.

Wind patterns are somewhat more reliable. From May to October the south-east trade winds blow on to the north of the continent, while the southern part is under the influence of the westerlies. From November to April the westerlies move southwards, blowing through Bass Strait, and the south-east trade winds cover the continent, except for the north-western part where cyclones become frequent. In the south and east, and particularly in the Sydney area, one gets quite awesome wind storms when the sky turns yellow and the air becomes stifling and oppressive. Nature seems to be covered by a veil and animals become uneasy. Then suddenly the storm breaks, and the air is thick with a very fine dust the colour of bricks, which is why these dry storms are called 'brickfielders'. Then when the wind has shifted from the north to the south, one sees trees leaning away from it, the sky fills up with dark cloud and the southerly buster 'comes with a rush of cold air and a splatter of rain'. *

As a result of the earliest examinations of the continent's flora, botanists used to believe that the great majority of Australian plants were unique to that part of the world. The most recent conclusions are that Australian vegetation derives from the same origins as other plants, but that it has taken on its specific character under the influence of prolonged isolation.

There is no lack of variety. Species number more than 12,000, of which the eucalypts and the wattles are the most widespread. There are at least 500 different species of eucalypts, ranging in size from very small to very large, some as high as 100 metres in Victoria and Tasmania. When the wind blows, the strips of bark hanging from the trunk rub and rustle against each other making odd plaintive noises. The bluish-green, almost yellowy tint is what predominates in the landscape, giving it a strange monotony. Wattles, with about 600 species, are also found in all parts of Australia; they even figure on the country's currency. Their bright yellow flowers are as gay as the gums are melancholy. Wattle trees are usually smallish, but can grow to heights of thirty metres in certain rainy parts of the south-east.

Forests cover only a tiny proportion of the land mass, less than four per cent. On the east and south-east coasts, and in Tasmania, the forest is mainly eucalypts. In the north there is tropical rain forest, where palm trees stick up out of dense jungle. Cypress, box and gum-trees also grow in some inland forests.

These forested areas are however very much the exception. The bush is the Australian equivalent of the South African veldt. It may be grassland with clumps of wattles or dwarf gums sprinkled all over it; or it may be covered in impassable thorny bushes. Whatever it looks like, it gives the same fascinating impression of immensity, loneliness and silence. It has been described as follows :

There is no broad middle-distance to give the scene solidity – no fields, no little hill with a wood or a church spire. The middle-distance often looks monotonous and featureless. The beauty of the bush lies more in the sense of space and distance combined with the strange and vivid detail –

* Pringle, J.D., *Australian Accent*, Chatto & Windus, 1958, p. 187.

the shapes of trees and shrubs, strongly lit by sun and etched by shade, bizarre, weird, but endlessly fascinating.*

Australia has frequently been described as a country of living fossils. As Dr P.H. Fischer puts it, 'There is one thing that no listing can do justice to, and that is the wonderful feeling one has when one is right among these odd venerable animals, the most appealing in the world.'

The monotremes, quite unique to the continent nowadays, appeared on the planet during the Secondary era or possibly even earlier; they died out elsewhere but survived in Australia. They lay eggs, suckle their young and have a duck-like bill. One of them, the platypus, has a fine pelt, webbed feet which make it a good swimmer, and claws (one of them poisonous) which enable it to burrow. The echidna is a great consumer of ants; it has a back bristling with quills like a porcupine.

In addition to these two monotremes, there are no fewer than 150 species of marsupials. The marsupials emerged during the middle Cretaceous period. Some are herbivorous, others carnivorous. This sort of animal does not develop fully in the womb like placental animals. They are born while still in a very embryonic state, their mouths open but eyes closed, and with only the front legs developed so that they can claw their way to the mother's pouch and cling on to a nipple. The largest of the marsupials is a kangaroo that stands more than three metres high; its young, born after thirty-eight to forty days, is about twenty-five millimetres long. The smallest marsupial looks something like a mouse and is forty-five millimetres long. But there are many other marsupials apart from these ones. There is the possum, with some similarity to the northern squirrel; the Tasmanian wolf, which really does look like a wolf and has the same carnivorous habits; the Tasmanian devil, now almost extinct, reputed to be very fond of chickens and described as truly diabolical in appearance with its grin, its black coat and its sinister grunting; the charming koala, the epitome of laziness and self-indulgence, a peaceable and harmless creature which, once it has been adopted by men, is said to cry like a child if left alone.

In comparison with these creatures, placental animals seem

* Pringle, *op. cit.*, p. 31.

mundane indeed. They are few in number, if one excludes animals that have been imported. There are rats, mice, bats, and dingoes, the wild dogs that seem to have arrived on the continent with the Aborigines. As for the birds, they are dramatic in their variety. One geographer who had a poetic turn of phrase says that 'when the myriads of birds settle, the ground seems to be suddenly strewn with flowers.' They come in all colours and there are 700 species of them, including any number of parrots, cockatoos with red or sulphur-coloured crests, pink and grey galahs, red, yellow and green rosellas and long-tailed parakeets with pink heads. No list of Australian birds would be complete without the kookaburra with its sudden gales of hearty, good-natured, very human-sounding laughter; or the lyrebird with its magnificent curved feathers which the male can spread like the frame of a lyre; or, last but by no means least, the bower-bird, a seducer who builds a little bower of twigs to attract a mate. In front of it he will set out blue ornaments and fresh flowers, and he even paints the sides of his love-nest with charcoal or the juice of plants. When his job is finished, he shows his satisfaction by bowing, strutting about, swelling his chest, dragging his wings and spreading his body feathers as he blows or whistles. As soon as a female has succumbed to these charms, he chases her away and starts trying to attract another one.

Black swans and emus are both typical of the Australian scene. To appreciate the fine plumage of the swans, one must see them at dusk, preferably flying. The emus are picturesque, running at full tilt on tremendously powerful legs, with their strong bodies, their rather scrawny necks and ridiculously undersized heads. The cassowary (which has given its plume to the military cadets at Saint-Cyr) is capable of sudden unprovoked attacks which can stun or even kill a man.

There are 300 species of lizards, some of which, the monitors (or goannas as they are called in Australia), can reach two or three metres in length and are related to creatures from the Cretaceous period. Snakes come in 140 different varieties, crocodiles in two, fish in 2,200 and molluscs in 10,000. The most abundant group is undoubtedly the insects – of the 750,000 different types of insect known, more than 40,000 of them have been found in Australia. The 2,000 species of Australian flies are particularly aggressive. But Nature, who does all things well, has given them 1,400 different kinds of spider to contend with.

About a century ago, Australian flora and fauna inspired the following comment from a contributor to the *Revue des Deux Mondes:*

When one considers the weird plants and animals that inhabited this southern continent before Europeans took possession of it, one could almost agree with Cuvier's apt comment that this country Australia is more like a fragment of some other planet which just dropped on to our globe by chance. *

* Blerzy, H., 'L'Australie', *Revue des Deux Mondes*, Paris, 15 December 1864.

Part One
From Myths to Reality

Chapter One

Terra australis incognita

The ' Southern Continent' as seen by the Ancients – Ptolemy's world-view – rival theories in the early Middle Ages – Marco Polo – general agreement on the existence of a terra australis incognita *– role of the Asians: Malays, Hindus, Arabs, Chinese – Portuguese voyages of discovery – Gonneville – were the Portuguese and French the first to sight Australia? – the great Spanish voyagers: Mendaña, Quirós, Torres – Australia undiscovered*

Men thrive on the fascination of mystery. For more than two thousand years, the possibility that there existed a southern land whose precise location, nature and size were all unknown quantities, gave rise to legend upon legend. Both the Greeks and the Romans attempted to rationalize scientifically the hazy promptings of their imagination. Aristotle was one of the first to prove that the Earth was round. But this then raised the question: if the planet really was spherical, surely somewhere, far beyond the regions already known, there would have to be other continents, whose weight would serve to keep the globe in equilibrium? For otherwise surely it would be in danger of tilting? Hence the notion of the Antipodes. No sooner had it been thought of than the visionaries took it up. There was the historian Theopompus who prided himself on being the successor of Thucydides. He jumbled facts and fantasies. Beyond the three islands which bounded the horizon of his contemporaries, Europia, Asia and Libia, beyond the Ocean Sea which girded them, so far away that it was impossible to measure the distance, he described a vast, fabulous continent. Everywhere there were 'green meadows and pasture plots ... big and mighty beasts ... [men who] in the same climate exceed the stature of us twice ... many and divers cities, [with] laws and ordinances clean contrary to ours.'*

* Quoted by Wood, G.A., *The Discovery of Australia* (revised by J.C. Beaglehole), Macmillan, Melbourne, 1969, p. 1.

13

Who told him so? 'The son of a nymph', who was supposed to have told the story to King Midas (although strangely he doesn't seem to have said anything about those gold mines).

Be that as it may, the notion of the Antipodes crops up throughout the Ancient World in a variety of forms. Philosophers reasoned its existence from theories of harmony, poets found their inspiration in it and geographers their research material. There were three questions above all which were thrashed out again and again: first, in that part of the world, was there more dry land or more water on the surface of the earth? Second, did human beings live there? Third, if so, would it be possible to reach them? There were as many contradictions as there were opinions on the matter. Let Ptolemy speak for them, Ptolemy whose conclusions more or less sum up the state of knowledge among the Ancients. At that time Asia, as far as it was known (or supposed), stretched beyond India as far as Malaya. As for the Indian Ocean, it was a lake. At about latitude 15° south of the Equator, this lake washed the shores of a *terra incognita*, which was still as attractive and still as mysterious as it had appeared a few centuries before. It was out of the question to try to go there. Pliny had said so and his word was law. Between the Mediterranean and the unknown land stretched a torrid zone which made any navigation quite impossible. But that was not the only obstacle. There were also fogs, shoals, treacherous currents and tides, not to mention the sea-serpents – all sorts of dangers to daunt the boldest mariners.

During the centuries which followed the fall of the Roman Empire, this hypothesis sparked off vehement polemics. It was seen by Christians as an attack on the truth of Scripture. How could one reconcile with the theory of the single origin of the human race a concept which took for granted a plurality of worlds? Saint Augustine pointed out that even if one accepted that the earth was spherical, it would not necessarily follow that the area opposite to Europe would be dry land. One Church Father, less temperate than the Bishop of Hippo, dismissed the Antipodes idea as 'witless old wives' tales'. The sorts of notions which were generally believed by Christians are well documented. For example: the earth was in the shape of a parallelogram, indented by gulfs and seas, twice as long from east to west as from north to south, and with Jerusalem at its centre. However, there was one point on which emerging Christianity saw eye to eye with the paganism of the later Roman

Empire: woe betide any rash mariner who trusted himself to that immense untrustworthy ocean which encircled the earth.

Marco Polo was not daunted by these terrors. Professor G.A. Wood says that when Marco Polo got back to Venice in 1295 after being away for twenty-four years,

for the first time, and at one magic stroke, there stood revealed all the kingdoms of the world, and all the glory thereof. From Constantinople to Pekin, from Pekin to Java, from Java to Colombo and to Aden, from Cairo to Madagascar, the whole eastern world was described in convincing detail. *

One of Marco Polo's tales in particular gave a new lease of life to the theory of the southern continent: 700 miles from Java, in the south-south-west direction, you came first to two islands, Sondur and Condur, but they offered nothing of interest, says the narrator. However, the next stages of his journey were different. For example, Locac, 'a good country and a rich', in which there was 'gold in incredible quantity'. Or the Island of Pentam, 500 miles farther south, with 'odoriferous trees'. And finally, 100 miles farther on, Java the Less, with 'a compass of 2,000 miles and more', and which offered 'great abundance of treasure'.† Marco Polo's contemporaries wondered: was this the unknown world of which the Ancients had spoken? And much later another question was to be asked: was it in fact what we nowadays call Australia? In fact it was neither. Modern experts have established that Locac was Cambodia and that Java the Less was Sumatra.

At all events, the legend had been revived. At the very moment when an explorer had made it believable again, thinkers and poets set about revitalizing it. There was Roger Bacon, who argued that this 'place beyond the Tropic of Capricorn' not only existed but was also 'of best habitation, seeing that it is the higher part of the world, and the more noble; and hence the opinion of some that Paradise is there.'‡ The master of Saint Thomas, Albert the Great, was no less positive: down there to the south, he believed, lay 'the fourth part of the Earth'. The descendants of Adam could quite well have reached there since, with all due respect to the Ancient

* Wood, G.A., *op. cit.*, p. 22.
† Quoted by Wood, G.A., *op. cit.*, pp. 27–8.
‡ ibid., p. 10.

World, it would not be absolutely impossible to go through the tropics. Even Dante, with his unmatched imagination, boosted this fascinating belief in the southern world. For Dante, it will be remembered, comes up from the Inferno on to the mount of Purgatory at the antipodes of Jerusalem. At the top he sees the earthly Paradise and in the sky 'four stars ne'er seen before save by the ken of our first parents'. Professor Beaglehole has accurately summed up the total effect of these discoveries and dreams :

The great southern continent was to most thinkers of the time more than mere knowledge founded on discovery and experience – it was a feeling, a tradition, a logical and now even a theological necessity, a compelling and inescapable mathematical certitude.*

All that remained to be done was to locate this world, for nobody now doubted its existence although nobody yet knew of it for certain. And it was then that the era of the epic voyages began.

The Asians, for their part, had not been by any means inactive, although the hallucination of the unknown southland had not haunted them to the same extent. The odd thing is (and no historian seems to have given an adequate explanation of this) that they never went east of a line from the Celebes to Timor. Perhaps they too had heard the sort of fables that the storytellers of the western world had made up, about 'the magnetic mountains', 'the clotted seas, with their thick, murky waters', the sea-serpents, especially the horrific 'odontotyrannus' which could easily have swallowed up an elephant in its gaping maw. The fact remains that from Timor to the northernmost tip of Arnhem Land is only about 800-odd kilometres, which is a stone's throw for the sort of mariner who had already managed to cross the Indian Ocean. If only some stout-hearted sailors had decided to sail farther eastward, Australia would have been discovered hundreds of years before any European made landfall there.

Be that as it may, experts speak of two waves of Malay migration into the general area, the first possibly in the fourth millennium, and the other in the third century B.C. These invaders were to be followed by many others.† They came into the region at a time which

* Beaglehole, J.C., *The Exploration of the Pacific*, A. & C. Black, 1934, p. 11.
† It is highly probable that on several occasions Malay fishermen had made a fleeting acquaintance with the continent. In 1802 (see page 126), Flinders dis-

is really very recent when compared with the period when the Aborigines had reached Australia (see Chapter 4). After the Malays came the Hindus, in the first century A.D. They too, like the Malays, went no farther than the East Indies archipelago. However, they dreamed up very similar legends to the ones which were beginning to take such a hold on the imagination of Europeans. From generation to generation they handed down, in ever more alluring detail, needless to say, descriptions of islands which were full of palaces built of solid gold, where dwelt indescribable beauties in the midst of perfect landscapes, and diamond stairways led down to pleasant lakes. However, the problem was, how could one get there? For any ship would be sucked down helplessly into inescapable whirlpools and would founder in the realm of Garuda, that bird in the form of a gryphon which flew only at night and carried off elephants, tigers and rhinoceroses in its talons.

The Arabs, a few centuries later, felt much the same fears at the thought of those unknown, perilous seas. They had taken over the Greek concept of the roundness of the earth and, like the geographers of antiquity, they too had deduced from it the existence of antipodes. However, also like them, they were convinced that there existed a torrid zone which made it quite impossible to go from the northern to the southern hemisphere. Sinbad the Sailor, the hero of the *One Thousand and One Nights,* by being tied to the foot of a fabulous bird, was able to fly from Madagascar to India. He was seen in Japan, the Moluccas, Java, but once again his odyssey came to its end in Timor.*

Did the Chinese, long before everybody else, ever manage to cross the seas which separate Indonesia from Australia? One of their historians has recently claimed that as long ago as the sixth century B.C. this route was already familiar to them. Not having been able to study their archives, we can only note the scepticism on this

---

* When Torres discovered the straits which bear his name in 1606 (see page 25), he is supposed to have met 'Moors', to the west of New Guinea. But the expression 'Moors' was a flexible one and the explorers of the time had only a very sketchy grasp of ethnology.

covered wreckage of Malay-type boats along the coat of the Gulf of Carpentaria. Their crewmen, if they ever managed to get back home, cannot have taken away a very happy memory of the landscape they had glimpsed, because they are supposed to have called it 'the land of the dead'

point of the noted Australian historian, G.A. Wood. However, as for the seas of the Malay Archipelago, there can be no doubt: Chinese navigators were often to be found in those waters in the fourteenth and early fifteenth centuries. We know that they could use the compass long before Europeans. However Sinologists have noted that after a palace revolution in the first half of the fifteenth century, a tendency to isolationism put a temporary end to the seafaring enterprises of the Chinese.

And it was at this juncture that Europeans, compelled by their passionate inquisitiveness, were to set about piecing together a solution to the mystery of the southern seas.

Let us give credit where it is due: the Portuguese were there first. It was Prince Henry the Navigator * who gave the first impulse to their breathtaking saga, which was to go on for more than a century. By 1445 they had reached Cape Verde. Forty-three years later Bartolomeu Diaz caught sight of a sharp promontory at the southern tip of Africa. He gave it the ominous name of the Cape of Storms. Soon, however, optimism took the place of this pessimism. It was that same cape (which from then on was to mean Good Hope) that Vasco da Gama sailed round twice, the first time in 1497, the second in 1502, on his way to India. But India itself was soon left behind. By 1511 Albuquerque was established in Malacca, a site of vital importance, because it was there that the routes from China, the East Indies and the Mediterranean intersected. By 1512 the Portuguese were familiar with the northern coastline of Java. About fifteen years later they were sailing in the waters north of New Guinea.

Did they find Australia ? The question has been debated at length. In the *Bulletin of the Paris Geographical Society* for 1878 one reads : 'Everything suggests that we owe the first reliable data on Australia to one of the many Portuguese navigators who, as early as 1512, were exploring the seas near India.' Fifteen years later Professor Rainaud, who devoted 500 pages to the southern continent, still shared that assumption. But, over the years, ideas have changed with the progress of research. The reader will be grateful to be spared the detail of the debates which this uncertainty gave rise to – in a period of sixty years, eight conflicting opinions were

* One of the sons of John I, King of Portugal from 1385 to 1433.

expressed. The most reliable conclusion is no doubt that which Professor Wood reached in 1922, and which A. Sharp confirmed ten years ago :

It may, I believe, be affirmed with confidence that we have no news of any voyage in the sixteenth century at all likely to have led to knowledge of any part of the Australian coast. And this fact seems to me good reason for entertaining a strong sceptical prejudice in respect to arguments that seek to prove that the Australian coast was well known.*

Not that this means the Portuguese played an insignificant part in the search for the elusive *terra australis incognita*. After their voyages round Africa, who could go on believing in that impassable torrid zone ? Had not their explorers made landfall on the tip of Senegal and found the land there to be so hospitable and pleasant that they called the cape they had just sailed round 'Green Cape' (*Verde*) ?

The fame of Jacques Cartier tends to obscure the fact that at this period the French did not restrict their exploration to North America. There was no shortage of brave men, although it must be said that their exploits have been somewhat romanticized by legend. For instance: Binot Paulmyer de Gonneville, who seems to have been a Norman knight of sorts, happened to be in Lisbon, and was dazzled by the wealth brought back from India by Vasco da Gama. He chartered a vessel, which he called *Hope*, took on two Portuguese guides and weighed anchor. It is known for certain that he rounded Cape Verde and, in September 1503, crossed the Equator. But what then ? A tempest forced him to put into some mysterious country, which could be any one of the half-dozen that have been suggested. Was it West Africa ? Possibly Maryland or Virginia ? Perhaps Madagascar ? New Zealand ? What about Australia ? Why not ? Certainly this was the hypothesis which was most eagerly believed by commentators in the eighteenth century. Whatever the truth of the matter, Gonneville had a fine tale to tell : the land was fertile and the natives friendly – they had received the French 'like angels from heaven'. The fortunate navigator had brought from his wonderland 'a local prince' who longed to learn the arts of war, in which, he had been told, the Europeans were without peers. But Venus was stronger than Mars. The prince was

* Wood, G.A., *op. cit.*, pp. 58–9. Cf. Sharp, A., *The Discovery of Australia*, Clarendon Press, 1963, Chapter 1.

baptized and fell for the charms of a lady relative of Gonneville who married him. A century and a half later, in 1663, a memoir was published bearing the signature of one 'J.P.D.C., an Indian priest' and arguing that a religious mission should be sent to 'the southern lands'. The author claimed to be the great-grandson of Gonneville and was consumed with the desire to take the true faith back to the land that his ancestor had discovered. But the great Louis XIV was not convinced, and this worthy aim was to remain unrealized for another seventy-five years, until the next great wave of colonialism. *

J. Dunmore is probably much nearer the mark in suspecting that Gonneville must have made land somewhere along the coast of South America. And that, after all, in the earliest days of the sixteenth century, was no mean feat.

The role played by the French and by the Portuguese begins to raise doubts and difficulties when one notes the comments of experts on a series of maps of 'Java la Grande', done between 1530 and 1570. The most famous of these maps, drawn by Jean Rotz, published in 1542 and dedicated first to Francois I, then to Henry VIII, shows a coastline that bears an uncanny resemblance to Australia's. One can even make out several names, including, in the north-east, 'dangerous coast', and in the south-east, 'coast of grasses'. Curiouser and curiouser ! One of Captain Cook's detractors was to use this map in an attempt to belittle the accomplishments of the brilliant explorer. According to him 'dangerous coast' must be the Great Barrier Reef and the 'coast of grasses' Botany Bay. Modern specialists are more suspicious. They believe that these maps with their French names are in fact just copies of Portuguese originals. In any case, they maintain that it is wishful thinking to recognize the outline of Australia in these crude sketches. The view of M. Marcel Chicoteau seems the most tenable : 'There are too many imponderables in the whole subject. If one looks at nothing but the historical documentation, one cannot avoid the conclusion that it makes little sense to see "Java la Grande" as Australia.'†

The conclusion seems inescapable: the Portuguese and the French may well have skirted parts of the Australian coast. But they never discovered the land.

In 1519, when Magellan sailed through the straits that now bear his

---

* See page 36. Needless to say, no one ever again set eyes on 'Gonneville's Land'.

† Chicoteau, M., *Australie Terre Légendaire*, Brisbane, 1965, p. 71.

name and led his ships all the way to the Philippines, did he have any
idea of the geographical revolution he had caused ? For the first
time it had been proved that the classic route via the Indian Ocean
was no longer the only way to seek the 'southern continent'. One
could look for it just as well by sailing from east to west. The
Spaniards, having taken over Mexico and then Peru, found that the
west coast of Central and South America was the perfect starting-
point. Adventurers by the dozen set off, from Acapulco in the
north and especially from Callao in the south. As hot-headed as they
come, these men were a cross between crusaders and conquistadors.
Some of them also had the poetic gift of leaving gripping accounts
of their deeds. Most of these expeditions set out during the reign of
Philip II. With his usual inability to match his ambitions to his
means, Philip saw the expeditions as a way of realizing his vague
grandiose schemes for a universal empire.

The first expedition left in 1567 : two ships, 150 men, and four
Franciscans, who were the spiritual brothers of those who were
soon to take part in the 'mystic epic' of French Canada. The two
leaders, Alvaro de Mendaña and Pedro Sarmiento, were chalk and
cheese. Mendaña has been described as 'a Spaniard of the nobler
type ; humane, self-controlled, courteous and tactful, yet firm, when
firmness was necessary'.* His second-in-command, Sarmiento,
was of a more dubious sort. He had not been sorry to shake the dust
of Peru off his feet – the native ladies found him irresistible, which
had been put down to magic and had got him into a tight corner with
the Inquisition. Eighty days out from Callao they sighted land. It
was, says Mendaña, 'so large and high, that we thought it must be a
continent'. Could it possibly be the *terra australis incognita*, they
wondered ?

Everybody received the news with great joy and gratitude for the Grace
that God had vouchsafed to us, through the intercession of the Virgin
of Good Fortune, the Glorious Mother of God, whom we all worshipped,
and whom we all praised, singing the 'Te Deum Laudamus'.

Then they disembarked. The Franciscans erected a cross. The place
was baptized and called Santa Isabel, after the saint on whose day
the expedition had set out from Callao. Mendaña took possession of
the country 'for Christ and for Spain'. The only trouble was, as

* Wood, G.A., *op. cit.*, p. 86.

they found out before long, that all they had discovered was the group of islands later to be called the Solomons. After a few weeks dissension was rife among these men, whose imaginations were as active as their enthusiasm was strong. Should they turn back or push on westwards ? They plumped for the first. Had they pushed on, Captain Cook might never have been heard of – from the Solomons to the eastern seaboard of Australia is not much more than 1,800 kilometres, and this, when compared with the Pacific that they had already crossed, is an insignificant distance. Although they had not in fact found the supposed southern continent, their expedition did reinforce the belief in it. The famous map of Mercator, published at this time, shows the outline of a land of immense proportions in the South Pacific. It was called the Magellanican continent, in honour of the man who, according to the courteous cartographer, had proved its existence.*

Twenty-six years were to pass before the Spaniards resolved to equip another such enterprise. For they had discovered that sea-serpents were not the only peril lurking in the ocean which had been rather hastily called 'pacific'. The dawn of greatness was at hand for Good Queen Bess's England. No fewer than three times, her sailors, who were more like buccaneers than missionaries, had spread havoc in the part of the world where the Spaniards thought they ruled the waves. John Hawkins, Thomas Cavendish, and especially Francis Drake had shown the world that, when they felt like it, the mariners of Her Britannic Majesty were quite good at helping themselves to other people's (ill-gotten) gains.

Perhaps the debacle of the Invincible Armada in 1588 had something to do with that long period of Spanish inactivity. Whatever the case may be, it was not until 1595 that Mendaña, now aged fifty-three, set out again for the South Seas. This time he took a more sizeable company with him : four ships, 287 crewmen and soldiers, ninety-eight 'civilians', many of whom were married. The idea was to set up a permanent colony, if not on Santa Isabel which had been discovered twenty-eight years before, then somewhere else. The flamboyant Sarmiento had been dropped. In his stead there was a man of a markedly different stamp : Quirós. Pedro Fernández de Quirós, by profession a pilot, by inclination a writer

---

* Tierra del Fuego, to the south of the Straits of Magellan, was supposed to be the northern tip of the 'continent'.

of sorts, was essentially an idealist, a man of great vision and keen faith. He has been seen as a second (but unsuccessful) Christopher Columbus, and a Don Quixote in the sunset of Spain. Their sailing date was 9 April; 103 days later, on 21 July, they sighted their first land. Mendaña believed he was back in 'his' Solomon Islands – in fact he was more than 5,000 kilometres off course, a typical example of the very hazy calculations of longitude in the vastness of the Pacific. Anyway, after he had realized his mistake, he named his new discovery the Marquesas Islands. Quirós, in optimistic vein, saw women who were even prettier than those in Lima (which was saying something), and a young boy 'who looked like an angel'. They lost no time in converting these beautiful beings : 'Mass was said and the natives were taught to make the sign of the cross and to say "Jesus, Mary", which they did with pleasure and with much mirth.' But the Spaniards had to be away again, to seek the elusive Solomons. Their next landfall was another disappointment – 'but we are not sorry to have found this land, for it resembles Andalusia.' They called it Santa Cruz. Meanwhile, continued frustration was sapping the crews' confidence. Quirós reminded them, to no avail, that 'we have come this far for the love of God and the sake of unsaved souls.' An evil spirit whispered to him to say no more. An unlucky stroke of fate was the death of Mendaña, whose wife then took command of the expedition and somehow managed to bring it to the security of Manila. * As for Quirós, he was more than ever convinced that somewhere down there lay the southern continent, with its hapless pagans impatiently awaiting the revelation of the Good Word.

One cannot help admiring the combination of great willpower and passionate conviction in one man. Quirós spent ten years badgering the temporal and spiritual authorities. The Viceroy of Peru was glad to see the back of him. He left for Rome, in abject poverty. There the Spanish Ambassador took an interest in him. He got navigators to check on his expertise and men of religion to test his piety. They pronounced themselves satisfied. Quiros was granted an audience with the Pope, who gave him a letter of recommendation for His Most Catholic Majesty, consecrated rosaries and a splinter of the True Cross ('this last only with some

---

* What a pity that historians have not dwelt a little on Señora Mendana. She must surely have been something of a colourful character.

difficulty', pointed out the recipient). Back in Madrid at last, he wrote endless reports and managed eventually to convince the government. Perhaps it was just that they, too, were relieved to be rid of him. In any case, after great trials and tribulations he got back to Lima on 10 March 1605. It took him another ten months to sway the doubters and make ready. He set sail at last on Saint Thomas' day, 21 December. He was in command of three vessels, with close on 300 men armed with muskets, arquebuses and several bombards. An important contingent was his six Franciscans and four friars of the Order of Saint John of God, to act as medical orderlies. The commander of one of his caravels was an officer who before long was to become famous : Admiral Luis Vaez de Torres.

On 10 February 1606, more than 300 kilometres east of Tahiti, the first land was sighted. A native chief came aboard, to be accorded 'three salutes with the flutes, the same as a Spanish Grandee'. Quirós made sure of the main things – the visitor was dressed in European costume and a medal was hung about his neck ; he was then taken back ashore and the cross was set up. They set off again and put in at various islands. None of these was Quirós' heart's desire ; and the Solomons of 1567 were as elusive as ever. Then on 1 May the lookout called 'Land ho !' And sure enough, land it was – land that stretched so far that it could not possibly be an island. So at last they had found the 'great continent' that men' had dreamed of and sought over the centuries. Saint Philip and Saint James had blessed the expedition, for God had chosen their day on which to grant Quirós this supreme joy !

The missionary-explorer went ashore and took possession. It was decided that the country must be named *Austrialia del Espíritu Santo*, in honour of the Austrian origins of the Spanish King, Philip III (who was of course a grandson of Charles V). A river ('as wide as the Guadalquivir at Seville') was called the Jordan ; the city which it was planned to build there would be called Jerusalem. They set up a government of nineteen 'ministers'.* 'In the name of the Most Holy Trinity, of the Roman Pontiff and of His Most Catholick Majesty', all members of the expedition were dubbed Knights of the Order of the Holy Ghost (one trusts they were mindful of the honour). The Franciscans heard their confessions. A church of greenery, consecrated to Our Lady of Loreto,

---

* A pity that they left no Hansard of their deliberations.

was built ; Quirós knelt in it on 14 May, Whit Sunday, to worship :
' To God alone, all honour and glory are due ! ' He kissed the earth :
' Oh, land that has been sought for such a long time, that so many
others might have found and that I have yearned for so much ! '
Mass was celebrated and Spanish dominion ceremonially enacted,
salutes being fired from the ships' guns.

But there was no gold, and the crews soon tired of spiritual joys.
As Professor Wood says : 'Don Quixote must acquiesce in the
tyranny of facts.'* The tribulations of the journey back home need
not detain us. By 9 October 1607, Quirós was back in Madrid, with
two *maravedís* in his pocket which he gave to a beggar. Once again,
if only they had persevered a little longer, the Spaniards might well
have discovered Australia. Espiritu Santo† is one of the New
Hebrides group ; from there to Sydney is just under 3,000 kilo
metres, as against 13,000 from Peru, which the expedition had left
twenty-two months earlier.

Torres was another one who came within a hair's breadth. He
and Quirós had split up, for reasons that historians do not seem to
have clarified. He had headed north-west, sailed along the southern
coastline of New Guinea and discovered the strait that bears his
name. A letter to the King, sent from Manila on 12 July 1607,
proves that he got as far as the Philippines. Little more is known of
him, for he seems to have died not long afterwards. Did he sight
Australia ? Some lines from his report read as though they might
be referring to the Great Barrier Reef and Cape York. But again,
one falls back on conjecture.

Quirós lived for another eight years, most of which he spent in
Madrid ; he went back to Peru and ended up in Panama, where he
died in 1615. He turned out more than fifty reports ; he drew more
than 200 maps. There is something intriguing in the workings of
his imagination. His good faith cannot be put in doubt, unless of
course he felt that any means would be justified by the end : to
ensure that other expeditions would be sent *ad majorem Dei gloriam*.
He had come to see his discovery as a new Eldorado. According to
him, it was

a quarter of the Earth's surface, with peaceable, virtuous natives whose
only lack is the true Christian faith ; the land is fertile, the climate healthy,

---

* Wood, G.A., *op. cit.*, p. 126.

† The island still bears the same name.

it never snows, there are no swamps, no crocodiles, no reptiles, caterpillars, ants or mosquitoes ; there is fruit, there are fishes, there is silk, ivory, marble, silver, pearls and gold . . .

It is a mouth-watering description. But since the death of Philip II, the Escorial had turned a deaf ear. In the first years of the seventeenth century the Spaniards had had enough of these fantastic dreams. They felt they could live the good life with their American possessions. Anyway, the growing might of France promised them enough problems without going to look for other ones somewhere else.

Others were to take the Spaniards' place. They would not be such great dreamers, but they would have the knack of getting things done. In that very year when Torres had been sailing through the Strait, other Europeans – and this time nobody questions it – set foot for the first time on the soil of Australia.

Chapter Two
The first discoveries

The Dutch first to reach the west coast of Australia – Van Diemen and Tasman – unfavourable impressions of the land and its people – Dampier, 'pirate and hydrographer' – his influence in France – Maupertuis, Buffon and de Brosses – Bougainville's circumnavigation – 'New Cythera' – Bougainville's near miss – more British expeditions: Byron, Carteret, Wallis – Callander's and Dalrymple's vulgarizations – the end of the beginning

The Dutch are an astonishing people. The tighter the corner they are in, the tougher their determination seems to be. In the sixteenth century, after a bitter struggle, they had finally managed to wrest their freedom from Philip II. That freedom, dearly bought as it was, turned out not to be an unmitigated blessing. Ever since the discovery of the East Indies, it was Dutch ships that had been in the habit of ferrying to ports throughout Europe the goods brought back by the Portuguese. This brokerage business supplied a great part of the wealth of the Low Countries. But it was a business that Philip II put a stop to in 1580. That was the year when His Most Catholic Majesty succeeded in annexing Portugal. To take revenge on his former Protestant subjects in Holland, he closed the port of Lisbon to them. Others might have despaired. But there was no shortage of men or means in Amsterdam, and their will to live was strong. Since the Dutch could no longer be the middlemen, there was nothing for it but to go in for exploration on their own account.

And so, their flag began to be seen along the route made famous by Vasco da Gama. The way they gradually ousted the Portuguese from their conquered territories and established a definitive settlement at the Cape in 1652 is well known. But what is not so well known is that, forty-seven years before then, the Dutch had made another voyage that attracted no notice at the time. On 18 November

1605 a small three-masted vessel, the *Duyfken*, left the north coast of Java under the command of one Willem Janssen. His mission was to reconnoitre the west and south coasts of New Guinea where, so he had been told, there was a good chance of finding substantial amounts of gold. The ship's log-book shows that, having sailed eastward through the waters of the Malay Archipelago, Janssen had at length reached a coastline that he took for part of New Guinea. Being unaware of the existence of the passage that Torres was to discover only two months later,* it never entered his head to go any farther east. So he chose to change to a southerly course, skirted the unknown shoreline for about 300 kilometres, had a brief encounter with some unprepossessing natives, found no sign of any precious metals, then turned back to the north-west to report on his mission. A glance at a map is sufficient to show that what the *Duyfken* had stumbled on all unawares was the northern tip of Australia. The coastline that the ship had followed was in fact the coast of the Gulf of Carpentaria, down the western edge of Cape York Peninsula.

This brief trip earned no fame for Janssen as a second Columbus. It was a close call. But it was only the first step. Not long afterwards the Dutch were to revolutionize the science of navigation. Until then they had always taken the traditional route eastward from Europe : down to the Cape, then up the coast of Africa as far as Mozambique, where they caught the trade winds which took them across the Indian Ocean towards the East Indies. In 1611, one of them discovered that by sailing eastward along the latitude of the Cape for four or five thousand miles, a skilful navigator could catch southerly winds which, if he used them properly, would blow him all the way up to the Malay Archipelago. The advantage of this route was that it was shorter ; the disadvantage was that there was no land at which to put in. For, of course, nobody yet knew that on this route there was a strong chance of sailing right into an undiscovered country. A. Sharp writes : 'The first ship to make contact with the west coast of Australia did so without design.'† This was the *Eendracht*, out of Amsterdam, commanded by Dirk Hartog.‡

---

* And Torres kept the news to himself. See page 25.

† Sharp, A., *The Discovery of Australia*, p. 32.

‡ A tin dish on which a sailor had scratched the date 25 October 1616 was found on the island now called Dirk Hartog.

She made landfall about 700 kilometres north-west of Perth. After that, it became the regular thing for ships bound for Batavia to reconnoitre in greater or lesser detail these mysterious shores. Certainly the Dutch East India Company took them quite seriously, judging by the instructions it issued to its ship-masters :

You are charged with discovering and taking the bearings of all capes, promontories, shoals, lands, islands, rocks, reefs, sandbanks, dangerous passages, winds, currents and everything to do with these, and with calculating their exact latitude and longitude and the lie of the land. You shall land at different spots to examine the country carefully and see if it is inhabited or not ; if there are any inhabitants, you shall observe their ways, their villages, the different parts of their kingdom [*sic*], their religion, politics and wars, what sorts of boats they have, their fisheries and industries [*sic*]; you shall pay particular attention to any gold, silver, tin, iron, lead, copper or precious stones, and such vegetables and animals as there may be . . .

One cannot help admiring the worthy civil servant who drafted that text ; it certainly does not sin by omission. Indeed everything had been thought of, except shipwreck. And shipwrecks, alas, were quite frequent, since the coast was inhospitable. One of these wrecks is famous. During the night of 4 June 1629 the *Batavia*, under a Captain Pelsaert, bound for Java, ran on to the reefs of a group of recently discovered islands. There were women and children on board. The master put them ashore with a party of crewmen, then, in the ship's boat, set out with the rest of the men for the mainland, about thirty kilometres away. He was looking for fresh water, but failed to find any. A month later he managed to reach Batavia. He set off again from there at once to rescue the survivors of the wreck, whom he found to be in perfect health, but in the power of a group of mutineers who had shared out the women among themselves and killed any of their shipmates who had refused to join them in rebellion. Virtue triumphed in the end ; and a bitter end it was – the leader of the mutiny and some of his henchmen had their right hands chopped off and were then hanged. The punishment of two other offenders was even less enviable : they were marooned on the island and left to whatever fate had in store for them.

These various incursions were all somewhat haphazard. Then, in 1636, Anthony Van Diemen was appointed Governor-General of the Dutch East Indies. The story goes that he had absconded from

Holland to avoid paying his debts. Thanks to his uncommon intellectual gifts, and in particular to a talent for writing that was unmatched among the other employees of the East India Company, his promotion to the top rungs was rapid. He had plenty of foresight and will power and had read Quirós. Though he was quite devoid of the latter's compulsive mysticism, he too had an ambition to leave the great southern continent to posterity, discovered and stamped with his name.

In the very first year of his tenure of office, an initial attempt at finding the continent ended in failure. The main aim of this particular expedition was to find out whether the Gulf of Carpentaria (which had been known, of course, for the past thirty years) might be in fact the opening of a sea-passage. At the very outset the commander of the expeditionary party was murdered by Aborigines. The second-in-command, a cautious man no doubt, turned back, taking with him only a sketchy but unfavourable impression of the unwelcoming Gulf coast.

Giving up comes hard to a Dutchman. Nothing daunted, Van Diemen decided to have another try, but with better men this time. He chose them well. His men were Frans Visscher, a pilot, who knew the eastern seas like the palm of his hand, and a captain by the name of Abel Tasman. Tasman, more interested in finding sources of wealth than in expanding his knowledge of geography, let alone anthropology, was the sort of man favoured by 'the Seventeen'.* He set out on his first voyage on 14 August 1642, with two ships (one with a crew of sixty, the other of fifty), rations for a year, plus an extra six months' rice.† As a further precaution, Tasman sailed first for Mauritius (a mere twenty-two days away; time being no object!) to take on more varied victuals. Then he set course, first, due south; next, due east; but there was no sign of any 'continent' to be seen. At last, on 24 November, land was sighted. They called it 'Anthony van Diemensland, in honour of our great Governor-General, our illustrious master'. (It was later renamed Tasmania.) They skirted the coastline for ten days until they found

---

* This was the name of the central executive body of the Dutch East India Company in Amsterdam.

† The rations included meat (twice a week) and bacon (once only), both salted, of course. It will be seen (p. 50, footnote) how Cook managed to overcome the deadly scourge of scurvy.

a place where they could land. There was something odd about the place. The soil was apparently of good quality ; in the distance, they heard a dull sound something like the beat of a gong ; there were trees, twenty to twenty-five metres tall, with notches cut into their trunks at intervals of one and a half metres (what a height the natives must be !) ; and, last but not least, tiger-like spoor on the ground. Even so, the forms had to be respected. One day the expedition's carpenter swam from the ship to the shore (the sea was running too high for even a ship's boat to make it), there to set up a pole on which he hoisted the Dutch flag, 'leaving for posterity and the inhabitants of this land (none of whom showed themselves, although we surmise some were not far away and were with watching eyes on our goings-on) the above things as a memorial.'*

They decided to leave on 4 December. Nine days later a massive rocky coast loomed up ahead. It was the west coast of the South Island of New Zealand. The country was a tremendous sight, but their welcome was unpleasant. Four men were killed by natives.† Tasman cut short the visit. For one thing, he was pretty sure that he had carried out part of his commission, taking this newly dis- covered land to be a section of the north coast of the great 'South- land'. For another, he hoped to add to his success by rediscovering the Solomons. However, once again they were nowhere to be seen. Instead he sighted a group of islands which he called the Friendly Islands,‡ perhaps by contrast with the previous landfall. Then, setting course due west, he sailed along the northern coast of New Guinea and got back to Batavia on 15 June 1643.

For a journey lasting ten months, his results were not insigni- ficant. But the authorities had been counting on better things. It was difficult to make the businessmen of Amsterdam, who were not given to doing things on the grand scale, see what was in it for them. Even so, Van Diemen managed to secure their approval for the financing of a second expedition ; once again it was Tasman who was appointed to lead it. To begin with his commission was of tremendous scope : since he claimed to have discovered the northern edge of the unknown continent, he was to check whether it might

* From Tasman's *Journal*, quoted by Sharp, A., *op. cit.*, p. 78.
† The Maoris, of course, came to be known for their military prowess.
‡ The Tonga archipelago, 1,000 kilometres east of Fiji.

be possible to find some route via that part of the world which would facilitate trade with Chile. Later, his expedition's aim was reduced to a smaller scale : all that had to be done was to find out for certain whether New Guinea was or was not an island. In 1644 Tasman did not match the feat of Torres thirty-eight years earlier. But he did managed to explore in very great detail the northern coastline of Australia. A historian says of him : 'His voyage as a whole was one of the most impressive in the exploration of Australia's coasts, involving a traverse of thousands of miles of unknown, dangerous, and complicated waters.'[*]

Perhaps it was the death of Van Diemen in 1645 which marked the beginning of the end. Perhaps Amsterdam had had enough of these expeditions which led to discoveries of solely geographical interest. Or they may have felt that they would only attract others to the region, who would compete with them and beat them at their own game. At all events, about the middle of the seventeenth century, the Dutch lost interest in the area. One more expedition did leave (from the Netherlands itself) to pick up survivors of a shipwreck. It was in 1696. The captain, Willem de Vlamingh, limited himself to spending a few weeks along the west coast of Australia. He was not sorry to leave what he called 'that wretched Southland'.

Admittedly, descriptions of 'New Holland', as it was called, were unflattering. A few examples, firstly, on the land itself :

... a dry and poor district, without any fruit trees or what men could derive benefit from ; it is low and uniform without hills or heights, wooded in various places with undergrowth and brush ; with little fresh water ; ... it extends mainly north-east and south-west with shallow clay- and sand bottoms.

Or this :

... no sign of running water, and moreover the high land was very bad, and the land was dry, without trees, leaves or grass, and everywhere high ant-hills, of earth thrown up, which from afar were not unlike men's huts. There were also such swarms of flies which got about our mouths, and in our eyes, so that we could not get away from them ;

Others noted 'the coast showing very uniform, without any fore-

* Sharp, A., *op. cit.*, p. 91.

land, or inlets* as other lands have, but seems a dry cursed soil without leaf or grass '; . . . a desolate region . . . without animals† or birds of note . . . '; 'In our view, it is the most arid and God-forsaken country that it would be possible to find anywhere on the face of the Earth . . . ' Need one go on ? As for the inhabitants, they were 'pitch black, thin of body and quite naked, with a woven basket or net on their head . . . They have absolutely no knowledge of gold, silver, tin, iron, lead, copper, and also of nutmegs, cloves and pepper.' The best that could be said of them was that they seemed 'not so hostile, bold and vicious in disposition as the blacks of the west part of Nova Guinea.'‡ They were 'as black as coal and naked from head to toe ; their noses are pierced with bones, being more like monsters than men . . . the poorest, most wretched creatures I have ever set eyes on.'§

There were still two questions unanswered. Was New Holland joined to New Guinea ? Was it split from north to south by a sea-passage ?

Once again the veil of mystery was to descend on the continent, this time for a full forty years. It was not until nearly the end of the century that the English were to solve a small part of this mystery. Up until this time, the Union Jack had been almost wholly absent from the scene. The only sign of it had been in 1621 when a British vessel, en route from Plymouth to Java, had been blown off course and had found itself on the west coast of Australia, roughly in the area that the Dutch were soon to reconnoitre. However, this chance discovery had led to nothing. Sixty-six years later it was another lucky chance that led to the presence of one William Dampier, on another ship out of Timor in search of New Holland. Dampier was a colourful character, equally remembered for his doings and writings. Born the son of a Somerset peasant, he was clearly not cut out to remain a tiller of the soil. He had a lust to travel, educate himself and see the world. It has been said of him

* Apparently these very earliest explorers did not set eyes on the sound which has contributed so much to the present expansion of Perth and Fremantle.

† However a kangaroo was first sighted in 1629.

‡ i.e. Cape York Peninsula.

§ These are extracts from Dutch captains' logbooks, quoted by Sharp, A., *op. cit.*, pp. 48, 49, 51, 52, 60–1, 62.

that he was 'dowered with an everlasting curiosity, an insatiable appetite for new experiences, the thorough instincts of the scientific student, and an admirable capacity for describing what he called "observables" in plain, accurate, vivid English.'* The portrait of him that hangs in the National Portrait Gallery in London bears the simple legend : 'William Dampier, pirate and hydrographer'.† Not an unfair description. He really was a pirate, as we shall see, and nobody disputes that he had a masterly grasp of marine topography. But two other epithets would not have been out of place : for one thing, he was a writer whose travel books were widely enjoyed by his contemporaries ; and for another, he was a naturalist whose descriptions of fauna and flora are classics of their kind.

In 1670, at the age of eighteen, he left his father's farm and went off to Newfoundland. There he found the inclement climate not to his taste. From then on he was to spend the greatest part of his life in the tropics, in Java and Sumatra as well as in Jamaica where he tried the way of life of the planter. It was here too that he discovered his true vocation – piracy. The island has been called 'the metropolis of the pirate-world' by Professor G.A. Wood, who also says : 'Every sensible Jamaican seaman was a pirate, and Dampier went with the others.'‡ We need not dwell here on his skirmishes with the Spanish in the Caribbean and along the Pacific coast. One wonders why he gave up privateering. It may have been a sudden urge to broaden his mind. 'When he should have been thinking about murder and loot, he was thinking about crocodiles and beetles.'§

Whatever the reason, he turns up in 1688 on the north-west coast of New Holland, having come across the Pacific. He stayed thereabouts for three months and eventually went back to England via Tonkin, Cambodia, Sumatra, Malacca and India, thus having gone right round the world. With him was his travel journal, full of descriptive detail and scientific observations. He published a part of this journal, which brought him immediate celebrity. And then in 1699 the Admiralty put this sometime pirate in command of one of Her Majesty's ships. A poor ship she was too : the *Roebuck*, of

* Wood, G.A., *The Discovery of Australia*, p. 214.

† Quoted by Wilkinson, C.A., *William Dampier*, John Lane The Bodley Head, 1929, p. 4.

‡ Wood, G.A., *op. cit.*, p. 215.

§ *ibid.*, p. 217.

34

296 tonnes ; Dampier said she was so old, ' the plank was so rotten it broke away like dirt,'* and she was manned by a crew which was not over-endowed with virtues. The captain had as his objective to circumnavigate New Holland. In fact he never managed to do this. But he did manage to explore in great detail the north-west coast of Australia ; he also supplied further proof that New Guinea was an island, by discovering new land to the east of it which, in the time-honoured manner, he dubbed New Britain. On the homeward voyage the worm-eaten *Roebuck* went down in mid-Atlantic, off Ascension Island.†

Dampier's impressions of Australia confirmed those of the Dutch : the countryside was arid and dusty ; there was no water, short of digging wells, nor were there any fruit-bearing trees ; the only food was turtles, sharks and possums. In fact, there was only one redeeming feature about the place – out in the bush, now and then one came across beautiful scented flowers, ' for the most part unlike any I had seen elsewhere '. As for the inhabitants, Dampier's accounts of them make previous descriptions read almost like eulogies :

Setting aside their human shape, they differ but little from brutes ...
Their eyelids are always half-closed, to keep the flies out of their eyes ;
... They have great bottle noses, pretty full lips, and wide mouths. The
two fore-teeth of their upper jaw are wanting in all of them ... They are
long visaged and of a very unpleasing aspect, having not one graceful
feature in their faces ... Their costume consisted of a piece of the rind
of a tree, and a handful of grass or bough ... They have no houses, but
live in the open air, without any covering ; the earth being their bed, and
the heaven their canopy ...

The arms they carried were wooden swords and a kind of spear.

---

* Wood, G.A., *op. cit.*, p. 232.

† The crew was saved but Dampier, on the complaint of one of his officers, was court-martialled. His judges pronounced that he was ' not a fit person to be employed as commander of any of Her Majesty's ships '. This did not deter merchants from putting him in command of two later expeditions to the Pacific. It was during the second of these, of course, that one of his officers picked up Alexander Selkirk from the island of Juan Fernandez, off the Chilean coast. Selkirk, the interesting character on whom Defoe was to base *Robinson Crusoe*, had had himself marooned there four and a half years earlier, after a quarrel with Dampier, and had lived in total isolation.

Dampier and his men tried to clothe some of them, but it seemed that this was not to their liking, for they took off at once the old breeches, the worn-out shirt and the equally ancient jacket that he had put on them. As well as which, he says, ' I did not perceive that they had any great liking to them at first, neither did they seem to admire anything that we had.' On another occasion, having come across a group of other Aborigines, he summed them up thus: ' they ... have the most unpleasant looks and the worst features of any people that ever I saw, though I have seen great variety of savages.' *

In France, the tales of Dampier's travels met with tremendous success. The first translation had appeared in 1698, just one year after the original English publication, and by 1712 there had been seven more editions. In fact, as Professor A. Rainaud has pointed out, *terra australis*, though still *incognita*, had gone on intriguing and whetting Frenchmen's appetite for new discoveries throughout the seventeenth century. In 1626 Richelieu had been presented with an anonymous memoir on the subject. Then, in 1656, a gentleman by the name of Flaucourt claimed that Gonneville (see pages 19–20) had established the Most Christian King's rights to that part of the world. Thirteen years later the Ministry of the Navy received two submissions on the same question. And in 1676 a work bearing the title *La Terra Australe* and deriving directly from Quiros gave a rhapsodic description of the mysterious continent. All of which means that there was already a public eager for the stories of adventures that Dampier had to tell. However, in the unhappy years that led up to the death of Louis XIV in 1715, and during the honeymoon period of the Louisiana venture under the Regency, it was impossible for anything practical to be done. It was not until 1730 that the French India Company lent a willing ear. Under the administration of Cardinal Fleury, one Bouvet de Lozier was commissioned to go and look for ' Gonneville's land '. Having sailed down the Atlantic to the fifty-fourth parallel, farther south than Tierra del Fuego in fact, all he could see through the fogs were penguins and icebergs. He did manage to discover an island – it bears his name to his day – and then sailed back home to France. Although he had not really brought an answer to the problem any nearer, Bouvet de Lozier was

---

* Dampier's impressions quoted by Wood, G.A., *op. cit.*, pp. 221–2, 228, 230.

sure in his own mind that he had skirted the southern continent.

Scientists and philosophers now brought their own lights to bear on the enigma. Buffon was the first. In the introduction to his *Natural History* he wrote : ' It seems likely that, by sailing due east from the Cape of Good Hope, it should be possible to locate some part of those lands, which constitute a veritable separate world.' Maupertuis was of the same opinion. Frederick II having appointed him Director of the Prussian Royal Academy in 1746, he took the opportunity of impressing his patron with his *Letter on the Progress of Science*. He explains to Frederick that ' in the southern hemi-sphere there is an unknown blank, extensive enough to contain a whole new part of the world which could be greater in area than any of the known parts.' Maupertuis was amazed ' that no ruler is curious enough to explore this immense and lonely fastness '. But Frederick the Great was more concerned with the fastness of Silesia. Voltaire, as one might have expected, was interested, and in his great *Essai sur les Moeurs* he advocated the discovery of what he calls ' that fifth of the surface of the earth '.

It was left to a talented amateur to bring the question really alive in France. This was Charles de Brosses, who at the time was first president of the provincial *Parlement* at Dijon. He had an inquiring mind ; it was this which prevented him from staying within the narrow confines of his legal training. He turned his keen interest to topics as diverse as contemporary Italy (which gave him the subject of his celebrated *Letters*), Rome under the Republic, the study of languages, even fetishism. His first published work, which came out in 1756 in two hefty quarto tomes, was called, significantly, *Historie des Navigations aux Terres Australes*. De Brosses took for granted the existence of no less than three unexplored southern continents : in the southern Atlantic there was ' Magellanica ', in the South Pacific ' Polynesia ' and, to the south of the Indian Ocean, 'Australasia '. Convinced that France was presented with a unique chance to win glory and great wealth by discovering and exploring these unknown lands, de Brosses urged Louis XV to ' turn his gaze entirely to his navies . . . , at a time like the present when a neigh-bouring power, caring not a whit for the interests of any other nation, has the manifest ambition of being sole ruler of the seas.' Histori-cally, it would be difficult to fault such advice, offered as it was right at the beginning of the Seven Years War.

Of course Louis XV was consumed by European rivalries and

was more interested in upsetting opposing alliances than in upsetting his order of priorities. And when that war was over, the 'neighbouring power' had indeed become 'sole ruler of the seas', a role it was to retain against all comers from then on. None the less, a few years later, between 1766 and 1769, for the first time the French standard circumnavigated the globe. Bougainville, who did it, was an appealing character. He had been first a secretary in the French Embassy in London, and then an aide-de-camp to Montcalm during the war, in Canada. The diplomatic service and the military life having afforded him little advancement, he heard the call of the sea. As soon as he had returned to France after the war, he had been commissioned by the King to found a colony in what were then called the Malouine Islands (nowadays the Falklands), which both the British and the French saw strategically as the key to the Pacific. He established his colony of exiles from Nova Scotia there. Their parents had already been evicted from their homeland by the British fifty-two years before ; they must soon have come to believe that the British were inescapable, for they were dispossessed of this new home by a Royal Navy expedition in 1765.

The French Admiralty was stung by this setback. It was known that there were British expeditions already on the seas, bound for the Pacific. The French naval authorities decided that the British had stolen enough marches on them, and sent orders to Bougainville to head for the East Indies via the South Seas. He set out in November 1766, in command of two frigates with poetic names, *La Boudeuse* and *L'Étoile*.* His impressions of Tahiti† are too well known for us to dwell on them. However, we must just glance at the inhabitants of this 'New Cythera' as seen by the expedition's botanic-cum-physician :

They are born under the fairest skies ; their rulers are more like fathers to them than like kings ; their only god is Love itself. Each day is the feast-day of this deity, the whole island is his temple, all the women are his idols and all the men his disciples. And such women, too ! As for their beauty, they are the rivals of the Circassians, the sisters of the Graces, and quite unveiled ! The tyranny of shame and modesty has no sway here ; the flimsiest gauze is no obstacle to any breeze or desire ... A severe censor may see their behaviour as rank immorality, outrageous

---

* 'Sulky' and 'Star' (*translator's note*).

† Discovered by Wallis. See page 41.

prostitution, the most brazen cynicism ; but is it not rather man's natural state, in his essential goodness, devoid of all prejudice, responding spontaneously and guiltlessly to the sweet promptings of an instinct which, because it has not yet degenerated to the level of Reason, is ever sound ? *

Bougainville had the good sense to stay only a fortnight in this earthly Paradise. Sailing westward, he landed first in Samoa ; then he discovered that Quirós' *Austrialia del Espíritu Santo* was in fact only a group of islands. He knew that if he stayed in those latitudes on a westerly course he was bound to come across New Holland. But only a week later he sighted, to the south-west, an unbroken sandy shoreline, from which he was separated by shallows and reefs ; and to the north-west an ominous line of tell-tale breakers. He writes : 'We could see the tops of rocks over which seas kept breaking with the utmost violence. In this discovery we saw a warning to us from God that we could not disregard.' As well as that, 'we were by now down to our last two months' bread ration and had dried vegetables left for no longer than forty days ... It was high time to put about and head northward.'

This impressive seascape was of course the Great Barrier Reef. If Bougainville had been so bold as to turn south instead of north at that point, he would most likely have landed on the east coast of Australia, two years before Cook. One wonders whether he was ever to regret his decision to go north. In any case, having got back to France in 1769 after a round trip of twenty-eight months, he urged the Versailles bureaucrats to equip other expeditions. He prefaced his narrative of the voyage with a dedicatory *Epistle to His Majesty* :

The Spaniards, Portuguese, English and Dutch may well have won the rights of first-comers in discovery and exploration. However, this does not preclude French navigators from justly claiming a share of glory in these inspiring but exacting enterprises ... Gonneville, a native of Dieppe, was the first to set foot on the southern lands.† After that, diverse causes, both internal and external, seemed to abate the nation's interest and activity in these matters.

* Shades of Rousseau ! One wonders whether Jean-Jacques ever heard of this letter (sent to the astronomer Lalande in 1769) ; if so, he might well have seen it as another sign of the spread of his ideas.
† The Gonneville legend, endorsed by de Brosses, died hard in France. After

Bougainville wrote these lines in 1772. No great knowledge of history is needed to appreciate that the 'internal and external causes' which he mentions were still as strong as ever.

The English too had read Dampier with intense curiosity. Interest in *terra australis incognita* reached such a pitch that speculators made disastrous losses by getting involved in the bizarre episode of the South Sea Bubble. In this aptly named affair, a company had persuaded thousands of trusting souls to hand over their funds – in 1718 the King himself, extraordinarily enough, had agreed to be patron of the company – and had assured its investors of fabulous profits from its trade monopoly in the South Seas. And sure enough the dividends did reach 100 per cent ; shares in the company, which stood at 128 points in January 1720, had reached 1,000 a mere seven months later. A glance at 'Law's system' tells what happened next – share prices fell more suddenly than they had risen, bringing down in the general collapse even the safest stocks, including those of the Bank of England itself. The whole thing, needless to say, led to financial ruin, suicides and scandals, with the Chancellor of the Exchequer even ending up behind bars.

It may well have been this prevailing interest in the Pacific region which caused two great writers to take that part of the world as the setting for their works. In 1719 Defoe published *Robinson Crusoe*, the origin of which we have touched on (see page 35, footnote); and five years later, drawing once again on Dampier, he wrote his *General History of the Pyrates*. In 1726 Swift produced *Gulliver's*

Bougainville, three further expeditions set out to find the elusive 'Gonneville's land'. In December 1769 the ships of Cook and Surville came close to meeting, north of New Zealand. Two years later Kerguelen discovered the island now called after him, and his co-commander, Saint-Allouarn, skirted part of the west coast of Australia. At that same time another Frenchman, Marion du Fresne, was the first white man since Tasman to set foot on Tasmania, where his memory is kept to this day. He was killed by Maoris in the North Island of New Zealand, of which his second-in-command, Crozet, took possession (or so he imagined), giving it the name of 'South France'. After his return to France, Crozet was to tell Rousseau of the misgivings he felt about the 'noble savages' who had murdered Marion du Fresne. Jean-Jacques could scarcely believe his ears : 'What ? Is it possible that the goodness of Nature's children should be compatible with a certain perversity ?'

Travels. The itinerary of Gulliver has been established. Lilliput was situated to the north-west of Tasmania, near Lake Torrens i.e. 400 kilometres north of Adelaide. Next, Gulliver sailed through what is now known as New South Wales. There he was captured and taken to Brobdingnag, the land of giants, which is more difficult to place with any precision, but which we may say was to the east of Japan, in which area it was still believed that another civilized country might exist. Similarly, Balinbarbi, the empire under the floating island of Laputa, was in the north Pacific, on about the forty-sixth parallel, stretching eastwards as far as the unexplored parts of California. Even for the generation after Swift's, none of this geography seemed in any way fanciful.

The involvement of Great Britain in European conflicts between 1740 and 1763 prevented her from giving the encouragement that any further exploration of the South Seas would have required. However, the ink on the Treaty of Paris was barely dry when a series of expeditions got under way. In 1764 John Byron (the grandfather of the poet) began a voyage through the Pacific, but after two years he had only managed to discover a handful of insignificant islands. He returned to England via Java. Soon afterwards two other expeditions circumnavigated the globe. Then, in 1766, it was Samuel Wallis' turn. He discovered Tahiti a short while before Bougainville got there, and annexed it for Great Britain under the name of 'King George III Island'.* Apart from this, Wallis' contributions to the advancement of geography were about as limited as Byron's. His comrade, Philip Carteret, was more successful. Crossing the Pacific farther to the south, he came upon Santa Cruz and the Solomons ; he did not realize what they were, no European having set eyes on them since Mendaña 200 years before (see page 21). He went on to circumnavigate Dampier's 'New Britain', established that a neighbouring piece of land was in fact an island, which he called 'New Ireland', and then, having called at the Philippines and in Indonesia, sailed back to his home port.

This new series of voyages to an ocean which was still full of mystery, in search of equally mysterious lands, also caught the fancy of writers. In 1766 and 1768 John Callander brought out a three-

---

* History does not say whether the first Englishmen in 'New Cythera' were as susceptible to its charms as the first Frenchmen under Bougainville.

volume bare-faced crib of de Brosses.* He was so certain of the existence of a vast continent in the South Pacific that he called his work *Terra Australis Cognita*. Needless to say, he denied the glory of having discovered this great land to the incompetent French ! *Vae victis !*

Vain are the repeated exhortations of the French writer,† addressed to a nation which is so far from being able to prosecute new discoveries that they have been stripped by the late war of the best foreign settlements they possessed ; and by the ruin of their marine seem totally disabled at present to attempt anything of moment in this way. Far other is the case of this happy island. United among ourselves, respected by foreigners, with our marine force entire, and (humanly speaking) invincible, aided by a set of Naval officers superior in every respect to those of the nations around us, with a Sovereign on the throne who is filled with the most ardent and laudable desire of seeing his native country great and flourishing. These, I say, are incitements that seem to render everything possible to Great Britain.' ‡

Such a hymn *ad majorem Britanniae gloriam* was bound to have a sequel. Not long after, an agent of the East India Company, one Alexander Dalrymple, published a *Collection of Voyages in the South Seas*, which on the one hand continued Callander's arguments and, on the other, revealed the author's strong desire to become the Columbus of the Pacific.

So it was that, in the late 1760s, the southern lands were a subject of keen interest in England. Nevertheless, when compared with the next part of the story, everything that had taken place up to that time was little more than a curtain-raiser.

---

* It even included the Gonneville hypothesis.
† De Brosses, of course.
‡ Quoted by Wood, G.A., *op. cit.*, p. 253.

Chapter Three

The voyage of the *Endeavour*

Cook's background – his character – the two aims of his mission – the
Endeavour *– Joseph Banks – Venus observed at Tahiti – Society
Islands discovered – New Zealand circumnavigated – towards the east
coast of New Holland – landing at Botany Bay –* Endeavour *aground
on the Great Barrier Reef – weeks of observation of the land and its
inhabitants – Cook's and Banks' opinions frequently differ – astonishing
flora and fauna – Cook takes possession of New South Wales – the
return to Britain via Batavia, the Cape and St Helena – Cook's second
voyage south destroys definitively the myth of the 'southern continent'
– Cook's third voyage – discovery of Hawaiian islands – his death at
the hands of natives – Britain uninterested in Australia*

On 5 May 1768 the Councillors of the Royal Society* interviewed
a naval officer, Lieutenant James Cook, aged thirty-nine. He was
no stranger to them. They had done him the honour, the previous
year, of publishing his study of an eclipse of the sun in their *Philosophical Transactions*, a journal with readers throughout Europe.
They were convinced that the author of this piece of work was 'a
good mathematician, and very expert in his business'.† They
decided to entrust him with a mission to which they attached great
importance. It was known that 1769 would be an ideal year for
observing the transit of Venus and working out from it, along the
lines suggested by Halley at the beginning of the century, a more
accurate measurement of the distance between the earth and the sun.
Scientists having established that this observation would be of no

---

* The Society had been founded in 1660 with the aim of advancing human
knowledge through experimentation. It was held in universal esteem and fostered
the arts as well as science and technology.

† Quoted by Wood, G.A., *The Discovery of Australia*, p. 271.

value unless it was carried out in the Pacific (or rather on Tahiti itself, not long since discovered – see page 41), the person to do the job properly would have to be both a man of science and a sailor.*

There can be no doubt about Cook's qualifications. He had been born into the family of a day-labourer but had not remained long on the land. At the age of eighteen he could not resist the urge to go to sea. During the summer he plied the Baltic in a merchantman ; during the winter he buried himself in scientific books. The outbreak of the Seven Years War gave him the opportunity to join the Royal Navy. His rise was rapid. By 1757 he was already in command of a vessel of sixty-four guns. He took part in the siege of Louisburg,† and was in the fleet under the command of Admiral Saunders which sailed up the St Lawrence river – in fact it was in this action that he proved himself as a hydrographic surveyor, for it was Cook who charted the shoals in the St Lawrence and thus enabled the fleet to get up as far as Quebec without mishap.‡ After the war he was put in command of a flagship. By that time, 1763, his reputation was so firmly established that he was given the task of charting in detail the coastline of Newfoundland and Labrador. When he published the results of this survey, specialists were so impressed that the Royal Society itself accepted him, four years later, as a contributor.

What can one say of this man, as he stood on the threshold of fame ? Most of the descriptions tally : a tall man, a good six feet and more, with a determined face, thinnish lips and sharp eyes which seemed to express stubbornness rather than gentleness. He was not an emotional man. Though married for seventeen years, he only lived for a total of six years with his wife, just long enough to have six children. He makes no mention of his family in his travel writings. But they were not meant as a personal diary and this does not mean he was devoid of passion. Far from it. But certainly he was

---

* Dalrymple also applied but was not selected, on the grounds that he did not belong to the Royal Navy.

† Louisburg, which had been captured in 1745, then given back to France by the Treaty of Aix-la-Chapelle, surrendered again in 1758.

‡ This was in fact a most valuable service to his country. A previous attempt, in 1711, to take the city by attacking up the river had come to grief on the shoals in the St Lawrence.

as indifferent to religion as he was to love.* There was only room for one divinity in his life, to which he made the offerings of his discoveries : Science. He was methodical and meticulous almost to a fault. Nor did he put up with weakness in others. He was a man of few words and his bearing was so commanding that few would have dared question his authority unless looking for trouble. And when anyone did, trouble was what he got ! It has been said of him : 'Cook's temper was Scotch – "good but short".'†

On one of Cook's infrequent stays in London the snobbish Boswell, as usual wanting to hob-nob with the famous, managed to meet him (with Mrs Cook as well, which was something of a rarity). He gives a vivid description of the man :

A plain, sensible man, with an uncommon attention to veracity. My metaphor was that he had a balance in his mind for truth as nice as scales for weighing a guinea .... He seemed to have no desire to make people stare ‡... It was curious to see Cook, a grave, steady man, and his wife, a decent plump Englishwoman, and think that he was preparing to sail round the world.§

The Royal Society's instructions were not the only ones that Cook carried, nor were his observations to be purely scientific. The Admiralty had given him sealed orders : on leaving Tahiti he was to sail due south, to about the fortieth parallel, and seek the undiscovered southern continent. In fact he should consider the discovery of this land his 'main object'. If he succeeded where all others had failed, and actually found land, he was instructed to 'take possession for His Majesty', but to be sure that it was 'with the consent of the natives' (not an insignificant irony). Should the *terra australis* remain *incognita*, however, he was to sail westward to 'the land discovered by Tasman and now called New Zealand'. It was to be left to Cook himself to decide whether to return to England via Cape Horn or the Cape of Good Hope. As Professor Wood has pointed out, Cook's brief made no mention of New Holland.

---

* He had no chaplain aboard *Endeavour*. At Tahiti he took on board a native 'priest', out of curiosity.

† Wood, G.A., *op. cit.*, p. 272.

‡ Which one could hardly have said about the diarist himself !

§ *Boswell : the Ominous Years 1774–1776* (ed. C. Ryskamp & F.A. Pottle), Heinemann, 1963, pp. 308–9.

The Navy Board gave close thought to the type of vessel best suited to such an expedition. They plumped for a ship of the type known to sailors at the time as a ' cat-built bark '.* She was of 375 tonnes, had round bluff bows which could take plenty of rough treatment, a wide deep waist tapering towards the stern, and a short keel enabling her to sail in shallow waters.† She was re-christened *Endeavour*, a name which speaks volumes for her purpose. Her crew was hand-picked and was largely made up of men under thirty. There was a cook who had lost his right arm. But, more importantly, there was on board one Joseph Banks, who was to achieve such fame‡ that we must give him some space here. Alan Moorehead gives the following description of Banks :

He was only twenty-five when the *Endeavour* sailed from England, and great wealth (he had £6000 a year from his country estates) had combined with good looks and a buoyant, affable nature to turn him into the very prototype of the *beau jeune homme* setting out on the grand tour from eighteenth century England. He had the easy, likeable manners of Eton and Oxford . . . §

However, he was not just a socialite. Ever since his childhood he had been keenly interested in botany and zoology ; later on in life, he was to go on scientific trips to all parts of England, and even as far as Newfoundland. He spent much time cataloguing and describing birds, fish and plants. As soon as he heard of the *Endeavour* expedition he could not resist the desire to go on it. As a member of the Royal Society he had Lord Sandwich (former, and future, First Lord of the Admiralty) pull a string for him, and had no trouble in being included in the ship's company. He must have caused a stir when he went aboard, with a retinue which included a Swedish botanist, Dr Solander (who had studied under Linnaeus),

* A corruption of the Norwegian word *kati* (meaning ' ship ').

† Details for those who like details : she was thirty-two metres long on her top deck, twenty-seven metres along the keel, and almost ten metres wide.

‡ In 1778 he became President of the Royal Society, a position he was to occupy until his death forty-two years later. As a friend of George III he wielded influence in government circles, being consulted on all sorts of matters, especially on things Australian, although he never returned to the southern continent. He was also elected an associate member of the *Institut de France*.

§ Moorehead, A., *The Fatal Impact*, Hamish Hamilton, 1966, p. 12.

two artists, a secretary, four servants (two of them Negroes) and even a brace of greyhounds.

Endeavour weighed anchor on 26 August 1768. She followed the time-honoured route to the Pacific, via Madeira, Rio de Janeiro and Cape Horn. Banks noted philosophically on Christmas Day that ' all good Christians, that is to say all hands got abominably drunk so that at night there was scarce a sober man in the ship. Wind, thank God, very moderate, or the Lord knows what would have become of us.'* On Tierra del Fuego they had a bizarre misadventure. Eager to botanize, Banks set off on an expedition to some hills. He made the mistake of taking the two Negroes with him, and then the second mistake of letting them get hold of a bottle of rum. They drained the bottle, ventured out of their tent and froze to death

Cook crossed the Pacific on about the thirty-ninth parallel. They saw plenty of whales and seals, penguins by the score, but no sign of any continent. Cook, who was already sceptical of Dalrymple's claims, was more dubious than ever. They reached Tahiti at length on 13 April 1769 and stayed for three months, observing Venus† and the natives. *Endeavour*'s captain noted laconically that they were free from the curse that was laid on Europeans' forefathers, for they did not have to earn their bread by the sweat of their brow. Banks saw in this ' New Cythera ', as Bougainville had called it, an 'Arcadia of which we were going to be Kings '.‡ The women, too, with ' fire in their eyes ', impressed him !§ However, science was not forgotten ; historians agree that the observations of Cook and his collaborator were excellently carried out.

They left Tahiti on 13 July 1769. Not quite 200 miles to the west they came on a group of islands that Cook called the Society Islands

---

* Moorehead, A., *op. cit.*, pp. 13–14.

† Who would be a historian ? G.A. Wood wrote in 1922 : ' The observation was made with complete success on a day " perfectly clear without so much as a cloud intervening "' (*The Discovery of Australia*, p. 277). Whereas, thirty-two years later, his colleague J.C. Beaglehole wrote that the observation of Venus was a failure, because of a dusky shade hanging about the planet.

‡ Quoted by Wood, G.A., *op. cit.*, p. 277.

§ Unfortunately, when they left Tahiti half of the crew were to be afflicted with venereal disease. Opinions differ on who had brought it to Tahiti – Wallis and the English, or Bougainville and the French. Alan Moorehead suggests it was both.

'because they were close together'. After that there was nothing in sight except the vast empty ocean. As far as the eye could see, there was no hint of any land. The seas became so heavy that Cook decided to alter course, first to the north, then back to the south-west. On 7 October the cry 'Land ho!' went up. They knew it had to be 'New Zeeland'. Cook still had to disprove the theories of Tasman and Dalrymple that this land was really the west coast of the undiscovered continent. And disprove it he did, in short order, by discovering that 'New Zeeland' was in fact two islands, which he circumnavigated. With his customary common sense Cook noted that they gave every sign of being admirably suited to European settlement.

The choice of the itinerary for the homeward voyage, it will be remembered, had been left to Cook himself. He could return either round Cape Horn or via the Cape of Good Hope. The route round the Horn had the advantage that if offered the explorers another chance to demolish for good the myth about *terra australis incognita*. The trouble with this course, however, was that *Endeavour* had taken a battering from storms of late and was no longer in a fit state to survive the gales in the South Seas. It had to be the western route. But if they had made straight for the southern tip of Africa, it would have been a journey devoid of any scientific or geographical interest. The ship's provisions would last for another six months, if rations were reduced by a third. So they decided to try to locate the east coast of New Holland and follow it north towards Indonesia. The greatest discoveries are almost all like that, a mixture of chance and purpose.

Endeavour left New Zealand behind on 1 April 1770. On 20 April, at 6 a.m., the officer of the watch, Lieutenant Hicks, caught sight of land. There were hills covered in trees and scrub and interspersed with sandy areas. Cook named it Point Hicks; it is roughly halfway round the coast from Melbourne to Sydney. The shoreline hereabouts offered no spot where a landing could be made. So Cook coasted on northwards for nine days, until a bay was sighted which Cook says was 'tolerably well sheltered from all winds, into which I resolved to go with the ship'.* The explorers stayed there until 9 May, studying the odd human beings (see Chapter 4), venturing some distance into the interior,† catching

---

* Quoted by Wood, *G.A.*, *op. cit.*, p. 290.

48

countless fish and above all (from Banks' point of view at least) collecting a great many specimens of the richly varied flora. When they decided to name the bay, it was not the plants but the fish which were singled out – Professor Wood has noted that Cook in his journal had originally called it Stingray Harbour. However, the words were later amended (presumably at the suggestion of Banks) to the name which time was eventually to endorse : Botany Bay.

They skirted the coast northward for another five weeks, without untoward incident. Then on 11 June, at about 11 p.m., in full moonlight and on a high tide, there came a sudden violent impact – *Endeavour* had struck a submerged coral rock,* which was so sharp that her hull was pierced. Cook behaved with his wonted coolness, as did his men. As Banks put it : 'The seamen worked with surprising cheerfulness and alacrity ; no grumbling or growling was to be heard throughout the ship, not even an oath, though the ship was in general as well furnished with them as most in His Majesty's service.'† They jettisoned ballast, forty to fifty tons of stores, half of the guns.‡ The ship was refloated twenty-four hours later and sailed gingerly to the nearest shore, where she was beached and examined. It took them until 6 August to make her seaworthy again. This meant nearly two months of hard work ; but the time was also spent in reconnaissance and observation, the results of which were to prove invaluable to future colonists. Then, when the ship was ready, they set off again towards the north. They were the first to sail up the east coast of Australia, covering a distance of some 4,000 kilometres. Before arriving in Batavia, which they reached on 11 October, they passed through what is now called Torres Strait, thus proving conclusively that New Holland and New Guinea were separate land masses. When asked where he had come from, Cook replied merely, 'From Europe'.

His route 'from Europe' had not been exactly direct. However, for the homeward voyage, he followed the common course via the

---

* The ship had by now reached the Great Barrier Reef that runs parallel to the east coast of Australia for some 2,000 kilometres.

† Quoted by Wood, G.A., *op. cit.*, p. 299.

‡ Six of them were salvaged in 1969 by an expedition from the Philadelphia Academy of Natural Sciences.

---

† Cook walked some five or six kilometres in the general direction of present-day Sydney. He says he found nothing of note.

Indian Ocean and the Atlantic.* Banks was pleased with Cape Town, and with the Dutch women. 'In general,' he wrote, 'they are handsome ... and when married (no reflection upon my countrywomen) are the best housekeepers imaginable, and great childbearers.' When they got to St Helena, Banks had another opportunity to sing the praises of the Dutch : 'Were the Cape now in the hands of the English it would be a desert, as St Helena in the hands of the Dutch would infallibly become a Paradise.'†

Endeavour dropped anchor near Dover, two years, ten months and seventeen days after she had left. Cook wrote to the Admiralty in his unassuming way : 'I flatter myself that the discoveries we have made, though not great, will apologize for the length of the voyage.'‡ His discoveries, he says, were 'not great' – one wonders what he might say if he could see Australia today and the promise it has for the future.

At the northernmost tip of the Australian coast, not far from Cape York,§ the maps now show an island which bears a symbolic name : Possession Island. It was here, just before sunset on a southern winter evening, 22 August 1770, that Cook laid formal claim, in the name of His Britannic Majesty, to the lands he had discovered. The proper rites were observed, the colours were run up and three volleys of small arms were fired from the shore, to be answered by three from the ship. The land thus annexed was called, first, New Wales (the reason for this choice is obscure) and later, New South Wales.

Cook saw no reason to comment on this ceremony ; he took it for granted. However he and Banks, like the conscientious professional and scientific men they were, did record enough about their observations for one to have an idea of what each of them thought of this strange country and its inhabitants. Their impressions were much more detailed and observant than those of the Dutch ; they

---

* The stay in Batavia had catastrophic effects on the health of the crew. Until then Cook, by maintaining inflexible standards of hygiene, had managed to keep his men free of disease, including the dreaded scurvy. But the miasmic Indies put an end to this exceptional state of health. Between their arrival in Batavia and their arrival in Cape Town, twenty-three of the ship's company were to die.

† Both quotations from Wood, G.A., *op. cit.*, p. 313.

‡ Wood, G.A., *loc. cit.*

§ Cook called it 'York Cape' after George III's late brother.

have the added interest that comes from the fact that the opinions of the two men do not always coincide.

Take Botany Bay, for example. As Banks saw it, 'The country consists of either swamps or light sandy soil' and its products were eucalypts 'and vast quantities of grass'. Cook's impression was more favourable : the country, he says, was

diversified with woods, lawns and marshes ... The woods are free from underwood of every kind, and the trees are at such a distance from one another, that the whole country, or at least great part of it, might be cultivated without being obliged to cut down a single tree. We found the soil everywhere, except in the marshes, to be of a light white sand, and produceth a quantity of good grass, which grows in little tufts about ao big as one can hold in one's hand, and pretty close to one another ; in this manner the surface of the ground is coated.

Some distance inland his impressions were even more favourable :

I found in many places a deep black soil, which we thought was capable of producing any kind of grain. At present, it produceth, besides timber, as fine meadow as ever was seen ; however, we found it not all like this, some places were very rocky, but this I believe to be uncommon. The stone is sandy, and very proper for building.*

Elsewhere, Banks' view was as follows :

In the whole length of the coast we sailed along, there was a very unusual sameness to be observed in the face of the country ... the fertile soil bears no kind of proportion to that which seems by nature doomed to everlasting barrenness. Water is a scarce article ... Even the timber was so hard that the carpenter who cut firewood complained that his tools were damaged.†

For all that, Banks the naturalist had his mind more on observing the flora and fauna than on exploiting the thankless land. And this task was a rewarding one. Each time they landed he came back on board with ever more varied collections of plants. There were birds, too, in great numbers, and the ocean was well stocked with turtles, dolphins, great sharks, sea-snakes and oysters.

The enthusiasm of the future President of the Royal Society was

* Quoted by Wood, G.A., *op. cit.*, p. 291.
† *ibid.*, pp. 307–8.

at its strongest during the weeks of their enforced stay near the Barrier Reef. 'It was a time of zoological romance,' says Professor Wood. The Barrier Reef itself was an amazing thing to look at, ' ... a wall of coral rock ... always overflown at high water, generally seven or eight feet, and dry in places at low water. The large waves of the vast ocean, meeting with so sudden a resistance, make a terrible surf breaking mountains high.'* No less fascinating were the countless creatures living in the labyrinth of the reefs: green turtles so large that the flesh of one of them fed the whole crew; cockles so enormous that *Endeavour*'s coxswain, albeit a small man, could get inside the shell; crocodiles lying in wait for prey; sharks gliding past menacingly; while the sky above was full of great flocks of multi-coloured birds, thousands of them.

Their trips ashore were equally rewarding, except for the fact that the inescapable mosquitos and the bull-ants made life unpleasant. But it was worth putting up with these torments to be able to see, close to, white ants' nests so tall that they looked like 'Druidical monuments'; dazzling butterflies, of which there were literally millions, Banks noted; birds of every sort of plumage, parrots, parakeets, white and black cockatoos, cranes, pigeons, crows, bustards, doves, geese, black swans the like of which were unknown in Europe, pelicans by the shore and the magnificent lonely albatross in the distance. It was a dreamlike existence; after a time one stopped being amazed by anything, however amazing it was – the 'fox' they saw (actually a dingo); or the mud-skippers flipping about from stone to stone and even climbing trees; or that strange beast crawling through the grass 'about the size of, and much like, a one gallon cagg [*sic*]. It was ... as black as the devil, and had wings,' said the sailor who spotted it ;† or a creature that looked like nothing on earth – one of Banks' greyhounds which chased it was hampered by the tall thick grass, whereas the creature had no difficulty in the long grass at all; instead of fleeing on all fours, it made its escape by taking enormous leaps on its hind legs which were out of all proportion to its front ones. An officer 'had the good fortune to kill the animal which had so lóng been the subject of our speculation. To compare it to any European animal would be impossible, as it had not the least resemblance to any one I have

---

* Wood, G.A., *op. cit.*, pp. 303–4.
† Probably a flying-fox.

seen.'* Whatever it was,† it was a point in favour of the country, proving to be 'excellent meat' and providing the hunter and his companions with a good dinner.

As for the natives ('the Indians', as the explorers called them), they were even more out of the ordinary. Banks and his men never managed to see many of them, thirty-odd at the most at any one time, but they did see them at close enough range for Banks to satisfy his scientific curiosity. He was particularly intrigued by their colouring and wondered if they were as jet black as they looked. He rubbed and scratched at the skin of one of them, got through the layer of filth and discovered that the colour of the person underneath was nearer to chocolate than to coal. In other respects, too, he found that Dampier's descriptions did not always tally with his own observations. The natives were, admittedly, quite odd and stark naked, although now and again they did seem to feel some sort of modesty and they would conceal certain parts of their anatomy with their hands. None of them was minus the two front teeth. They had holes cut through their noses, fitted with bones about eight inches long, 'like sprit-sail yards rigged across' as the amused sailors put it. Most of them were skinny, standing about five feet eight inches, had bright eyes and good beards, and their faces and bodies were painted here and there with white and red stripes. To Cook they seemed much less unappealing· than he would have expected ; according to him, their features were 'far from being disagreeable' and he thought they had 'soft and tunable' voices.

The explorers were especially intrigued by their way of life. 'They seem', says Cook, 'to have no fixed habitation, but move about from place to place like wild beasts in search of food . . . Where they stop, they build mean small hovels, not much bigger than an oven . . . They have not the least knowledge of iron or any other metal ; their working tools must be of stone, bone and shell.' ‡ Their weapons he describes as consisting of spears, barbed with wood or splinters of shell, eight to twelve feet in length, and tipped with the poisoned spike of a stingray ; and a curved hardwood throwing stick, which they could launch with prodigious accuracy over a distance of fifty yards, never missing the target by more than about four feet. Cook

* Wood, G.A., *op. cit.*, p. 300.

† And it was, obviously, a kangaroo.

‡ Wood, G.A., *op. cit.*, p. 302.

saw them as a peaceable people, timid and harmless, quite without cruel instincts.

However, the captain of *Endeavour* would have been unfaithful to the spirit of his age if he had not philosophized on them in terms which would never have occurred, say, to Dampier :

They may appear to some to be the most wretched people on earth ; but in reality they are far more happier than we Europeans ; being wholly unacquainted not only with the superfluous but the necessary Conveniences so much sought after in Europe, they are happy in not knowing the use of them. They live in a Tranquillity which is not disturbed by the Inequality of Condition : The Earth and the sea of their own accord furnishes them with all things necessary for life ; ... they live in a warm and fine Climate and enjoy a very wholesome Air : so that they have very little need of Clothing ... ; they seem'd to set not value upon anything we gave them nor would they ever part with any thing of their own.*

Banks summed them up as being ' content with little, or rather with all but nothing.'

One can easily imagine the eager welcome given by ' enlightened ' circles to these reports. Cook's name was made overnight. What he had not discovered may have increased his fame more than what he had in fact seen. One of his comments, almost a passing remark, was to attract considerable attention : 'Although I have failed in discovering the so much talked of Southern Continent (which perhaps do not exist) ... 't The words in brackets had their importance ; they relegated to the rank of a hypothesis what had been a universally accepted certainty. It was decided to get to the bottom of the mystery once and for all. One year later Cook set off again, in charge of two ships this time, with more purposeful names than *Endeavour* : *Resolution* and *Adventure*. He traversed the Antarctic oceans as far south as the Polar Circle, criss-crossed the Pacific, from New Zealand to New Caledonia, the New Hebrides, Tonga, the Society Islands, the Marquesas and Easter Island,‡ and then the Atlantic, where he discovered two new territories ; he called them

---

* Quoted by Clark, C.M.H., *A Short History of Australia*, Mentor, New York, 1963, p. 19.

† Quoted by Wood, G.A., *op. cit.*, p. 311.

‡ One notes that he had no desire to revisit the Great Barrier Reef.

South Georgia and the South Sandwich Islands. He arrived back in England on 30 July 1775, the voyage having lasted three years and eighteen days and covered nearly 70,000 miles.*

This time his conclusions were firm and based on sound geography. He knew that if there was a continent in the South Pacific, it 'must lay with the Polar Circle where the Sea is so pestered with Ice, that the land is thereby inaccessible.' †

This was the end of the myth which had haunted men's imaginations for 2,000 years. Manning Clark says that Cook seemed to have been 'the gravedigger of "terra australis" '.‡ For London was no more interested in New South Wales than it had been in New Holland. Everyone's mind was on the disturbing rumours from the North American colonies. The land which was one day to become Australia seemed doomed to relapse into that same obscurity in which it had existed for so many millennia. And yet, before ten years were up, it was to be the solution to one of the most serious problems facing His Majesty's government.

---

* Mrs Cook and her children saw about as little of him, this time back, as three years before. Less than a year later he was at sea again. First the Pacific, with stops in Van Diemen's Land (although again he stayed away from New South Wales), in New Zealand, Tonga, the Society Islands and the Hawaiian group, which he discovered in 1778. Then he turned this attention to the north, skirted as closely as possible the west coast of America, surveying it as he went, circumnavigated the Aleutians and sailed along Bering Strait until he was stopped by the ice. He decided to go south to winter in Hawaii, and there he was killed in a skirmish with natives on 14 February 1779. He was fifty-one. Historians are still unsure whether or not his body was eaten by the men who killed him.

† Quoted by Clark, C.M.H., *A History of Australia*, vol. I, Melbourne University Press, 1962, p. 54.

‡ *ibid.*, p. 55.

Chapter Four
The Aborigines

When did they arrive? – where did they come from? – why did they migrate? – their settlement of the continent – their appearance – the search for food – nomadic existence – sources of food – weaponry – skill at hunting – social organization – the tribe – language – family relationships – women and marriage – sex and reproduction – children – initiation – death – the creation of the world – magic and witchcraft – legends – art-forms – the Aborigines and Europeans

Over the last fifty years, advances in research have made it possible to hazard reasonably accurate answers to the main questions about the strange Australians whom those first Europeans described in such unflattering terms. When did they arrive? Where did they come from? What was their habitat? And what was their way of life?

It must be pleasant to be a prehistorian. Their time-scale is a flexible one, to say the least. When they attempt to date the period at which human beings first settled in *terra australis incognita*, they can play with thousands of years at a time. Was it 35,000 years before our era? No more than 10,000 perhaps? Or somewhere between 10,000 and 20,000? Professor Mulvaney's estimate of 25,000, which he calls 'a conservative figure',* seems reliable enough. Which would mean that, if one takes Birdsell's estimate of sixteen years as their average life-expectancy,† there would have been close to 1,600 generations of Aborigines before the advent of white men.

Such figures boggle the mind. But there are other questions no

---

* Mulvaney, D.J., *The Prehistory of Australia*, Thames & Hudson, 1969, p. 66.
† Is there not something arbitrary about this figure of sixteen?

less fraught with uncertainties. Was the continent colonized at one go ? Or were there successive waves of 'first Australians', as the ethnologists call them ? The latter hypothesis does seem far and away the more likely. Some scholars even maintain that the process of their immigration was spread over many centuries. Whatever the case may be on that score, there is general agreement that mysterious developments began to take place about the sixth mellennium B.C. About then, there were rapid strides made in technology, as has been deduced from the discovery of tools which are seen as similar to ones being used at the same period in Asia, if not in Europe. One wonders whether this marked the ending of countless centuries of adaptation and the beginning of what has been called 'the age of inventiveness'. Or it may be that such artifacts were brought by other immigrants of whom all other traces have disappeared. As yet, nobody seems to have found the key to this enigma, and to many others like it.

Then there is Tasmania, to confuse the issue. At one time Tasmania was joined to the mainland. It was not cut off by the sea until about the eleventh or tenth millennium B.C. The Aborigines who used to live there may have been only a first wave. Otherwise how did they come to be so different from the others ? They were, for example, the only ones of negroid type ; they were also more primitive, being ignorant of the axe, the boomerang and the shield ; and they were not accompanied by the dingoes which were always to be found with their mainland counterparts. It may be that they had come in from an easterly direction, making an accidental land-fall on a voyage down from Melanesia. Or even that they came in on a southwest course, from the direction of New Caledonia.

If one accepts that last hypothesis as a probability, then that makes the Tasmanians unique in yet another respect : they would have been the only Aborigines who did not enter Australia from the north. On this general route, opinions do not differ for once – Southeast Asia was the starting-point for these prehistoric migrants.* It is possible that they may not always have lived there. Professor A.P. Elkin has traced their migration from India and Ceylon to Malaya and Indonesia. Less cautious estimates suggest that their origins were in the Caucasus, that they were a branch of the numerous

---

* It has been said that Australia's interest in that region nowadays is merely a return to its own origins.

racial groups which swarmed out of the high central Asian plateaux and spread either westward or southward. But does their starting-point matter that much ? The route they took seems to be more important. They could have come via New Guinea (which was joined to Australia in prehistoric times) and settled the lands round the Gulf of Carpentaria. Or perhaps via Timor, going in a south-easterly direction, either overland or by canoe. As can be seen, there are large areas of doubt in this whole question.

The question of what might have caused them to migrate in the first place raises even greater doubts. Was it simply out of something like a spirit of adventure ? Judging by their characteristics in the following centuries, one would say not. Or is it more likely, as has been suggested, that they were fleeing from a more aggressive invader ? The trouble with that theory is obvious : if the Aborigines were moving to safer areas, why did their enemy not pursue them ? At least this last question does provide some minimal certainty for the historian. The Australoids, as the specialists call them, were the sole inhabitants of Australia for thousands and thousands of years.

If one can reach no hard and fast certainty on the date of their coming, their origins or the motives behind their migration, one can at least try to imagine how they spread over the country. Some of them, having arrived in the north-west corner, seem to have spread along the coasts, then gone inland. At the north-east corner their movement has been reconstructed more accurately. Some, leaving Cape York behind, reached the Queensland river systems ; from there, via the Diamantina valley and Cooper's Creek, they came down as far as Lake Eyre, which was to become a sacred site for them ; the whole region is believed to have been green and fertile, not becoming arid until some time between the tenth and fifth millennia B.C. Others must have come down the Murray, an easy way right down to the Bight. The landscapes probably bore little resemblance to those that we know, as tremendous volcanic erup-tions were to transform the face of the country.

What is certain is that, throughout the continent, space was plentiful. Ethnologists have estimated that, by the time of Cook's arrival, there were no more than 300,000 Aborigines, averaging about one to every twenty-five square kilometres. Their possession of the land's resources was undisputed. There being no other races of men there, they had no human enemies ; nor were they threatened by any man-eating predators, which were non-existent in Australia.

What they owned was a land which, despite its aridity, they were to exploit with amazing ingenuity ; and which, with its endless, timeless, silent horizons, was to bring to flower the mysterious seeds of myth they carried within them.

As for their appearance, the earliest explorers seem to have been unkind in their descriptions. Obviously the Aborigines did not meet aesthetic canons based on ancient Greece. Nor did they look like anything that Europeans had set eyes on up till then. The only racial types that resemble them at all are to be found in parts of southern India, Ceylon, Malaya, Timor and New Guinea. Almost without exception, they showed the same features : thin legs and arms and an abnormally protuberant abdomen ; heavy, thick, purplish lips and a prognathous jaw ; fine strong teeth ; a flat triangular nose with a narrow bridge ; the eyes close together and deep set, beneath a receding brow ; their skulls thick and covered in long, frizzy hair, as black as their skin. The surprising thing is that, by the nineteenth century, those who describe them seem to have a much more favourable impression of them than their predecessors of a century or two before. Let two examples suffice. A former British officer, Colonel E. Warburton, describing a group of Aborigines in 1873, said they were ' fine well-made men, most of them bearded, and considering the wretched hand-to-mouth life they lead, were in fair bodily condition.' *

And ten years later a Dane by the name of Carl Lumholtz, who lived among them for four years, said that the women ' carried themselves in a dignified manner '.† This may not prove much. Except that one should not generalize. And that ugliness is in the eye of the beholder. In any case, it is well established that there was a great range of types among these primitive people. In the south there were men whose bodies were covered with hair nine inches long and women with beards and moustaches. In northern Australia the breed was taller and stronger, there was less of a difference between them and the Europeans and there were coppery tints in the women's hair.

---

* Quoted by Elkin, A.P., in *The Australian Aborigines*, Angus & Robertson, Sydney, 1938, p. 44.

† Lumholtz, C., *Among Cannibals*, John Murray, 1890, p. 131. Not that Lumholtz was attracted to any of them. In fact he had scandalized his hosts by declining their hospitable offer of a girl.

There was one great perennial problem facing these Australoids : food, and where to find it. They have been described many times, walking in groups of twenty to forty, the men in front, carrying their few weapons and a shield, the women bringing up the rear, burdened with the youngest children and the barest minimum of utensils that the community needed. It has been estimated that, depending on the sort of ground they were traversing, they would cover some twelve to twenty kilometres a day. Some observers, seeing such behaviour as having obsessional characteristics, have sought to explain it in psychiatric terms as arising from *angst*. The real explanation is more trite : hunger. The Aborigines could not stay long in one place because if they did they could never be sure of keeping body and soul together.

Two basic facts of their life emerge from this. Firstly, in view of the climate, clothes were unnecessary. Admittedly, in the south, in parts where the winter can be severe, animal pelts were worn ; and at night when they felt the cold they slept by camp-fires which were never allowed to go out. However, this was luxury compared with the lives of those who lived elsewhere. They went about completely naked ; they never covered their bodies with anything more than a smearing of animal fat, which was meant not to keep away the cold but to discourage the persistent mosquitoes. Secondly, the idea of a village, a place where they might settle for good, was utterly inconceivable. Now and then they sheltered for the night in caves. But more often than not they simply made rough humpies out of a few branches and pieces of bark. Sometimes they went as far as to daub clay on the roof or build them on stilts in flood areas.

It is extremely unlikely that anyone stayed in these humpies during the day. If they were fortunate enough to find a river or reach the sea, they lived well on fish. With their great skill and eyesight much sharper than Europeans', they could catch fish by hand. More usually they fished with nets, with line and hook (made of wood or bone), and especially with harpoons which they could throw with extraordinary accuracy. It is known that in certain regions they knew how to smoke fish. However, this was the exception rather than the rule, as was the practice of sun-drying fruit or kangaroo meat, which was the fare of only the most prudent gourmets. In general, though, the first inhabitants of Australia were of necessity neither prudent nor gourmets. They lived from day to day, going without if they had to, eating their fill and more when they had the chance. They ate anything and everything – kangaroos, koalas, rats, wombats, snakes, bats, lizards (especially goannas, some of which can be almost as long as crocodiles) ; they ate birds' eggs when they could get them ; but they particularly enjoyed insects, ants and grasshoppers, including the grubs, some of which were believed to have magic properties.* Prehistorians say they were more vegetarian than carnivorous, and that their special delicacies were honeycombs, the roots of water-lilies, and yams, the juicy relative of the sweet potato. Their diet included certain sorts of leaves which their monkey-like ability to climb trees enabled them to pick.

It was in the procurement of this nourishment that the division of labour between the sexes proved its usefulness. The women were allotted the less exacting tasks. They were expert at getting fruit, roots, insects and small rodents, which they dug up with their nulla-nullas, heavy hardwood sticks about sixty centimetres long, serving as both pick and club. The hunt for water, which was rare and precious, was more difficult. Every Aborigine seems to have been a full-time dowser. Professor Elkin says, 'Nature is to him an open book compiled in a language he has learnt from birth.'† In places where Europeans died of thirst, the Aborigines always managed to find something to drink. They knew the secrets of drinking the dew, of finding the precious liquid inside tree-trunks, of tapping the little reservoirs of frogs' bellies. It was clearly most sensible for them to drink as soon as they had found water. But some original thinkers had managed to invent containers that were sufficiently watertight to carry a little liquid. As a last resort, at times of severe drought, they were capable of walking unbelievable distances overland, like wild animals in the African veldt, to reach a life-saving waterhole.

The men, of course, looked after the hunting. The favourite weapons were boomerangs and spears. The boomerang was not used throughout Australia ; in western areas of southern Australia, in certain parts of Arnhem Land and in Tasmania, it was unknown. Elsewhere it was a versatile article – a short, slightly curved implement, the shape of which varied according to whether it was

---

* One observer, who is not hostile to them, reports that they enjoy eating the vermin on their own bodies and on others' bodies. He adds that they eat the fleas on their dingoes.

† Elkin, A.P., *op. cit.*, p. 37.

meant to come back to the thrower or not ; the ones which did come back were actually less common than the others. There were also two different designs of spear. The first was made of one single piece of wood ; the other sort was tipped with a stone barb, secured to the shaft by resin and wax, and sometimes dipped in rotting matter so as to poison the wounds inflicted by the weapon. The shaft was about three metres long. The weapon could be thrown a distance of sixty metres, especially when it was launched from a spear-thrower (a sort of artificial extension of the arm that added great strength to the flick of the wrist). We talk of the cunning of Red Indians ; the cunning of the Aborigines was just as remarkable. They were unequalled in the skills of imitating bird-calls, stalking, camouflage and leaping suddenly on their prey ; they covered themselves in mud to disguise their scent, swam with a nest of reeds on their heads, took meticulous care to stay down-wind from their quarry.

When the men and women gathered again after their respective hunting expeditions, their first golden rule was to pool and share equally whatever game had been brought in. They lit their fire by rubbing two pieces of wood together, one hard, one softer. A certain minimal preparation was necessary ; with tools of stone and wood, scrapers and spears, they made stone ovens which could half-cook the meat. If they had killed a kangaroo, it was carried to the camp where, after the fur had been singed off, it would be gutted and, usually, eaten raw. If they were not too famished, they would roast it for a while.

The Aborigines have been called stone-age men. Literally speaking, this is true, in that they never reached the stage of using metals. And yet this primitive level of existence was not incompatible with a highly complex social organization and a spiritual life of astonishing richness.

It has been estimated that, by the time Europeans began to settle Australia, there were some five or six hundred tribes. The word 'tribe' should not be taken too strictly. All the term means is a group of a few hundred individuals sharing a common language, the same beliefs and customs. The most potent of these beliefs was that they all looked on themselves as the descendants of the same ancestors, who were mysterious beings, half spirits, half men, and whose constant reality and presence they took for granted. Within

the tribe there was no hierarchical order and no clearly defined leader ; but the authority of the elders was recognized by all. The extent of the territory they saw as theirs was related to its fertility. In the less arid regions it would be no more than a few hundred square kilometres ; in other parts it might be a few thousand – the extreme case was the lands of the Aranda people to the north of Alice Springs, which covered an area of 60,000 square kilometres.*
Naturally these nomadic zones were not clearly marked off from one another ; the tribes which owned them had no frontiers or border guards. However, they did have an intense attachment, which was both physical and metaphysical, to the soil that they felt belonged exclusively to them, their relations, forefathers and descendants. If any outsiders attempted to encroach on their rightful domain, the only possible result was conflict. Bloodshed was common, but did not breed lasting hatred. Reconciliation was as prompt as the outbreak of violence that had led to it. Conquest was not followed by atrocity ; rape, burning and massacre seem to have been unknown among them.

If the tribal lands were vast, their inhabitants lived in enforced isolation ; if they were smaller, different tribes could meet from time to time. Neighbouring tribes (if the concept of 'neighbours' has any meaning in a country as huge as Australia) came together, either to exchange gifts,† or to hold sacred ceremonies in which they could recognize the similarity of their faiths. In this way the barriers of language were crossed. On the point of language, as on so many other things, estimates vary widely. Some say there were 200 languages, some say 300, some 500. Professor Elkin mentions the 'wealth of vocabulary, the variety of grammatical forms and the power of expression of Australian languages'.‡ There must have been countless dialects. These languages existed in no written form, although some people believe that certain symbolic signs, looking something like hieroglyphs, may be evidence of some script. It has also been said that, when they could not understand sounds uttered by others, they used non-verbal forms of communication, such as the sign language of the deaf-and-dumb, notches of different sizes

* More than a tenth of the area of France.

† Professor Stanner says they attached more importance to the idea of giving than to the gifts themselves.

‡ Elkin, A.P., *op. cit.*, p. 29.

cut in sticks, or smoke-signals when the range was too great for the voice to carry.* But much of this is guesswork.

These problems of communication did not arise within a single tribe or among the smaller groups (say, forty or fifty people) which lived together on a day-to-day basis. The family ties which gave them their feeling of belonging together were so complex that it would be extremely difficult to describe them in detail. The family was the central nucleus. Usually, several families joined forces to form a clan, or a local group. Legend has it that the womenfolk were brutalized mercilessly, but this seems to be untrue ; however they were certainly kept in a state of strict subservience. It appears that in certain communities they were forbidden to speak to anyone but their husbands or to take part in any of the religious rituals. The possibility of a woman remaining unmarried was inconceivable. Marriage, which was the universal rule,† was contracted as soon as a girl reached puberty, a custom which led to certain problems, since boys did not marry until they had gone through a long initiation period (see page 66). This meant that a very young girl was often given to a very old man, whose first wife could no longer render the sort of service that he was entitled to expect from her. Professor Elkin explains that the Aborigines, in justification of the wide disparity in the ages of man and wife, would say : 'Poor old man must have young wife to get honey and water for him.'‡ It was also possible for a girl to be betrothed from the moment of birth, or even from before birth. As she grew up, she gradually became used to being near her future lord and master, who brought her up the way he wanted her to be and trained her to keep her eyes lowered when dancing. Most marriages were devoid of ceremony, the beginning of cohabitation being the only announcement required. Now and then a token ceremony took place – the woman would present food to her man as an earnest of her usefulness, and the man would tap her once or twice with an ember, as a sign of his omnipotence over her.

---

* Their traditional 'cooee' may have been a rallying-cry, a call of welcome or a distress-signal. Again, opinions differ. All the explorers mention it. One of them says that on a still night the cry of 'cooee' could carry farther than three kilometres.

† For all that, less permanent liaisons were not unheard of.

‡ Elkin, A.P., *op. cit.*, p. 159.

Both monogamy and polygamy were common (not to mention homosexuality) ; in all cases marriages were arranged. There were certain rules, although these were not always obeyed. The only unbreakable taboos seem to have been incest, marrying one's mother-in-law and marrying the latter's sisters. The ideal marriage was between a man and his first or second cousin. But even with them one had to watch one's step, because there were 'crossed' cousins and 'parallel' cousins. For example, it was legitimate to marry the daughter of one's mother's brother, or the daughter of one's father's sister. But it was not possible to marry a child of one's mother's sister or a child of one's father's brother, for such cousins were considered as having the same standing as brothers and sisters of the direct line. A man could start with one wife, then contract marriage with several more. When tribes met, the women might be swapped, presumably to relieve the monotony of matrimony ; courtesy might also decree that a woman be lent to a visitor to the tribe. No marriage was necessarily a once-for-all arrangement. If a man tired of a wife, he could repudiate her ; but a rejected wife did not remain in her enforced spinsterhood for long. Indeed, such women could belong to a series of husbands. However, an abduction was a serious crime ; it led to Trojan-type wars, but no *Iliad* ever sang them.

Ethnologists have described the sex-life of Aborigines somewhat crudely. It does not seem to have been completely without refinements ; but kissing was certainly considered bad form. They saw coitus and reproduction as two completely separate things. Sexual intercourse itself was an agreeable pastime, which a woman could make more erotic by painting symbols of masculinity on her body. However, having children was a more serious business. It involved freeing the soul of a future human being from its totem and sending it into the womb of its mother. Its essence, which was a purely spiritual entity to begin with, was to be converted into matter by the action of a man. It would not have occurred to any of them that a man might be the physical agent of conception ; his role was merely to 'prepare the way' and facilitate the coming of an already existing spirit.

This way of thinking may explain why children were treated with such indulgence.* Punishments or beatings were unheard of ; their

---

* This did not preclude the killing of newborn children who had caused their mothers too much pain.

life was spent in play. This pleasant atmosphere changed at puberty, which marked the beginning of the time when the growing girls and boys would have to take up the mystical role of continuing the tribe into the next generation. The celebration of the girls' arrival at puberty was uncomplicated. They were painted red and yellow and the growth of their breasts was welcomed by the older women who sang to the fertility spirit to hasten their development. The boys, the coming generation of men, did not get off so lightly. As the first step of his introduction to the life of a man, an Aboriginal boy of ten or eleven might have his head stuck into a wooden bowl full of yam shoots ; still in the bowl, it would be pulled back and forth ; his chin and cheeks were rubbed with roots to make the hair grow, and finally his face was painted black. At the age of about fourteen, there came the great day when the boy was admitted to the secrets which had been handed down for thousands of years. Perhaps it was believed that pain would quicken their understanding. This could explain why pain was an ingredient of the initiation ceremonies. These ceremonies were too complex and varied to be detailed fully here. The elders of the tribe, wearing their long multicoloured feathers, impressed on the youths the solemnity of the moment. It was then that what we must call the liturgy began. Sometimes the nasal cartilage was pierced and a bone fitted through it as a symbol of maturity ; sometimes one or two upper teeth were pulled out and smashed by stones ; sometimes they slashed the body or pulled out hairs from the most sensitive parts. The climax, circumcision, almost always took place at sunrise. The novice was anointed with human blood which, having been drawn from the arms of the elders, was sacred ; he also drank some of the blood, which he was told would given him greater strength and a longer life. The ceremony took place to the accompaniment of chanting, singing, shouting and dancing. The new man was now qualified to hear the revelation of the mystery of his origins and his destiny. He learned that he belonged to a tribe, which had been shaped by his ancestors and continued by their descendants. It was now up to him to ensure the survival of the tribe ; this was to be his duty until his dying day.

It has been said that death itself was probably the most significant and important social event in the life of any Aboriginal community.*

---

* Elkin, A.P., *op. cit.*, p. 336.

When a member of the tribe lay dying, he was surrounded by his wives, children and relatives, who sang and moaned and slashed their own bodies. They would work themselves into a hysterical frenzy, in the belief that the violence of their yelling and gesticulation might chase away the powers of evil. The end of a life meant only one thing to them : it was caused by black magic or witchcraft. Their uneasiness could only be allayed by finding a scapegoat, an unfaithful wife, a son who had neglected his duties to his father or an enemy of long standing. Such revenge as they took rarely went as far as murder ; the supposed 'criminal' was punished sufficiently by the shedding of blood.

Although burial services took many different forms in different tribes, they had the common purpose of helping the dead on their way to their spirit-home. Some tribes buried their dead ; some mummified theirs ; others cremated them. Sometimes dead bodies were simply left to decompose. Death, according to R.M. and C.H. Berndt,* was always the occasion of a ritual oddly like a European wake. These proceedings were always supervised by special celebrants, who handed the office down from father to son. They sat on a platform beside the corpse, their arms outstretched in a posture which suggested supplication. In some areas, members of the tribe would eat some of the flesh of the dead person, intending thus to preserve something of him. This was done especially by the mothers of stillborn children, who thought that by doing this they could ensure the rebirth of the spirit which would enable them to conceive again in the future. Whatever rites were practised, the ceremonies lasted a long time so as to impress on the community what had happened to it and to enable it to adjust to the trauma it had just suffered.

Many Aboriginal groups believed in reincarnation. However, the rebirth of the same person in a different form was of secondary importance to them. What mattered was the continuity of a spiritual essence, which was already present in a foetus inside the womb, never lost its power throughout a lifetime, remained present but invisible after the disappearance of the matter that had embodied it, and was for ever indestructible.

The questions 'Where do we come from ?' and 'Where do we go ?'

* Berndt, R.M. & C.H., *The World of the First Australians*, Ure Smith, Sydney, 1964, p. 386.

were as perennially perplexing for these primitive peoples as for us. They had evolved no precise chronology for their notion of Genesis. However, they did believe that there had been a beginning of the world. Mysterious beings had created everything, heaven, earth and men. Men partook of the same essence as all things and were an integral part of a natural system that had been given its shape in 'the dream-time'. A human being was doomed if he lost touch with this natural system, for it was both the source of his own life-force and his purpose in living. He was watched over by his totem, which was not only a link with the world of the spirits, but also a companion ('mate', as later Australians were to put it – see pages 155–6), a brother, friend and protector. This totem was usually an animal, a kangaroo, an emu or a pigeon. It would warn him of imminent danger, help him to get better when he was ill, prevent him from catching the diseases of others. Sometimes it worked through dreams ; sometimes through its physical manifestation. These totems were not always the companions of individuals. At times they protected a whole tribe ; at others there was a totem for the men of the tribe and another for the women – and woe betide any who tried to use for their own purposes the patron spirit of the opposite sex.

Although these beliefs were vaguely formulated, they were so vital and vigorous that they were bound to breed magic and witch-craft. These took many different forms. If one pointed a certain bone at an enemy he was bound to die ; the same thing happened if one threw some of his hair into the fire. Those who go in for classifying behaviour see the different magical practices as falling into three main categories. There were, firstly, the beneficent 'productive' spells, which were meant to make the search for food easier, or to make rain, or to inspire love. Then there were the 'protective' spells, calculated to allay jealousy, to put an end to a quarrel, to keep somebody in good health, to discover who had 'murdered' a person who had recently died, to neutralize the powers of evil, to keep misfortune at bay or to uncover enemies. The third group of spells were the purely 'destructive' ones, aimed at making an enemy fall ill, or even causing his death.

Living as they did a life that was full of supernatural forces, the Aborigines had many reasons for holding communal ceremonies in which they gave expression to this mystic element of their life through dances, singing and gesture. Aborigines say these ceremonial practices had the purpose of bringing back the past and projecting the present into the future. When they relived scenes from tribal mythology, this did not mean they were just play-acting or putting on a show. The men and women who took part in them took it all extremely seriously and firmly believed that their own well-being and the well-being of their neighbours depended on their acting. Aborigines would add to such an explanation the maxim : 'He who loses his Dreaming is lost.' * If not only the individual but the tribe is to be sure of surviving and of being continued, it must know that its food supply will not run out and that the generations will follow one another in the way the ancestors have decreed. This is why the two richest and most common themes of the corroboree are food and fertility. It is also no doubt why the corroborees give such an awesome impression of a powerful living faith.

The actors and dancers colour their faces and bodies red, yellow, white and black. Their songs, which have very few words, are repeated again and again, telling sometimes of the exploits of their totems, or beseeching them not to desert their protégés. When they dance, Elkin says, 'they stamp their feet into or "scrape" them along the soil, and beat their rhythm-sticks on the ground, and so raising the "new earth" to enfold them as in its emanations symbolized by the dust.'† The mythological scenes that they enact, to the accompaniment of music, are meant as an intense supplication to the creative spirits of the dream-time. As for the music, their instruments are few. In the north they have a sort of wooden trumpet. But the most common is, of course, the didgeridoo, a hollow wooden or bamboo tube anything up to three metres in length, which when played properly can produce notes ranging from very low to very high.‡ There is also the bull-roarer, which is spun round in the air above the player's head, and so called (by Europeans) because to them, obviously but erroneously, it sounded like the roaring of a bull. But to the Aborigines it is the voice of the spirits. The usual rhythm instruments are sticks or boomerangs, struck against one another or on the ground.

* Elkin, A.P., *op. cit.*, p. 43.
† *ibid.*, *loc. cit.*
‡ One explorer notes that when white men try to blow it, the only noises produced are laughable or disastrous.

The lives of the Aborigines were full of legends. According to Dr P. Fischer their animal stories are bettered by none, Kipling's included. The old myth-makers knew how to combine a profound feeling for nature with imaginativeness and amusement. Some of the animals that turn up in these legends were completely imaginary. For example there was the bunyip, which had a great liking for the flesh of humans, especially humans of the female sort ; like the Loch Ness monster it lived in lakes, creeks or marshlands ; it had a blood-curdling cry and was as large as an ox ; it was a cross between a man and a fish, and its body was covered with scales, feathers and fur, while its hair was made of reeds ; 'eyewitnesses' spoke also of its long ears, sharp teeth and curved tusks. Or else there was the *kadimakara*, which was a reptilian monster, living beneath three enormous gum-trees that held up the sky and protected the earth from the sun's rays. There were fabulous snakes, like the huge *myadi*, the mere name of which can still to this day strike fear into an Aborigine ; or the *kaitchlam*, an ancestor of the Arnhem Land tribes, whose head was crowned with a rainbow ; or the *moha-moha*, with its tail four metres long, its body two and a half metres wide, its shiny head, its saw-toothed jaws, greenish neck and chocolate-coloured fins.

As well as these eerie beings, there were many other sorts of fables full of charm. The reason why fish have such pretty colours is that they were once birds ; they had to take refuge in the sea to escape the brush turkey which, in a fit of jealousy at not being able to fly, set fire to their forest. When a koala moans, it is taking after its ancestor Koob-borr, which wept because men had refused to give it anything to drink and forbidden it to eat anything other than gum leaves. There are countless other tales. Long ago the sky was so close to the earth that people had to crawl about in the dark ; but gradually the magpies managed to lift it with twigs held in their beaks. The kookaburra has been laughing ever since he saw a bird escape from the jaws of a python that had had to yawn. Spencer Gulf, in South Australia, would never have come into existence if a kangaroo (which at that time was actually a man) had not used a bone to break the isthmus separating it from the open sea. The forever-whispering bluebirds are extremely timid, which is under-standable, since they were in fact formerly men and are still being terrorized by the giant Nurunderi who was responsible for turning them into birds in the first place. This giant was devoid of pity ; his

70

two wives had fled ; he caught them and unleashed the fury of the ocean to drown them ; but their bodies were turned into the small twin islands, not far from Kangaroo Island, off the South Australian coast. Windulka, the bandicoot, on the other hand, was luckier – he hid from a pursuing dingo in a ditch but, realizing that he was still going to be discovered, he dug and dug until he was deep down and out of danger, by which time he had located a spring and made an arid region fertile. The gecko, Ipilya, also deserved gratitude. He was one hundred metres long and had an unquenchable thirst. Having consumed vast quantities of wet grass and water, he was able to squirt the mixture into the sky and in a short time the monsoon rains began to fall.

The Aborigines also sensed a sort of identity between man and nature. For a European a stone is just a stone ; but for an Aborigine it is the embodiment of a being with which he feels a spiritual link. The same goes for the stars. The two brightest stars in the Southern Cross are actually two brothers who got cut off by a bushfire while out hunting and managed to take refuge up in the sky. Some Aboriginal groups had a similar explanation for the Pleiades. For them these seven stars (which the Greeks saw as the daughters of Atlas and Pleion) were the Makara, fair-haired women of uncommon beauty. They married the men of Orion and disappear westwards one hour before their husbands so as to have time to make ready the fire on which the game will be cooked. In winter, when they appear in the east, their bodies are hidden by icicles ; when the ice drops from their bodies the earth is covered in white frost.

This mythology and the accompanying rituals were not transmitted solely by oral tradition. There were artists who communicated them in creative works as well. They had all the tools required, such as chisels, similar to those used by sculptors, woodcarver's wedges, axes and stones for polishing and sharpening. They made their colours from red or yellow ochre, white clay, with powdered charcoal for the black ; they had no blues, greens or greys. They did their drawings on the ground, or on weapons and shields, on wood, bark or on rocks. The best of these rock-paintings are at the Oenpelli caves, in Arnhem Land, 250 kilometres east of Darwin. There the landscape still has a prehistoric look. There are free-ranging buffalo, lagoons covered with water-lilies, millions of brightly coloured birds. The caves are to be found in cliffs. The drawings are on the ground, the walls and the roofs. Some are lifelike, some more stylized. The patience put into them is obvious. They represent humans in animal shapes, snakes from legends, the aforementioned *kaitchlam* included, kangaroos, emus, lizards, all those unique animals of the Australian continent. There are many 'spirits', bearing uncanny resemblances to human beings, as well as depictions of sexual behaviour and witchcraft. Professor Mulvaney writes :

Aboriginal rock art is best comprehended in its natural setting, and alone ... The site itself must be comprehended as frequently more meaningful than the art which covered it ... The drawings on significant sites were simply the medium through which ancestral creation beings continued to influence every-day life ... as tangible evidence of the dream-time and of abiding totemic beings. *

One feels perplexed at the disparity between an almost animal-like level of life and a metaphysical system of thought. The temptation to draw a facile parallel is strong. At no other time in history has there been such rapid and far-reaching material progress as in our own time. But spiritual awareness is outdistanced and moves at its ancient snail's pace. The Aborigines, on the other hand, had put the spirit before matter. Their civilization was poised, static and enduring ;† whereas ours is forever opening out into the future. The question must be asked whether these stone-age men, with their mystical habits, led a fulfilling life. A European of the twentieth century certainly finds their fulfilments difficult to imagine and well-nigh impossible to envy. The least one can say of them is that they had no desire for change and that they had no inkling of the shattering experience that was now in store for them.

---

* Mulvaney, D.J., *op. cit.*, pp. 171–2.
† It was one of their axioms that what was done in the dream-time must continue to be done today.

Part Two
Australia as a Penal Colony
1788-1821

Criminality and prisons in Great Britain – American War of Independence ends transportation to North America – where should the convicts be sent ? – choice of Botany Bay – Phillip's appointment – departure of the First Fleet – meeting with La Pérouse – landing in Sydney Cove – two years of tragedy – the Governor's energy – threat of starvation – arrival of the Second Fleet – growth of population – improvement in conditions for convicts – development of private holdings – currency problem – outline of future Sydney – Phillip returns to England

The misfortune of some of the people does not make for the well-being of others. The statement is too true for us to find any comfort in it nowadays. We think our cities are unsafe – but what would we have thought if we had lived in London 200 years ago ! The chief of police stated that one in every eight of the population was a criminal. He may have had reason to exaggerate his problems, but the fact remains that the streets of London were infested during the day by the most efficient pickpockets in the world, and after dark by footpads who thought nothing of murdering the people they robbed. Juvenile delinquency was rife. It has been estimated that there were as many as 2,000 to 3,000 boys between the ages of ten and fifteen organized in gangs which stopped at nothing.*

* The question of the crime rate was still acute at the beginning of the nineteenth century. Calonne, who had taken refuge in London from the French Revolution, wrote a book about it in 1801 – *A Proposal to Eradicate Highway Robbery in the London Area*. He recommended the setting-up of a body modelled on the *maréchaussée* (mounted constabulary) of the Ancien Régime, and on the *gendarmerie* that Napoleon had just established. If Calonne is to be believed, the area round London was even more dangerous than the city streets : 'The vagabonds break in between eleven p.m. and one a.m. .... They all enter the house together, while

English society in the eighteenth century offers an amazing spectacle. There was a landed aristocracy, growing more influential all the time and with an appreciation of public well-being that has rarely been seen in any other privileged class. There was a merchant class which was building the British Empire. And there was an intellectual elite that gave the English a position of unquestioned pre-eminence in Europe. However, the rest of the picture was ugly. Historians have familiarized us with the rabble of illiterate, homeless unfortunates, devoid of the most elementary notions of hygiene, going from ale-house to ale-house. This was the wretched proletariat, that class of victims already being produced by the Industrial Revolution which was to bring to Britain a greatness unknown since ancient Rome.

No proper solution was offered to this problem. The police force was to most intents and purposes non-existent. If any transgressors were caught, they were sure of an inhuman fate. The criminal laws were so harsh that it would be impossible to imagine what they were like if the original statutes were not extant to prove it. Professor Manning Clark has taken the trouble to draw up a list of offences that were punishable by death – it occupies two full pages in an octavo-sized volume. There were, of course, murder, arson, rape, treason, forgery, mutiny, desertion and so on. But there were all sorts of other crimes which were looked on as equally serious. For example, you were sentenced to hang if you stole a sum in excess of one shilling, if you stole cattle or horses, or if you were caught in the act of breaking and entering, or if you had stolen goods worth more than forty shillings. Seducers were also frowned upon and, if they abducted an ' heiress ', their necks were at risk. Such harshness was not totally unrelieved. In theory, condemned criminals were entitled to the consolations offered by a minister of religion. But in 160 cases (the legislators were fond of statistics), these last rites were denied them. As always at that period, a hanging was a performance enjoyed by great numbers of spectators (and also, according to cynics, by great numbers of pickpockets). In 1783, when it was decided to do away with the public processions which always followed condemned criminals to the scaffold, Dr Johnson saw this as an infringement of the rights of the people.

---

the owners are at supper ; then, without regard to age or sex, they murder everybody most abominably and leave one hour before sunrise.'

The letter of such inhuman laws was tempered in practice by different forms of leniency. Judges would often take it upon themselves to reduce the severity of a charge, thus avoiding having to pronounce the death penalty. The King himself was free with his pardon. However, even if convicts could escape the death penalty in these ways, plenty of other torments awaited them : irons, the stocks and the lash. This last was the cruellest of them all ; as many as 500 strokes might be inflicted, crippling a person for life. Any wretch who survived such ordeals could look forward to prison. And the prisons of the time beggar description. A visitor to one of them in 1767 complained in the *Gentleman's Magazine* that 'The felons in this country lie worse than dogs or swine ... The stench and nastiness are so nauseous ... that no person enters there without the risk of his health and life.'* All other witnesses agree. The few who agitated for reform agitated in vain. Some gaols were so overcrowded that men and women were not segregated and the risk of epidemics was high and obvious. One solution to the whole problem came to seem very attractive : would it not be possible to get rid of these prisoners by sending them all somewhere else ? This was the beginning of the idea of transportation.

Transportation had in fact been practised on a small scale ever since the beginning of the seventeenth century, but it was not to be legalized for another hundred years. As for where to send the convicts, this was no problem. The North American colonies, close enough and sparsely populated, were the very place. Professor A.G.L. Shaw writes, 'All the American colonies except those of New England received some convicts at some time, but most went to Maryland and Virginia.'† Between 1715 and 1776, it has been estimated, some thirty to forty thousand were sent. Both the government and the transporters made money out of the business. The government sold the surplus prison population at £5 per head to the transporters, who resold them in North America at £10 per man and £8 or £9 per woman. Trained tradesmen could fetch as much as £25. The only risk to the investment was the wastage during shipment, as the death rate was about thirty per cent.

The only thing that went wrong with this brainwave was that the

* Quoted by O'Brien, E., *The Foundation of Australia*, Sheed & Ward, 1937, p. 113.
† Shaw, A.G.L., *Convicts and the Colonies*, Faber, 1966, p. 32.

'rebels' put a stop to it. Francis Bacon, more than a century before, had already shown up the cruelty involved in this disguised form of slavery. Benjamin Franklin was to take up the cause, pulling no punches, complaining that it was an insult for the British government to pour the overflow from its prisons into the American colonies. London tried to persuade the southern states, using the argument of their perennial labour shortage ; but the offer was declined. During the War of Independence a stop-gap solution to the problem was worked out : pending the defeat of the rebellious colonists, the surplus of prisoners was to be accommodated in sub-standard temporary conditions aboard hulks moored in the Thames.* However, as the crime rate, and the conviction rate, went on climbing, such stop-gap arrangements soon proved grossly inadequate.

After the peace was signed, the problem was still there. According to Edmund Burke, the fate of 100,000 convicts was in the balance. He called on the government to declare what it intended to do with these wretches and to which part of the globe it meant to dispatch them. The great orator was getting rather carried away ; it has been established that in England and Wales there were in all not many more than 4,000 convicts awaiting transportation. However, even if the problem had been exaggerated, it still lacked an answer. The government did what would be called nowadays a 'feasibility study'. The various possibilities were canvassed : in Africa there were Gambia, Angola, Algiers, the 'Kaffir coast' in the vicinity of the Cape of Good Hope,† the islands of Tristan da Cunha and Madagascar ; in North America there was still Canada ; in England itself, even the coal-mines were considered. But there were objections to each of these possible solutions.

Parliament had begun to study the problem in 1779. A committee of the House of Commons had invited Joseph Banks to express an opinion. Having sailed with Captain Cook, he was to be an acknowledged expert on all things Australian until he died in 1820. Banks' opinion was categorical. If they wanted a place of exile for convicts, Botany Bay was the perfect spot. It was remote enough to make escape impossible ; it had soil that was fertile enough to make it

---

* A good instance of the bureaucratic concept of the temporary – the hulks were still there more than eighty years later.

† The Cape was a Dutch possession at the time.

independent of assistance from the home country within a year ; it enjoyed a pleasant climate (the same as that of Toulouse in the south of France, he said) ; the natives were harmless ; there were no beasts of prey ; and there was an abundant supply of wood. Last but not least, Banks suggested that there could be little doubt that a land-mass as extensive as New Holland would offer possibilities of profit. The Commons committee was properly impressed by such assuredness and came to the conclusion that the scheme satisfied both humanitarian precepts and the principles of sound policy ; in addition it might prove to have advantages in the fields of shipping and trade. And then nothing was done.

The idea lapsed, in fact, until 1783, when it was raised again by another member of the *Endeavour*'s company, one James Matra. In favour of Botany Day Matra put forward the argument that it might help the government solve the problem of how it was to assist those of its former subjects in North America who, because they had remained loyal to it, were now resented by the newly independent states. Cook's former shipmate had no hesitation in guaranteeing that New South Wales would be the ideal new home for the Loyalists.* Although Matra's proposal found favour, Pitt, who had just become Prime Minister, remained unconvinced. Meanwhile, time was passing and the overcrowding in the gaols and hulks was becoming even more acute. In 1784 it was formally proposed that the old system of transportation be reactivated. But the problem of where to transport the convicts remained. The following year Sir George Young, an admiral, once again advocated Botany Bay. He used the same arguments as had been used before, but put them more forcefully : was England to accept unprotestingly the loss of America and content herself with her present colonies, dissatisfied as they were with their lot ? Should she not seek other possible colonies ? Surely Cook had not made his discoveries in vain. If England were to exploit these, even in a small way, it could only be of advantage to all mankind.

When a problem has remained unresolved for a lengthy period, sheer weariness usually has a lot to do with the eventual decision on it. This may well have been the case in 1786. Or the urgency of the

---

* This was their own name for themselves : the 'rebels' called them 'Tories'. They made up a good third of the population. In fact it was not to New South Wales but to Canada, in particular Nova Scotia, that most of them were to go.

situation may have been brought home to officialdom by an uprising on one of the hulks and by the increased likelihood of epidemics breaking out. Whatever the reason, on 18 August the Home Secretary, Lord Sydney, notified the Lords Commissioners of the Treasury by letter that they were to take all the necessary steps to transport 750 prisoners to Botany Bay. This decision was ratified in the Speech from the Throne in the following January and approved by Parliament without debate.

At this point it would not be out of place to pause and glance at the relevant documents. In recent years they have given rise to a controversy which says much for the vitality of historical studies in Australia. The question is : is it really true that the main reason for the settlement of Australia by Great Britain was that she wanted to get rid of a surplus of convicts ? Until quite recently the answer to this question was always 'yes'. However, about twenty years ago a doubt was first expressed on this point. It was suggested that the reason for choosing Botany Bay was actually a strategic one. Then, in 1966, Professor Blainey put forward the hypothesis that the really decisive factors had been of a commercial and military nature. He pointed out that flax and timber were as necessary to navies in those days as steel and oil nowadays. And it happens that in 1786 the British, doubting the reliability of their alliance with Russia, were beginning to fear that their traditional sources of supply along the Baltic coast might soon be closed to them. During his second voyage to the South Pacific, Cook had realized that Norfolk Island, about 1,500 kilometres north-east of Botany Bay – which is not far, compared with a voyage from Britain itself to the Antipodes – could supply both of these raw materials. The conclusion had been, according to Blainey : 'Norfolk Island was the plant nursery ; Australia was to be the market garden and flax farm surrounded by gaol walls.'*

This is a stimulating and ingenious hypothesis. Space does not permit a more lengthy exposition of it or of the counter-arguments advanced by Bolton and Shaw. Suffice it to say that these arguments

---

* Blainey, G., *The Tyranny of Distance*, Sun Books, Melbourne, 1966, p. 33. It must be added that the attempts to carry out this plan were so unsuccessful that by 1824 flax from the Baltic had to be imported into Sydney. The timber project was no more successful.

are no less convincing. Nevertheless, one is tempted to see the truth somewhere between them. After all, what government has ever had a very clear grasp of its own motives, or even a clear idea of what results its decisions may lead to ? In 1786, Pitt had many other more pressing problems than what to do with Botany Bay. It must surely make sense to assume that he was influenced in his decision by all sorts of reasons, more or less ill-defined, as well as by a clearly-defined central one. No doubt the main concern was to hear the last of all those bothersome convicts. As for other reasons, it is quite possible that, in settling New South Wales, there was some intention, however imprecise, of getting in before the French. La Pérouse (see page 84) had sailed from Brest on 1 August 1785. It is extremely probable that British intelligence, which was prodigiously efficient,* not only knew of his departure but also assumed that the expedition had a purpose which it had not. It would be surprising, too, if the Cabinet had not lent an ear once more to Sir Joseph Banks, who was by now a man of influence and could have been relied on to extol once again the commercial potential of any new colony. The possible use of flax and timber is expressly alluded to in the appendix to Lord Sydney's letter to the Treasury, although at the very end and as though in passing, suggesting perhaps that these were not of such fundamental importance. Need one add that the Admiralty, for its part, would not have been worth its salt if it had not been struck by the strategic worth of Botany Bay ? A glance at any map would have told them that it lay where the routes from Europe via the Horn and Cape Town crossed the routes to Calcutta, Canton and Kamchatka and the routes towards California (the importance of which was to become clear in 1790 when the Nootka Bay occupation all but led to a war between Great Britain and Spain).

All that was by the way. The pressing need was to find a man who was capable of conducting a load of unsavoury passengers to the ends of the earth, there to turn them into colonists and possibly

* In 1777, for example, the British secret service had managed to get hold of the whole correspondence between the French government and the American plenipotentiaries. The following year, less than forty-eight hours after the treaty of alliance was signed between the 'rebels' and His Most Christian Majesty Louis XVI, the terms of the treaty had been passed on to London.

even to demonstrate, as a true son of the Enlightenment, that men and women freed from the yoke of civilization could revert to their state of natural purity.

The man chosen was Captain Arthur Phillip. He was now forty-eight, having joined the navy at the age of seventeen. He was given an imposing and precise title :

Captain-General and Governor-in-Chief of the territory called New South Wales, from Cape York in latitude 10° 37′ to the southern extremity of the said territory of New South Wales in the latitude of 43° 39′ south, and all the country inland to the westward as far as the one hundred and thirty-fifth degree of longitude,* including all the islands adjacent in the Pacific Ocean.

He was also given powers which, in the nature of things, were extensive. As for the man he was, let Manning Clark describe him :

He was in many ways a fine flower of the eighteenth-century, a common-sense man with a contempt for the consolations of religion but, at the same time, a belief in the established church as a means to promote the subordination of the lower orders in society. The members of the upper classes, he believed, should cultivate the Roman virtues of self-discipline, self-mastery, and endurance. Phillip's face, as it has survived in the portraits, suggests that, like other worshippers at the shrine of 'cool reason', he was also driven by darker passions, though the dignity of his bearing and the high-mindedness that informed his every action provided eloquent testimony both to his nobility of mind and to his success in sublimating such darker passions.†

The First Fleet (as the first convoy of convicts transported to Australia is called) sailed from Portsmouth on Sunday, 13 May 1787. The convoy comprised two men-of-war and nine transports of between 279 and 461 tonnes. The previous evening, at the Royal Circus Theatre in London, the event had been celebrated by the performance of an aptly entitled opera – *Botany Bay*.

It is to be hoped that the writers of the opera had the good taste

---

* The north-south line would pass roughly through Darwin and Adelaide nowadays. This line was an implicit recognition of Holland's claim to the west of the country. In any case, nobody could be sure whether there was not some inland sea separating the two sides of the continent.

† Clark, C.M.H., *A Short History of Australia*, p. 21.

to make it a serious work and not a flippant one. For the atmosphere in which the First Fleet sailed was ugly. The convicts were crammed into the ships' holds, chained in pairs to the walls. Some of them had been there since the month of January. Phillip was outraged by the conditions. Two months before the sailing date he was still requesting that, if he was to be sent any more prisoners, they should at least be washed and clothed. The state of the women convicts he found especially squalid, half-naked and so disgusting that he suspected an epidemic must soon break out. All necessary precautions were taken so that none of these wretches, fit or unfit, could start a revolt. Iron bars prevented anyone coming up through the hatchways ; holes were cut in the walls of the holds so that shots could be fired in if necessary. When they were a week out from Portsmouth, Phillip took a humane decision and established a roster to allow the convicts to spend a few hours on the upper deck, without chains.

The voyage passed without serious incident. From time to time recalcitrants were flogged, of course, with greater or less severity.* But this punishment was so often meted out, to sailors as well as convicts, that everybody took it for granted. The fleet spent a week at Tenerife. In Rio de Janeiro, where they stopped for a month, the stauncher Protestants were revolted by ' the sloth, the ignorance, and the bigotry 't of the Papists. Another month was spent at Table Bay on the Cape of Good Hope, in October and November, where the shrewd Dutch traders gave them further cause for complaint, increasing threefold the price of everything needed by their fellow Protestants. When they had left the Cape behind, they had 7,000 kilometres sailing in front of them, through the Roaring Forties, on the tremendous swell of the southern Indian Ocean.

The ships dropped anchor at Botany Bay on 18 January 1788. The voyage had lasted only eight months and a week. It says much for Phillip's ability that he had lost no ships and that the mortality rate, at three per cent, was very low. However, the new Governor-in-Chief's problems were only beginning. He took stock of his company. After disembarkation, he would lose the transports ; this would leave him with the two warships, *Sirius* and *Supply*, and a

---

* The women too were flogged, naked, to begin with. Later they were put in irons and their heads shaven.

† Clark, C.M.H., *A History of Australia*, vol. I, p. 84.

peace-keeping force of marines made up of nineteen officers, twenty-four N.C.O.s, eight drummers and 160 privates. There were thirty wives and twelve children. Twenty-one of the convicts had not lived to see Botany Bay. Those who had were made up of 365 men, 153 women and eleven children (six boys and five girls). In all, this gave Phillip the charge of some 1,000 souls. Unsure as they were of what the future held for them, they certainly had no idea that for more than two full years they were to hear nothing of their home country.

It took Phillip no time to realize that Botany Bay fell far short of the glowing descriptions that had been given of it. Being a man of initiative, he explored the coastline to the north. There, three days later, to his relief, he came upon 'the finest harbour in the world, in which a thousand sail of the line may ride in the most perfect security'.

It was here that the city of Sydney was eventually to be built.* Phillip made up his mind without further ado that he would put his charges ashore at this spot in preference to the original destination.

On 24 January he got back to Botany Bay where he had left his fleet. What should he see but two more ships, flying the *fleur de lys* ! He could well have done without these unexpected guests. His officers reassured him that it was only a scientific expedition, under the command of a gentleman whose name was not unknown in England, the Comte de La Pérouse had made his name six years before during the American War of Independence, with a daring raid in Hudson's Bay. However, now the two countries were at peace. Both sides made a point of observing the code of naval politeness. Phillip left this duty to his junior officers, however, as he was anxious to sail at once for Sydney Cove. The English officers learned from the French that the two vessels, *La Boussole* and *L'Astrolabe*, had left Brest two and a half years before, that they had sailed round the Horn and across the Pacific, and that their knowledge of Cook's exploits had led them to explore Botany Bay.

* This was the harbour that Cook had discovered but had not explored. He had called it Port Jackson after a secretary at the Admiralty in whose family he had worked as a stable-boy. Phillip, not to be outdone, baptized one of the bays in this harbour Sydney Cove, thus immortalizing the name of a Home Secretary.

La Pérouse could not praise Cook too highly : 'Mister Cook did so much that all anyone else can do is admire his work.'* More practical matters were then raised ; the English were sympathetic but unforthcoming. La Pérouse says :

Their commander had authorized them to render me all possible service. They added however that since he was about to set sail northward, he could not afford to give us meat, munitions or sails, so that their offers of service amounted to nothing more than their good wishes for the remainder of our voyage.

The commander of *La Boussole* was too sensible not to appreciate that the English had good grounds for this attitude. He stayed at Botany Bay for six weeks, during which time a priest who had accompanied the expedition, Father Le Révérend, died † At the end of these six weeks, La Pérouse sailed away and was never seen alive again.‡ In Australia nowadays one sometimes hears it said that if La Pérouse had arrived a week earlier, the country could well have become a French dependency. Such courtesy is worthy of note ; but it must surely be said that the belief is unfounded. It is difficult to see how the government of Louis XVI, and the various revolutionary regimes that followed him, could ever have managed to establish a colony in Australia, let alone keep it viable over the years.

Such considerations were far from the mind of Governor Phillip on 26 January 1788 when the landing of his convicts began at Sydney Cove. The men landed without untoward incident. The disembarkation of the women, some days later, led to scenes of wild debauchery which were only ended by a violent thunderstorm. No doubt it needed more than rain to restore order ; and no doubt a modicum of decorum was eventually restored to the scene. On 7 February the Union Jack was raised, volleys were fired, the band of

* Clark, C.M.H., *A History of Australia*, vol. I, p. 55.

† He was the second European to be buried in Australian soil. To this day, an annual ceremony of remembrance takes place at his grave on 14 July.

‡ Because of the mystery surrounding the fate of the La Pérouse expedition, the Constituent Assembly commissioned Bruny D'Entrecasteaux in 1791 to lead a search-and-rescue expedition. It failed to find any trace of La Pérouse. It was not until 1827 that an Englishman, Peter Dillon, found the wreckage of La Pérouse's ships on the small island of Vanikoro, between the New Hebrides and Santa Cruz. This discovery was later confirmed by Dumont d'Urville.

the marines played 'God Save the King' and the first Governor of Australia formally took office. He took the opportunity to deliver a brief sermon to the convicts, promising clemency as the reward for good conduct and severe punishment for all offenders.

The matter of first importance was to establish some sort of settlement. The land looked unpromising ; there was no sign of the 'meadows' mentioned by Cook. There were, it was true, flowering shrubs which one officer saw as surpassing in beauty, perfection and number any that he had ever seen in an uncivilized country. However, for the rest, the country was uninspiring. Marjorie Eldershaw gives this description of the atmosphere of the place :

The first settlers found the fringe of the coast barren, unusable, bedrock. In some places there were swamps with silvery tussocks of coarse grass ; in others white sand-dunes ... A little inland the bush began ... ; it was just one tree after another *ad infinitum*, with some spiny undergrowth ... stretching out endlessly, green in the foreground, grey-green in the middle distance ... The bush was sinister in its monotony ; it was trackless and unremembering. It closed like water over anyone who strayed into it. Men were lost a few yards from the settlement. And it was silent. There were sounds – the laughter of the kookaburras, chatter of parroquets, other birds, the crepitation of branch on branch, of leaf against leaf – but these things were cushioned on a silence as vast as the bush. They rested on it and never penetrated it.*

Men would have had to be made of steel not to despair at times. Two years after the original landing, an officer could still write that the country was 'past all dispute a very wretched country'.†

Phillip was undaunted. He had a belief in the future of this queer place. Even at his lowest ebb, the sort of things he reported must have made the bureaucrats in the Colonial Office think that everything was fine. He speaks of certain small problems that they had encountered and which, given time, more hands and in particular more men able to till the soil, he was sure would be overcome.

His 'small problems' were actually none too small. Before leaving England, Governor Phillip had declared that convicts could not be used to lay the foundations of an empire. And yet, of course, the only labour force at his command, once they had reached Sydney

* Eldershaw, M.B., *Phillip of Australia*, Harrap, 1938, pp. 94–6.
† Clark, C.M.H., *A History of Australia*, vol. I, p. 121.

Cove, was the convicts. They were of diverse origins. A handful of them, mainly Irish, were political prisoners. There were a few people of quality who had somehow found themselves on the wrong side of the law and who, in the new situation in Australia, were soon to show what they were made of. Many of them were poachers, many more pickpockets. The rest were a mass of hard-core crim- inals and professional thieves, who would have done anything rather than a day's work. But these were the very people who were expected to till virgin soil that was so stony that it broke tools ; and to cut down trees for wood that turned out to be either too hard or else too brittle to be of much use in building. Phillip himself recognized that, though the majority of the convicts were well behaved, many of them would sooner face punishment than work. They have been called 'a dead weight' on the colony. After all, they had been chosen pretty much at random; prison governors had taken the opportunity to get rid of their most undesirable inmates. This meant that there were hardly any who were skilled at any- thing. Phillip complained that there was not a single gardener, let alone a competent botanist, in the whole colony. He was convinced that fifty free men, accompanied by their families, would accomplish more in a year than a thousand convicts.

In any case, it was out of the question to expect any assistance from the troops. From the outset they asserted their exclusiveness. They would not hear of any duties over and above those which they performed under normal garrison conditions. The officers were exceedingly loth to take part in the proceedings of any court other than a court martial. The other ranks felt that guarding convicts was beneath them. Their commanding officer, Major Robert Ross, was no help. He had been dignified with the title of Lieutenant- Governor of New South Wales, and disagreements between him and Phillip became frequent. These incidents foreshadowed the scenes of violence that the budding colony was to witness.

All these factors made for an atmosphere of tension. For one thing, the shortage of women was not calculated to calm the passions aroused by an appalling fate in so many exiles of different back- grounds. Thoughtful officialdom had toyed with the idea of recruit- ing womenfolk in sufficient numbers from the islands in the Pacific. Fortunately for the *vahines*, they were spared this ordeal. This left a few married women, who were of course not freely available, and the other female convicts, who were not at all reluctant. The latter, if one can judge by the contemporary pictures, were anything but beauty queens. As well as which, the sexes were strictly segregated, at least in theory. This may be one reason why the men quickly turned to the abuse of alcohol. However, this substitute turned out to be equally unsatisfactory, being rather hard to come by. For more than two years they could only draw on the supplies of liquor brought out from England by the First Fleet. Needless to say, such precious liquid was worth its weight in gold. Phillip once remarked that the promise of a swig of alcohol was the only sure way to get work done.

Though himself an unbeliever, Phillip was not above using religious persuasions to help him in his difficulties. For the first six years, religion was embodied in one man, the Rev. Richard Johnson. One of his contemporaries describes him as a just, pious and mild man. Perhaps he also lacked a sense of humour – for his first sermon, delivered under a tree a week after the landing, he took as his text verse twelve of Psalm 116 : ' What shall I render unto the Lord for all His benefits towards me ? ' What a pity that nobody thought of noting the reaction of the assembled convicts. The worthy chaplain dinned into his charges the evils of drink, that easy road to hell. With his faith in predestination, he seemed to believe that all the convicts were already damned ; the posthumous fate which he promised them could not have given much weight to his remonstrances on earthly things.

Johnson became a protector of Aborigines. To begin with the ' Indians ', as they were called, gave little trouble. Both sides were watching each other. Even when closer contact had been made, there was no improvement in mutual understanding. Phillip was a humane enough man ; he also took his orders conscientiously, like the good civil servant he was, trying to win their trust and make sure that all his subjects would live in amity and kindness with them. This, however, was easier said in Downing Street than done at Sydney Cove. The usual method (trinkets and trash) was tried, but without impressing the natives. For one thing, their conception of private property was quite different from the Europeans' ; they saw nothing wrong in simply taking whatever they felt like taking. When the newcomers blithely did the same to the natives, the Governor decided to set an example to the Aborigines. In the presence of the tribe whose fishing lines had been stolen, Phillip had the culprit flogged. The result of this experiment was a great surprise to the Europeans. The Aborigines, to a man, showed symptoms of disgust at the flogging ; their sympathy for the victim was so intense that a woman even took a stick and threatened the man wielding the lash. The British found this behaviour incomprehensible and wondered whether it was motivated by scorn or fear. Phillip tried in vain to fathom the ways of the native mind. After eighteen months he had an Aborigine by the name of Bennelong live with him. Bennelong picked up a smattering of English, a taste for European food and more than a taste for grog. He ran away after six months but came back before long, to live in a small hut that was built for him near the Governor's quarters. He was highly unpredictable in his behaviour.* The general conclusion among the British was that the only way to treat the ' Indians ' was harshly. Unfortunate incidents became more and more frequent. By December 1790 things had reached such a pass that Phillip reluctantly authorized a punitive expedition. This was to be the first in a long, sorry series of blood-lettings.

However, all these were quite minor problems. The real difficulty was survival itself. Within a month of arriving at Sydney Cove, Governor Phillip had sent one of his most trusted officers, Lieutenant Philip Gidley King (one day to be Governor himself), to reconnoitre the resources of Norfolk Island, in accordance with Colonial Office intentions. This reduced by fifteen convicts and eight sailors the numbers that Phillip had in his charge. He now had more than 900 men and women to house, clothe and feed. The convicts were housed in ramshackle lean-tos, where they were probably no worse off than in His Majesty's gaols and hulks back home. The soldiers lived in tents, of course, or in huts ; the sailors lived on board the two warships. Only the King's representative had the right to a house made of bricks. All these living arrangements, needless to say, left much to be desired in the way of elementary decency. Still, the convicts were used to rags and to roughing it ; and the barefoot sentries who presented arms outside the official residence were a long way from Buckingham Palace.

* Phillip was to take him to England on his return there in 1792. He presented Bennelong to George III. This did not make the Aborigine's fortune. He went back to his native country in 1795, taking with him almost his sole legacy from civilization – an addiction to alcohol.

The biggest headache of all was food: This thankless land refused to take the seeds they planted. All it grew were a few herbs, spinach and parsley. Admittedly, what with birds and the kangaroos, there was a meat supply of sorts ;* fishing also brought in a welcome addition to the diet, except in winter. But these local products were inadequate. The colonists had to rely on the stocks which they had brought with them ; and the speed with which these stocks dwindled was a constant worry. Phillip instituted a system of rationing, which he was gradually forced to make more and more stringent. It gave no favoured treatment to anyone and Phillip himself was the first to abide by it. Characteristically, when he had guests to dinner, he expected them to bring their own bread. He sent off many appeals for help which, with luck, were acted upon within a year. In October 1788 he sent the *Sirius* under Captain Hunter to the Cape of Good Hope. The ship arrived back the following May (having sailed right round the globe), bringing supplies which lasted only four months. *Sirius* set off again for China at the beginning of 1790, but foundered on the Norfolk Island reefs. At this point the colony's morale was probably at its lowest ebb, as by now scurvy was raging. A relief ship, *Guardian*, sent from London, also came to grief. The only ship left was *Supply*. Small as she was, she represented the colony's last chance. In April the Governor sent her for help to Batavia. It is hardly an exaggeration to say that, if their isolation had continued much longer, the first Australian colonists would have starved to death.

The evening of 3 June 1790 was quite unlike any other. It has been described by Captain Watkin Tench, the sort of historian's godsend who keeps a diary :

I was sitting in my hut, musing on our fate, when a confused clamour drew my attention. I opened my door, and saw several women with children in their arms running to and fro with distracted looks, congratulating each other, and kissing their infants with the most passionate and extravagant marks of fondness.

He ran to a hill, looked through his pocket-glass and realized that

---

* Professor Shaw quotes some significant figures : the First Fleet landed one bull, one cow, four calves, one stallion, three mares, forty-four sheep, some pigs and poultry. After six months there remained a grand total of one sheep ; the rest of the livestock had been lost in the bush.

their prayers were answered. One of his brother officers was beside him ; they were speechless, overcome with emotion, wringing each other's hands, openly weeping. It was a British transport, the *Lady Juliana* ; she had sailed from Plymouth eleven months before. They had letters which they tore open with trembling fingers. News hit them 'like meridian splendour on a blind man'. They learned of the illness of their sovereign and his fortunate recovery.* They read in amazement of the outbreak of the French Revolution of 1789, which to Tench was 'a wonderful and unexpected event'.†

Once they had got over the first excitement, they could see their situation in a more matter-of-fact way. The risk of starvation was now averted ; and the arrival of more ships, over the succeeding months, was to solve that problem for good. However the Second Fleet, as it was called, not only brought supplies, it was also laden with convicts. One out of every four of them had died during the voyage. When the survivors were landed they were a sorry sight. An observer of the scene at Sydney Cove describes it as distressing and miserable. A great many convicts were unable to walk or even to stand up. They were thrown bodily over the side, like crates or baggage. Some of them fainted on being brought up into the fresh air. Some died there and then on the deck. Some died in the boats as they were rowed ashore. The evidence of this witness may be exaggerated. But even six weeks later, when Phillip wrote a dispatch, he said that more than 100 prisoners were still quite incapable of doing any work at all, because they were too old or suffering from chronic illness. One of the women had been unable to walk for three years ; there were two men who were total imbeciles.

Despite the quality of some of these new recruits, the colony's fortunes were soon to change for the better. New hope had arrived with the supplies and the new workforce. Since the dark days of January 1788, the colony had struggled for bare survival. But the next two years were to be a period of constant growth and consolidation, albeit slow and painful.

In December 1792 the resourceful Phillip who, because of his state of health, had requested to be relieved, sailed for England. He had

* George III's intermittent bouts of insanity had begun in 1788.

† Tench, W., *Sydney's First Four Years*, Angus & Robertson, Sydney, 1961, pp. 169–70.

been in charge of New South Wales for not quite five years. By the time he left, the colony numbered some 3,000 inhabitants. On Norfolk Island there were about 1,000 more. In all, about 4,000 British subjects were now living in that part of the world, about four times as many as had come on the First Fleet. In some measure this growth was due to a high birth rate. Despite the fact that women were a small minority, there were many families, and child mortality was low. However, the increase in the numbers of convicts transported was the principal cause of the population growth. From 750 in 1788 they had reached 2,300 by 1792, making up about three quarters of the population.

The word 'convict' held a variety of different meanings. It was applied to those prisoners whose original sentence (usually seven years) had to run its full term. But there were many others whose sentences were commuted in one way or another. The most lenient reduction of sentence was the conditional pardon, which restored a convict to full citizenship, but under one important condition : he was forbidden to return to England before the expiry of the original sentence. Another, less liberal, form of provisional freedom was granted to 'ticket of leave' men : these convicts had no legal rights and were forbidden to hold land or move out of their police districts. There was, however, one great difference which marked them off from the common convicts, which was that they were exempt from the forced labour system and could actually hire themselves out to employers. To begin with, of course, they had no choice, as the government was the only possible employer.

The chain-gangs have often been described. They worked for nine hours each weekday and for five hours on Saturdays. On Sundays they had no work to do, except to attend, if not actually listen to, the Rev. Johnson's sermons. The harshness of this system varied according to the gang overseers, most of whom were either convicts themselves or former convicts. The labour, which consisted of clearing the ground, putting through roads, erecting a few buildings, was not marked by any great efficiency. Now and then convicts who could take no more of it tried to escape. Tench estimated that in 1791 a total of thirty-eight convicts had managed to abscond to the wilds. That same year, some of them aspired to more distant havens and made their escape in the belief that China was close by and the ideal place to go. These unfortunates presumably perished in the bush. In another escape that almost succeeded, nine

92

convicts made it as far as Timor in an open boat. There the Dutch authorities welcomed them at first; then after looking into the matter further, handed them over to the captain of a British warship.

The development of a class of employers and landholders was essential to the future growth of the country. The earliest members of this class were soldiers and sailors-cum-farmworkers. As time went on their numbers were augmented by what were called 'emancipists', convicts who had been granted an unconditional pardon before they had served out their full term. Phillip had the power to grant them land. Bachelors got thirty acres (13½ hectares), married men fifty (22½). Just before his departure, at the end of 1792, he was empowered to extend a more advantageous form of this privilege to officers and administrators. R.M. Crawford has estimated that by 1792 one-third of the land under cultivation was in the hands of private owners, who drew on the convicts for their labour force. Under this arrangement, relations often grew up between masters and convicts that were more humane than the latter had known in the chain-gangs.

In this way the Governor was gradually relieved of the necessity of providing food for a considerable proportion of the population. For he had been not only the sole employer of labour, but also the sole supplier of foodstuffs and clothing. The supplies of food and clothing were issued free (and frugally) to both the troops and the convicts by the government stores. These stores also supplied the landholders with tools, livestock and seed, buying in return their meat and crops. Currency was a problem. There was an almost total lack of money, apart from the few coins brought out from England by soldiers or sailors (or even by convicts). Now and again a foreign ship or two might put in for supplies at Sydney Cove. But the payment received for these sales did little to increase the monetary reserves; over the first four or five years, according to S.J. Butlin, the currency brought in this way was negligible. And so other forms of payment were devised. There were, firstly, I.O.U.s signed on any piece of paper and bound to disintegrate in a short time. The most reliable and popular currency were the drafts, payable in gold, which the Governor drew on the Treasury in London, especially for the officers, in lieu of the salary paid to them at home. Payments in kind and barter were no doubt more common than any other form of currency. The favoured commodities were tea, sugar, tobacco, flour and, above all, alcohol.

Thus life in the colony gradually prevailed and took shape. There were even social gatherings of a sort when officers' wives came out from England. Royal birthdays were celebrated with as much pomp as could be mustered. On the King's birthday and on the Prince of Wales', Phillip would give a banquet—a pity that the menus have not survived. Public buildings gradually rose. By 1791, apart from the Governor's official residence, there were already a hospital, a barracks and three government warehouses ;* the first streets had been roughed out on the site where modern Sydney's magnificent thoroughfares now run.

Robert Ross was relieved as Lieutenant-Governor in February 1792 by Major Francis Grose. On 2 April, Grose wrote to the Under-Secretary of State, Nepean, expressing his amazement at the state of the colony. Instead of the bare rocks he had been expecting, he found himself amid gardens which were flourishing and producing all sorts of fruit. There were great quantities of vegetables, too, and he lived in a house which he found completely to his taste. He suggested that all that was needed for the colony to become self-sufficient was a shipload of livestock and corn ; all its difficulties would then disappear. Grose freely acknowledged that on arrival he had been full of prejudices and bias against this unknown country, yet, since leaving England, he had seen no country that pleased him as much as this one.

Grose's description may be somewhat fulsome. Perhaps it was meant to impress Governor Phillip. The fact remains that, although the penal settlement of New South Wales was still very far from being a paradise in 1792, it was no longer the hell it had been in 1788.

---

* The first church was not built until 1793.

Chapter Six

Problems of growth

New South Wales without a Governor for three years – army ascendancy – army monopoly in trade – John Macarthur – appointment of Hunter – his difficulties with the army officers – King replaces Hunter – growing conflict with Macarthur – Macarthur expelled – revolt of Irish convicts – Macarthur's triumphant return – King recalled – Bligh succeeds King – Bligh's career – the Bounty *mutiny – Bligh's violent streak – tension grows – Bligh deposed by* pronunciamiento *– military rule for two years – arrival of Macquarie*

It is fascinating to think that, throughout the years after the departure of Phillip, while Europe was convulsed by the Revolutionary and Napoleonic Wars, a handful of Englishmen, engaged in bitter dissensions, rivalries and in-fighting, somehow managed to found a new nation at the ends of the earth. The 'problems of growth' of the title are the series of crises that shook early Australian society, albeit without halting its development.

After Phillip had gone, there was no Governor in Sydney for the next three years. Various theories have been advanced to explain this : that it was an economy measure ; that the choice of a replacement for Phillip posed too many problems ; or even that the new appointee might be captured en route by enemy pirates.* For whatever reason, New South Wales was administered by the local military authorities between 1792 and 1795. From 1795 until 1810 there was a succession of three naval men in charge. These men, although very different types, had to face the same difficulties, the origins of which we must now examine.

---

* For one thing the Cape, though a Dutch possession, was under French control. It was not taken over by the British until the autumn of 1795.

Three years after the First Fleet had landed its charges at Sydney Cove, Pitt pronounced himself satisfied with his decision. In 1791 he told the House of Commons that it had been absolutely essential to rid the kingdom of some of its most unredeemable criminals and that the solution chosen had been the most justified on economic grounds. In other words, Pitt was saying that the matter was now closed. This tendency of His Majesty's government to wash its hands of the new colony was bound to be reinforced by subsequent events. When Great Britain found itself in arms first against the 'revolutionary hydra' and then against the 'Corsican ogre', it clearly had more pressing troubles than the affairs of a penal colony in the South Seas. From the Cabinet's point of view, the best Governor would have been one whose name was never mentioned at their meetings.

However, this was close to wishful thinking. After all, the colony was now controlled by army and navy officers who found themselves in positions of power for which their training had given them no preparation. Not only had they little or no administrative experience, but they had hardly anyone to turn to for advice. If they sent requests for instructions back to London, they could not expect an answer for a year and more. And yet, if they took certain responsibilities upon themselves, they were for ever in danger of being reprimanded for it, since the administrators at home were quick to take offence. The Prime Minister and his Cabinet might well wish to forget all about Australia, but their subordinates were more watchful. At least four Ministries were responsible for the colony ; the Home Office, because it owned the convicts ; the Admiralty, because it had the job of conveying them ; the Exchequer, as always on the lookout for economies ; and the Ministry of Supply, which owned and provisioned the transports. The correspondence that passed between Sydney and London, written in that period's admirable administrative prose, inspires constant wonder at the myriad minutiae that occupied those civil servants.

Certainly there was no shortage of problems. But there was one particular problem which nobody had to face : at least in New South Wales there were no Frenchmen, as there were in Canada, and no Dutchmen, as in South Africa. And as for the natives, they resembled the Red Indians as little as they did the Kaffirs. Before long the newcomers just gave up trying to understand the Aborigines. Manning Clark says :

They were disgusted by their personal habits, by the filth, the flies, and the stench that surrounded the aborigines. They were angered by the indolence of the aborigine, by his inability and absence of desire to exert himself to raise himself out of his material squalor.*

This attitude was deplored in London. In 1802 Lord Hobart, Secretary for War and the Colonies, complained high-mindedly that the humanitarian injunctions of his predecessors had not been properly obeyed. There was little that Hobart could do, for at that same time his representative in Sydney, like most of his colleagues, had come to the conclusion that the Aborigines, because of their resistance to change and their inability to comprehend and accept the boon of British civilization, deserved stiff punishment.

Seen in this light, the Aborigines were a mere nuisance. The convicts, too, were a minor problem. The numbers transported were reduced by the wars. From 4,000 in the first four years, the rate dropped to about 2,500 between 1793 and 1810. The system of differences in status among the convicts, as already described (see page 92), was continued more or less unchanged and without too many problems in the years after Phillip's departure. Those convicts known as emancipists (see page 93) were beginning to make their presence felt. However, they were not yet numerous enough for their status to give rise to the sort of polemics that will be described in the next chapter.

The real problem, the one which far outweighed all others, was the army. The military men were the only organized body, the only disciplined body, the only body that wielded any real power in the colony. Certain historians have given the New South Wales Corps a name for extraordinary corruption and immorality. But one does wonder whether it was in fact worse than any other. In any case, during European wars it was never the crack regiments of the British Army that were garrisoned overseas. And the officers stationed in Sydney, like those elsewhere, well knew that their posting there was for a fixed period and tried to make as much as possible out of it in the shortest possible time. The lengths they went to brought down no fewer than three Governors.

Two centuries later, what takes one's breath away is not so much their profit instinct as the violence of their passions. Australia nowadays is a mild enough place ; but in those days it simmered

* Clark, C.M.H., *A Short History of Australia*, pp. 37–8.

like a cauldron. The army gentlemen were not the only hot-blooded ones ; their opponents were just as extreme in their emotions. Sociologists can have a field day with the effervescence of these earliest years in New South Wales. May an outsider venture to suggest that this effervescence may have been a result of a combination of loneliness and claustrophobia ? For there was something of the prison in the very nature of this place, even for bold men who had not been sent to it against their will – they were 24,000 kilometres from their own country, unsure of ever being able to hear from it as long as the wars lasted ; they were closed in to the east by the ocean, and on the other three sides, only about fifty kilometres away, by a mountain range that bade fair to be impassable.*

The problems began to crop up soon after Major Grose arrived, as Lieutenant-Governor, to take over from Phillip. The power that this unknown soldier thus acquired must have gone to his head. He very quickly used it to the advantage of his fellow officers. He opened to them two new ways of getting rich : landowning and trade. In theory officers were barred from both, but in such a place at such a time who was there to quibble about such niceties ? Grose, in whom men noted 'the lack of distinction, the amiability, the joviality',† used this policy of land allotments and trade concessions as a way of gaining popularity with his subordinates. In all he allotted 6,070 hectares, most of it to military officers. He even gave them the services of convicts free of charge, up to ten men and three women per officer, according to Professor Pike. This land policy of Grose gave the officers a privileged position compared with that of the few free settlers who had already decided to try their luck in the Antipodes, mainly retired soldiers or sailors plus a very few immigrants. The problem with cultivation, however, was : what to do with the crops ? The officers soon realized that it would be more profitable to sell alcohol than flour. This led to an increase in the abuse of liquor. Profitable as this trade was, it was not the only way in which the obliging Lieutenant-Governor allowed his brother officers to fill their coffers. Although the risk of starvation was a thing of the past, the docking of a cargo vessel was still very much an event. The

* These were the Blue Mountains. They remained impassable until 1813. See pages 115 and 128–9.

† Clark, C.M.H., *A History of Australia*, vol. I, p. 132.

masters of these ships would have preferred to sell their goods for hard cash. But in Sydney, cash was of course hard to come by. What the military gentlemen could offer, though, was what nobody else could offer : payment via drafts on the Treasury in London (see page 93). They therefore had no trouble in acquiring the lion's share of trade. Not that they were the only possible buyers. Slowly but surely private businesses were growing and beginning to compete with them. D.R. Hainsworth remarks that when these officers decided to declare a monopoly of trade for themselves, in 1798, after six years of commercial experience, 'it is at least as reasonable to see this agreement as a desperate attempt to shore up a crumbling dyke as to see it as the formal establishment of an anti-social cartel.'*

There was one man who was farsighted enough to think beyond these petty manoeuvres. His name was John Macarthur. He was a lieutenant in the New South Wales Corps, having come out with the Second Fleet in 1790 at the age of twenty-three. Vance Palmer speaks of him as 'a restless and dissatisfied' young man.† He was certainly not an easy person to get on with, having fought a duel during the voyage out and later having had difficulties with Phillip, the upshot of which was that he declined to accept any of the Governor's invitations to dinner. This martinet was undaunted by the likes of Grose. Within a few months he was Paymaster of the Corps and Inspector of Public Works as well as the owner of a farm of 40 hectares of the finest land. This farm he graced with the name of Elizabeth Farm, after his good wife, who seems to have been as mild and placid as he was irascible and passionate. In 1795 he was promoted to Captain by Paterson, who succeeded Grose as Lieutenant-Governor.

John Macarthur was already a man of importance in the colony when the first Governor since Phillip, John Hunter, arrived to take up his post. Hunter certainly seemed a wise choice for the job. He was now fifty-eight, having spent the previous thirty years in the navy. His seamanship was impeccable, his integrity unimpeachable, his zeal indefatigable, his judgement sound and unbiased. He was, in addition, no stranger to the new country, having come out in the First Fleet with Phillip and stayed for three years.

* Hainsworth, D.R., *Builders and Adventurers*, Cassell, 1968, p. 12.
† Palmer, V., *National Portraits*, 3rd ed., Melbourne University Press, 1954, p. 2.

Hunter did not notice the problems besetting him until some time after his arrival. The truth was revealed to him only gradually. Having realized the state of affairs, he attempted to re-establish the civil power, break the officers' monopoly and control the rum trade. But Hunter, though trying to clean up an Augean stable, was no Hercules. Acutely aware of his own impotence, he poured out his complaints in dispatches which were not to be read for another eight months. In his opinion the officers of the garrison would have dishonoured any other regiment in His Majesty's service ; he saw them as being lower than the lowest of the convicts. This may well have been true ; but it was dangerous to put it in writing. For at the very same time John Macarthur and his associates were sending letters of a very different sort to London. The recipient of these letters, the Duke of Portland, who because of his indecisiveness has been likened to 'a tennis ball, to be tossed from side to side ',* eventually lost patience with Hunter. In that autumn of 1799, the return of Bonaparte to France from Egypt was seen in Downing Street as ominous, foreshadowing troublesome events compared with which Botany Bay was a tiresome trifle. On 5 November, four days before Napoleon's 18 Brumaire, Hunter was informed of his dismissal from his post by one of those missives that governments like to send to their appointees as reminders of the insecurity of their tenure.

The next Governor was Philip Gidley King. He took up his post ten months after the dismissal of Hunter. He was forty-two years of age and had joined the navy at twelve as a cabin-boy. Like his predecessor, he was no stranger to New South Wales, having also come out originally with Phillip. When he arrived back in Sydney as Governor-in-Chief, he was appalled at what he found and reported in heartfelt terms that all the nations of the world seemed to have conspired to flood the country with spirits. The cellars, he said, were full to overflowing with this fiery poison. Vice, debauchery and an inexplicable slackness seemed to have taken hold of everyone. He resolved to get to the root of the problem. This was no doubt a wise policy. It was also the policy of his predecessor. Even so, for a while it looked as though King might make it work, as he had greater authority than Hunter. But he was up against

* Clark, C.M.H., *A History of Australia*, vol. I, p. 147.

formidable opponents. As soon as he forbade the officers to continue
the traffic in spirits, they gave it up nominally but went on as before,
using their mistresses (women convicts) as cover. As soon as he
banned the import of spirits, an army smuggling-ring kept the trade
supplied. The Governor-in-Chief soon came to see Macarthur as
the kingpin in the opposition. Macarthur is a difficult man to assess.
This is how one historian sees him, perhaps too kindly :

It no doubt earned him little credit with his fellows that, in a loose age,
his was the first stable home in Australia, that the roof of Elizabeth Farm
sheltered a wife legally wedded and a family living the life of an ordinary
English domestic *ménage* in the midst of a community in which nearly
the whole of the rest of the ruling class, civil and military, lived squalidly
with concubines ... when others began to become rich by trade, they
still found cause for envy, since his was solid and material wealth and
theirs was mainly ephemeral paper riches, born of speculation and
dissipated in speculation ... It has been held against [him] that [he]
obtained [his] first property through the use of official opportunities and
Government money at [his] disposal. But this was merely the normal
custom of [his] times ... Macarthur certainly traded in spirits to some
extent – he admitted this openly ... [But] it needs to be said that his own
papers do not disclose any abnormal liquor trading in his private capacity ... Governor Sir Ralph Darling wrote of him that he was 'a man
of strong passions, and observes no medium in anything. He is equally
ardent in his exertions to serve as he is to injure ... a man who embarks
in his cause must go all lengths.' He declared that he 'knew no medium
between friendship and enmity '.*

The Governor-in-Chief certainly did not share in the first of these
two responses. As far as King was concerned, Macarthur did not
fit the description just quoted either – he called Macarthur the
'Perturbator'. One year after taking up his appointment, he found
a way to rid himself of this troublemaker. Macarthur had wounded
the Lieutenant-Governor, Paterson, in a duel. If King were to
court-martial him, he would simply give him a forum, widen his
popularity and more than likely guarantee him a resounding
acquittal. King therefore decided to ship him to England for court-
martial. He sent with Macarthur a 53-page report couched in
unflattering terms : 'Experience has convinced every man in this

* Ellis, M.H., *John Macarthur*, Angus & Robertson, Sydney, 1955, pp. xiv-xvi.

colony that there are no resources which art, cunning, impudence and a pair of baselisk [*sic*] eyes can afford that he does not put in practice to obtain any point he undertakes.'* When he saw the ship taking Macarthur weigh anchor, King must have heaved a sigh of relief at the end of the struggle. But it was really only round one that was over.

Life in the colony continued, as frustrating for King as before. Like the worthy administrator he was, the Governor-in-Chief dutifully issued rules and ordinances. Having turned his hand from seafaring to enlightened despotism, he drew up regulations governing prices, wages, hours of work, the employment of convicts, the baking of bread and selling of meat, interest rates, weights and measures, the issue of banknotes. One wonders whether anyone bothered to read his new laws – certainly, nobody much bothered to see that anyone else obeyed them. In any case the officers were now turning their attention towards newer things. Since their monopoly had attracted more and more competition from private enterprise, it was becoming less profitable. So they decided to go in for animal husbandry, following the example of a handful of daring pioneers who, early as these times were, had foreseen the potential of such a venture.

Four years after his arrival, King found himself faced with a situation which, for a few hours, must have made his troubles with the 'Perturbator' seem tame indeed. For the first time since the arrival of the First Fleet there was a concerted attempt at a rising among the convicts. These were Irish, and so heirs to a tradition of desperate measures. When they had arrived, in September 1791, Phillip had seen no special significance in the fact that they were Irish. But of course they were different from his other charges, in that they brought with them the unvanquished faith of their ancestors and a nationalistic tradition that had been tempered by misfortune. The 1798 rebellion in Ireland had been savagely suppressed and this had led to a sharp rise in the transportation rate to Botany Bay. By the turn of the century more than 1,200 Irish convicts had been landed in New South Wales. Hunter had harboured suspicions about them and had eventually convinced

* Ellis, M.H., *op. cit.*, p. 207. According to Dr H.V. Evatt, the report never reached London. See Evatt, H.V., *Rum Rebellion*, Angus & Robertson, Sydney, 1938, pp. 65–6.

himself that they had hatched a seditious plot. He had one of the 'plotters' arrested and flogged. The flogging was particularly savage, but the man refused to give the names of his 'accomplices'. The 1804 rising was a more serious affair. During the night of 4 March a mob of 200 which soon grew to 400, led by a former soldier, set about burning and looting at Parramatta, in those days a small settlement close to Sydney. The repression was swift. A detachment of soldiers was sent in the morning ; they opened fire as soon as they came up with the rioters. The casualties were fifteen killed and several wounded ; the remainder gave themselves up. Nine of the ringleaders were hanged forthwith, nine others were given 500 lashes ;* several dozen were sentenced to hard labour, cutting coal. However the great majority of the rebels, some 300 or more, who were seen as 'deluded but not wicked men ',† received only a caution and a reprimand.

By the end of 1804 the Irish had been brought into line, the Aborigines had been taught a lesson, the convicts in general were giving no trouble and the threat from the French had passed (see pages 85 and 124). Just when all King's problems seemed solved, who should reappear on the scene but the 'Perturbator' himself, now a civilian. John Macarthur had not let the grass grow under his feet. Although his trial had misfired, it had convinced him that he had little future in the army. He had resigned his commission and taken up an idea which had already been mooted by others but which he was to put into practice in an exemplary fashion. Despite the scepticism of Banks, the revered expert on everything Australian, Macarthur had managed to convince the British government that there was a great future for wool in New South Wales. His return to Sydney was triumphal. He had brought with him some of the most valuable sheep from the royal flocks. More importantly, he also had an order authorizing him to receive an allotment of 5,000 acres (2,025 hectares) of the best grazing land, as well as a promise of a further concession of the same size if the first venture proved a success. This was a great blow to King. But he contented himself with thinking of another nickname for Macarthur ('the hero of the

---

* Father Dixon, who had been the first Catholic priest to be permitted to celebrate Mass, in 1803, was present at the floggings. The sight of the bleeding backs made him faint.

† Clark, C.M.H., *A History of Australia*, vol. I, p. 172.

fleece') and also by drowning the frustrations of the administrative life in the drink that he had tried to proscribe. His discontents were short-lived, as it turned out ; he learned in August 1806 that it was now his turn to be recalled to London.

Whatever else might be said of the man to whom it fell to be the next Governor, no one could accuse him of having a weak personality. He arrived preceded by his legend, which to some made him a hero and to others a monster. William Bligh had been born in 1754 ; he became an officer in the Royal Navy in 1771. He was in command of one of the ships in Cook's final, fatal expedition, a rapid rise which suggests his superiors thought highly of him. He had also seen active service in the American War of Independence and then gone over to the merchant marine for some years. He had come back into the King's service in 1787, which was to be a decisive year in his life. It was the year when he met Sir Joseph Banks (who was to become his protector), and when he was offered the command of a ship called *Bounty*. His mission was to sail for Tahiti and convey specimens of the breadfruit tree from there to the West Indies, where the British government hoped to transplant them and start a crop. On the voyage out, which lasted eleven months, there were numerous incidents. Witnesses' versions differ : some say Bligh was a tyrant, a man of harsh cruelty, with a streak of sadism ; others suggest he was no worse than many another captain, with his lurid range of curses and a staunch belief that a touch of the cat-o'-nine-tails would do nobody much harm. The ship's tense atmosphere was relaxed by the stay in Tahiti. Perhaps they stayed too long ; after six months in paradise the *Bounty* must have been too much like hell. Seventeen witnesses have left seventeen different versions of the mutiny ; which means, paradoxically, that it is difficult to tell what actually happened. What is beyond question is that the mutineers dumped their captain and eighteen loyal members of the ship's company in a boat just over seven metres long and two metres wide. Bligh's achievement was to navigate this craft for forty-one days, through mountainous seas, to Timor, a distance of more than 5,800 kilometres. On some days they were limited to half a loaf of bread and a few mouthfuls of water. When he got back to London, Bligh was court-martialled and acquitted on all charges arising out of the loss of his ship. Banks, who was full of Bligh's feat in surviving the open boat, even managed to have him presented at Court. In 1791 he set off again on another breadfruit mission, which was accomplished without a hitch.

Despite being cleared, Bligh's character was not unsullied by the *Bounty* affair, and he commanded no other ship until 1795. In 1801 he saw active service again at the battle of Copenhagen with Nelson, who mentioned him in dispatches. Three years later he was involved in another incident on his quarterdeck, when one of his officers accused Bligh of insulting and ill-treating him. This time the court-martial found that the charge was partly proven ; Bligh was reprimanded and admonished to be more circumspect in his language. The judgement may have caused Bligh to smile. As for Sir Joseph Banks, it did not alter his high opinion of the man. When the Governorship of New South Wales fell vacant, Banks recommended his protégé. Bligh got the job and arrived in Sydney on 8 August 1806.

One can imagine the sort of comment that greeted his arrival to take up his duties. Macarthur prepared for the fray. To begin with, his relations with the new Governor were cordial. However the aims of the two men were so opposed that this precarious understanding was bound to end before long. The 'Perturbator' had visions of a colony run along seigneurial lines by a landed aristocracy using convict labour to ensure economic success based on wool. Bligh was not so far-sighted as this. Dr Evatt stresses the basic simplicity of his character. Bligh's instructions were to put some order into the affairs of New South Wales and especially to put a stop to the illegal traffic in rum. Like the well-trained officer he was, he was determined to carry out these instructions to the letter ; like the disciplinarian he was, it never occurred to him, despite the *Bounty*, that anyone might cross him. He used dictatorial methods. For example, if anyone reminded him of what the law said, his reply was that whatever he wanted *was* the law. Or if he was re-minded of the Colonial Secretary, he was apt to say, 'To hell with your Colonial Secretary ! He can give orders in London if he likes, but I give the orders here !' Reports of this sort of language may well be apocryphal, but they were certainly given currency by his opponents in the full knowledge that, because they corresponded with what was known of his character, they would most likely be believed. His relations with all and sundry were soon poisoned. Mrs Macarthur saw Bligh as violent, rash and tyrannical. The 'tyrant' himself saw the lady's husband with no more indulgence.

The words he uses to describe his adversary recall Hunter's and King's – an arch-fiend, a constant disturber of public society, a venomous serpent to His Majesty's Governors.

The incidents which led up to the explosion of the Rum Rebellion need not be detailed. The situation came to a head on 26 January 1808, a day of oppressive humidity and heat. Bligh had managed to have Macarthur arrested, basing this decision on a series of grievances. This act incensed the officers. The Commander of the New South Wales Corps, Major Johnston, set the prisoner free. Then came, as Dr Evatt puts it, 'the intrusion of these drunken and half-drunken troops who were walking along with guns loaded, bayonets fixed, and the fife and drum giving a feeble imitation of "The British Grenadiers".'* Character assassination was the order of the day – the opponents of Bligh put it about that he had hidden under his bed to escape them. They even circulated a caricature purporting to show the scene. The truth was, however, that Bligh managed to evade arrest for some time so as to destroy certain papers. After Bligh's eventual arrest, Macarthur was acclaimed and the triumph of 'liberty' was celebrated by bonfires and illuminations. Johnston may not ever have read Napoleon's addresses to his troops, but in his speech to the Corps after the deposition of Bligh there is something of the tone of the victor of Austerlitz, as he thanked the gallant soldiers and implored them to 'persevere in the same honourable path and you will establish the credit of the New South Wales Corps on a basis not to be shaken'.† The 'Perturbator's' comment was that the 'tyrant' could only gnash his teeth in humiliation.

Macarthur was now in a position of unquestioned hegemony. Johnston, with doubtful legality, took the title of Lieutenant-Governor‡ Bligh was kept under house arrest and then allowed to return to England. No sooner had he stepped on board the ship that was to take him home than he proclaimed himself once more Governor and Commander-in-Chief and declared that New South Wales was in a state of rebellion. He then repaired to Hobart Town

* Evatt, H.V., *op. cit.*, p. 220.

† *ibid.*, p. 257.

‡ Acts of insubordination seem to have been not infrequent at that time in the British army and navy. A.G.L. Shaw has noted several more, from this same period, in India, Santo Domingo and Europe.

to await a more favourable turn of events. The rebels, for their part, felt some anxiety about the reactions to be expected from London. But London was much more taken up with European affairs than with the Antipodes and reacted with chilly indifference. For the next twenty-three months the military authorities, under three different commanding officers, held de facto power.* Legitimate government was not re-established in the colony until the arrival of a new Governor on 23 December 1809. This was Lieutenant-Colonel Lachlan Macquarie.

* Johnston was subsequently court-martialled and cashiered. He was permitted to go out to New South Wales again where he settled and made good as a farmer and stock-breeder. Bligh went on to become a Rear-Admiral. The wily Macarthur avoided trial. He stayed in England for eight years, from 1809 to 1817, then went back to Sydney. The last had not been heard of him.

Chapter Seven
Towards a new destiny

*Macquarie's career and character – the reign of virtue – public works –
years of peacefulness – new problems arise – confrontations with Marsden and the Bent brothers – the Treasury criticizes the Governor's
expenses – development of wool-growing – conflict between emancipists
and exclusives – Macquarie's support for the emancipists – London's
anxiety about the future of New South Wales – the Bigge inquiry –
Macquarie recalled – the penal settlement becomes a colony*

One has only to look at Macquarie's record in Australia to see that
he was a man of a very different stamp from those who had preceded
him. He inaugurated four years of unwonted calm and, despite some
dissensions, he had a total of twelve constructive years in a job which
nobody else had managed to hold for nearly as long.

One of his portraits shows him as he was at the age of forty-four.
He has just been appointed to an important position in London,
which his expression suggests is a pleasure to him. He also looks
as though he enjoys the red uniform with its gold braid and epaulettes, and the open neck showing a broad cream-coloured tie, very
elegant if standard garb. Even without the uniform one could guess
at a glance that he is a disciplined soldier, from the way he holds
himself, standing there almost at attention, from the straightforward
gaze of the man used to being obeyed and the face tanned by the
open-air life. The whole study suggests a man who takes a dignified
professional pride in respecting duty and the hierarchy to which he
belongs. Need one add that the face betrays not the slightest trace
of a sense of humour ? This is a point on which, for once, historians
agree. Nobody disputes the man's integrity, the purity of his intentions, the sincere cast of mind. But at the same time everybody
stresses the vanity of the fifth Governor.

Macquarie was forty-seven when he took up his Sydney posting.

He was no stranger to foreign parts. Remoteness was in his blood, the forlorn remoteness of the wind-swept Hebrides where his undistinguished roots were (his mother was reputed to be illiterate ; the family worked a wretched farm) and which he had left at the age of fourteen. He joined the army and saw the world, serving in America during the War of Independence and then in India. His rise from ensign to the rank of captain was rapid. As well as seeing new countries, he married and found a new, undreamt-of social world opening to him. The marriage lasted three brief years, his wife dying in 1796. Whatever the Bombay Sans Souci Club may have been, the fact that Macquarie was president of it in 1800 says much for his rise in society. His career – Egypt in 1801, India again the following year, then back to England – continued to be a success. Such a success, in fact, that he was presented at Court, where he met the most beautiful ladies in the world. Lord Castlereagh even asked him his opinion on the Hindu question ! He was off again in 1805 to Bombay, only to learn that he had been promoted lieutenant-colonel in the 73rd infantry regiment which was on its way back to garrison in England. He reached London again in 1807.

He had met the woman who was to be his second wife two years earlier. She was actually a distant relative of his, belonging to the noble branch of his own clan. As soon as he set eyes on her he summed her up as the perfect wife for a soldier. She was twenty-seven. He had told her they would have to wait four years before being married, a condition which she accepted with remarkable equanimity. However, as it turned out, they were married by the autumn of 1807. As London became aware of the events in Sydney Town and the need to find a successor to Governor Bligh, Macquarie made sure of bringing his qualifications for the job to the attention of Castlereagh. He was appointed Governor in the spring of 1809 and sailed with his wife, on the storeship *Dromedary*, on 22 May.

His orders were wide-ranging – 'to improve the morals of the colonists, to encourage marriage, to provide for education, to prohibit the use of spirituous liquors, and so to increase agriculture and stock as to ensure the certainty of a full supply to the inhabitants under all circumstances.' * Nothing could be clearer or more pointed, especially the last recommendation, as Downing Street hoped to be bothered as little as possible by New South Wales. The

* Clark, C.M.H., *A History of Australia*, vol. I, p. 265.

law that the new Governor was to uphold was now strengthened by a persuasion that his predecessors had lacked. His regiment, the 73rd, had come out with him. They were the first regular army troops to be seen in Sydney Town and with their brand-new uniforms and brass band they caused a sensation.

Before drawing up the list of his problems, Macquarie called for the latest statistics. In New South Wales there were just over 10,000 inhabitants, approximately 48 per cent of whom were convicts. There were a further 1,000 people colonizing Van Diemen's Land, where the proportion of convicts was greater. In theory, at least, the social order was inflexible : at the top were the military men ; then came the civil servants, the landowners and their tenants, then the free workers, and right down at the bottom were the convicts. But in practice, members of these apparently rigid classes often moved freely from one to the other.

Macquarie's first years were good ones. The new Governor benefited from the general weary reaction against the recent troubles. There was a moralizing tone to his announcement of his intentions. On 1 January 1810 he issued a proclamation-cum-New-Year's-greeting in which he hoped that the higher classes would set an example of subordination, morality and decorum, and that those in an inferior station would endeavour to distinguish themselves only by their loyalty, their sobriety and their industry.

It was to be the reign of virtue and hard work. One of Macquarie's first acts was to declare illegal all the decisions and measures taken by the self-appointed provisional authorities. He issued precepts of good conduct that were much needed. The proportion of illegitimate children has been estimated to be as high as two thirds, and alcohol continued to be as important as before in the life of the colony. The number of drinking-shops was reduced from seventy-five to twenty, and these twenty were made to close during church services. The unreligious were reminded that to work on the Lord's Day was a shameful and indecent custom. Unmarried couples living together were told that it was time to put an end to their immoral and illicit relations. M.H. Ellis in his life of Macquarie says that many young people, who had been happily cohabiting until then, paid up the three guineas needed to regularize their marital status.[*]

Macquarie had in him something of the Roman pro-consul. The

* Ellis, M.H., *Lachlan Macquarie*, Dymock's Book Arcade, Sydney, 1947, p. 221.

town which would one day become modern Sydney was laid out by him on a grand scale. He put roads through, erected public buildings and hospitals, encouraged the building of churches and schools. Even the Aborigines benefited from this virtuous dynamism. A school was provided for them ; with great difficulty, six boys and six girls were persuaded to attend it. The number of these young candidates for ' civilization ' was never to rise beyond twenty ; they were for ever regarded askance, not only by the colonists but by their own people.

As a wise administrator, the Governor knew the value of a planned ration of entertainment as a help in maintaining the balanced but monotonous well-being which he saw it as his function to promote. A racecourse was opened ten months after his arrival, and regular balls were held from then on. The *Sydney Gazette*,* which was usually full of cautionary tales of evangelical tone, says of the first of these balls that the Governor and his lady honoured the function with their presence, that the ladies vied with each other in beauty and elegance, that the band of the 73rd gave a perfect rendition of *God save the King* and then filled the room with melodious dance-tunes, and that the Governor and his party withdrew at 2 a.m. Apart from horse-races, balls, dinners, card games and cricket matches, there were kangaroo hunts to give those who took part in them the impression of belonging to the real upper crust. The Governor also held his dinners and receptions once a fortnight, inviting 100 to 150 guests. The fare was probably not *cordon bleu*. A dissatisfied guest wrote home to England that the Macquaries, being Scots and consequently close-fisted, kept a shabby table. Another, Ellis Bent as it happens, said that the service at the Macquaries' dinners was so poor that one might have danced a reel between courses.

For various reasons Macquarie's popularity, in London as well as in Sydney Town, lasted for four years. Whitehall was pleased at receiving fewer contradictory complaints from New South Wales ; and New South Wales itself felt that there now resided in Sydney Town a Governor who knew how to govern.

It was too good to last. The honeymoon period came to an end with personality problems and, more seriously, with problems of

* The paper first appeared in 1803.

principle. In his capacity as defender of the faith, Macquarie had a bone to pick with the Rev. Marsden, the official representative of Protestant orthodoxy. This minister was an odd character. He had come out in 1794 and, after the departure of his colleague the Rev. Johnson in 1800, had stayed on as the sole representative of his faith in the colony. By all accounts Sydney Town was not noted for piety. Marsden, according to the historians, was as strong as an ox and did not know the meaning of fatigue. His energies were not fully consumed by the demands of evangelism and he saw no contradiction between earthly profit and the eternal bliss promised by his faith. Which may be why he became the largest stock-breeder in the country after Macarthur. He seems to have been something of a Jack-of-all-trades, as he also held an appointment as magistrate. 'Spare the rod, spoil the convict' may have been his motto ; certainly he was not loth to sentence them to the lash. He had no belief in any rehabilitation of the convicts, and their redemption struck him as equally unlikely. About the Aborigines he was no more sanguine. He lamented the fact that they did not think, were attached to no belongings and had no need of anything, which was a mystery to this early member of the 'consumer society'. Surprisingly enough, he had nothing but praise for the Maoris, whom he saw as intellectually superior to the Aborigines, lacking only a knowledge of trade and the arts and enjoying a nature which predisposed them to pick up European work habits and morality as well as to welcome the word of God. The big difference was that, in New Zealand, Marsden was a law unto himself, whereas in Sydney he had to contend with Macquarie. And Macquarie's authority soon came to irk Marsden very much. This incompatibility of the two men gave rise to a sequence of incidents, the upshot of which was a summons to the Governor's office. There, in a stormy scene, the minister was given a dressing-down and was called the leader of a below-stairs conspiracy. He was also forbidden thenceforth to have any contacts with the representative of the Crown beyond those which could not be avoided by reason of the positions they both occupied.

Such language did not go down too well in London, where Marsden had important connections in religious circles. The news of Macquarie's set-to with Marsden did the Governor's reputation no good, especially since it arrived about the same time as a report that he was having just as violent a confrontation with the representatives of the judiciary. The law courts of New South Wales were under the jurisdiction of two brothers, Ellis and Jeffery Bent. The former had come out with Macquarie to take an appointment as Judge Advocate. To begin with he and Macquarie got on well, but gradually they came to interpret their respective rights in conflicting ways. The arrival of Jeffery Bent in 1814 to take up the newly created post of Judge of the Supreme Court aggravated things further. He had an unbounded self-esteem.* For his part Macquarie, after four years of omnipotence in the atmosphere of Sydney Town, had not become any more willing to see another's point of view. The two men collided head-on over questions of important principle as well as over trivia. The end came only when Macquarie threatened to resign if the two brothers were not recalled by Whitehall. He had his way eventually, but Ellis Bent having died in the meantime, Macquarie had to sit through a funeral oration by the Rev. Marsden which was a barely disguised indictment of his Governorship. An additional source of tension was the return of Macarthur not long afterwards. The 'Perturbator' had been permitted to go back to New South Wales on the loosely worded condition that he take no further part in politics. Macarthur's reports to friends in London, after the Governor had refused to grant him a new allotment of land, were just as unfavourable to Macquarie as those sent by Marsden and the Bents.

Macquarie was so highly thought of in government circles that these squabbles might well have been overlooked, or put down to the torrid Antipodean atmosphere. However, other infinitely more serious difficulties arose which did cast some doubt on the Governor's abilities.

As the Napoleonic Wars drew to a close, the Treasury was out of sorts and England out of pocket. Economy was the order of the day, now more than ever. At a distance of 20,000 kilometres, the bills for Macquarie's expenditure on public works and buildings seemed exorbitant. People were beginning to say that such outlay of funds had never been envisaged thirty years before when Pitt had made the decision to use Botany Bay to accommodate the overflow of the prison population. It was beginning to be asked :

* On arrival, he had refused to disembark unless he received a salute of thirteen guns.

what sort of a possession should New South Wales be? There were those who preferred still to see it as a penitentiary and who wondered whether it was run on harsh enough lines. They were put out by the constant reports of former convicts who seemed much better off than a great many of His Majesty's subjects at home in the British Isles. According to another view, the new possession should be considered as a colony, on a par with any of the other colonies. This meant that there should be no half-measures, that the colony's growth must not be restricted to the status of a mere prison settlement. Such a view was obviously wise. Profound and far-reaching socio-economic developments were bound to transform New South Wales in ways that would have left the crews of the First Fleet speechless.

The question of exports had arisen from the outset. Unless the young colony was to prove a never-ending liability to the home country, it had to produce goods for foreign exchange. The plans for flax and timber production had come to nothing. There was some expectation of discovering and mining coal, but the proverbial 'coals to Newcastle' objection could be put up against any suggestion that England might be a market for it. Sandalwood was found in Fiji, which – in spite of being 3,000 kilometres away – was supposed to belong to the maritime territory of Sydney. China would have been a profitable market for sandalwood, in exchange for tea and silks, but the East India Company's monopoly ruled out any worthwhile trade. In fact, for years the new colony's only appreciable resources were sealing and whaling. Unfortunately the sealing did not last long, as the animals that were the basis of the trade were massacred indiscriminately. There was more future in whaling, certainly, but it required the support of considerable investment and was subject to foreign competition.

It is against this background that one can assess the interest shown in the possibility of developing a wool industry. The first merinos had been imported from the Cape in 1797. A handful of resourceful men, including of course Macarthur and the monetarily minded Rev. Marsden, had started raising sheep. Three years later Governor King was already talking of considerable wool-producing potential. In 1807, a first consignment of samples of merino wool (weighing 111 kilograms) was sent to England, where it met with indifferent success. However, only three years later, the mercantile evangelist sent off more than 1,360 kilos. Even so, development of sheep-farming was hampered by lack of space. As long as it was thought that New South Wales was restricted to the coastal strip between the sea and the mountain ranges, further expansion seemed extremely limited. This view was radically altered in 1813 (see pages 128–9) when the mountain barrier to the west was finally crossed, giving the colony vast new spaces which were eventually to make sheep-farming the greatest source of wealth in modern Australia. *

Macquarie did not favour this development. He saw sheep-farmers as men who were careless of their appearance and behaviour, who did not settle in any one place and were therefore difficult to govern. He had a very different view of the colony's future, putting much more hope in agriculture than in sheep. Tilling the land he saw as the best way of ensuring the regeneration of former convicts. These ex-convicts, as it happens, were by now more and more numerous, because they had either served their full terms or been granted remissions. They took no exception to being given the name of 'emancipists', although there were other people who used it as something of an insult. Emancipists were becoming a force in the life of the colony, diverse and colourful as many of them were. There were, for example, the Scottish martyrs – the five men sentenced to fourteen years transportation for having advocated reforms in Edinburgh in 1792 – who enjoyed provisional freedom from the moment of their arrival. They, it must be said, were exceptions to the rule, for the great majority of convicts had to serve out at least a part of their sentence. Many of these people must have been blessed with wills and constitutions of iron, since ill-treatment and humiliations did not prevent them from coming to occupy places of some importance in the community. Take George Barrington – the so-called 'King of the Pickpockets' – a character if ever there was one. His background is misted with legend. One wonders whether he really had emptied all those pockets, or lived in such exalted aristocratic circles, as he was reputed to have. What is certain is that it was the theft of a gold watch and chain at a race-meeting that led to his discovery of Australia. Having arrived in 1791, he had become chief of police in Parramatta five years later. But he was not the only felon to become a senior law-enforcement officer. Andrew Thompson, whose crime was the theft of cloth

---

* Development was slow. By 1821 wool contributed only £11,977 to a total budget of £471,375.

worth £10, was appointed commandant in Parramatta six years after his arrival. He held the job for ten years, managing also to become the biggest producer of cereal crops.

Having more than one string to their bow seems to have been characteristic of the emancipists. Francis Greenway, for one, began as a forger and ended up as a famous architect. His first job was the design and construction of a lighthouse. Macquarie was so impressed that he entrusted to Greenway the construction of a new Governor's residence. Greenway's original brainchild was a castle, with stables on such a scale that the Treasury vetoed the design. Nothing daunted, Greenway endowed Sydney Town at Macquarie's behest with barracks, churches and law-courts. His work is still visible in Sydney to this day. Ex-convicts also made good in the other professions. There was one William Bland, who had killed a man in a duel in 1813. He became a doctor, and later went on to be a philanthropic educationalist and even a politician. Another who distinguished himself as a doctor was William Redfern. He had been accused of having taken part in the Nore mutiny of 1797, but his moral standing was such that in 1817 he was to be selected as one of the original directors of the Bank of New South Wales, the first banking house to be established in the colony. As for Michael Robinson, transported as a blackmailer in 1796, he turns up thirty years later in the guise of the colony's Poet Laureate, one of the perquisites of his office being two cows. There was Joseph Lycett, another forger, who turned his hand to painting ; and Richard Read, who left a series of portraits of Macquarie. *

It is in no way surprising that men of such vitality were attracted to commerce. James Towell (yet another coiner) made a successful business of selling whale-oil.† Samuel Terry, who owed his acquaintance with Australia to the theft of 400 pairs of stockings, accumulated such a fortune that he became known as the 'Botany Bay Rothschild'. A widow with seven children, Mary Reibey (transported at the age of thirteen for horse-stealing) specialized in seaborne trade. Another who became wealthy through exports was Simeon Lord, perhaps the best known of them all. At nineteen he had stolen some lengths of calico and muslin ; in New South Wales

---

* However, it is not certain that the Governor actually sat for him.

† He went back to England where he lived in poverty and twenty years later murdered a woman.

he was the first to set up factories for the production of hats, shoes and blankets as well as soap and candles.

The problems created by such people were many and varied. What attitude should one have to this unprecedented category of citizens ? There were some (the 'exclusives') who saw fit to treat them as untouchables. The exclusives were so called because they sought to exclude from polite society, if not from public service, anyone who at any time and for any reason had been sentenced to transportation. Macquarie had loftier ideals.* He could not help believing, he said, that every emancipated and deserving convict should feel at home in the colony. His principle was that, once a man had earned his freedom, his past should be forgotten and not held against him. He practised what he preached, too, inviting emancipists to his dinners and receptions, commissioning buildings from Greenway, making the redoubtable Rev. Marsden share his bench with two ex-convicts and insisting that Judge Bent be addressed in court by barristers who had themselves once been in the dock.

To resolve the status of New South Wales as a penitentiary or a colony and the question of the emancipists, London decided to appoint a commissioner to make an inquiry into them. The man chosen was John Thomas Bigge, whose main experience was as Chief Justice at Trinidad. His terms of reference were so wide that it has been said of Bigge that he was not only a Commissioner

---

* Perhaps he had read the touchingly optimistic thoughts inspired in the good *abbé*, Father Delille, some years earlier :

Who doth not know the comforting sight

Afforded by that great receptacle of bandits,

Botany Bay, Albion's bilge,

Where robbery, looting and sedition are spewed in abundance

To purge old England and to make the new land fertile.

There, in remote exile, an indulgent law-giver

Turns dangerous subjects into wise colonists and happy citizens,

Smiles on repentance, encourages industry,

Gives back freedom, civil habits and nationality.

On all sides I see marshlands reclaimed,

Deserts made to bloom and the woodland tamed.

(from *Malheur et Pitié* [*Woe and Pity*], London, 1802, canto II, lines 80–91).

of the Crown but he was also a private investigator.

He arrived in Sydney in September 1819. Macquarie gave him his thirteen-gun salute and a cordial welcome. But he was worried. He had even tendered his resignation, feeling that Westminister was losing confidence in him. As ill-luck would have it, Lord Bathurst's reply, requesting him to reconsider his decision, went astray. Moreover the Governor had only a very sketchy notion of the purpose of Bigge's inquiry into his administration. Relations between the two men got rapidly worse, which might have been expected. One of them, at fifty-nine, was a soldier of humble extraction, prudent, pragmatic and humane, with a thorough knowledge of local conditions ; while the other was a professional lawyer, of upper-class background, with a theoretical cast of mind, given to judging everything on English lines and totally ignorant of the matters he was to study.

Bigge's inquiry took two years. The evidence he collected ran to thousands of pages, although he does not seem to have been guided by complete impartiality in his selection of it. His great labours produced three reports which are milestones in the history of Australia. Broadly, they condemned the road-making and the erection of public buildings, as well as the policy favouring the emancipists. To Bigge, New South Wales was still a penal settlement. Nevertheless he pronounced in favour of immigration, and this was to have far-reaching consequences. He recommended that immigrants be granted land in proportion to their capital and that convicts be used as shepherds on the wool-growing properties. This was not only a vindication of Macarthur's ideas, it was also a step away from the penitentiary concept towards colony status. For the new immigrants would have to be accorded the same rights as any other British subjects who settled elsewhere throughout the Empire.

Macquarie, of course, was unimpressed by Commissioner Bigge's criticisms of his policies. At the beginning of 1822, his resignation having been accepted, he sailed for London, where he arrived just at the time when Bigge's first report was tabled in the Commons. The Governor lost no time. Having arrived on 5 July, he submitted his defence to Lord Bathurst by the twenty-seventh. This was an account of his administration which, though predictably biased, gave in the main an accurate picture. One certainly finds Macquarie exaggerating things to his own credit, such as when he says that on

his arrival in New South Wales the colony was 'still in its infancy'.*
Even so, the contrast between 1810 and 1821 was striking. One need
only look at the figures quoted by Macquarie : population (including
troops) in 1810, 11,590 as against 38,778 in 1821 ; head of cattle,
12,442 and 102,939 ; sheep, 25,888 and 290,158 ; pigs, 9,544 and
83,906 ; horses, 1,134 and 4,564 ; area under cultivation, 7,615
(3,084 hectares) acres as against 32,267 (13,068). Perhaps the growth
was most vividly exemplified by Sydney Town itself. For years the
place had been called 'The Camp', because of the impression of
the makeshift and the temporary that it gave. In 1820 two Frenchmen, Jacques Arago and Louis de Freycinet, on a voyage round the
world, put into Port Jackson. Arago described Sydney as follows :
'The town looks like an amphitheatre and presents a beautiful
spectacle ... The older wooden houses are now replaced by fine
stone dwellings, adorned with handsome sculptures and with
balconies of remarkable beauty and taste.' They were equally
impressed with the public buildings and the general appearance of
the town. Marjorie Barnard writes : 'Sydney was a blue and white
town, blue water, white walls, blue roofs and blue skies.'† Another
description of Sydney written in the early 1800s gives one the same
unforgettable impression that the city still gives to travellers to this
day :

The views from the heights of the town are bold, varied and beautiful
The strange irregular appearance of the town itself, the numerous coves
and islets both above and below it, the towering forests and projecting
rocks, combined with the infinite diversity of hill and dale on each side
of the harbour, form altogether a *coup d'oeil* of which it may be safely
asserted that few towns can boast a parallel. ‡

* This hardly tallies with the letter (quoted by Hainsworth, D.R., *Builders and
Adventurers*, p. 163) from Macquarie to his brother four months after taking up
duty : 'Notwithstanding the arrest of Govr. Bligh and the late Disturbances in
this Country, I found the Colony on my arrival in a perfect state of tranquillity
and in a thriving flourishing condition. Indeed the whole country is much more
advanced in every kind of improvement than I could have supposed was possible
in the time it has been settled.'

† Barnard, M., *Macquarie's World*, Melbourne University Press, 1946, p. 25.
‡ *ibid.*, p. 25.

One wonders at the thoughts of the departing Governor, aboard the *Surry*, as that landscape gradually receded. There can be no doubt that he was a man of greater vision than he has sometimes been given credit for. He it was who first suggested the name 'Australia' for the still unexplored continent. In fact, though they may not have been aware of it, Macquarie and Bigge, despite the irreconcilable differences of their views, each had an important contribution to make to the development of the country. Macquarie, by enabling ex-convicts to take their place in society, promoted essential social cohesion. And if Bigge had not foreseen the necessity for great landholdings in the development of the economically vital wool industry, the future of New South Wales would no doubt have been unpromising. The confrontation between these two men marks the opening of a new era in the history of Australia.

Part Three
Australia as a Colony
1821-1901

Chapter Eight
The search for the continent

*Exploration by sea : Bass, Flinders, Baudin – exploration by land – the
Blue Mountains crossed – the south-east explored : Cunningham, Hume
and Hovell, Sturt, Mitchell, McMillan, Strzelecki – John Eyre's trek
from Adelaide to Albany – the search for 'the Inland Sea' : Sturt,
Leichhardt – south-north crossings : McDouall Stuart, Burke and
Wills – the explorers' faith, patriotism and scientific curiosity – their
different methods – the 'tyranny of distance' – the Aborigines – major
difficulties : lack of navigable rivers, shortage of water and food, harsh
climate – by 1860 more than half of Australia discovered*

When Macquarie left Sydney in 1822, although the whole coastline
of Australia had been reconnoitred, the hinterland was still largely
unknown.

In October 1795 two young men, George Bass, a surgeon of
twenty-four, and Matthew Flinders, a naval ensign of twenty-one,
decided they had seen enough of Sydney Cove, where they had
arrived seven weeks before. They obtained Governor Hunter's
permission to broaden their horizons. In a tiny craft less than three
metres in length (aptly enough called the *Tom Thumb*), they explored up the river which runs into Botany Bay. It must have been an
eventful trip – Bass, who was close to two metres in height, took up
almost all of the boat's length when he lay down. However, the
discomforts of this journey did not deter them. Eighteen months
later, in another boat not much larger, they explored almost 1,000
kilometres down the coast southward from Port Jackson. On meeting some Aborigines, Flinders carried out an odd experiment,
cutting off their hair and beards with a pair of scissors. They were
so frightened at this, staring and grinning fixedly at one another,
that Flinders saw them as 'not unworthy the pencil of a Hogarth'.*

* Quoted by Scott, E., *The Life of Captain Matthew Flinders, R.N.*, Angus &

These two journeys of exploration were only a beginning. In 1798 the two men were given a ship of twenty-six tonnes, which must have seemed like a flagship to them, and were the first to circumnavigate Tasmania, thus proving that it was an island separated from the mainland. After this Bass and Flinders split up. Bass went in for business activities in which he received more than his share of hard knocks. Flinders pursued his interest in the sea and exploration. He is reported to have said that, if he was lying in his grave and there was talk of a voyage of discovery, he would rise straight away from the dead. But he was far from dead when he sailed from England in July 1801, in command of the *Investigator* (of 341 tonnes!). His orders were to make a detailed survey of the coasts of Australia. 'The Indefatigable', as his officers nicknamed him, charted the southern coast from Cape Leeuwin, at the south-west corner, to a point eastward of the present site of Adelaide. On 8 April 1802, four months after his arrival in southern waters, he had a surprise that was reminiscent of Phillip's encounter with La Pérouse fourteen years earlier – what should he see but an unfamiliar sail on the horizon. As it approached, the flag became clearer and turned out to be the tricolour of the Revolution. It was a delicate situation, France and Britain being, as far as Flinders knew, still at war.*

Flinders realized soon enough who these untoward visitors were. He knew that, nine months before his own departure, a certain Captain Baudin had sailed from Le Havre with two ships, *Le Géographe* and *Le Naturaliste*.† Flinders went aboard and paid a visit. Baudin found him cold and reserved. Was Flinders just being British, or was he suspicious? For a period of half a century, Westminster governments had the greatest difficulty in ridding themselves of their obsession that the French had designs on Australia. But if that had been the case, the question would undoubtedly have been raised in 1802 at the Amiens peace negotiations; which it was not. Of course, Napoleon may have had some scheme at the back of his mind; it would not have been surprising in such a many-sided genius as Bonaparte. Be that as it may, the

* In fact, the Treaty of Amiens had been signed on 25 March. But the news of this had of course not yet reached the Antipodes.

† Baudin actually had a British Admiralty passport, thanks to Sir Joseph Banks. In those days, courtesy was not a casualty of war.

Robertson, Sydney, 1914, p. 90.

aim of Baudin's expedition was primarily scientific. He had twenty-four scientists aboard, who gave the crew no end of trouble. The captain said : 'They clutter up the deck, they suffer from seasickness, they do nothing useful and they panic at the slightest gust of wind.'

The two explorers separated on 9 April, apparently on good terms. They had only been able to communicate via interpreters. Their meeting had been brief and it is extremely unlikely that Flinders learned in any great detail of the Frenchman's doings, though they would have interested him. Baudin had taken his time. He had been 220 days (which included a stop of more than a month in Mauritius) on a voyage that had taken the *Investigator* seventy-eight days less. For one thing, he was as fond of reading as of the natural sciences and his ship's library contained more than 1,100 volumes. For another, as one of his officers is supposed to have said to one of the Englishmen, if they had not lingered to collect butterflies, they would have beaten Flinders to it. The implication is unfair ; Baudin's achievement shows he was not lacking in conscientiousness or pride in his work. He was also not lacking in jingoism, and had given the name 'Napoleon's Land' to the stretch of coast from Wilson's Promontory, in the south-east, to Cape Adieu (near the 130th meridian which bisects the continent from north to south). He had scattered French proper names along the coast like a paper-chase. One historian remarks that to look at a map of 'Napoleon's Land' is like looking at the index to the Paris Panthéon or the Père-Lachaise cemetery. * There were Richelieu, Desaix, Montaigne, Volney, Montesquieu, Talleyrand, Decrès, Cambacérès, Lacépède, Laplace, Buffon, Maupertuis, Pascal, Berthier, Lafayette, Descartes, Racine, Molière, Bernadotte, La Fontaine, Condillac, Bossuet, Colbert, Rabelais, d'Alembert, Sully, Bayard, Fénelon, Joan of Arc, Massena, Turenne, Jussieu, Murat, Jérôme, Louis, Hortense, Joseph, Lucien, Joséphine.† No doubt the men

---

* The Panthéon and the Père-Lachaise cemetery contain the graves of many illustrious Frenchmen (*translator's note*).

† In 1807 the geographer on the expedition, Louis de Freycinet, published the first detailed atlas of Australia. Five years later, after Napoleon had exchanged his first wife, Joséphine, for his second, Marie-Louise, 'Josephine Gulf' had become 'Marie-Louise Gulf'. By 1824, most of the French place-names had been dropped, except in the south-east corner.

of science enjoyed adding to this list. As for the crew, their morale was at its lowest, sapped by raging scurvy : if only Baudin had taken the same precautions as Cook. He decided to make for Port Jackson. By the time he reached there, on 20 June, he was in dire straits. He says : ' I had four men in a fit state to work, including the officer of the watch.' At least he had the compensation of finding in Sydney his second ship, *Le Naturaliste*, with which he had lost contact a few months before in Tasmanian waters. The British, fully aware now that peace had been signed, could not do enough to help him. François Péron, the great naturalist, who was to bring back an invaluable collection of specimens from this voyage, wrote : ' The English received us with that great cordial open-handedness that can only be attributed to the perfection of European civilization.' It may be that Péron and Freycinet went further than natural science and geography and dabbled in political matters. Perhaps they were merely clumsy. Whatever the truth, their activities and the questions they asked roused Governor King's suspicions and led him to expand his occupation of the continent, by way of precaution. *

Flinders had been in Port Jackson at the same time as Baudin. He sailed from there on 22 July 1802. The rest of his voyage is an epic, if ever there was one. He sailed up the east coast of the continent, along the Great Barrier Reef and through Torres Strait. By this time, *Investigator* was in such bad condition that she could not have survived a gale. Even so her captain pressed on westwards, right along the north coast, then turned south down the west coast, to come back eastwards through the Bight. He reached Port Jackson again on 9 June 1803, the first man to have circumnavigated the continent. Nevertheless he was unsatisfied, feeling that his charting of the coastline was incomplete. So he sailed for England, with the object of exchanging his unseaworthy ship for another, sounder vessel. The ship he was on, the *Porpoise*, was wrecked and Flinders, like Bligh a few years before him, had to cover hundreds of kilometres in an open boat. He managed to make Sydney, from where

---

* See Chapter 10. After a stay of six months, the two French ships left Sydney in November 1802. Baudin died in Mauritius the following year, on the way home. Between 1807 and 1813 Péron and Freycinet published their *Voyage of Discovery to the Southern Lands*, in which they had unkind things to say of the leader of the expedition.

after a brief stay he set out again in a flimsy twenty-tonner. Following his original course northwards again as far as Timor, he then turned south-west across the Indian Ocean. Here he met another setback. His ship was leaking like a sieve. He decided to put in at Mauritius, where he dropped anchor on 17 December 1803, all unaware that France and Britain had been at war once more since the previous May.

The island's Governor was General Decaen, one of the volunteers of 1792, a brave officer who had served in the Revolutionary wars under Kléber and Moreau. He hoped that this remote posting would give him the opportunity to show his worth and had dreams of expanding French influence into Asia. He saw something sinister in the arrival of Flinders, and harboured against him the same suspicions as King against Peron and Freycinet.* However, he went further than the Governor of New South Wales and placed his English visitor under arrest. He also invited him to dinner. The scene begins to look somewhat like comic opera, as Flinders stood on his dignity and declined. When Decaen received his refusal he took it as an insult and decided to detain him as a prisoner-of-war. Flinders had to stay for seven years on the island, and was only allowed to return to England in 1810. He was then thirty-six. He spent the last four years of his life writing his monumental *Voyage to Terra Australis*. The final irony that fate had in store for Flinders was that the day after the book was published, on 18 July 1814, he died.

These maritime discoveries were to have a considerable bearing on the future of Australia. Until then, ships coming to Sydney from the Cape had sailed south of Tasmania, on the assumption that it

---

* He probably suspected that Flinders had been sent to reconnoitre the island, in preparation for a British invasion. Such suspicions were far from absurd ; the island did become a British possession in 1810, when its former French name (île de France) was changed to Mauritius. On 9 July of that year, Napoleon sent Decaen an extraordinary letter, informing him of his decision to double the number of troops garrisoned on the island and adding, 'which would give a total (including inhabitants and the frigates' crews) of 5,000 to 6,000 men, and would require the English to mount a most substantial expedition.' The Emperor, needless to say, was not in the habit of making plans to remain on the defensive : 'The dispatch of these 1,500 reinforcements on store-ships and frigates strikes me as most important, especially since the frigates themselves will be of great

was part of the mainland, before turning northwards. Now they could sail through the strait called after George Bass, which shortened the voyage by some 1,200 kilometres. On journeys northward from Sydney, too, time could now be saved. Once Flinders had charted Torres Strait in detail, navigators returning to Europe or making for China no longer avoided it as they had previously. Some of them had been in the habit of making the long detour via the Solomons and the north of New Guinea to get to the Dutch East Indies. Distance may not have been tamed; but it was certainly less daunting than it had been.

The men who explored the inland also found distance their worst enemy. Three distinct phases have been discerned in this discovery of the hinterland. In the first period, lasting about thirty years, a series of expeditions opened up an area in the south-east corner bounded by the sea and a line drawn between Adelaide and Brisbane, approximately. The second stage was the search for the mysterious ' new Caspian Sea '* that many were convinced lay at the heart of Australia. When that expectation had been proved false, the various expeditions crossing the continent from one side to the other completed the cycle of adventures. It all took about fifty years.

For twenty-five years after the arrival of the First Fleet, little if any progress was made. The colonists and convicts at Sydney Cove could see a bluish mountain range on the horizon. These mountains seemed to forbid any expansion inland. Between 1789 and 1804, seven attempts were made to cross the range. But each time the expeditions met such a dense and intricate mesh of gorges, escarpments and ravines that they had to give up. Governor King's conclusion was that they had to abandon all hope of ever developing agriculture on the far side of this dispiriting landscape. At that time, as recent studies have shown, there was no pressing economic necessity to open up the inland.

Civil servants should know not to commit themselves to any hard and fast opinions. In the autumn of 1813 three men, Gregory Blaxland, William Lawson and William Charles Wentworth,

---

* Moorehead, Alan, *Cooper's Creek*, Hamish Hamilton, 1963, p. 13.

usefulness there. The plan would be to equip them to invade and take the English colony of Jackson [*sic*], which lies to the south of the Ile de France [*sic*], and which would furnish us with considerable supplies.' As can be seen, the suspicions harboured by one side were not as unfounded as those of the other side.

accompanied by four servants, five dogs and four horses, triumphed at last over the seemingly impassable barrier. Unlike their predecessors, they had kept to the crowning ridge of the mountains, instead of getting lost among the valleys. What they saw, when they eventually got through to the other side, filled them with excitement – grassland sufficient to support the stock of the colony for the next thirty years; they thought it was the most varied landscape they had ever seen. Macquarie, ever eager to expand his public works programme, decided immediately to put a road through. It led to the site of present-day Bathurst. Unfortunately, the high hopes raised by this opening up of the plains were tempered two years later by a discouraging report from John Joseph Oxley, the surveyor-general of lands. Oxley had followed two recently discovered rivers and found that they kept dissipating in lagoons, swamps, sandbanks or 'an ocean of reeds'.* Oxley drew two conclusions which for a time were looked on as certainties: the first was demoralizing – 'that the interior of this vast country is a marsh and uninhabitable' west of the 147th meridian;† but the other seemed more promising – Oxley felt that they were not far from an inland sea.

The impetus to explore the inland had been given. In 1823 Allan Cunningham found a way northward from Bathurst to the Liverpool Plains, halfway from Sydney to the future site of Brisbane. Four years later he got to the Darling Downs, within 100 kilometres of the future capital of Queensland. At the same time, Hamilton Hume and William Hovell led an expedition in the opposite direction, managing to reach a point beyond the site where Melbourne would one day rise. They were very favourably impressed by the region, finding its soil magnificent and its climate much more like that of England than any other part of Australia.

Then it was the turn of Charles Sturt, one of the most heroic figures in the annals of Australian exploration. He is usually seen as a Tory gentleman, with an unshakeable faith in God. He joined the Army in 1813 at the age of nineteen and had the standard career: the war in Spain, then the Canadian campaign against the Americans, followed by garrison duty in France during the allied

---

* Quoted in Fitzpatrick, K. (ed.), *Australian Explorers*, Oxford University Press, 1958, p. 66.
† *ibid.*, p. 61.

occupation that followed Waterloo, and finally Ireland. He sailed for Australia in 1826 as part of the guard on a convict ship. In Sydney the Governor chose him as his secretary, a way of life which one may imagine did not satisfy him. He was fascinated by the Australian wilderness and soon obtained permission to set off adventuring into the bush. During the most torrid weeks of the summer of 1828 he trekked down the valley of the Macquarie River, only to confirm that it led nowhere. By way of compensation he came upon a ' noble river' to which, like the good officer he was, he gave the name of the Governor of the day, Darling. But it turned out to be another disappointment, as its water was salty.

Sturt led a second expedition in 1829. This time he at least came across constant navigable rivers, first the Murrumbidgee with its Aboriginal name, and then another river which was both 'broad and noble'.* Since this one was bigger than the Darling, Sturt called it after the Governor's hierarchical superior, the Colonial Secretary, Murray. He navigated downriver for twenty-five days, with the constant expectation of reaching the sea. But, like many another Australian exploration, this one was a sequence of hopes and disappointments. This broad and noble Murray River flowed into a lake which proved to be inaccessible from the sea.† They had to return by the way they had come. That return journey was to be one of the most heroic episodes in the history of Australia. Sturt and his companions were already suffering from exhaustion and were living on reduced rations. They had to cover more than 1,400 kilometres upstream, rowing hard every day from dawn until 7 p.m., and taking only one hour's rest. When they got back to Sydney, Sturt was in such a weakened state that he suffered from blindness for some months. But he was undaunted, and fifteen years later was still actively seeking the answer to the riddle of Australia's inland.

Three further expeditions completed the exploration of the south-east. In 1836, Thomas Mitchell penetrated a region to the north and west of Melbourne that was so different from the usual

* Quoted in Fitzpatrick, K., *op. cit.*, p. 104.
† This time it was the turn of the royal family to supply a place-name. The one chosen for this vast reservoir, about seventy kilometres south-east of Adelaide, was Lake Alexandrina, after the ten-year-old girl who was later to accede to the throne as Queen Victoria.

Antipodean landscapes that he dubbed it 'Australia felix'. There was something of the bard in Mitchell. He says it was

one of the most beautiful spots I ever saw, [with] the appearance of a well kept park ... The earth indeed seemed to surpass in richness, any that I had seen in New South Wales ; and I was even tempted to bring away a specimen of it ... of this Eden I was the first European to explore its mountains and streams – to behold its scenery – to investigate its geological character, and, by my survey, to develop those natural advantages, certain to become, at no distant date, of vast importance to a new people.*

A less lyrical Scot, Angus McMillan, gave the name of 'Australian Caledonia' to a forested region 200 kilometres east of Melbourne. Finally, in 1840, Paul Strzelecki, a geologist of Polish extraction, blazed a zigzag trail through the Australian Alps, even climbing single-handed the highest peak in the Snowy Mountains, to which, in a burst of nationalist fervour, he gave the name of Mount Kosciusko.

By 1840, the explorers had managed to join up the various centres of population dotted round the south-eastern seaboard. The interior still resisted them. They now redoubled their efforts.

First there was John Edward Eyre. At twenty-five he was one of the most experienced explorers in Australia, having trekked south from Sydney to the Murray and Port Phillip Bay, crossed from Melbourne to Adelaide and ventured into the desolate region north of Adelaide.† Discouragement comes hard when you are young and ready for anything. In 1840 he set out to open up a stock route round the Great Australian Bight from Adelaide to King George's Sound in the west. With him went one European, John Baxter by name, three Aborigines, nine horses and six sheep. He had resolved to do it, or die in the attempt – which he almost did. After a five-month-dogged trek through the arid, forlorn wilderness of the Nullarbor Plain, two of the Aborigines murdered Baxter and fled with most of the supplies and weapons. Eyre describes his predicament as follows :

At the dead hour of night, in the wildest and most inhospitable wastes of Australia, with the fierce wind raging in unison with the violence

---

* Quoted by Fitzpatrick, K., *op. cit.*, pp. 138–9.

† Here he named Mount Hopeless, in token of that desolation.

before me, I was left, with a single native, whose fidelity I could not rely upon.*

This Aborigine, Wylie by name, turned out to be fearless and above reproach. The two men have been immortalized in local mythology, trudging through the sands of that God-forsaken coast, the white man supported by the black man. They were in luck. In an inlet they came upon a whaler flying the French flag, whose master (an Englishman, as it happened) gave them hospitality for two weeks.† Eyre was not one to rest on his laurels. They pushed on, covering another 500 kilometres, through pouring rain, to arrive at the small settlement of Albany on 7 July 1841. They had walked 2,000 kilometres in almost nine months; they had discovered nothing.

At this same period, Charles Sturt led another expedition which was just as abortive as Eyre's. He set out from Adelaide on 10 August 1844, only to return there on 19 January 1846, after trudging many hundreds of kilometres through the hottest, most arid parts of the Simpson Desert. It has been said of this trek that never has so much dogged courage been expended to so little purpose.

Sturt's expedition may have achieved nothing; but at least he did not perish. Ludwig Leichhardt was not so fortunate. He was a Prussian who had come to Australia in 1842 at the age of twenty-nine. It has been conjectured that he emigrated so as to avoid military service. A counter-theory is that, like so many others, he was lured to Australia by the mystery of the continent. Whatever the case may be, the quiet life was not for him. By 1844 he had scraped some funds together and was planning a journey of exploration to the north-east of Australia, which was still completely unknown. He set out from somewhere near the spot where Brisbane would one day be built, taking eight people in all with him, including a sixteen-year-old youth, a convict, and three Aborigines, of whom one was partly civilized and the others were quite primitive. They covered 4,500 kilometres in four months and four days and got as

---

* Quoted in Fitzpatrick, K., *op. cit.*, p. 190.

† This was early in June 1841. The master, Rossiter, made Eyre promise not to tell anyone of his presence there, fearing that war might have broken out once more between France and England. It is a fact that in the autumn of 1840, the Eastern question did almost provoke a general outbreak of war in which France would have been without allies, as in 1815. Louis Philippe's wisdom defused the crisis.

far as the present site of Port Essington, on the Coburg Peninsula in the far north of the continent. This first expedition was fruitful, and the thorough Leichhardt brought back a great many observations of scientific value. He made a second journey in 1846, a mere stroll of 1,000 kilometres. Two years later, disaster struck. Having gone from Brisbane to Port Essington, he decided to attempt an east-west crossing of the entire continent, from Sydney to Perth. He set out and disappeared for ever. Neither he nor any of his six companions, nor any of the seventy-seven animals they had taken with them, was ever seen again. Several rescue expeditions were sent out, but they were unavailing in the search for the lost Leichhardt, although some of them (especially the expedition of Charles Gregory in 1858) filled in important gaps in knowledge of the northern inland. The mystery of what had become of Leichhardt made such a profound impression on Australians' minds that, as late as 1938, a further attempt was made to get to the bottom of it. The searchers did find a few human bones and some coins, but were forced to the conclusion that these relics could just as plausibly have come from some other expedition.

The tragedy of Leichhardt could have quenched the lust for exploration. In fact, it caught the public imagination and increased the desire for discovery. So far, nobody had ever crossed the continent from one side to the other. Now adventurous men began to dream of crossing Australia from south to north, of setting out from the safe, inhabited parts and plunging into the mysterious central deserts. Out of three attempts, John McDouall Stuart scored two misses and one success. He had gained some experience of exploration in smaller expeditions with Sturt. In early 1860 he left Adelaide and made for the heart of the continent. He scotched the legend of the inland sea, but was forced to turn back by lack of food and water and the exhaustion of his horses. His achievement was to reach a point 150 kilometres north of Alice Springs, where he raised the Union Jack on a mountain, some thousand metres high, which is now called after him. He got back to Adelaide in October 1860 after seven months of exhaustion and privation. He was off again before the end of November, this time to spend eleven months attempting to find a way through the centre, and meeting with no more success than before. On returning to Adelaide a second time, he took less than a month's rest – having arrived back at the end of September 1861, he set out for his third attempt at a crossing in

October. This time his efforts met with success. On 24 July 1862 he and his companions reached the shore of the Timor Sea, not far from the place where Darwin now stands. They had blazed a trail which was to become the standard route to the north coast.

South Australia and Adelaide took pride in Stuart's achievement. The colony of Victoria* had been hoping to beat South Australia in the race to cross the continent. This rivalry ended in perhaps the most notorious, certainly the most often debated disaster in the history of Australian exploration. Melburnians liked to do things on a large scale – having heard that Adelaide was prepared to subsidize Stuart to the tune of £2,500, Melbourne decided to offer no less than £12,000 to any local explorer who entered the lists. To this day, historians still wonder how on earth an eminently responsible body such as the Royal Society of Victoria managed to narrow down its choice to Robert O'Hara Burke, a police inspector who was as ignorant of exploration as he was of the sciences. For all that, Alan Moorehead speaks of his Irishness, his charm and dare-devil nature, his eccentricities, his mercurial, head-strong, reckless temperament.† As well as which, at nearly forty, he was head over heels in love with a fetching young lady by the name of Julia Matthews, who was prominent in theatrical circles, but somewhat unready, from all accounts, to requite the policeman's passion.

Perhaps he hoped to impress the lady. This could explain why he moved heaven and earth to be chosen for the job of leader of an expedition which he knew would bring him fame. He set out from Melbourne in mid-winter, on 20 August 1860, with a lavishly equipped expedition consisting of John Wills, his second-in-command (who was a competent astronomer and meteorologist), twelve other companions and twenty-one tons of baggage carried by twenty-five camels, which were being used as pack animals for the first time. To begin with, everything went well. At Menindie on the Darling, 600-odd kilometres to the north-west of Melbourne, Burke established a base where he left most of the supplies and the majority of his companions. He pushed on northwards with six men and fifteen camels. At Cooper's Creek he established another depot and sent for the bulk of the expedition to come up from Menindie. After six weeks of waiting for them, Burke's patience wore thin. On 16

* See Chapter 10 for the development of these newer colonies.

† Moorehead, A., *op. cit.*, pp. 28–9.

December he set out into the unknown, accompanied only by Wills and two others, King and Gray, with one horse, six camels and supplies for twelve weeks. Their marches were from 5 a.m. until 5 p.m., with one hour's rest ; the order of march was Burke and Wills in the lead, reading the compass, followed by Gray leading Billie, the horse, and with King and the camels bringing up the rear. The weather could not have been better. Full summer as it was, the rains that year had been heavy and the desert was like a garden, covered in greenery and water-lilies. They reached the Gulf of Carpentaria within two months. They turned about and started back by the same way, at the same pace. But their supplies and staying-power were running out. Burke, Wills and King made it back to Cooper's Creek ; Gray died of exhaustion.*

The three survivors reached Cooper's Creek again on 21 April 1861, having walked almost 2,500 kilometres in just over four months. At the Creek they hoped to find their companions and much-needed supplies. But the camp was abandoned. It was half-past seven in the evening. They found a note which they read by moonlight – the depot party had left for Menindie only seven hours earlier ! Having expected Burke and Wills to be away only for three months, and being at a loss to know what to do, they had taken with them all the clothing and most of the food. Burke and Wills were now in a perilous dilemma. With only two weak camels left, to try to follow and overtake their companions would have been foolhardy. Burke decided to make for Mount Hopeless, 250 kilometres away, where there was a police post. They left a note and then, exhausted as they were, set out. They did not get far, although they managed to trudge on for two months more. Wills' diary is a moving document. They started their march on 23 April. On the 29th a camel got bogged and had to be shot. On 7 May the sole surviving camel died. It was the beginning of the end. On 22 June Wills noted : ' I am so weak today as to be unable to get on my feet.' Three days later : ' The cold plays the deuce with us, from the small amount of clothing we have.' A last entry, dated 26 June (but probably meaning 28 June) : ' My pulse are [*sic*] at forty-eight, and very weak, and my legs and arms are nearly skin and bone. I can only look out, like Mr Micawber, " for something to turn up ".'† King was the only one

---

* It has been suggested that he was killed by Aborigines.

† Quoted in Fitzpatrick, K., *op. cit.*, pp. 371–2.

who lived to tell the tale ; he was saved by Aborigines. Burke and Wills died of hunger and exhaustion.*

The Burke and Wills expedition has been seen as a wanton, pointless sacrifice, and as more of an exploit than a proper exploration. However, it did play its part, along with many others, in raising a corner of the veil of mystery that shrouded the inland of Australia.

It is possible to sketch a general picture of these awe-inspiring exploits and of the men who took part in them. Professor Spate has examined their motivation and their backgrounds. Many of them were army officers bored by garrison life ; there were two sailors, no strangers to wide open spaces ; and there were scientists, eager to add to the fund of human knowledge. Although they came from a wide range of differing backgrounds, they also had much in common. They shared that keen curiosity which is found in all men through whom humanity progresses ; they shared the zest for adventure ; above all they shared a taste for the poetry of the undiscovered. As one of them, Ernest Giles, says : 'An explorer is an explorer from love, and it is nature, not art, that makes him so.' †
Many of them also had a mystical streak in them, which contrasts markedly with their predecessors of the Enlightenment. They were given to seeing the supernatural at work in their exploits. Here is a representative sample of their writings. First, Sturt :

Something more powerful than human foresight or human prudence appeared to avert the calamities and dangers with which I and my companions were so frequently threatened ; and had it not been for the guidance and protection we received from the Providence of that good and all-wise Being to whose care we committed ourselves, we should, ere this, have ceased to rank among the number of His earthly creatures.‡

Or, again from Sturt, there is an account of a perilous encounter with several hundred Aborigines : 'This was not the only occasion upon which the merciful superintendence of that Providence to which we had humbly committed ourselves, was strikingly mani-

---

* A search was made for their bodies which were taken back to Melbourne for burial.

† Fitzpatrick, K., *Australian Explorers*, p. 12.

‡ *ibid.*, p. 92.

fested.' Eyre, too, noted after a day of alarms 'At night, the whole party were, by God's blessing, once more together, and in safety'; and when he had struck water in the most infernal heat he wrote, 'That gracious God, without whose assistance all hope of safety had been in vain, had heard our earnest prayers for his aid.' Leichhardt, likewise, wrote that 'an Almighty Protector had not only allowed us to escape [privation], but had even supplied us frequently with an abundance.' And, lastly, Mitchell saw his discovery of a river as 'a reward direct from Heaven for perseverance'. *

These extraordinary individuals were as intense in their patriotic feelings as in their religion. When McDouall Stuart reached the centre of Australia, he noted :

Built a large cone of stones, in the centre of which I placed a pole with the British flag nailed to it ... We then gave three hearty cheers for the flag, the emblem of civil and religious liberty, and may it be a sign to the natives that the dawn of liberty, civilization, and Christianity is about to break upon them. †

The Queen's birthday was sacrosanct. On 24 May 1845, even Leichhardt notes :

It was the Queen's birth-day, and we celebrated it with what – as our only remaining luxury – we were accustomed to call a fat cake, made of 4 pounds of flour and some suet, which we had saved for the express purpose, and with a pot of sugared tea. We had for several months been without sugar, with the exception of about ten pounds, which was reserved for cases of illness and for festivals. ‡

Sixteen years later, to the day, Wills (who was to die within the month) says : 'Started with King to celebrate the Queen's birthday by fetching from Nardoo Creek what is now to us the staff of life.'§

From these moving and heartfelt words, one should not conclude that the men who wrote them were unalloyed idealists. To see them through, such men needed sound practical sense as well as idealism. Money, for one thing, was of prime importance. Some of them, as

* Fitzpatrick, K., *op. cit.*, pp. 109, 179, 185, 231 and 318.
† *ibid.*, p. 347.
‡ Leichhardt, L., *Journal of an Overland Expedition ... 1844–1845*, T. &. W. Boone, 1847, p. 265.
§ i.e. nardoo seeds. Quoted in Fitzpatrick, K., *op. cit.*, p. 369.

has been seen in the cases of Stuart and Burke, managed to get government subsidies. At the opposite extreme one finds other explorers, such as the trio who first crossed the Blue Mountains, who met their expenses out of their own pockets. The general rule was, however, that the expeditions were financed jointly by official organizations and private interests. Among the latter, of course, the subscriptions of squatters bulk large, anxious as they were to find new grazing lands.

Once the finance had been found, the final list of necessities for the march had to be drawn up. Scientific instruments were reduced to a minimum. Leichhardt, for instance, took only 'a Sextant and Artificial Horizon, a Chronometer, a hand Kater's Compass, a small Thermometer, and Arrowsmith's Map of the Continent of New Holland'.* Clothes, weapons and supplies were the next problems. Again Leichhardt is precise. Each of his men had two tough pairs of trousers, three thick shirts and two pairs of boots. Some of them also took ponchos, made of light waterproofed calico. Their ammunition consisted of thirty pounds of gunpowder and eight bags of cartridges of different calibres. As essential supplies they needed 1,200 pounds of flour, 200 pounds of sugar, eighty pounds of tea, twenty pounds of gelatine, 'and other articles of less consideration, but adding much to our comfort during the first weeks of our journey'.†

This made for a very heavy load, which had somehow to be carried. Some of the explorers set out at the head of veritable convoys. In 1844 Sturt took with him fifteen men, eleven horses, 200 sheep, six dogs, thirty yoked oxen pulling three wagons, plus a cart and, interestingly enough, a boat intended for use on the inland sea. Mitchell, on one of his trips, outdid Sturt, taking with him thirty men, 250 sheep, seventeen horses, eighty draught animals, eight wagons, three carts and two boats. Gregory, a few years later, with only eighteen men, fifty horses and 200 sheep, was quite outclassed. The advantage of these caravans was their greater safety; but this was almost outweighed by the disadvantage – the slowness of the pace. Leichhardt says that it took two hours every morning to load up the horses and yoke the bullocks. Some of the

---

* Leichhardt, L., *op. cit.*, p. xiv. Without having seen it, one can only suppose that, the year being 1844, his map was somewhat rudimentary.

† *ibid.*, p. xviii.

explorers concluded that speed and travelling light were the most important elements in any success. Eyre seems to have been the first to put this principle into practice. John McDouall Stuart followed his lead, taking with him only six companions, five of whom were convicts. Gradually the practice became generally accepted as exploration became less and less a pastime for amateurs.

Whether they travelled light or saw safety in numbers and large expeditions, all of the explorers had to cope with awesome difficulties. One experienced fellow maintained that 1,000 miles of exploration in Australia was the equivalent of 10,000 miles anywhere else, except in the polar regions. The first and foremost of the difficulties was the sheer vastness of the continent. This is a point that has been stressed again and again. May one be forgiven for wondering whether it has not been somewhat exaggerated ? After all, the distance from the Pacific to the Indian Ocean is no greater than from New York to San Francisco. If one were to judge merely by the map, one could well assume that it was no harder to explore and open up Australia than it was North America. It may even have been easier in some respects : for instance, the opposition put up by the Aborigines was paltry compared with the resistance of the Red Indians. Kathleen Fitzpatrick says of the Aborigines :

At their first encounter with white men the aborigines were not hostile, but they were amazed and terrified, though less by the men than by their horses. When they saw a mounted man for the first time they naturally supposed man and beast to be one ; when they discovered this was not so they wondered whether the horses might be the white men's women ... Very soon, however, the news spread among the aboriginal peoples that the coming of the white man spelt disaster – the use of firearms which terrified the kangaroos from their accustomed hunting-grounds, the abuse of aboriginal women ...*

The greatest ill-effect on the Aborigines was that the water-holes, on which the survival of the explorers and their numerous animals

---

* Fitzpatrick, K., *op. cit.*, pp. 8–9. If one can judge from one of Sturt's descriptions, this may not have happened often. A tribe had gathered to meet him, ' ... and all, without exception, were in complete state of nudity, and really the loathsome condition and hideous countenances of the women would, I should imagine, have been a complete antidote to the sexual passion' (*ibid.*, p. 115).

depended, were drained dry by these strangers who arrived out of nowhere. Incidents were bound to occur. They may not have been as frequent as one might think, since very few explorers were killed in this way In fact, when they surmounted their fear of one another, Europeans and Aborigines got on quite well, as is attested by the composition of the expeditions or by the good Samaritan who saved the life of the sole survivor of the Burke and Wills tragedy.

Nor were there any wild animals to fear, apart from the wild dogs. Insects, admittedly, were something of a problem. One account left by George Grey says :

To sleep after sunrise was impossible, on account of the number of flies which kept buzzing about the face. To open our mouths was dangerous – in they flew, and mysteriously disappeared, to be rapidly ejected again in a violent fit of coughing, and into the eyes, when unclosed, they soon found their way ... *

Another explorer says that they prevented him enjoying the shade. In desperation, he was forced to go and lie out in the burning sun which was too hot for them.

Such drawbacks were minor. But geography and climate made for complications and perils which were much more serious. One only has to remember the importance of the St Lawrence basin and the Mississippi basin in the opening-up and settlement of North America to imagine the thoughts of the Australian explorers when they realized the lack of navigable waterways with access from the sea. Such rivers as they did find too often turned out to be water-courses which looked as though they would broaden and deepen, but petered out into mere trickles or strings of stagnant ponds, or just vanished into the sand leaving only their dried-up beds. Not that they had disappeared for ever, because they might surface again farther on, luring the hopeful after them. But there was one thing which was worse than these vanishing rivers, and that was the total lack of water. Eyre trekked more than 2,000 kilometres along the coast of the Bight without once finding running water. At one stage his sheep went without drinking for six days, and his horses for five. Leichhardt gives a striking glimpse of the sort of tricks of the trade they had to learn, such as drinking the water which dripped from their sodden blankets when it rained.

* Fitzpatrick, K., *op. cit.*, p. 7.

Hunger was another danger which drove the explorers to unappetizing experiments. One of them reports having devoured the bones and feet of a pigeon ; roast lizard was a not uncommon fare. Another one tells of a baby wallaby that he found dying. Having only recently left the mother's pouch, it weighed a mere two ounces (fifty-seven grams) and had not yet grown much fur. He ate it alive, skin, bones, fur, skull and all.

The temperature was almost always inclemently hot, and often subject to great fluctuations. Mitchell recorded 54° Celsius. Sturt noted one reading of 56° and became so used to that sort of heat that he found a mere 35° pleasantly cool. However, Sturt also notes :

The horn handles of our instruments, as well as our combs, were split into fine laminae. The lead dropped out of our pencils, our signal rockets were entirely spoiled ; our hair, as well as the wool on the sheep, ceased to grow, and our nails had become as brittle as glass. The flour lost more than eight per cent of its original weight, and the other provisions in a still greater proportion.*

And then, during the night, the temperature could fall below zero.

Such wide fluctuations in temperature were not the only desert phenomena they had to cope with. Mirages were also frequent. Many of the explorers believed they had seen with their own eyes the legendary inland sea that so many men had sought. But at least these illusions gave them hope, and a little hope went a long way among so many heartbreaks. The three most demoralizing aspects of the outback were the distance, the silence and the loneliness. Oxley, right at the beginning of the great adventure of Australian exploration, had been appalled by these features of the inland : 'Nothing can be more melancholy and irksome than travelling over wilds, which Nature seems to have condemned to perpetual loneliness and desolation.' Sturt was overpowered by a similar impression :

My companion involuntarily uttered an exclamation of amazement when he first glanced his eye over it. 'Good Heavens,' said he, 'did man ever see such country !' Indeed, if it was not so gloomy, it was more difficult than the Stony Desert itself ; yet I turned from it with a feeling of bitter disappointment.†

* Fitzpatrick, K., *op. cit.*, p. 7.
† *ibid.*, pp. 60, 305.

McDouall Stuart felt the landscape to be so utterly inhuman that it almost seemed aggressive. Perhaps the most moving document of all is his cry of anguish when, having fallen ill in this setting and thinking he was going to die, he begged two of his companions to stay with him, so that he should not feel too abandoned if death should come for him during the night.

And yet, by about 1860, nearly all of the inland had been explored, except the vast desert which stretches away from the centre towards the north-west.

Chapter Nine

The pastoral age

British woollen industry saved by Australia – influx of capital and immigrants – Wakefield's theories – the government's application of them – origin and development of the term 'squatter' – squatters of different kinds the search for grazing lands – the difficulties of wool-growing – ways of life – Aborigines and bushrangers – mateship – wool-selling – economic crisis – simultaneous rise in official price of land – conflict between squatters and government – squatters victorious – rapid recovery – rise of a landed aristocracy

The explorers were only the vanguard. A great army of stock-raisers followed them, ever eager for new grazing lands. With this unexpected potential of the new country, a colonial Australia was gradually taking the place of the old penal settlement, as more and more immigrants and capital flowed in.

History is often little more than a set of random coincidences. The development of wool-growing in New South Wales would not have been so rapid if it had not been for the troubles in the British woollen mills. After 1815, British wool-producers found they could no longer keep up with their foreign competitors, especially the Germans. Before the Napoleonic Wars, the British monopoly in wool had been threatened only by the Spaniards, and that only in a small way. But the ambition of the Emperor of the French had unforeseen consequences. When he occupied the Iberian peninsula, he exported merinos to other parts of Europe, in particular to Germany, where the conditions of soil and pasture happened to suit them. As S.H. Roberts has pointed out, the export of this breed of sheep was to be one of the more significant of Napoleon's legacies to Europe. The result was a vast improvement in the quality of Continental wool.

By 1820 British mill-owners were in desperation. Even though they had lowered their prices and managed to have import tariffs raised, the German producers still succeeded in undercutting them. A deterioration in the quality of English wool resulted in a further drop in the already low reputation of the British producers. They were to be saved by Botany Bay, the place which everyone had despised. It will be remembered that in 1807 John Macarthur had first sent a sample of his wool to London, where it was greeted with fairly general scepticism. However, the wool-growers on the other side of the globe had not lost heart. They went on sending consignments of wool, in greater and greater quantities ; and the British diehards went on maintaining that the wool was rough and of poor quality. But the day came when it was judged to be every bit as good as the wool from Saxony or Silesia, the reputation of which was by now firmly established. The point was finally won for Australia in 1822 when the Duke of Sussex awarded Macarthur two of the Royal Society's gold medals.

About that same date, people in Sydney had reached the conclusion that wool, and nothing else, was going to be the essential export that they had been looking for ever since the arrival of the First Fleet. Beyond the Blue Mountains, which had been crossed eight years earlier, grazing lands seemed to stretch on for ever. To use them for cattle-raising seemed a doubtful prospect. The amount of beef that could be consumed by the population was limited, as was the quantity of salt meat that would be taken as supplies by ships. Sheep-farming was the ideal solution. The climate and the type of soil were just right, and the demand for wool from the British mills ensured a vast market. Prices, too, were just right – a ton of wool sold in London for ten times the price of a ton of wheat – and made for certain profits, even allowing for shipping costs. These costs were, in fact, so low that the Australian wool-growers were very soon able to produce wool of the same quality as their German competitors, at lower prices.*

Three simple figures tell a revealing story. In 1821, wool exports stood at 79,275 kilograms ; in 1830 they exceeded 900,000 kilos ; and by 1840 they had reached 4,530,000 kilos. This means that in less than twenty years wool exports had grown more than fifty

---

* Australia did not outdo Germany until after 1840. But by mid-century, the victory of the Australian growers was complete: they supplied half of British imports, five times more than Germany.

times. Such phenomenal development can be explained by several factors. For one thing, there was no lack of space for expansion, though to make full use of it funds and manpower, both in short supply, were needed. These needs began to be answered once Australia became known. The prospect of profits turned the colony from a despised liability into a desirable asset. Capital, as might be expected, turned out to be the hardest thing to attract. In 1824, when Governor Brisbane took up the suggestion of the Colonial Office and decided to adopt the Spanish dollar* as the unit of currency, the resulting confusion had an adverse effect on investment.† The situation settled down three years later when the colony reverted to sterling. Over the next ten years, no fewer than thirty-one banking houses opened their doors to the funds which were arriving from the home country.‡ There was one measure in particular that warmed the hearts of British capitalists: in 1834 the High Court ruled that the usury laws did not apply to the colony.

The other great need, immigration, had begun to be met earlier. At the end of Macquarie's governorship, the number of free settlers (excluding emancipists) was insignificant: after thirty-two years of British occupation there were only 1,307 of them. However, about 1820 the question was being asked in Britain: might it not be possible to siphon off towards New South Wales some of the excess population in the home country? As Sir Keith Hancock says: was it really necessary for someone to turn thief before going out to Australia? There was a gradual flow of applicants, either down-and-outs hoping to escape the empty misery of their lives, or adventurers seeking excitement. There were even a few victims of the period's fashionable world-weariness, looking for an Antipodean antidote to their disenchantment. Eventually, all classes were attracted to the mysterious new land.

---

* This currency, which was still widely used, inspired the Colonial Secretary to tell the Governor of the boundless benefits which it showered on all mankind, facilitating the transportation of goods from one end of the earth to the other, and bringing great blessings alike to Protestant North America, Popish French Canada and Muslim India.

† In 1800, King had fixed the rate at five shillings to the dollar, but it was subject to constant fluctuation in response to the availability of metallic currency.

‡ It must be added that almost two thirds of these institutions eventually collapsed or were taken over by more successful competitors.

To begin with, the Colonial Office, which was second to none in the techniques of indecision, contented itself with uttering encouraging words. When it became apparent that words were not enough and that Sydney was crying out for more manpower, the Colonial Office managed to persuade the Treasury to provide subsidies. The government paid the travel costs of any emigrants whose characters were guaranteed by references from members of the clergy and other respectable persons. Women were included in this policy of munificence, with the aim of increasing the very small numbers of them in the colony ; they had to be spinsters or widows, between the ages of eighteen and thirty, in good health and in possession of certificates of morality.*

Statistics being indispensable nowadays, it has been estimated that between 1831 and 1840, 65,000 immigrants arrived in Australia ; and over the next ten years a further 108,000. These 173,000 free settlers outnumbered by 90,000 the convicts who were transported during those same years. In 1841 the 'government men' (the euphemism that was coming to be used of the convicts) made up only 23 per cent of the total population, as against 43 per cent ten years earlier.

This influx of population brought with it political and social transformations which will be dealt with in the next chapter. Here we shall deal with the experiences and adventures of the new arrivals. Most of them, after all, had not uprooted themselves from their native soil and voyaged 20,000 miles from England, just to take up the same sort of life from which they had escaped. If one wanted to make a fortune, one did not stop in Sydney. And so they set out into the unknown hinterland, seeking the places where wealth grew out of the ground. But the ground itself was a problem. Who owned it ? How should it be shared out ? The Crown was the sole landlord and it was therefore up to it to decide the conditions in which it would give up its rights to its subjects.

It was a thorny problem and there was no shortage of theorists

---

* One is reminded of the French minister, Colbert, sending out to New France his 'healthy sturdy girls'. He expressed himself in a more earthy fashion than the civil servants in Victorian England : 'We are readying the 150 wenches, the brood-mares, stallions and ewes who must be sent to Canada.' These new arrivals in Australia did create a problem, as will be seen.

to speculate and pontificate on it. The case of someone like Edward Gibbon Wakefield is particularly revealing. Wakefield was a complicated character, who still intrigues biographers. Although at home with ideas, he was also at the mercy of his passions. In later life he became a specialist in sociology ; but he started as something of an expert in the abduction of young ladies. In 1816, at the age of twenty, he had eloped with a girl of sixteen who, it is said, was a paragon of beauty and grace. They made for Gretna Green where they were married. The seducer's bride being still a minor, he used his charm to get her an annual pension of £2,000. The marriage lasted four years, produced two children and left Wakefield a widower. The success of this first venture may well have encouraged him to try again. In 1826 he found another innocent who was not altogether unconsenting. She was still at school, the same age as his first victim and, strangest of all, her family too was wealthy. However, this time things did not turn out so well for Wakefield. The girl's parents tracked her down to France, where she was living, married to the seducer, and talked her into returning home with them. Her husband behaved like a gentleman. In the full knowledge that British justice looked severely on such escapades, he returned to England in 1827 and gave himself up, a noble gesture that earned him three years' gaol.

Hence, at thirty-one, Wakefield found himself behind bars in notorious Newgate Prison. Conditions there seem not to have been too harsh for him, and in any case he was not one to remain idle for long. He set himself to study, first of all, the problem of capital punishment, before going on to the question of emigration, which was a topic of growing interest. He concentrated particularly on the case of Australia. His research must have been prodigious. He became the Jules Verne of political economy and eventually was more of an expert on New South Wales than if he had actually gone there. Readers of the *Morning Chronicle* in 1829 were the first to discover this, when that newspaper published a series of unsigned articles on the colony, called *A Letter from Sydney*. Shortly afterwards these articles appeared in book form, purporting to be edited by one Robert Gouger. This 'editor' was, of course, our erstwhile seducer of maiden ladies. His comments on the system of colonization cannot have been very pleasing to the government. He was of the opinion that the policy was ill-considered. To exploit the land solely by sending out convicts, as had been done for the past thirty years, was bound to end in failure, as it could not be expected that the crime rate would keep pace with the development of society. The conclusion was obvious: the government must foster the emigration of free workers. Not only that, but once they arrived in Australia, they must not become landowners too soon. In Wakefield's view, the only way of ensuring this was to put a stop to the allotment of land and change to a system of selling land at prices that some people would not be able to afford. Profits from these land sales were to be put into a fund for the subsidizing of emigration, with young married couples being given first priority – for Wakefield 'the greatest evil of all' was the 'great disproportion between the sexes' that had come about through the transportation of men in far greater numbers than women.

In addition to this, settlers should not be allowed to scatter too widely over the country, for sooner or later there was bound to be a shortage of labour. ' The *scarcity of labourers* was an insuperable bar to any mode of cultivation that requires the employment of many hands.'* The important thing to avoid was population scatter. This was to be avoided by reaching 'a just medium' between 'superabundance of people' and 'superabundance of land'. And the way to achieve this was by fixing a 'proper' price for land. This was Wakefield's famous 'sufficient price'.† His logic was indisputable. But it did raise practical problems to which this forerunner of the technocrat could offer no real solution. How could one arrive at a formula that would ensure a 'proper' dispersal of settlers? How 'sufficient' were 'sufficient' land prices? Where should the level be set?

Wakefield's ideas, in all their imprecision and coherence, made him an extraordinary propagandist. Although he was an unimpressive public speaker, in private he had extraordinary powers of persuasion. His manner, his gestures and voice gave off a sort of magnetism that people found difficult to resist. His 'sanguine and combative temperament' was perceptible even in his writings, which were prolific – letters, articles, pamphlets, books – all of them showing the Wakefield aptitude 'for writing vividly about distant countries, never seen except with the eye of the imagination'.‡ He

---

* Quoted by Bloomfield, P., *Edward Gibbon Wakefield*, Longmans, 1961, p. 100.
† *ibid.*, p. 101.
‡ *ibid.*, pp. 130–1.

was best at founding societies for the furtherance of his ideas. The best known of these was the National Colonization Society, which was to play a fundamental part in the founding of South Australia (see pages 170–71).

Such mental activity naturally irked the officials at the Colonial Office, who were given to rather more leisurely ways. 'Mr Mother Country', as Wakefield called this ministry, had no clear ideas on the problem. Its various changes of heart on the matter made life difficult for its representatives in Australia. According to Fitzpatrick, 'Much of the economic history of Australia during the Crown Colonial period is ... an account of sudden rapid adjustments of Australian economy attempted at Whitehall with scant or secondary reference to the colonies themselves.'* Some of Wakefield's ideas eventually reached Australia. His theories on population dispersal were welcomed by Governors who were anxious not to lose their authority through the over-mobility of colonists. In 1834, when His Majesty's government, in its best high-and-mighty manner, declared that it was not prepared to allow the population to spread beyond the permitted territorial boundaries, one may be sure that London and Sydney saw eye to eye on this question.† These boundaries had been laid down in 1829, and enclosed the so-called 'Nineteen counties', an area round Sydney of about 20,000 square kilometres.

These administrative obstacles turned out to be flimsy and ineffective. But the whole problem of population and concentration of settlement seemed a simple one compared with the difficulties inherent in the distribution of land. The first governors, with the lordly largesse that comes from the possession of limitless property, had started by granting land more or less to all comers. This system of distribution was prone to anomalies and uncertainty and by 1820, of the 260,000-odd hectares granted, only a minute proportion had been cleared or cultivated. An attempt had then been made to relate the area of lands granted to the means of the persons applying, £500

* Fitzpatrick, B., *British Imperialism and Australia, 1783–1833*, Sydney University Press, 1971, p. 21.

† It is interesting to note that the Governors of the Cape had done the same thing in the eighteenth century, following the lead of their French counterparts in Canada a century earlier, in an attempt to curb the spirit of adventure of the famous backwoodsmen.

being the minimum which qualified one to apply for a grant. However, the same £500 would be used several times to guarantee a succession of different applicants. In addition, it became common for more and more immense grants to be made. The record in this respect was probably held by the Australian Agricultural Company, which the Macarthur family had been instrumental in founding in London in 1824 and which, for a nominal sum, held 500,000 hectares.

The New South Wales authorities were thus forced to the conclusion that there might be something in Wakefield's theories. Recently, in 1827, a new system of land concessions had been tried. Every landholder was to be subject to annual dues of £1 per 100 acres (40 hectares), and was under an obligation to surrender his lease on six months notice. It is possible that the first of these measures was actually enforced ; but the second was certainly unenforceable. 'Here I am, here I stay,' could well have been the motto of the bold men whose colourful story we must soon relate. Since the system of granting and renting land had failed, all that remained was to accept the suggestion of the ex-inmate of Newgate and try selling it. A start was made in 1831. The civil servant who wrote out the instructions for dispatch to Sydney most likely had the feeling, familiar to his colleagues, that he was settling this business once for all. The new ruling was that land should henceforth be distributed only by auctioning it, the minimum price to be five shillings per acre. Every eventuality had been thought of : the lease would be valid only if no other buyer offered better conditions ; buyers would pay 10 per cent of the purchase price at the time of the sale and the balance as soon as possible, at the latest before taking possession of the land.

But this new arrangement was a flimsy dyke that was to be swept away by a tidal wave of squatters.

The word 'squatter' has even found its way into French.* In English, by the Middle Ages, it already had its extended meaning, and in Scotland and Wales was applied to anyone, such as gipsies, who settled on any land to which they had no right. At the end of the eighteenth century, in America, it was current in the sense which concerns us here. Usage in Australia varied considerably within a period of a few years. To begin with the word was derogatory,

* Cf. the *Robert* dictionary, 1966.

meaning roughly the same as 'vagrant'. Both of these terms were the opposite of 'settlers', who were respectable people, living on land that had been granted to them by the Crown. This verbal distinction between good and evil lost its point when the alleged evil had become so widespread that it was no longer possible to see it as such. At a time when ex-convicts and free immigrants were setting out to discover a continent that the explorers themselves had barely more than glimpsed, it was difficult to see such enterprise as a bad thing. These people certainly did not see themselves as bad. They were opening up a virgin land, so why should they not be allowed to settle in it wherever they liked ? They argued that they should be freely allowed to settle wherever they could find unoccupied grazing land and for as long as their stock needed it. Another notion that was shared by almost all of them was that the people who cleared the land and made it produce had surely more rights to it than the Queen of England or any official organization. Not quite the sort of opinion to recommend itself to civil servants in Whitehall or Sydney Town.

The great movement of the squatters did not really get under way until after 1830. Men of all different backgrounds took part in it, contrary to the time-honoured belief that these *conquistadores* of the wool industry were all penniless. As S.H. Roberts says :

The striking feature about the first squatters was how many of them were men of good birth, education and capital ... First were the sons of the successful officials and colonists of the settled parts – the first local-born generation of good stock. Then came the small capitalists who had been caught in the English crises and had been attracted by the Wakefieldian campaign ... Lastly, a large – many would say, predominant – proportion of Scotsmen and a fair sprinkling of Army officers.*

Such men were not uncommon, but they were far from being the only sorts ; squatting would not have given rise to the colourful legend if it had been a pastime reserved for worthy bourgeois. There was no lack of thrill-seekers, original characters and black sheep.

Despite the differences in their backgrounds and make-up, their common aims gave them a degree of uniformity in their ways. They

* Roberts, S.H., *The Squatting Age in Australia, 1835–1847*, Melbourne University Press, 1935, pp. 371–2.

even dressed alike, looking not unlike cowboys and wearing what almost amounted to a uniform : trousers with under-straps, blue shirts, long boots, spurs, a leather belt on which were slung tobacco-pouch, knife and pistol, and on their heads the great broad-brimmed cabbage-tree hat,* reminiscent of the Texan's ten-gallon hat. What especially marked off the squatters from their American counter-parts was that they all wore full beards and moustaches, like the Boers a few thousand miles away who at that very time were pre-paring for their Great Trek.

Such sartorial details were unimportant to the squatters, of course. Their minds were fixed on the one objective : the coveted grazing runs. With regard to these, there were two schools of thought. There were the men who, either from caution or because they had no capital, would reconnoitre the run before making a full-scale expedition. They would set out on horseback with their saddlebags stuffed with tea, sugar, tobacco and flour, their billy-cans and tinder-boxes slung from the saddle, and their blankets in a roll behind the cantle. They set off in all directions, westward, north-ward, southward, looking for their never-never land. They would push on and on, in the belief that the farther they went the better their chances were of finding good land. Squatters who had already settled on a run regarded the arrival of these new competitors with a mixture of sympathy and suspicion. The generous ones would help with advice about land ; the indifferent ones would say as little as possible. There were those who were ill-disposed enough to the newcomers to send them off on wild goose chases. However, the fact was that, whether they had been helped or misled, there was so much space that the new arrivals sooner or later found a run that suited them. They would take nominal possession of it. But, for them, this was only the beginning. They had then to trek back to the town from which they had started, and take some very necessary steps. Firstly, they had to comply with (or at least pay lip-service to) legal requirements. Secondly, and more importantly, they had to find a backer. A common arrangement was the so-called system of Thirds,† under which a capitalist would put up the money to buy the sheep and the equipment, in exchange for which he earned a one-third share of the profits. The whole undertaking depended for

---

* Woven from dried leaves.
† Roberts, S.H., *op. cit.*, pp. 343-4.

its success, of course, on the soundness of the buyer's judgement. He not only had to choose good stock, he also had to be a judge of men, able to select reliable shepherds and in particular good bullock-drivers.* These 'bullockies' have come to epitomize the folklore of that period. They were colourful characters in their red shirts, moleskin trousers and the inevitable cabbage-tree hat, with a whip five metres long and an unsurpassable command of profane language which they used to encourage their bullock-teams.

The second method was used by the more adventurous, who dispensed with the preliminary reconnaissance and set out with all their stock, belongings and household. This method had the obvious advantage of being a considerable time-saving. It also had its drawback : the great risk one took in setting out into the unknown with a full-scale expedition. After all, these journeys were not pleasure outings, although not all of them involved the eleven men, two children, 1,650 sheep, eighteen bullocks, two drays, one cart and four horses that made up the caravan of one would-be squatter, a former navy man, mentioned by Professor Blainey. But even if they were not all as sizeable as that one, these prospecting expeditions usually comprised a fair number of persons and animals, and took provisions for a year. Each dray carried a ton of supplies and was drawn by three pairs of bullocks. One shepherd was required to every 600 or 700 sheep ; and one hut-keeper to every two or three shepherds. Roads, or tracks even, were non-existent. Here is Manning Clark's description of a typical trek :

At times the way lay across deep gullies ; the drays descended easily into these depressions and were pulled up the other side by the bullocks to a volley of oaths from the driver. At times they were halted by rivers in flood, or by swamps through which they could only pass by frequent unloading. At times the drays sank up to the axles in mud, and at other times bullocks and men laboured against flies and dust. On a good day they travelled twelve miles, on a bad day as few as three or four, so that the journey to a run took between forty and sixty days.†

When they had selected a run, these men of endurance had to set their shepherds to guarding the grazing sheep. At night they would

---

* The bullocks were imported. Pairs of bullocks of the same colour were especially sought after.

† Clark, C.M.H., *A Short History of Australia*, p. 88.

round up the animals into a very rudimentary corral, where a watchman would take charge of them. To begin with, masters and men lived in unbelievably primitive conditions. The first structures were rough bark huts which gave little or no protection from the elements. When a more advanced state of civilization had been reached, these precarious dwellings were replaced by wooden structures.* There were usually three men to a hut, two shepherds plus the hut-keeper who was responsible for the domestic arrangements. Heating and lighting were supplied by dingy oil-burning lamps. At night, the men slept on the bare earth. Their blankets kept out the cold, but not the flies and mosquitos and the countless insects attracted by the sheep-droppings.

In any case, it was as well not to sleep too soundly, as there was a constant possibility of danger. There were the dingoes, for one thing. These dogs were cunning hunters, quite capable of stalking in silence and cutting off a mob of sheep which they then slaughtered by the dozen. The men they would only threaten in self-defence. It appears that one cannot say the same for the Aborigines, although one must stress that on this matter the truth is difficult to come by. What one can say for certain is that there was a total breakdown in understanding between whites and blacks. It was understandable that the Aboriginal owners of the land, whose freehold went back countless centuries, should not take kindly to the new settlers. And in the same way, it was no doubt natural for the newcomers to fail to comprehend why such a potentially wealthy and fertile land should lie fallow for ever. This mutual incomprehension gave rise to dirty work on both sides, in which the Aborigines came off worst. They were shot on sight and even (reportedly) given flour poisoned with arsenic. One particular massacre, at Myall Creek in 1838, was especially notorious, twenty-eight of the natives, apparently harmless, being murdered in cold blood. At least this time the authorities did something about it, and seven of the murderers were eventually hanged. But it is difficult to draw any sure conclusion. S.H. Roberts says that after this Myall Creek drama,

the natives became unbearably impudent, and no longer were flocks or even human life safe. Seven or eight years of virtual terror set in ... Twelve white men were either killed or severely wounded in 2 months of

---

* Originally, the word 'station' meant only the quarters of the squatter and his men. The meaning was later extended to include the run itself, regardless of area.

1842, and at least 3500 sheep driven off. Scarcely a station was exempt from outrages or menace.*

The problem of the bushrangers was more clear-cut. The word 'bushranger' had originally been applied to escaped convicts who took to the bush and managed to survive by raiding the settlements. This happened especially in Tasmania, where the hardest cases among the convicts were sent and where the countryside, densely wooded and cut by deep valleys, offered the escapee all sorts of ready hideouts. From Tasmania the practice spread to the mainland. One suspects that legend has magnified the doings of these people. No doubt a few bushrangers would rustle some livestock from time to time. But they only resorted to violence as a last extremity. And they were not the only sheep-stealers, often making secret deals with shepherds. These shepherds, like the bushrangers, were at home in the vast and lonely unknown. Like them, they were dedicated individualists, rigorously rejecting the bondage of civilized society. Both sorts of men shared a distaste for all binding rules and regulations, and reacted with the same vehemence to the sight of troopers in uniform.† Their common proletarian origins gave to them both a deep-rooted instinctive aversion to any hierarchical order.

In any case, the law of the bush prescribed that you did not inquire too closely into a comrade's origins. Especially when you met in the only entertainment establishments available, those squalid drinking-shanties where the rum flowed like water and the aim was to get obliviously drunk in as short a time as possible. Here they played poker and sang those sentimental or cynical ballads which have left such a mark on Australian folklore. Women were as rare, it was said, as black swans in Europe. Some men took Aboriginal mistresses ; others dreamed of the day when they would go down from the bush and become the Casanova of Sydney, Melbourne or Hobart. But while they remained in the bush, their unrecognized sentimental and spiritual needs required some sort of outlet. The convention of what has been called 'mateship' grew up. Russel Ward, in an analysis of the complex of motives underlying mateship, says :

* Roberts, S.H., *op. cit.*, pp. 407–8.
† The troopers' reputation, it has been said, owed more to their savagery than their bravery.

Perhaps, as the habit of freedom and independence increased his self-respect, the typical bushman, blessedly ignorant of psychological theory, appeased this spiritual hunger by a sublimated homosexual relationship with a mate, or a number of mates, of his own sex.*

Any man who was worth his salt looked on himself as bound to his mate for better or worse, sharing everything with him and keeping nothing from him. The greatest thing in life was loyalty to one's mate whatever the circumstances ; and the worst thing one could ever do was to desert him.

Once a year, the great event in the lives of these men was the wool sales. The life of a squatter being very much a business speculation, the sales were the object of a great deal of anxiety. A good year's wool clip could be suddenly threatened by a prolonged drought, or a flash flood, to say nothing of bushfires and the constant danger from disease among the sheep. When things had gone well, they loaded the wagons with as much of the precious cargo as they could hold and set out for Sydney. In boom times they might be met along the road by horsemen, sent out by city buyers to steal a march on their competitors. Not that this meant that payment for the purchases would come through any sooner. Many months could pass – up to three years in extreme cases, according to Professor Blainey – before the deal was finalized, a London-bound ship was found and the return from the sale was assured. Only then would the squatter cover his outlay and find out his exact profit.

The late 1830s were the best years. Despite the fact that the price of land had risen in 1838 from five shillings to twelve shillings per acre, there was still a large gap between the letter of the law and its enforcement. Also, two years previously it had been established that for an annual flat rate of £10 a grazier could occupy under precarious tenure any run, of whatever area. The body of Crown Commissioners which was set up at the same time had in theory powers so wide that they have been described as judges, jury, policemen,

* Ward, R., *The Australian Legend*, Cheshire, Melbourne, 1965, p. 93. But as Ward himself states, at times the homosexuality was not all that sublimated, either. He quotes (see p. 92) J.C. Byrne's *Twelve Years' Wanderings in the British Colonies* : ' . . . where black *gins* are unobtainable, there is alas ! too much reason to believe, that the sin for which God destroyed "the doomed cities" prevails amongst the servants of the squatters.'

sheriffs, treasurers and barristers. But in practice this body was ineffectual, comprising as it did a hundred or so men to police half the continent. By this time, too, the status of squatter was no longer looked down on. It would have been unthinkable that the word should retain its old derogatory flavour when it now referred to a way of life that everybody aspired to. Sheep and wool were the only important topics of conversation. Newly arrived immigrants were advised to 'put everything in four legs'.*

The colony's dynamic rate of growth was retarded for a while by an economic slump and by a Governor's attempt to regulate the uncontrolled expansion in the industry. There was also a long period of drought, accompanied by a credit squeeze which resulted in the collapse of some banking houses and in ruin for a great many squatters. Sheep prices fell to rock bottom, some animals being sold off for as little as a shilling a dozen. One solution to the disaster was the process known as 'boiling down'. It was an expedient adopted by optimists whose wool was now worthless and who hoped to turn it into a different product. The term 'boiling down' could not be more exact. The animals (which had presumably been slaughtered first) were piled into containers which were then tightly sealed and in which they were boiled down until everything, fleece, meat and bones, had disappeared and all that was left was the fat. This fat was made into tallow. In 1844, boiling down accounted for some 200,000 sheep ; in 1845, the number rose to 750,000. By the late 1840s this figure had been tripled.

This 'solution' in fact solved nothing. The depression reached its lowest point in 1843. This plight of the squatters was further aggravated by the fact that they were simultaneously involved in a heated confrontation with the government. The Colonial Office had seen fit to put up the price of land to £1 per acre.† Wool-growers maintained that they could not possibly afford such a high price, while protesting vehemently against having to pay the annual rate which, as they rightly pointed out, gave them no security of tenure. The Governor of New South Wales at this time was Sir George Gipps. He put forward a compromise proposal : over an eight-year period, squatters would pay a licence fee of £40 per

---

* Roberts, S.H., *op. cit.*, p. 338.
† Four times the price of land in Canada, twelve times the price of land in South Africa.

annum for every twenty square miles of grazing land,* in exchange
for which they would enjoy security of tenure over those eight
years. Pandemonium broke out in the colony. It was the American
Revolution all over again, and the cry 'No taxation without representation' was heard. Governor Gipps' proposals were described
as an exaction worthy of the Bey of Algiers. Eventually, the squatters
were to win their point. In 1847 an Act of Parliament guaranteed
them the right to leases ranging from one to fourteen years at a rate
of £2.10.0 per thousand sheep, and also opened to them the option
of buying their runs.

Two or three years before these measures were taken, Australia had
found her economic feet again. Recovery was as rapid as the collapse
had been. After all, the country was young and rich in untapped resources, and an industry such as wool-growing was enormously
profitable under normal conditions. Once the teething troubles were
over, the metamorphosis was bound to happen. This early slump
and recovery is a typical example of the several but brief crises that
the liberal economy was prone to. Some people suffered as a result
of them, but for the bulk of the population they were less harmful
than the stagnation endemic in modern guided economies.

The difference between the squatters of 1830 and their predecessors at the beginning of the century was significant. The concept of
the vast property had already taken root. With this trend, there had
been a corresponding development of a landed aristocracy, which
was as conservative as the first generation of squatters had been
innovative. Even so, they were not the class of the future. For even
at that early stage, there was a potent egalitarian instinct at work in
the Australian community, which was to become the motive force
of a class of small property-owners, tradesmen and farm-workers.
They were ultimately to ensure the triumph of an aggressively
democratic spirit.

---

* S.H. Roberts estimates that an average run covered 5,000 acres (2,023 hectares)
and that runs of 500,000 acres (202,343 hectares) were not unknown.

Chapter Ten

New colonies and political transformations

Anti-French feeling hastens the settlement of Australia – occupation of Tasmania – Tasmania becomes independent of New South Wales – Governor Arthur – first attempt at settlement of Port Phillip – British take possession of Western Port, King George's Sound and parts of the north coast – foundation of Western Australia – a colony without convicts – more setbacks than achievements – squatters and the origins of the colony of Victoria – their success – South Australia as a testing-ground for 'systematic colonization' – 'the Paradise of Dissent' – five Governors of New South Wales in thirty years: Brisbane, Darling, Bourke, Gipps, FitzRoy – emancipists against exclusives – the end of transportation – gradual granting of political rights

At the same time as the explorers were solving the mysteries of the unknown continent and the sheep-farmers were beginning to tap its rich resources, Australia as a body politic was also developing. New colonies were founded, each of which in its turn was to follow the example of New South Wales and win from the mother-country its own parliamentary government. Eventually, the partial cessation of transportation was to put an unregretted end to half a century of Australia's existence as a penal colony.

Tasmania* was the first to become a separate territory in its own right. It will be remembered that Baudin's expedition in the early 1800s had aroused British suspicions. It may be too far-fetched to suggest that it was the French who made Australia British. However, although one can only make such a statement with great reservations, it is not entirely unfounded, as will be seen in this chapter. Certainly, when Governor King landed troops and convicts on the northern and southern coasts of Tasmania in 1803 and 1804,

---

* The name is used here for convenience, although it did not officially replace 'Van Diemen's Land' until 1855.

there can be no doubt that it was to prevent the old enemy from getting there first. Baudin himself witnessed one of the landings and the customary ritual that went with a formal act of possession – the hoisting of the Union Jack and the salute of guns. The commander of the *Géographe*, innocent as he was of the slightest designs on any British territory, dismissed the ceremony as 'childish', which can scarcely have endeared the Frenchman to His Majesty's officers.

The British, having taken possession of the island, were there to stay. They discovered that their new acquisition was about four-fifths the size of Ireland. They were especially struck by the marked difference between it and New South Wales, for the island was a place of mountains and great forests, with many lakes and rivers and with lush green landscapes which came as a surprise to them after the unrelieved greyish bush of the mainland. They were also surprised, and reminded of home, by the amount of rainfall and the temperate climate. Despite this, the settlement of the island proceeded extremely slowly. In the earliest days, almost its only inhabitants were the most dangerous and refractory of the convicts, who had been sent there because it seemed likely to be an excessively difficult place from which to escape. Even so, some of them did manage to make good their escape. Once they were at large, they could only survive by raiding and plundering the isolated farms of the island's few settlers. At least one of these first bushrangers is said to have resorted to cannibalism. As for the natives, they were just as reluctant as those on the mainland to accept the bounties of Anglo-Saxon Protestant civilization.

For a period of four years, between 1813 and 1817, the local representative of that civilization was no shining example, it must be said. The job of Lieutenant-Governor had been given to an officer, one Thomas Davey, who had come out on the First Fleet and spent five years in the colony and thus was no stranger to these parts. Davey seems to have been an eccentric, with a pronounced taste for material gains. Macquarie, under whose orders he was, judged him severely as a frivolous buffoon. But between Sydney and Hobart Town, where 'Mad Tom', as he was known, was posted, communication was infrequent. In his southern isolation, Mad Tom's eccentricity came to the fore. Manning Clark says of him:

He often drank to excess with convicts at the 'Bird in Hand' in Argyle

Street, walked the streets in his shirt-sleeves, called all and sundry by their Christian names, and cohabited openly with convict women to the great pain of his long-suffering wife and the scandal of the few respectable families in Hobart Town.*

After Davey's departure, there followed a less colourful period of seven years. In 1824 Colonel George Arthur took charge of Tasmania. Under Mad Tom's successor the island's resources (wheat, grazing and fishing) were developed sufficiently to attract a growing number of immigrants. Whitehall had also realized that Hobart Town was separated from Sydney by almost 800 miles of difficult sailing, and it had been decided to sever Tasmania from the jurisdiction of New South Wales. The most significant thing about the new Lieutenant-Governor was that he was a man of a quite different stamp from his predecessors. At forty years of age, he had spent half his life in the infantry. When the Napoleonic Wars came to an end, he had seen service in Jamaica as a quartermaster and had commanded the garrison in Honduras. As a dyed-in-the-wool Puritan, he had a stern view of life and looked on human nature without indulgence. He saw men as innately vicious, and the only thing capable of countering this flaw in mankind was the strictest moral code. Nobody enjoyed his receptions, which were niggardly, solemn and boring. When settlers saw the new Lieutenant-Governor riding down the streets of Hobart Town, dressed in his black, semi-military, semi-civilian greatcoat, buttoned to the neck, his black trousers with their red stripe, his black beaver hat and his sword by his side in its shining scabbard, they knew that a new era of law and order was at hand.

Arthur, the enlightened despot, had an opportunity to show the colour of his authoritarian and moralistic principles. Whitehall was beginning to wonder whether transportation really was the cure-all it had been made out to be thirty years before. There had been no reduction in the crime rate in the British Isles. And at the same time, the news from Australia was that many a convict could turn out to have a worthy career in the Antipodes. The conclusion arrived at was that transportation as a punishment should be either abolished or made harsher. The time being not yet ripe for abolition, it was the second solution which was chosen, the one which Bigge had recommended not long before (see page 118).

* Clark, C.M.H., *A Short History of Australia*, p. 46.

Tasmania seemed the ideal place to try out this new experiment. It was as far away as Botany Bay, and much easier to police. Also, it was under the command of a man who was convinced that stern discipline was a necessary condition for the redemption of sinners. For the punishment of the worst and the reformation of the best (or, as Arthur no doubt saw them, the less evil ones), two different systems operated. The most dreaded punishment was to be sent to the penal establishment at Port Arthur, in the far south of the island. It was situated at the tip of a peninsula which was joined to the island by a narrow isthmus where half-starved wild dogs were said to roam free. Another feature of the place was the forced labour for making roads, often done by prisoners chained together in gangs. There was, however, a chance of being assigned to private owners, and this was a fate that held less fears and more hope for the convicts. The Governor believed that such work would still be hard enough to bring home to the miscreants all the abomination of their wrongdoings, while at the same time setting them the example of a righteous master from whom their black hearts might well pick up a sense of goodness. This was a sound idea. But it did rely for its success on the co-operation of the settlers who, as W.D. Forsyth says, were transformed into 'amateur warders' from whom the strictest efficiency was expected. They were given

half the prisoners as assigned servants and were held responsible by Arthur for their punishment and reform . . . The Governor looked on the colony as primarily a gaol and on free settlers as an encumbrance unless they bore a share in convict management.*

Arthur was inclined to follow a line of reasoning through to its logical conclusion. For example, on the question of race relations, the solution that appealed to him as the least pernicious was to segregate the blacks and the whites. Until that time, wholesale slaughter had taken the place of a policy on the problem. It has been estimated that, of the 3,000 to 7,000 Aborigines who inhabited the island in 1804, no more than 300 remained by 1830. Governor Arthur, as though he was a naturalist attempting to save a species of animal threatened with extinction, decided to contain the few surviving Tasmanian Aborigines on the peninsula where the Port

* Forsyth, W.D., *Governor Arthur's Convict System*, Sydney University Press, 1970, p. 61.

Arthur penal settlement was located. The manhunt was organized : 2,000 soldiers and colonists acted as beaters across the whole island ; it lasted for seven weeks and cost £30,000 ; and it resulted in the capture of one woman and one little boy, fast asleep. They tried persuasion next. A missionary talked some Aborigines into going with him to one of the smaller islands in Bass Strait. But spiritual succour and material assistance did not prevent their extinction. By mid-century, their numbers were down to forty-seven ; by the 1870s the race had died out.

Arthur has been called a second Macquarie. By the time he left the governorship, in 1836, the island's population had increased threefold, its income was six times greater and the annual trade figure had grown from £75,000 to £900,000.

Interest in other parts of Australia was growing. Lord John Russell, Colonial Secretary from 1839 to 1841, describes in his inimitable manner a visit he received from a gentleman attached to the French government. This 'gentleman' having made so bold as to inquire of Lord John over which parts of the Australian continent Her Majesty's government claimed sovereignty, the Colonial Secretary replied, 'All of it'. Whereupon, the gentleman left.

Colonies were becoming fashionable again in London.* And the growth of the new colonies was to be much less hesitant than the early development of New South Wales had been. The American debacle of 1776 had faded from memory, and the growing belief in theories of free trade could only encourage overseas ambitions. There was, however, one thing that remained unchanged : Great Britain's suspicions of French aspirations. Feeble as the French governments of the Bourbon Restoration period were, Great Britain still had misgivings about French expansionism inherited from the days of Louis XIV and Napoleon. Thus it was that a combination of commercial ambitions and political disquiet made Downing Street take a series of steps which, though they were unco-ordinated and somewhat ad hoc, eventually bore out Lord John Russell's words.

The first move dated from 1803. As a precaution designed to assist the landing in Tasmania, an observation post was established on

* A.G.L. Shaw has counted more than 300 debates at Westminster on the colonial question between 1830 and 1840, as against some 200 between 1815 and 1830.

Port Phillip Bay.* This post was supposed to secure Bass Strait against the Machiavellian designs of Bonaparte. But this occupation of the Strait's northern shore was, to begin with, far less successful than the landing on the southern shore. The officer in charge of the operation was lacking in foresight. He formed the opinion that the desolate landscape and the infertile soil would never support the 300 convicts under his command and, after sticking it out for three months, requested (and was granted) permission to join the main body of the expedition in Tasmania.

There followed a ten-year lull in activity, while Great Britain dealt with the other problems associated with the Napoleonic Wars. Soon after the end of hostilities, there was a revival of interest in the Far East. The East India Company established itself in Singapore in 1819. This was a place of prime strategic importance and a trump card in the contest between the British and the Dutch for the Far Eastern markets. The coasts of New Holland were included in its ambit. There was even talk of developing a ' Singapore in Australia '. In quick succession, three trading posts were established in the north of Australia, not far from where Darwin stands today. These initiatives, in fact, had no immediate significance, but their establishment did have important consequences, since in order to legalize them His Majesty's government simply moved the western limit of its rightful possessions from 135° longitude over to 129°.† As Professor G. Blainey says : ' With a stroke of the pen, and more in the interests of uniformity than acquisitiveness, Britain claimed ... land equal to one sixth of Australia or nearly as large as Saudi Arabia.' ‡

This westward encroachment of British dominion continued slowly but surely. As before, it was the French who were the unintentional cause of it. Ships flying the *fleur de lys* were a frequent enough sight in. Australian waters, whether on straightforward scientific missions, looking for a suitable place to set up a penal colony (as J.P. Faivre has suggested), or simply on routine naval cruises. There was Louis de Freycinet, Baudin's old shipmate, who

* About forty kilometres from the present site of Melbourne and a hundred-odd kilometres from the goldfields.

† Phillip's original authority, it will be remembered, did not reach westward of 135 (see page 82).

‡ Blainey, G., *The Tyranny of Distance*, pp. 95–6.

was on Australia's west coast in 1818. There was Captain de Bougainville, the son of the great explorer, who sailed into Sydney in 1825 at the head of a French fleet. While he was there, he laid the first stone of a monument to the memory of La Pérouse. He was welcomed and made much of, and no doubt people speculated about the real reasons for his visit. This curiosity was reawakened the following year with the arrival of Dumont d'Urville. He had actually visited Port Jackson before, spending ten weeks there in 1824, as a lieutenant aboard *La Coquille* under Captain Duperrey. This time, he himself was in command ; and it was the same ship, under the new name of *L'Astrolabe*. Again, rumour was rife about the intentions of the French. Dumont d'Urville made no secret of his instructions, but one never knew what these Frenchmen might be up to. In London the Colonial Secretary, Lord Bathurst, was alarmed. Three times in one day he wrote to his representative in Sydney, Governor Darling, requesting that he proceed with all diligence to occupy Western Port, to the south-east, and Shark Bay, nearly 4,000 kilometres away on the west coast. Ten days later Bathurst had second thoughts and changed the latter part of his instructions – Darling should occupy, not Shark Bay, but King George's Sound,* at the south-west corner of the Bight. Darling did not hesitate and dispatched soldiers and convicts at once. When *L'Astrolabe* put in to Western Port and King George's Sound in the spring of 1826 and left again without raising the French flag or landing troops, the French threat was deemed to have been forestalled. Bathurst's quick thinking may well have been justified by events. But the Treasury, looking for economies to make, found the expense involved in the occupation unwarranted ; Western Port was evacuated in 1828 and King George's Sound in 1831.

One result of this activity was the realization that New South Wales and Tasmania were not the only possible colonies. Another result was the founding of Western Australia.

In 1827 a naval officer, Captain James Stirling, was sent on an anti-piracy mission in the Timor Sea. Stirling took the opportunity to sail down the west coast of New Holland, which was still largely unknown and which the Dutch, it will be remembered, had described in such unflattering terms. Captain Stirling was, by all accounts, a man of great good humour and optimism. He was in for

---

* The site of present-day Albany.

a surprise along the west coast, in the form of a navigable river. He explored it, seeing many black swans the like of which had never been seen in Europe, and finding that the land on either side seemed fertile, so fertile in fact that he could only compare it with Lombardy. He could not get over the disparity between his own observations and the opinions of his distant forerunners – he says that his report on the country 'differs so widely from that of the preceding Dutch and French navigators, that it will scarcely be believed that we undertake to describe the same country' * Perhaps the Admiralty staff included a historian or two, accustomed to reading conflicting reports. Certainly, it was the optimism of Stirling that won the day. Also, it was out of the question to give anyone else (i.e. the French) the opportunity of occupying a site that was so strategically placed on the route to the Malay Archipelago and China.

The Treasury, under protest, said they would finance one warship and no more. This was the first step. On 2 May 1829, Captain Fremantle raised the Union Jack on the southern bank of the river that Stirling had discovered and that now bears the name of the swans he saw. Then, in His Majesty's name, he proclaimed formal possession of all of that part of New Holland which had not yet been annexed, which amounted to one third of the entire continent and was bounded by more than 6,000 kilometres of coastline. All of Australia had now come under British sovereignty.

The first problems to be faced were finance and manpower for the development of the new colony. The government had pronounced its opposition in principle to the idea of duplicating Botany Bay on the Swan River. The founding of Western Australia was to be entirely the work of private interests. There proved to be no shortage of capital. One Thomas Peel, the type of man who would nowadays be called a promoter, made a secret arrangement with one of the richest men in Sydney, Solomon Levey by name, an emancipist of some years' standing. The government, after the customary hesitation (and no doubt taking some account of the fact that Thomas Peel was a cousin of the Home Secretary), finally approved a large-scale project. Peel was granted a land concession of 250,000 acres on the banks of the Swan River, on condition that he meet all the costs of conveying and settling 400 emigrants. There was a flood of excited applicants for these 400 places in 'Hesperia',

---

* Quoted by Battye, J.S., *Western Australia*, Clarendon Press, 1924, p. 69.

as the lyrical Captain Stiring had suggested naming his discovery.* The more prosaic civil servants in the Colonial Office were taken aback at the deluge of applications from would-be emigrants.

Disappointment followed hard on the first flush of enthusiasm. Forethought was non-existent. More and more immigrants arrived and land was distributed to them without reference to any master plan. As well as which, the soil itself turned out to be much less fertile than had been at first supposed. As Professor F.K. Crowley remarks, 'appearances were deceptive, and this was not the first time in Australian history that scenery had been confused with fertility.'† Nor did the immigrants possess any great agricultural skills. They were, for the most part, officers on half pay, younger sons of good families, tradesmen or members of the learned professions, all highly respectable but quite unsuited to the tasks of opening up a virgin land. Moreover, they began to hear the call of the unknown, as others had in New South Wales, and manpower dwindled away as though by magic. Wakefield saw it as the vindication of his theories and pointed out that, although Thomas Peel had arrived at the Swan River with 400 people, within six months he had to make his own bed and fetch and carry his water himself. Wakefield used Peel's experience in Western Australia as proof that, unless certain precautions were taken, too much land made too freely available resulted inevitably in dispersal of population. In 1840, some of those who accepted his theories decided to put them into practice. About 100 kilometres from Perth,‡ they founded their own community, which they called Australind. Their aim was to buy up land at Wakefield's 'sufficient' price and then sell it again in smallholdings, thus encouraging concentration of settlement. Australind was a failure and within four years it was nothing but a ghost village.

Stirling himself had been appointed Lieutenant-Governor of the territory in 1829. He administered the area for ten years, his confidence unshaken by even the worst setbacks. But after his departure, demoralization set in. There was a feeling of stagnation in the colony and it was apparent that it would never develop properly without more manpower. And, in the 1840s, manpower

* Battye, J.S., *op. cit.*, p. 66.

† Crowley, F.K., *Australia's Western Third*, Heinemann, Melbourne, 1970, p. 13.

‡ Established as the colony's capital as early as 1829.

was hard to come by as the enthusiasm that had fired the early immigrants had been extinguished. So it was that, in 1846, as a last resort, Western Australia came to ask that a consignment of convicts be sent out. Three years later this request was granted. Transportation to New South Wales had by now been abolished and London needed somewhere else to send its convicts (see pages 179–80). Thus the same steps were taken in the west as in the east, but in reverse order – Botany Bay, which had begun with prisoners, stopped using them half a century later; the Swan River, which had shunned prisoners to begin with, after twenty years of hardships and setbacks saw the advantages of having them.

Private initiative turned out to be more successful in the future colony of Victoria than it had proved to be in the west. It has been said that the development of Victoria is the sole example in Australia, and possibly in the whole British Empire, of a colony that succeeded without being planned.

This unwonted success story has its roots in the stubborn nature of a Sussex landowner called Thomas Henty, who was known for his breeding of sheep and horses, if not for his ten children. In 1828, at the age of fifty-three, he decided the time had come to see new horizons. Everybody was talking about New Holland. At first, he was tempted by New South Wales and Tasmania. Then he too succumbed to the Swan River contagion and decided that it was Western Australia for him and his family. He took the precaution of sending out his eldest boy, James, aged twenty-nine. Within two years, James Henty had reached the conclusion that 'Hesperia' would afford them all more frustrations than gratifications. He therefore went to settle in northern Tasmania, where his father and brothers came to join him. Here they were in for another disappointment, as land prices were too high, and anyway the best land was already taken. They decided to try the northern shore of Bass Strait. It was a family undertaking : one of the sons sailed for London to obtain the necessary authorization, while another one went ahead to look over the land. He urged his father to settle there without waiting for government approval. But Thomas Henty was not the sort to leap before he looked. He took a schooner of fifty-eight tonnes and explored almost 4,000 kilometres of coastline before deciding that his son was right. In 1834 the Henty family took possession of Portland Bay, some 200 kilometres to the west of Melbourne, the first of a gradual flow of squatters in the green and pleasant western district that Thomas Mitchell had called 'Australia felix' (see page 131).

It would have been inconceivable that they should be the only settlers in such promising countryside. About the same time two enterprising men, John Batman and John Fawkner, both of them sons of convicts, were attracted to the same area. Batman did things properly. With the support of capitalists he formed the Port Phillip Association and solemnly 'purchased 600,000 acres round Port Phillip from the aborigines in consideration of twenty pairs of blankets, thirty knives, twelve tomahawks, ten looking-glasses, twelve pairs of scissors, fifty handkerchiefs, twelve red shirts, four flannel jackets, four suits of clothes, and fifty pounds of flour.'* His competitor, John Fawkner, paid less attention to such niceties of the law. He and his men also crossed Bass Strait from Tasmania and reconnoitred the hinterland of Western Port which they found not to their liking. After spending twelve days looking over the land along the shores of Port Phillip Bay, they went a couple of kilometres up the Yarra River,† and settled at a place which struck them as ideal, on 23 August 1835. Batman and his men, who were already there, waved their 'treaty' at them and tried to keep them out – a pity that the ensuing brawl was not recorded for posterity. Eventually the code of the squatter – here I am, here I stay – prevailed and both of them remained. Thus was Melbourne founded.

In the government offices there was consternation – all this sort of thing was quite strictly forbidden by His Majesty's orders ! For a while, the law tried to prohibit a de facto situation. But soon practical good sense came to terms with reality, and Governor Bourke (see page 174) stopped insisting on the letter of the law. A year after these 'illegal' occupations, he made Port Phillip into a separate administrative district, thus legalizing the bold initiatives of Batman and Fawkner. Six months later, in March 1837, Governor Bourke even honoured this new district with a visit. He distributed names to the different places with a sure sense of protocol. Williamstown, at the mouth of the Yarra, was called after King William IV ;‡

---

* Clark, C.M.H., *A Short History of Australia*, p. 80.

† This river had been discovered during the original occupation of Port Phillip in 1803. It was named Yarra-yarra in 1835.

‡ Queen Victoria was to succeed her uncle within three months.

the place upstream was called Melbourne, so that the Prime Minister should not feel slighted. Development of the area was rapid, although the slump of 1842–4 (see page 157) hit the Port Phillip Association hard. Still, it is not always first-comers who are first-served. The influx of immigrants, from England and Sydney, continued apace, and the land being grazed grew steadily. In 1840 there were 10,000 inhabitants and 800,000 sheep; in 1847, 43,000 inhabitants and more than four million sheep; and by mid-century, 79,000 inhabitants and six million sheep. Such a phenomenal growth rate justified the desire for separation from New South Wales, but was to prove inadequate to cope with subsequent upheavals (see Chapter 12).

Believers in Wakefield's idea of 'systematic colonization' looked askance on the success of Port Phillip as well as on the failure at Swan River. Port Phillip they put down to good luck; Swan River they explained by the fact that their theories had been ignored. They decided to put these theories into practice somewhere else. This led to the founding of a fifth colony.

There was no lack of possible sites. Their choice fell on the southern coast of the continent, and in particular on Gulf Vincent,* near the mouth of the Murray River, the 'noble river' of which Sturt had given such an enthusiastic description. The originators of this new project were not out solely for material gain. Their aim was to found a colony which would be different from the others in every way. Their first stipulation was that there should be no convicts, whom they looked on as carriers of the germs of social corruption. They intended, also, to rely as little as possible on government assistance. They did not mind going through the forms of getting initial government approval, but thenceforward they intended to rely on the maximum of private initiative. Last but not least, these founding fathers, unlike those in Western Australia whom they saw as profit-hungry capitalists, looked on themselves as idealists of every sort, with a belief in human freedoms, social justice and religious tolerance, which they maintained had been the basis of British greatness but which their country seemed to have neglected somewhat. What they aimed at building was a better, more liberal and open Great Britain, a 'paradise of dissent' as Professor Douglas Pike calls it.

* The site of modern Adelaide.

These men who founded South Australia took account of realities as well as dreams. They knew everything about publicity. Having conceived the idea of the new colony in 1829, they made it a talking-point over the next five years. Wakefield, of course, supported it wholeheartedly. He saw it as a godsend, the opportunity to fix a 'sufficient' price, to prevent 'dispersion of settlement' and to encourage the emigration of young married couples who would make for social stability. One important concrete step that he took was helping in the formation of the South Australian Land Company, which was mainly composed of Opposition M.P.s who subscribed to his theories. In 1834 the government approved their proposals. By Act of Parliament South Australia was made a province and given a somewhat hybrid status : it was to have a Governor to preserve law and order (though by what means was left unstated) ; and the distribution of lands was to be the responsibility of three Commissioners. The colony was to receive a representative assembly when population growth and prosperity justified it.

Finance was the first necessity. Parcels of land were sold in advance, much as flats are sold nowadays while still on the drawing-board. The 'sufficient' price varied between twelve and twenty shillings per acre. In this way £35,000 was raised, a quarter of it from buyers who were eager to go out to South Australia, some of it from speculators who were equally eager never to set foot in the place, and the remainder from philanthropic subscribers whose altruism in the matter it would be unseemly to doubt. One of these men was George Angas. He was forty-seven years of age and had made his fortune in a shipping business left to him by his father. His 'great object', he said,

was in the first instance to provide a place of refuge for pious Dissenters*
of Great Britain who could in their new home discharge their consciences
before God in civil and religious duties without any disabilities. Then to
provide a place where the children of pious farmers might have farms in
which to settle and provide bread for their families ; and lastly that I
may be the humble instrument of laying the foundation of a good system
of education and religious instruction for the poorer settlers.†

* One wonders whether Mr Angas' care for Dissenters extended to the 'papists'
By the census of 1846, they amounted to 7 per cent of the population.

† Quoted by Clark, C.M.H., *A Short History of Australia*, p. 76. Angas was to
make good this aim in 1836 by founding the South Australian School Society

The first emigrants sailed in March 1836 ; in all, fifteen emigrant ships set out that first year. When they arrived, the new settlers met considerable hardships. Sturt's lyrical descriptions may have greatly influenced the choice of the site for the colony, but they were of little help to the colonists they had attracted. The explorer had said that he had never seen a more promising country or a more favourable site for colonization. But all that the disciples (or victims) of systematic colonization could see was hills and more hills stretching away, apparently for ever, towards the north. Hardly any surveying had been done and the land allotments were very difficult to locate. The unkindest cut of all was that there was no sign of the rolling pastureland that was making so many fortunes overnight in other parts. The immigrants had to make do with small farms, small runs and small flocks. The division of authority between the Governor and the Commissioners did not help things. These two branches of authority each claimed to be vested with the power to manage financial arrangements and to appoint administrative officers. They spent much energy in futile, bitter in-fighting.

The founders' idealism was beginning to look rather forlorn. In 1838, the sensible decision was taken to vest in one official the different powers of the Commissioners and the representative of the Crown. The choice for this new post fell on Lieutenant-Colonel George Gawler. Soldiering had been in his family for generations. He had seen service in Spain with Wellington and had been at Waterloo. Illness had changed the direction of his life : he discovered religion, which became his central preoccupation, and while garrisoned in Ireland, he actually managed to persuade some Catholics to change their faith. He was a man of courage and piety. With his arrival, the administration of the colony was brought back to the straight and narrow of its founders' virtuous principles. The new Governor had a difficult task and would have needed more than virtue to survive the polemics which surrounded him. The population growth itself gives some idea of the problems : 2,800 new immigrants in 1838, 4,600 in 1839, 3,000 in 1840. The fact that they saw themselves as the apostles of a new Enlightenment did not help house them or create work for them. Gawler, with the best of intentions, some naïvety and a total lack of training in solving such

---

and bringing out a party of Prussian Lutherans at a cost of £8,000, which he bore himself.

problems, did what he could. But events overtook him, the implacable Treasury accused him (unjustly, as it now appears) of overspending, and in 1841 he was unceremoniously recalled.

George Grey, who replaced Gawler as Governor, was less concerned about separating the wheat from the chaff. He too was an officer, but fired with none of Gawler's zeal. He had been attracted to Australia while still a young man. In his middle twenties he led two expeditions to the north-west. He must have been given to hard and fast conclusions, for his experience of the outback led him to the belief that the only real solution to the Aboriginal problem was a policy of forced assimilation. At that time, this was such a novel concept that it attracted the notice of the powers-that-be. And so, at twenty-nine, he found himself in charge of South Australia. In his tenure of four years he had little opportunity to put his ideas on the Aboriginal question into practice, as he was taken up with other problems. Hard fact was more to his taste than ideas. Six years had been enough to put Wakefield's theories to the test and disprove them. The Governor resorted to simple measures. He managed to balance a very precarious budget by increasing taxation and reducing expenditure, two unexpected measures which made Grey so unpopular that he was burned in effigy by settlers. At the risk of causing 'dispersion', colonists were encouraged to turn squatter. As a result, magnificent grazing lands were discovered in an area some 300 kilometres south-east of Adelaide.* And at the same time, it happened that mineable copper deposits were also discovered.

By the time Grey was posted to New Zealand in 1845, the colony of South Australia was at last beginning to develop. On the surface it seemed to bear little resemblance to the colony that the idealists had dreamed of in 1836. However, when ideas are sincerely held they never disappear without trace ; it is more likely that they change their shape. As Manning Clark has said : 'South Australia pioneered two great movements in the social history of Australia : how to appear radical and be conservative, or how to be a puritan without doctrines or principles.'†

From the vantage point of its half-century of existence, New South

---

* Near the bay that Baudin had called Rivoli. Although it had stuck, no doubt this Napoleonic name meant little enough to graziers in the 1840s.

† Clark, C.M.H., *A Short History of Australia*, p. 79.

Wales looked down on these Johnny-come-lately colonies with mingled sympathy and suspicion. While taking a pride in its seniority, it was to help them to win from the home country the political freedom to which they all aspired. At the same time, New South Wales itself was to experience problems associated with its own peculiar origins, for these origins aroused passions in New South Welshmen that their counterparts in the other colonies did not feel.

Between the departure of Macquarie in 1821 and the middle of the century, there were five incumbents of the Governorship in Sydney: Thomas Brisbane, Ralph Darling, Richard Bourke, George Gipps and Charles FitzRoy. Their average of six years in office compares favourably with the succession of short-term incumbents at the Colonial Office during the same period. For example, between 1827 and 1841 there were eleven different Colonial Secretaries, some of whom lasted for a mere four or five months.* One beneficial result of this continuity was a strong administration. The Governor's work was made easier, too, by the speeding up of communication with London, since ships could now make the journey in a little over three months. It must be added that these five men were all mature, Gipps at forty-seven being the youngest, and Bourke at fifty-four the oldest. Bourke was also the only one of the five to have had any experience whatever of public administration. All of them being army men, they lacked even that wider view of the world which seafaring can give. Brisbane and Gipps had actually known no other way of life than soldiering.† As for Darling, he had commanded Mauritius for four years, but his contacts with the few French settlers and the black slaves had given him little experience on which to draw in governing a population as heterogeneous and volatile as that of New South Wales. FitzRoy had had an easy time of it on Prince Edward Island and in the Leewards. Service in Canada and in the Caribbean made him see the honours of his new title as his due ; but it did not prepare him for the sort of thankless tasks that he found himself called upon to perform and which, in his view, were more suited to a junior

---

* The national hero, the victor of Waterloo himself, even had to turn his hand to the job for five weeks in 1832.

† Brisbane's sole passion was astronomy – ' the good Governor's hobby horse ', as the younger Bougainville called it after being received by Brisbane in 1825.

officer than to Her Majesty's representative, especially if (like him) that representative belonged to the noblest of the nobility. At least Bourke, for his part, knew something of the difficulties involved in such a job. He had spent the years 1826 to 1828 at the Cape, where he had learnt that a leader of men must expect to earn the ill-will of the men he leads. At the Cape, too, he had won the reputation of being a 'liberal', because he had tried to protect the 'noble savages' from the 'wicked Boers'. Such a reputation could only make his job easier in a colony whose intelligentsia was profoundly influenced by the democratic ideas of the Chartists.

These five men were equal in goodwill and unequal in their qualifications for the post, for as the Duke of Wellington is said to have remarked, there is many a brave man who is not fit to govern a colony. And in fact it is surprising that in the middle of the nineteenth century Great Britain should have been so short of professional administrators that she had to fall back on career officers. What one can say is that, although the selection of them was definitely haphazard, it adds an even more stirring touch to that great enterprise of the British Empire and the men who built it.

The first unpleasant surprise in store for these gentlemen, in their scarlet uniforms, loaded with gold braid and epaulettes and spangled with decorations, was their official residence. Until 1845 it was a decidedly modest house, comprising only six rooms. Brisbane moved out of it and took up residence on the outskirts of the town. Darling managed to extend the gubernatorial palace, but could not make it any more comfortable. Bourke, as soon as he saw it, complained that it was an excessively uncomfortable dwelling, subject to noxious smells and in a state quite beyond repair. His suggestion was to build a new residence, an idea that met with no favour at the Treasury. It did not relent until 1835, and even then it was another ten years before the official inauguration of the splendid building that was to be the admiration of every visitor to Sydney.

It is to be hoped, at least, that the Governor's office was spacious and that the desk was broad enough to hold all the files and paperwork that must have accumulated. These military gentlemen had no problems requiring a military solution, unless one counts a few sorties against Aborigines or a skirmish or two with bushrangers. Normally, there was no opportunity of practising the lessons of Sandhurst. On the other hand, there were any number of complaints and claims and grievances and protests. Apart from problems associated with squatting, dealt with in the previous chapter, there were three questions above all which cropped up again and again and again : the continuing rivalry between exclusives and emancipists ; the question of whether to continue or to abolish transportation ; and the question of political rights. These officers turned civil servants must often have longed to be back among their own kind, away from this hotbed of vested interests and undisciplined passions, where they were expected to do the impossible and reconcile points of view that were irreconcilable.

'Once a convict, always a convict' – this concept of the permanence of punishment had come under increasingly vehement attack ever since the beginning of the century. One wonders whether any of the Governors in Sydney ever had the curiosity to leaf through a history of Rome. They might well have benefited from it. Not that one can equate convicts and slaves, or emancipists and freemen. Nevertheless, there is food for thought in the points of resemblance. The Roman Empire at its height, in the first century A.D., had a problem which in some ways was close to one of the problems of New South Wales 1,800 years later. It has been estimated that, at that time, at least 80 per cent of the population of Rome were the descendants of slaves who had been emancipated at different periods. The ancient world seems to have been able to cope with these extreme variations in social status better than modern Australia. This may have been because the freed slaves could only change their status by a series of gradual steps. Emancipation certainly gave them immediate citizenship ; but it did not guarantee automatic access to public office and the magistrature.* And certainly they do not ever seem to have suffered the indignities to which the emancipists were subjected in New South Wales.

As more and more convicts won full or provisional freedom, the conflict mentioned in Chapter 7 increased in intensity. William Charles Wentworth took up the cudgels on behalf of the emancipists. Wentworth was a complex and paradoxical character who would have intrigued a psychoanalyst. He was the son of a surgeon (whose arrival in New South Wales is surrounded by some mystery) and of a convict mother. Despite these origins, he claimed descent from

* Originally, access to the full rights of citizenship took three generations. This time was gradually and almost imperceptibly reduced, without ever being defined officially by law.

a family of ancient lineage in England. He resolved that by his own achievements he would live down what was discreditable, and live up to what was respectable, in his chequered pedigree. He had first made his name as one of the party who found the way through the Blue Mountains. But his pride was rubbed the wrong way by an unrequited passion. He aspired to the hand of one of the daughters of John Macarthur (whose family had now become one of the most prominent among the local gentry), but Wentworth was given to understand that he was beneath them. He vowed revenge and thenceforward campaigned against the exclusives, calling them 'the yellow snakes of the Colony' and maintaining that the country belonged to those who were born and bred in it, namely the offspring of convicts. He even insulted Darling in public, because the Governor had not dared pronounce himself in favour of Wentworth's views. Over the preceding fifteen years, the emancipists had been steadily gaining ground. But the excesses of Wentworth's campaign on their behalf actually did their cause a disservice. Then, in 1840, with the epoch-making abolition of transportation to New South Wales, the whole question took on a new aspect. This conclusion, after fifty-two years, that the experiment of transportation had all been a mistake requires some examination.

It will be remembered that immigrants had been attracted to Australia in great numbers after the end of the Napoleonic Wars. These new arrivals had included a fairly high proportion of Irishmen. With them, of course, they brought their more volatile emotions and their staunch religious belief. A Presbyterian minister, John Dunmore Lang, whose fanaticism was equalled only by his sincerity, saw this influx of Irish immigrants as evidence of one of those diabolical schemes that the Papists were well known for. He declared that the Roman Catholic Church was attempting not only to enslave the misled people of Australia, but also to extend its realm of dire superstition into the neighbouring regions of the Pacific Ocean. For Lang, the time for action had come. Under this reverend gentleman's influence, other immigrants of anti-Roman persuasions were attracted out to Australia on a crusade to save the true faith.

Whether they were Protestants or Roman Catholics, the numbers of free settlers went on growing. A woman was to write one of the finest chapters in Australian history by rescuing some of them from destitution. In January of 1841 Governor Gipps, after much hesitation, finally agreed to receive a young lady called Caroline Chisholm, of whom he had already heard much. He was aware that it was her aim to found a charitable institution to help immigrant girls. Gipps, according to one historian, was an unlikeable man, with a certain inhumane and remote disdain in his manner. Another one describes him as 'a stern but handsome man, with keen black eyes and bushy black eyebrows. He looked every inch a Governor.'* And he preferred women to know their place, which was in the home. Margaret Kiddle gives Gipps' own account of his interview with Caroline :

I expected to have seen an old lady in white cap and spectacles, who would have talked to me about my soul. I was amazed when my aide introduced a handsome, stately young woman who proceeded to reason the question as if she thought her reason and experience, too, worth as much as mine.†

The Governor was inclined to dig his toes in. But Easter was approaching : the young lady vowed to devote her life to the good work she had undertaken, and within not many months permission was granted and the Female Immigrants' Home was founded.

At this time Caroline Chisholm was aged thirty-one. She had been converted to Roman Catholicism at twenty-two, on marrying an Indian Army officer. The young couple had lived in Madras for six years and had had three children. In 1838, when her husband was on leave, they had visited Sydney. What she saw there changed the course of her life and she decided there and then that she must take in hand the wretched girls who, having arrived in Australia, were 'turned loose in Sydney',‡ quickly found themselves reduced to poverty and took to prostitution. The question of where the money is to come from has never discouraged charitable instincts. Mrs Chisholm used her own house at first as a shelter until the Home took over. There was a gradual growth in the demand for her good works. It has been calculated that she helped or rehabilitated more than 11,000 women. It is no exaggeration to say, with Sir Keith Hancock, that it was thanks to her that the dignity of womanhood and the family was established in New South Wales.§

* Quoted by Kiddle, M., *Caroline Chisholm*, Melbourne University Press, 1950, p. 32.
† *ibid.*, p. 33.
‡ *ibid.*, p. 28.
§ Hancock, W.K., *Australia*, Jacaranda Press, Brisbane, 1961, p. 31.

Neither Mrs Chisholm nor anyone else could bring relief to the degradation of the convicts. Transportation went on, year after year. Between 1838 and 1840 they included a fair number of political prisoners, eighty-seven Americans, fifty-eight British Canadians and sixty-one French Canadians, who had been sentenced for their part in the 'rebellion' of 1837 and 1838 in the two French-speaking provinces of Canada. London had been shaken by this revolt. Did it mean that, after seventy years of experience of British institutions, these obtuse and incomprehensible Frenchmen still had not got it into their heads that things British were better ? Lord Durham was given the task of getting to the bottom of the affair.*

In Australia, which was still one hundred per cent British, such problems of race and nationality were almost non-existent, except where the Irish were concerned. But then, the Irish were so inured to oppression by the English that it was unlikely the religious difference would result in a political upheaval. On the other hand, the whole question of the rights and wrongs of the transportation system had been a running sore for so long that in November 1837 the Whig administration decided the time had come for a decision on it once and for all. It appointed a House of Commons committee whose terms of reference were to examine the efficacy of transportation as a punishment, the effect it was having on the state of morality in colonial society† and possible developments in the transportation system. After nine months deliberation the committee was categorical in its conclusions. Its report stated bluntly that transportation had two main features : it was 'ineffective in deterring from crime but remarkably effective in still further corrupting those who underwent the punishment.' It found the system was 'not susceptible of any improvement'.‡ When governments appoint commissions of inquiry, it is generally a way of avoiding a responsibility, a rule to which this government proved no exception. It delayed for two more years before accepting the committee's radical recom-

---

* Wakefield, too, infallible as ever, took part in the inquiry.

† Ever since the inception of transportation, this question of its impact on morality had concerned the defenders of virtue. One of these, a gentleman by the name of Frère, had won a prize at Cambridge in 1790 with a dissertation (in Latin) on the subject : 'Can one hope for an improvement in morality and in the exercise of virtue in the colony being born at Botany Bay ?'

‡ Clark, C.M.H., *A Short History of Australia*, p. 84.

mendations. And when it did do something about the problem, in 1840, it adopted only a half-measure. Henceforth, convicts were no longer to be sent to New South Wales, but only to Tasmania and Norfolk Island.*

The political trends that had been taking shape in New South Wales from the time of the Bigge report (see page 118) were bound to be encouraged by this decision to suspend transportation. Up until the time of the Bigge inquiry, the Governor had been next to God. In 1833 a Legislative Council was set up ; it had five to seven members, whose functions were purely advisory and who were all selected from the Civil Service. The representative of the Crown still retained the power to initiate legislation. But a measure could not become law unless the Chief Justice certified that the Bill was not repugnant to the laws of the United Kingdom and respected them as far as local conditions permitted. This was a cautious formulation, leaving scope for wide interpretation. The Crown was also empowered to disallow any Act within three years of its enactment.

A further step forward was taken in 1828. The Legislative Council was increased to not less than ten members and not more than fifteen. These members were still to be appointed, but some of them (the number was not laid down) were to be selected from among the more prominent landowners and merchants. Before any bill was presented to the Council, an abstract of it was to be printed in the public press. The most important advance of all was that no measure could become law unless it was passed by a majority of the Council. Once again, the Crown reserved its power of veto.

The principle of elected representation was finally recognized in 1842. The membership of the Legislative Council was increased to thirty-six, twelve of whom were government appointees (six of them from the Civil Service) ; but the other twenty-four were elected by citizens who possessed a high property qualification. This was the most decisive step of all on the way to proper parliamentary

---

* There was a later, unsuccessful, attempt to revive transportation to New South Wales. It continued to Tasmania until 1853, was introduced to Western Australia in 1849 and abolished throughout Australia in 1868. It has been estimated that, over the period of eighty years that transportation lasted, a total of 157,000 convicts were brought to Australia.

government in New South Wales. And that next development was just round the corner.

At this point it is appropriate to pause and glance at Australia as she was at the mid-point of the nineteenth century.

Chapter Eleven
Australia in the mid-nineteenth century

Population – territorial divisions – institutions – economic resources – rapidity of urbanization – Sydney, Melbourne, Hobart, Adelaide, Perth and Brisbane – social classes – lack of unity – controversies on religion and education – unsuccessful attempt to revive transportation – mediocre intellectual life – rejection of a suggested Federation – 'Quo vadis, Australia?'

Metternich was fond of saying that Italy was nothing but a geographical expression. His remark would have fitted Australia much better than Italy in the middle of the nineteenth century. The only links between its different colonies were their common attachment to the British Crown and a common source of prosperity, namely wool-growing. As for political unity, it was non-existent. Each of the colonies looked on itself as its own master and saw no reason to make any change.

By the late 1840s, approximately one third of the continent had been explored. Over the whole expanse of this vast land mass lived a total of about 430,000 inhabitants. It has been calculated that in 1840 the ratio of women to men was one to two; ten years later it was two to three. This growth in the female population was a stabilizing factor in Australian society; another was the increase in the numbers of free settlers. Down in Tasmania the proportion of convicts in the population was still 38 per cent. But in New South Wales the ratio was by now as low as two or three per cent. As for Victoria, there were only a handful of them there; in South Australia there were none at all; in Western Australia, admittedly, more were beginning to arrive, the proportion was growing, but all in all, the old penal colony of 1788 had almost completely disappeared. The growth of population was rapid, owing to a high birth rate as well as the influx of immigrants. Between 1831 and 1840, 65,000 settlers migrated to Australia (which was almost five times as many as in the previous forty years) ; between 1841 and 1850, more than 108,000 immigrants came. For all that, Australia was far from being the favourite destination for British emigrants. In fact, in 1850, only 6 per cent of those who emigrated from Great Britain chose to go to the Antipodes. America continued to attract the lion's share of them.

It is difficult, not to say impossible, to judge how many Aborigines there were at this period, for there is a total lack of figures. After sixty years of contact between whites and blacks, sometimes peaceful, sometimes hostile, there was still a complete absence of understanding between them. What Sir Paul Hasluck says of those in Western Australia was true of them all :

Their own law told them to kill when the British law said they must not kill ; it commanded them to go when the British law bade them stay ; it allowed them to take when British law ordered them to refrain from taking . . . Their law had come down from the great culture heroes of the past ages and must endure ; this British law was the unexplained and apparently contradictory series of commands given by white men when they were in a sulky mood.*

In the middle of the nineteenth century, the country was divided into four areas : New South Wales, which still meant more than half of the whole continent ;† Western Australia, separated from New South Wales by the imaginary line of the 129th degree of longitude ; South Australia, which amounted to about one third of the size of its western neighbour ; and Victoria, a dwarf among giants, covering an area equal to that of England and Scotland. To these four divisions must be added, of course, Tasmania, its dimensions being roughly those of Eire. The population density varied considerably : New South Wales had 187,000 inhabitants as against 97,000 in Victoria (where fifteen years before there had been only some 200), 70,000 in Tasmania, 66,000 in South Australia (which had also grown from about 500 in fifteen years) and 4,600 in Western Australia, where the rate of population increase was by far the slowest.

In 1850, the Australian Colonies Government Act set the seal

---

* Hasluck, P., *Black Australians*, 2nd ed., Melbourne University Press, 1970, pp. 122–3.

† In addition to which it included New Zealand up until 1841.

on Westminster's acceptance of the principle of representative government. This Act established legislative councils, like that in Sydney, for Tasmania, Victoria and South Australia. The Governor of each colony was vested with executive power, but the majority agreement of the Council was now necessary for the passing of laws. One third of the members of these legislatures were to be appointed by the Crown, the other two thirds elected on a very restrictive property-based suffrage. It was further provided that Western Australia would not have any such body unless and until one third of its landowners or leaseholders petitioned for it.

This constitutional development was completed between 1850 and 1860, by which time the principle of parliamentary government had been accepted by all the colonies, one after the other, with the exception once again of Western Australia which did not accede to this system of government until 1890.

As for the resources that provided a living for these 430,000 voluntary or involuntary expatriates from faraway Britain, there was of course, first and foremost, wool. This industry was based on sheep, sixteen million of them. To appreciate the full significance of this figure, it must be remembered that, forty years before, the total sheep population of Australia was less than one hundred thousand. Such a spectacular development in grazing should not, however, obscure the fact that progress was also being made, albeit much more slowly, in agriculture. By mid-century, 37 per cent of the arable land in Tasmania was under cultivation (the colony was looked on as the garden of the Antipodes), 32 per cent in New South Wales, 14 per cent in South Australia. In very good years, the colonies even exported cereal crops. Lastly, although the great days of whaling were past, Sydney and to a greater extent Hobart still served as depots for the courageous crews who hunted wild animals larger than their own ships. These primary products (wool, cereals and oils) supplied the colonies with sufficient exports for their balance of trade to reach a level of about four million pounds.

The increase in population was bound to lead to the development of local industry. The long distance from the home country may also have encouraged this development – Professor Blainey remarks, 'the ocean was Australia's first tariff wall.'*

* Blainey, G., *The Tyranny of Distance*, p. 137.

In the early days mills and breweries had been built, the latter in more considerable numbers, no doubt, to cater for the first settlers' appetite for alcohol. Many other types of industry were soon started. By 1850 the more important towns had soap and candle factories, potteries, tanneries, workshops producing clothing, hats and foot-wear. In the British tradition, there were shipyards ; in Tasmania alone 400 ships, as well as countless small craft, were launched between 1840 and 1849. None of this could have happened, of course, without credit arrangements. One of the most characteristic figures of the period is the rich capitalist, the banker-cum-merchant-cum-grazier. But the banks were reluctant to let private individuals of this sort play a very large part in financing industry. There were several banks in Tasmania and even more of them in New South Wales. Two of them, the Bank of Australasia and the Union Bank, dominated the market. The banknotes which they put out added to the coin in circulation. As for the stability of the currency, there was no question about it : as in the rest of the Empire, the pound sterling reigned supreme.

If one tries to imagine Australia as it was 120 years ago, the image that comes to mind is of vast grazing lands dotted with thousands of sheep ; a landscape bounded by unexplored horizons and inhab-ited by weird and wonderful native animals ; and in the foreground the rough and ready pioneers of a new breed of men. But such a stereotyped view only gives a fragmentary picture of what the reality was. Even in those early days the most significant feature of the next period was already apparent : the exceptionally rapid rate of urbanization. Close on thirty per cent of the population of New South Wales was concentrated in the capital. Two Australians out of every five lived in six towns : Sydney, Melbourne, Adelaide, Geelong, Hobart and Launceston. The remarkable thing about these six is that they were all seaports. In the interior, Wakefield's bugbear, dispersion of settlement, was still the rule. Two explana-tions of this phenomenon have been put forward. According to the first, the rapid development of the ports is related to the fact that, until after 1830, whale oil had been the major export. But even after wool replaced whale oil, the population density along the coastal strip went on increasing, and at an even faster rate. The conditions in which the wool-grower or the shepherd lived and worked were no doubt more suited to unmarried men than to men with families to care for. Women and children rarely if ever accompanied the men who chose to follow a way of life which was well known for its drawbacks and hardships. They usually preferred to stay in the towns, where they were likely to be less homesick and where there was at least a minimal standard of comfort and civilization. Reliable statistics from that time are hard to come by, but even without them, common sense tells one that in the under-populated bush the birth rate was bound to be much lower than in the towns.

In 1850 Sydney was, in fact, the only urban centre which deserved the name 'town'. Its situation called forth admiration from all who set eyes on it. One French visitor said there was something magical about it ; another saw it as spectacular and breathtaking. Nor was it only the natural beauty of Sydney's harbour setting that enchanted these Frenchmen ; they also exclaimed at the 'broad streets running at right angles to one another and lit by gaslamps, the elegant dwellings in stone and brick, the uncommonly imposing public buildings, the truly grandiose aspect of the Governor's residence'. One of them saw Sydney as a miniature London, 'London on a fine day, London with all its comforts, its beautiful shops, its luxury, sport and bustle, but London without the thieving element'. Another one (perhaps from Montpellier ?) says : 'The English have nicknamed Sydney "the Montpellier of Oceania" because of its fine healthy climate and the fertility of its soil.' Needless to say, these French travellers took an acute interest in things gastronomical and could find nothing wrong with the meat, the fruit or the fish. As for the wine,* one connoisseur pronounced it excellent ; another one, after a dinner at the Governor's, was more reserved : 'the wine seemed to me of good quality.'

The impressions of these French visitors may read somewhat optimistically : they do not seem to have looked much beyond the surface. The reactions of British travellers were more mixed. One of them describes Sydney, with perceptible condescension, as resembling a second- or third-rate town back home. Another one was of the opinion that there was more filth, poverty and vice in Sydney than in any other part of the Empire. As for the wine, whether it was 'of good quality' or not, the fact was that the vast

---

* The First Fleet had brought out the first vines. Wine production did not get properly under way until about 1820. John Macarthur had a hand in this important development, as in others.

majority of the population quite definitely preferred liquor of a more stimulating sort : ' The number of drinking-shops is unbelievable and drunkenness is rife.' So were gambling and, according to a demure Puritan, illicit sexual relations. One must presumably draw the conclusion that the French visitors' ignorance of English may have made it difficult for them to see anything but the more respectable aspects of the place. It is obvious that Sydney was already no exception to the rule that in cities, and especially in seaports, there can be a great disparity between appearances and realities.

There was no such range of conflicting opinions about Melbourne, which was still in its infancy. There is a document which gives a powerfully realistic impression of the Victorian capital about this time. It is a journal, with almost daily entries, kept over a period of years by the very pretty wife of an English lawyer, Georgiana McCrae. She had arrived in Melbourne in 1841, at the age of thirty-seven ; she was to live there until the end of her days, forty years later. She and her husband belonged, obviously, to the best society. Like others of their class, they were brought close to ruin by the slump of 1842–4. But through thick and thin, Georgiana continued to be a first-class witness to the time and events through which she lived. In her pages of concise prose, people and places are captured with an immediacy that brings them to life to this day.

From the moment she first arrived, she encountered a way of life which was quite foreign to her. As soon as they disembarked, 'we had to wade through mud and clay ... My good London boots quite *abîmés* !'* She and her family (four children aged from eight to two – three more were born in Melbourne) settled in. Their house consisted of

one tolerably large room, with four closets, *called* bedrooms, opening out of it. The walls of wood, about half an inch thick, and the ceiling of the same. The building raised on stumps to about two feet from the ground, and three wooden steps, like those of a bathing-machine, lead up into a

---

* ' Ruined ' The word appears in French in the text. Georgiana had received some of her education in a school run by 'some noble French ladies who had a shilling per diem allowed by the English government for their support'. The *supérieure* made 'soldiers' trowsers at a halfpenny the pair'. This was in London in 1809 ; they were apparently French *émigrées*. See *Georgiana's Journal*, (ed. H. McCrae), 2nd ed., Angus & Robertson, Sydney, 1966, pp. xvi and 25.

French window, which is the front door of the dwelling. At a little distance from the back door is a kitchen hut, *à rez-de-chaussée*. And for this accommodation the rent required by Mr Simpson is £100 per year !*

Some days after moving in, she ventured forth : 'Perambulated the town with Agnes, that is to say, we went up the north side of Collins Street, without any sign of a pavement ; only a rough road, with crooked gutters – the shops, built of wood, and raised on stumps.' Georgiana was soon to see why the gutter and the stumps were necessary : when it rained, the 'streets' were turned into raging torrents. This is a recurring theme – 'quite knocked up on my return from wading through the mud ; and my boots – *abîmés* ' ; 'Incessant rain. Grievous for the emigrants camped in miserable thin tents exposed to the south-west wind, while the flats are dotted all over with pools of water' ; 'The footpaths were terrible, and the road, all the way, like a bullock-yard' ; 'The road an everlasting chain of bog-holes' ; 'Lucia lost one of her shoes in a mud-hole'. †

The mud disappeared in summer, but was replaced by dust storms that prevented one breathing. When storms were approaching, she found the atmosphere reminiscent of London fogs, except that the wind was 'like the blast from a furnace'. The climate was not to Mrs McCrae's taste : 'At night thermometer 47°, and this, the Australian midsummer ! The boasted climate is a myth, and requires a constitution of india-rubber elasticity to sustain it '.‡ Perhaps that was why her children seemed to be for ever ill. Or it may have been the food, all fruit and vegetables having to be brought over from Tasmania. Even the water had to be carted in.

Georgiana's placid nature was unruffled by such hardships. When she had some friends round, '*Fortune-du-pot* dinners, which were then the vogue, tried my patience and ingenuity.' § If her husband had financial troubles, she consoled herself with proverbs remembered from her childhood : '*Me voilà sans sou ! mais non sans souci.*' ‖ She was careful not to get out of touch with intellectual things, of which she speaks in a rather highfalutin tone, believing it bad for one to read too many novels and reviews, since this distracts

---

* *Georgiana's Journal*, p. 26 '*A rez-de-chaussée*' (on the ground floor) is given in French in the text (*translator's note*).

† *ibid.*, pp. 26, 39, 41, 59, 95.   ‡ *ibid.*, p. 80.   § *ibid.*, p. 32.

‖ 'Money goes, worries come ', in French in the text (*translator's note*). *ibid.*, p. 92.

one from more stimulating activities that keep the mind alive.*

Fortunately, despite such lapses into the pose of the bluestocking, the young lady was fond of amusement. Her everyday life was usually spent in caring for her children and in exchanging visits with friends. Occasions for entertainment were not infrequent. The family might, for instance, go for excursions into the countryside, although these were not wholly without drawbacks, and one certainly needed stamina to stand up to a trap ride on the country roads : 'At one minute we were completely off the ground, at the next, suddenly down again – gutters three or four feet deep, and, everywhere, jagged tree-stumps interspersed with boulders !' †
Another distraction, less fraught with perils, was the official receptions. When Governor Gipps visited Melbourne, Georgiana says : ' I gave Lizzie my Chelle dress, and my wedding shoes, to enable her to go to the ball in honour of the Governor, at the Criterion, this evening. Went to the ball, but not to dance. Put on my best black satin dress, and a bit of ivy in my hair, so that I felt myself *comme il faut.*' ‡ This was in the spring, when the weather may have been fine. But at other times of year, going out in the evening was something of an adventure, and she had to pull on her husband's hunting-boots over her own shoes. On dark nights, a servant or her husband would walk in front with a lantern. The great annual event of the social calendar was the squatters' ball, an occasion when the city ladies might cast a demure glance of admiration at those men who had conquered the bush. Everyone was up very late that night, and the following day, a Sunday, only servants went to church. Georgiana must have looked delightful.

Hobart had no Georgiana. Having been in existence for well nigh half a century, its atmosphere was not as primitive as that of Melbourne. A French visitor found much to praise in it : he speaks of its ' fine waterfront ', its broad, well-paved streets lined with ' rich shops '. Even Englishmen were impressed, one of them thinking the customs-house and the market ' quite splendid' and ' imposing '. It even reminded him of home (praise indeed !) : ' The cabs and coaches have an Olde England air to them ; like ours, their coachmen are in red.' He did, however, have a few reservations : the St Mary's Hospital was the only place where one could have a bath ;

---

* Mrs McCrae was a talented painter.   † *Georgiana's Journal*, p. 30.

‡ 'Looking very proper' ; *ibid.*, p. 48.

the two theatres were places of ill-repute and there were only three inns in the whole town fit for a gentleman. On the other hand, there were dozens of public houses patronized by the lowest forms of human life. Some Englishmen were also put out by the inescapable presence of the convicts in the colony. But, on the whole, they found that Tasmania was 'as calm as any part of England and Hobart was an exceptionally peaceful town'.

In 1850, Adelaide and Perth were still in embryonic form. The former was composed largely of wooden or stone structures, hastily erected shanties rather than houses. Perth was not much better off. One traveller found himself put up in a room that was 'devoid of plaster on the walls or glass in the windows' and beset by hordes of flies. Despite the flies, which were a permanent nuisance, there was still a social life of sorts, including regattas, picnics, horse-races, kangaroo hunts, the Governor's ball (with a guest list of 180 ladies and gentlemen) and amateur theatricals (such as the epoch-making performance of a work by the improbable name of *Love à la militaire* !).

Brisbane, at this stage, is never mentioned by anyone. It had about 1,000 inhabitants. Until 1842 it was a punishment settlement for the hardest cases among the convicts. Yet, even then, the future development of the city that was later to rise there was already being determined by the shores of the magnificent Moreton Bay.

A group of human beings living together in which no ranking order evolves is well nigh inconceivable, a rule to which Australia was no exception. One visitor to the colonies in 1843 said that the Indian caste system was no more rigid than the Australian social structure. No doubt this is an over-statement. But it is true that New South Wales, in its capacity as Great Britain's eldest Antipodean offspring, was making some sort of effort to produce a society that was a replica of the home country's. At the peak of the pyramid, of course, there was the Governor with his civil and military staffs. Not that the Governor was automatically recognized as the first gentleman of the colony. If he did not belong to the aristocracy, but was of a less exalted rank, then the 'pure merinos' treated him as condescendingly as the peers of the realm had treated the first Hanoverians. The nickname 'pure merinos' was reserved for a very few 'old' families who could prove that no drop of convict blood had flowed in their ancestors' veins. Their aim was to establish a local nobility on the British pattern. Being unable to share the traditions of the real nobility back home, they followed a life-style which they hoped would foster the resemblance between themselves and their models. A prime example is provided by the Macarthurs. A friend who visited them in 1841 on their property at Camden, south-west of Sydney, has left a description of them. The property covered some 15,000 hectares. But it was not the land that counted so much as the house (the manor, one is tempted to call it). In its architecture and furnishings, in the grounds with their ornamental pond and their gardens, in the style of everything and everybody, servants as well as masters, the whole place was so reminiscent of old England that the visitor could scarcely believe he was 32,000 kilometres away from home. Tasmania, too, had its wealthy landowners living in the style of Virginian planters, supported by the slave labour of convicts. Such opulence was enjoyed by only a handful of families. There were in addition a great many other people, either former convicts or free settlers, who made a living from the land. Most were squatters ; some were farmers. Lower down the scale came the descendants of emancipists. And right at the bottom, shunned by everyone, were the 'canaries', the convicts, so called because of the yellow uniforms they wore.

It is probable that an accurate impression of Australian society at this time is conveyed by the following extract from a usually reliable French observer : 'In Sydney, in Melbourne and in the other towns, there exist all the elements of what could be called a good middle class such as is to be found in the main cities of England, outside London.' It was a society made up largely of middle classes, no doubt ; but this did not necessarily make for a united society. The 'small town' sketched by La Bruyère comes to mind * at a distance, it gives an impression of tranquillity and harmony – how delightful it must be to live under its peaceful sky ! Yet, as soon as you come into it, it turns out to be a hotbed of hatred and intrigue. One wonders whether the celebrated passage from *Les Caractères* occurred to any of the French travellers previously quoted. Certainly their impressions of the smaller Australian townships are

---

* Jean de La Bruyère, seventeenth-century French moralist, in his book *Les Caractères* gives a pretty picture of a small town which looks a peaceful and happy place from a distance. After spending two nights there, he finds he is like all the other inhabitants – he wishes he could leave *(translator's note)*.

strikingly different from their impressions of Sydney : 'Men who should be united by common interests are set against one another by quite arbitrarily devised categories with names calculated to give offence, and by a widespread and exceedingly obnoxious inquisitorialness.' Some years before, Hyacinthe de Bougainville had slyly suggested something similar :

In the society of New South Wales I met with nothing but kindness, politeness and amiability. If I had judged only on what I saw, I should have taken away the most perfect impression of everybody ; and if I had judged only on what they said about one another, I should have taken away the most damnable impression of them.

One may be tempted to dismiss this as the bias of a French naval officer taking a malicious delight in pointing out the faults of a British colony. But can one dismiss the impression of Darwin, who spent eighteen days in Sydney in 1836 ?

The whole community is rancorously divided into parties on almost every subject ... There is much jealousy between the children of the rich emancipists and the free settlers ; the former being pleased to consider honest men as interlopers. The whole population, poor and rich, are bent on acquiring wealth ; the subject of wool and sheep grazing amongst the higher orders is of preponderant interest. *

Professor S.H. Roberts gives a picture of a society at war with itself, a community of 98,000 souls split into rival factions. Petty functionaries were against more important functionaries ; merchants took unkindly to any sort of authority ; the squatters despised the town-dwellers ; the free settlers fought the emancipists ; the latter sought to live down their past by oppressing the convicts, who were as resentful of their former companions as of the free men. Professor Roberts' conclusion is that New South Wales was 'a pestilential little place overridden by a spirit of faction', and Sydney 'a distinctly unattractive mixture of all manner of types, not yet blended into a community, not yet possessed of any civic institutions and in no degree realizing its duties as the centre of the colony, and indeed, of the continent'. †

* Darwin, C., *Diary of the Voyage of H.M.S. 'Beagle'* (ed. N. Barlow), Cambridge University Press, 1933, p. 386.
† Roberts, S.H., *The Squatting Age in Australia, 1835–1847*, pp. 32 and 338. Such

As for the questions which so sharply divided the Australian subjects of Queen Victoria, first and foremost one must mention the continuing running sore of the exclusives-versus-emancipists squabble. However, the violent acrimony of thirty years previously had abated to some extent. Another generation had appeared on both sides and now, although the descendants of immigrants and convicts were still separated by a barrier of reciprocal scorn and resentment, at least they did not hate each other as cordially as their parents had. In the nature of things they were bound to feel more and more that they belonged to one and the same community.

The fragile unity that was gradually evolving was weakened rather than strengthened by religion. In 1851 there were 176,000 Anglicans in New South Wales, Tasmania and Victoria,* as against 47,000 Roman Catholics. The rest of the population was made up of Presbyterians, Wesleyans and a scatter of smaller sects.† The Protestants, though disunited on questions of religious principle, at least shared the conviction of their own superiority. There was a considerable difference between, on the one hand, the members of the Church of England (which still aspired to a privileged position in society and retained all its old hierarchical features), and on the other the members of the nonconformist churches, who were becoming more and more egalitarian and inclined to leave matters of faith to the conscience of the individual. What must also be taken into account is a powerful current of ideas, a survival from the Enlightenment, which was in the process of eliminating all the mystical content from religion. Moral enlightenment was the term for this unmetaphysical remnant of Christianity, with its rather tenuous link to an ill-defined Supreme Being. The Roman Catholics, of course, had no truck with any of this. They were the antithesis of other Christians in everything, their uncompromising faith, their intangible dogmas, their obedient passivity in belief and, more than anything else perhaps, the memory of the persecutions inflicted on their forebears. For, almost to a man, they were Irish, and the mere fact of having put ten thousand miles between themselves and

* The religious problem was more acute in these three colonies than in the others.
† Including 1,778 Jews, according to census figures.

---

language may appear too hard. It must be pointed out that it refers to Sydney as it was before 1840, but it is unlikely that the atmosphere would have been purified by magic in a period of ten years or so.

Ireland in no way changed the feelings they had harboured against the English and the Scots for centuries. Although Governor Bourke had decreed in 1835 that all religions were equal before the law, the practitioners of each of these different religions went on believing that their own was superior to all the rest. The mediocrity of them as sources of spiritual nourishment could not make up for the unChristian bitterness and bickerings of their adherents.

As might be expected, it was over education that these competing religions fought their nastiest battles. From the very earliest days until after 1830, church schools (basically Anglican or Roman Catholic) enjoyed a monopoly. In 1844, Gipps gave in to pressure from nonconformists and adepts of moral enlightenment and set up a committee to investigate the possibility of a state-run education system. This committee aroused a storm of protest and it was four years before the principle of state schooling was acted upon. According to Manning Clark,

> the Catholics branded the national schools as Protestant seminaries. Some Protestants were beguiled into accepting them as preferable to 'popish' domination. In an attempt to reconcile the irreconcilable both the denominational and the national schools were starved of funds, and so the quality of both types of education paid the price of sectarianism.*

This outcome of the education argument was disastrous enough. But the passions it aroused were not as divisive as the conflict that was coming to the surface between the supporters of egalitarian democracy and their opponents who favoured a more hierarchical social structure. Both of these schools of thought were in favour of a parliamentary system, but they understood by that two different things. The latter group looked on it as a way of entrenching the privileges they already enjoyed; the former group, although it would have been out of the question at that time to advocate universal suffrage, were trying to have the franchise extended so that a greater number of citizens could participate in the management of public affairs. Naturally this group included the trade unions. Recent research has shown that the influence of the unions at that period was far greater than used to be supposed. The conditions that workers enjoyed in Australia were, by comparison with contemporary European practice, favourable indeed. Austra-

* Clark, C.M.H., *A Short History of Australia*, p. 102.

lian workers were determined not to share this relatively high standard of living with other people. It was their qualms at the idea of competition that led them to originate the concept of a 'White Australia'. Their opposition to the immigration of workers from Asia was impassioned and adamant.

This same fear of competition from outsiders was behind a protest demonstration, attended by several thousand people, in 1849, against an attempt by the British government to make a new gift of convicts to New South Wales. From the top of a horse-tram Robert Lowe, an orator well known for his fiery eloquence, harangued the multitude, whose enthusiasm for the anti-convict cause was not dampened by the steady rain. According to Lowe, the injustice that the English had inflicted on their former American colonies was nothing compared with what they were now trying to do to New South Wales. He warned that Sydney could well witness scenes similar to those seen in Boston seventy-five years earlier. At about this same time another stormy petrel, the Rev. John Dunmore Lang, went so far as to advocate the establishment of a republic. However, the Australian air is somehow favourable to the spirit of compromise. When all the shouting had died down, the convicts were shipped to Moreton Bay, where there was no likelihood of any riots being aroused and where landowners could quietly acquire their unpaid services, out of sight of Sydney.

This may well be seen as a minor incident. For all that, it does have its significance, being a foretaste of the popular politics which were to have such an impact on the latter part of the nineteenth century. It was also the very last attempt by Downing Street to resurrect Botany Bay.

So it was that Australia in mid-century was racked by social feuds, religious wrangling, controversies on education and constitutional disagreements. These centrifugal forces at work in her society were not offset by any cohesive forces, either intellectual or political. For, even where opinions differ, the very existence of a vital intellectual tradition is invariably a force making for unity within a society. Even those who think they are divided by opposing ideas are in fact unwittingly held together by the intellectualism they have in common with one another. But in the young Australian colonies, literature, the arts and sciences were all but unknown. New South Wales, by virtue of its seniority, was more advanced than the rest.

Sydney did have a certain intellectual life, with its two theatres (opera being especially popular), its Philosophical Society and public library, its adult education institute and its university. One or two historians and poets could be mentioned ; but works of scholarship or creative imagination were greatly outnumbered by political pamphlets. The only glimpse one has of any artistic originality is in a school of painters. A French traveller sums up the situation in 1847 : 'Sydney seems bound to become the intellectual capital ... although at present it has no literary activity of its own.'

In any case, Sydney's intellectual life, such as it was, did not reach the rest of the country, since each of the colonies saw itself as a separate entity and clung to its individuality. One outsider says, in fact, that Sydney and Melbourne disliked each other so much that they were compared with Rome and Carthage. According to Professor John Ward

Until July 1851 the Port Phillip District was obsessed with the task of winning separation from New South Wales. After that date the new colony of Victoria was full of pride of independence. South Australia, which had never been a penal colony, abhorred the convict 'Sodom and Gomorrah' of the east. In Van Diemen's Land the struggle for enlarged self-government was complicated by the battle over convictism, which divided the free population of the colony and imparted a special bitterness to its relationships with Britain.*

Certainly, under such conditions, unity could not thrive. One Colonial Secretary, Lord Grey (he managed, amazingly, to hold the post for six years, from 1846 to 1852), did actually suggest the idea of federation. Less given than his predecessors to concentrating only on immediate problems, Grey was far-sighted enough to realize that, if the colonies remained separate entities, they would not have much of a future. Perhaps he was clumsy in putting this motion forward ; or he may have tried to impose it on the colonies. Whatever the case may be, they gave it a cool reception. It was to be another half-century before this sensible expedient was accepted, by which time it had become a crying need.

This then was Australia 120 years ago : no common heritage or

* Ward, J., *Earl Grey and the Australian Colonies 1846–1857*, Melbourne University Press, 1958, pp. 5–7.

religion ; little confidence in itself, despite its material success ; a great uncertainty about what the future held for it ; and a growing awareness among its inhabitants of what marked them off from their British forebears.

All the documents from that period speak of the future awaiting this mysterious continent. According to one Frenchman : 'Sydney may well become not only the monarch of the South Seas, but also the ruler of great states and powerful nations.' Another one says, prophetically : 'The geographical location of Australia will make the nation a natural intermediary between European ideas and the world of Oceania. If that mission is worthily carried out, the nation will go down in history as one of the best representatives of human society.'

Darwin, too, noted his opinions. His reflections are especially interesting as one senses a certain ambivalence in his feelings. His pride in being British is unmistakable :

In the evening I walked through the town and returned full of admiration at the whole scene. It is a most magnificent testimony to the power of the British nation : here in a less promising country, scores of years have effected many times more than centuries in South America. My first feeling was to congratulate myself that I was born an Englishman.*

But even great scientists are not always completely consistent. At the end of his stay in Sydney Darwin was dubious about the penal system : 'On the whole, as a place of punishment, its object is scarcely gained ; as a real system of reform, it has failed as perhaps would every other plan.' And his conclusion was emphatic : 'The balance of my opinion is such that nothing but severe necessity should compel me to emigrate.' But Hobart found more favour in his eyes. 'I suspect ... the society is much pleasanter than that of Sydney ... The Colony moreover is well governed ; in this convict population, there certainly is not *more*, if not *less*, crime, than in England.'† After he had sailed from Australia on 14 March 1836, in a mood of optimism laced with disenchantment, based on his recent experience and his intuition of the future, he penned these lines : 'Farewell, Australia, you are a rising infant and doubtless some day will reign a great princess in the South ; but you are too great and

---

* Darwin, C., *op. cit.*, p. 375.

† *ibid.*, pp. 388, 387 and 391.

ambitious for affection, yet not great enough for respect; I leave your shores without sorrow or regret.'*

On one score he was dubious – whether this complex country would have a great future: 'I formerly imagined that Australia would rise into as grand and powerful a country as N. America, now it appears to me, as far as I can understand such subjects, that such future power and grandeur is very problematical.'†

Whether Australia's future was to be 'problematical' or not, only time would tell. And could one really say at that period what it was to be an Australian ? *Quo vadis*, Australia ? In the mid-nineteenth century, there was no sure answer to such questions. Australia was already something of an enigma.

---

* Darwin, C., *op. cit.*, p. 394.

† *ibid.*, p. 387.

Chapter Twelve
Gold

Gold discovered in New South Wales and then in Victoria – the gold rush – arrival of European immigrants – official regulations drawn up – life at the diggings – Melbourne as a pleasure resort – Sir Charles Hotham Governor of Victoria – Hotham's enthusiastic reception – unfortunate decisions – growing discontent – the Eureka Stockade – immediate repression – the symbolism of Eureka – Melbourne's rapid transformation – influence of gold on the economy and society – a new direction for Australia?

The original Dutch mariners who touched the west coast had dreamed of gold. One of the reasons why they took no further interest in the country was that they found none. The British, for their part, had no interest in gold. To begin with, they were taken up with the penal settlement and later with wool. Now and then an explorer or two would make a haphazard discovery of the precious metal, but they attracted little attention. Then, in 1848, the gold strikes in California caught the world's imagination. More than 6,000 Australians crossed the Pacific to search for the wealth that their own country was soon to provide so abundantly.

Many of these expatriates returned sadder, wiser and none the richer. But one of them, Edward Hargraves, learned a lesson from his experience in America. Before setting off on his Californian adventure at the age of thirty-three, he had been a Jack-of-all-trades and master of none, a sailor, a wool-grower, a farmer, an innkeeper and a shipping agent. He had two gifts: stubbornness and imagination. These qualities did not make him a rich man, but they did earn him a sort of immortality. What he had seen in California convinced him that if one dug in similar soil in Australia, one would find the same thing. He was nothing if not single-minded. Having arrived back in Sydney on 7 January 1851, he set out less than a month later for a place near Bathurst, guided only by his instinct for the right kind of geological formations. His preliminary investigations convinced him he was on the right track. He felt the need to do things properly – it is firmly reported that when he struck real gold on 12 February he was dressed in top hat and tails. A little speech was not out of place. He told his astonished guide : 'This is a memorable day in the history of New South Wales. I shall be a baronet,* you will be knighted, and my old horse will be stuffed, put into a glass case, and sent to the British Museum !'† The name he gave to the site of his discovery had symbolic overtones : Ophir.

The news of the find was officially announced in May that year. The announcement set off the same reactions as three years before in America and thirty-five years later in the Transvaal. Pessimism and predictions of calamity were rife. As far away as Paris, the *Revue des Deux Mondes* noted that 'Australian newspapers are cursing the gold-fever in verse and in prose.' In fact, one of the most widely read Sydney dailies, whose readers were no doubt highly resistant to change, went so far as to compare the many catastrophes that were bound to befall the colony with an earthquake or the plague. The Governor, Sir Charles FitzRoy, took it all more philosophically and reported to London that any attempt to halt the rush to the goldfields was as absurd as trying to control the waves in the sea. This was a realistic view. Sydney, like San Francisco before it, emptied in next to no time. The Queen's representative had a brief moment of hope that his charges would soon come back, for many of the first to leave found nothing. But then the discovery of a nugget weighing about forty kilos in a block of quartz raised excitement to fever pitch.

Ophir was not destined to hold the limelight for very long ; Victorians could soon look down on New South Wales. The Victorian government, not to be outdone, had decided to award a bonus of £200 to anyone who found gold within about 300 kilometres of Melbourne. It would be interesting to know how often the sum had to be paid out, since before the end of that same year of 1851, an arc of places had been discovered, about 100 to 200 kilometres from Melbourne, which made very small beer of Hargraves' Ophir.

---

* In fact he was presented to the Queen in 1854. But no further honour came his way

† Clark, C.M.H., *A Short History of Australia*, p. 113.

Ballarat, Bendigo, Mount Alexander were the names which were destined to figure in the epic story of Victoria's gold-mining era. It is a story full of triumphs and heartbreaks, of noble and ignoble doings.

People converged on this new Eldorado from all sides. The first-comers, of course, were from Port Phillip. There, Governor La Trobe was more upset by it all than his counterpart FitzRoy in New South Wales. Everything was abandoned, he said, houses were up to let, business had come to a halt, even the schools were closed down ; in certain places not one man was left ; the whole structure of society and the machinery of government were breaking down. But it was not only Victorians who were the despair of the authorities. Early in 1851 the exodus had been from Melbourne towards Ophir ; now the current was running in the opposite direction, and the *Bathurst Free Press* lamented that madness seemed to have come over everybody. Tasmania told the same tale ; Governor Denison said that the ships sailing for Melbourne were full to the gunwales. Similarly, the 500-odd kilometres between Adelaide and the gold-fields did not discourage the South Australians from taking part in the rush and proving to the theoreticians of 'systematic colonization' that a little less planning and a little more initiative may be a better guarantee of success. They went by land and sea, forsaking their idealism in favour of Victoria's materialism.

These fortune-seekers presented a striking spectacle on the road to the goldfields. One witness says that some looked tense and impatient, and others looked almost ashamed of being there ; some looked downcast and preoccupied ; but all their faces showed the same determination. They went on foot, on horseback, in carts, pushing wheelbarrows, or in drays pulled by ten pairs of bullocks, all hurrying to reach Ballarat, Bendigo or Mount Alexander and all goaded on by the same fear of being too late. There were no roads or paths, only the barest tracks which became gradually impassable under the wheels of the many heavy vehicles. The diggers wore what almost amounted to a uniform : the inevitable cabbage-tree hat, a blue shirt, trousers of indeterminate shade usually turned yellow by mud and clay, and a leather belt bearing a knife and a pistol. Their tools were a short-handled shovel, a pick of the smallest design, a strongish rope, a washing-pan, a sieve, a bucket and a wooden basin. The more thoughtful also made sure of taking an axe, a frying-pan, a saucepan, a billy-can and a few yards of calico to

A Concise History of Australia

make a tent. Although wives rarely accompanied husbands, the caravans did include a few adventurous women, of the sort who were unperturbed by the attentions they attracted. Lord Robert Cecil, at the age of twenty-two,* paid a week's visit to the Victorian goldfields. This demure gentleman describes an unexpected sight along the way:

A digger in his jumper and working dress walking arm in arm with a woman dressed in the most exaggerated finery, with a parasol of blue damask that would have seemed gorgeous in Hyde Park. She was a lady (so the driver told us) of Adelaide notoriety, known as Lavinia, who had been graciously condescending enough to be the better half of this unhappy digger for a few days, in order to rob him of his earnings ... These women are no rarities at the diggings.†

By the southern autumn of 1852, the roads to riches had become less congested. But then there came another great influx of gold-seekers, attracted by the good news that had reached Europe and America at the beginning of the year, revitalizing the lust for gold that California had roused. The Americans (10,000 of them, reportedly) came because they had experience of hunting for gold which they thought they could put to good use. The Irish came because they believed that now, in the aftermath of the potato famine, their trials and tribulations must end somewhere. The Germans came because, after 1848, they were looking for a happier land; until 1852 they had chosen to go to America; now they plumped for Melbourne. The French were not immune to the gold-fever either; no doubt, one would have had to be singularly obtuse not to be infected by it. Once again the *Revue des deux mondes* disapproved: 'The reports from Australia read like dreams inspired by the *Arabian nights*.' It quoted the London *Standard* as saying that Ballarat was a solid gold plateau. A book published three years later as a guide for French emigrants was even more hysterical, referring to 'immense, fabulous, unheard-of wealth, a promised land where you step on gold as you walk and breathe gold-dust in the wind, where gold is so ubiquitous that it seems to grow on trees.'

* The future Lord Salisbury; he was to be Prime Minister of Great Britain during the Boer War.
† *Lord Robert Cecil's Goldfields Diary* (ed. E. Scott), Melbourne University Press, 1935, p. 13.

Nor was this all : ' In Bendigo there is a French hotel where the French flag flies ! ' The writer urged Napoleon III to ' Say the word, Sire, and Australia will be French ! '

Napoleon III did not say the word, and Australia continued to be British. The vast majority of the new immigrants, lured by the gold, were British subjects. Eighty-five thousand of them came in 1852, and almost as many in each of the two following years. For a brief period Australia actually displaced America as the favourite goal of British emigrants. These British emigrants came from all social classes. Wakefield took this fact as a text for a sermon, saying that a gold strike in a new country always results in the 'Jacobinization' of a society. However, nobody else paid any attention to that aspect of the phenomenon. The emigrants' most urgent consideration was to get places on the fastest ships available. These were the days of the legendary clippers, with their raked bows, their slim lines, their three great masts towering sometimes sixty metres high, and their tremendous spread of canvas of all different shapes and sizes snapping in the wind. In terms of comfort they were no doubt not up to the standard of liners of the future, but they were much faster than any other ship afloat at the time. They had captains like the famous ' Bully ' Forbes of the *Marco Polo*, whose motto was ' Hell or Melbourne '.* In 1852 he missed hell but got to Melbourne almost three weeks ahead of a steamer. His record was broken two years later by one of his rivals who made it from Liverpool to Melbourne in sixty-three days.

These great days did not last long. The steamers were soon requisitioned and converted to troop-ships for the Anglo-French expeditionary force to the Crimea in September 1854. Ships once again took three months on the Australian run. The passengers needed more patience, but the longer trip made their first glimpse of the Australian coastline all the more exciting – they shouted and jumped and looked as though they had gone mad. However their actual disembarkation was not so thrilling, as they had to walk part of the way to Melbourne through almost knee-deep mud. Accommodation was their next problem, as lodgings were few and far between and could be had only at exorbitant prices. Some took to sleeping out, in tents that were far from weatherproof, or under the bridges on the river ; some slept on tables or on bare floors, any-

---

* Blainey, G., *The Tyranny of Distance*, p. 190.

where out of the rain. Finding food was just as difficult. The hero of a widely read French adventure novel set in Victoria reports that he was charged thirty-seven shillings (excluding tip) for a meal consisting of kangaroo soup, an omelette, bread and one glass of beer.* Some of the immigrants lost heart there and then, gave up their plans to look for gold and took whatever work they could find. However, most of them survived the temporary ordeals of their introduction to the new country and set off for the goldfields with all the other fortune-seekers, ready to stake their lives on a lucky swing of the pick.

The authorities were concerned at this feverish activity. Having learned from the recent Californian experience, they were determined to control it from the outset. The letter of the law was unambiguous : both the surface of the ground and the subsoil belonged to the Crown and could only be mined with official permission. This permission took the form of a licence, the fee for which was thirty shillings a month and which entitled anybody to a grant of land eight feet square. This system was put into force in September 1851. Lord Robert Cecil commented that it was easy to see it was the Queen's government at work and not the people's. But this was surely an over-simplification of a difficult problem. No great imagination was required to realize that in these hordes of fortune-hunters, all obsessed with the dream of miraculous wealth, there must be all sorts of dangerous undercurrents at work.

There was a brief heady period of illusion. The very first men to arrive at the goldfields found gold in all sorts of places, in creek-beds, under tufts of grass, caught among the roots of trees. They felt like freeholders in Canaan. But very soon the precariousness of their tenure was revealed to them by the floods of new competitors. As the miners' way of life settled down, it turned out to be incom-

---

* This menu and the bill for it are mentioned in *The Gold Thieves* (*Les Voleurs d'Or*) by Céleste de Chabrillan. The novel was published in 1857 and was an immediate success. The authoress had led a chequered career (an illegitimate child, a circus performer, a notorious good-time girl). A scion of one of France's oldest families, Lionel de Chabrillan, having fallen in love with her, he was packed off to Australia to get over it. He saw life in the goldfields, even occupied a specially created consular post in Melbourne, and then went ahead and married Céleste. This was a social disaster for him, but she turned out to be a talented novelist (Dumas *pere* enjoyed her books).

patible with the notion of rank. One man who yearned after certain minimal social conventions was told by a spokesman for the popular opinion that if he expected to be treated deferentially, he should stay away. Equality was the order of the day, the only differences tolerated being those in sheer bodily stamina. Here too, as in the bush, the thing was to have a mate, with whom one was prepared to go through thick and thin. And thick and thin was exactly what they did go through, at least as far as living conditions and eating were concerned. To begin with, shelter was provided by tents, either simple cotton ones or sturdier ones of tarpaulin, and by shacks of gum-branches and bark which at least gave an impression of stability. Inside these structures, the better-off had straw to sleep on, but most diggers slept on the bare earth, rolled in a blanket.

In any case, lying-in was out of the question, as work began at sunrise and went on until sunset. Diggers usually worked in teams of four or six, one to wield the pick, two to wheel the loads of earth to the nearest water for washing and the others to dolly and cradle for the gold-dust. It was hungry work. One wonders whether there was, as legend has it, a real French chef on one of the goldfields, a man who had been 'well known in Paris'. What on earth must he have used to tempt the gastronomes' palates? The staple menu never varied : it was mutton and damper for breakfast, mutton and damper for lunch and mutton and damper for dinner, all washed down with endless billies full of tea. Alcohol does seem to have been banned from the goldfields, at least for a while. But this regulation was gradually breached and sly-grog sellers set up their unsavoury establishments to peddle temporary oblivion. Then there was drinking and singing and dancing, the hairy bearded men clumping about in pairs with all the gracefulness of polar bears. After dark, all sorts of musical instruments could be heard in the camps, fiddles and flutes, accordeons, trumpets, banjos, bagpipes and saxophones. In the first months, the Sabbath was pretty strictly observed ; in any case it was the day for household chores which the men had to do some time, having no women to do them for them. Sunday was a day for relaxation and reflection, a day for exchanging hopes and disappointments with one's mates.

Their hopes died hard. Discouragement did not come easy to most of these gold-seekers. And the reward was certainly worth persevering for. When diggers struck it rich, they were torn between jubilation and suspicion. It was frustrating not to be able to boast, but unwise to say too much. The denizens of the diggings were not choirboys, after all. The sensible thing to do was to hand over one's gold as soon as possible to the government representative who weighed it, gave a receipt for it and undertook to have it transported under guard to a safer place. The receipt was a passport to a brighter tomorrow. It might mean eventually a triumphal return to the old country, but more probably it led to a stay in Melbourne. By now Melbourne was unrecognizable as the town of only a few years before. One description, no doubt rather highly coloured, calls it the modern Babel, a part of hell on earth, a town of hooligans, drunks and gamblers. And certainly uncommon things were said to take place there. Stories (surely apocryphal ?) were told of horses being shod with gold, of games of ninepins being played with bottles of the finest wine, of men who lit their cigars with £5 notes. One reads also of sham marriages taking place, with couples sprawling dead-drunk in carriages driven by liveried coachmen, the 'groom' dressed in a suit of the finest broadcloth and with outsize gems on his beringed fingers, the 'bride' in her Sunday best, with long, dyed, unkempt hair, wearing a dress of silk or satin from which protruded a pair of grubby bare feet. One assumes that the folk tradition was embroidered such yarns a little. But certainly, times were difficult for 'high society'. One finds Georgiana McCrae complaining that even in the highest society, every man must be his own butler, polishing his own shoes and cleaning his own cutlery. Pessimists predicted the worst. One of them said it was the French Revolution minus the guillotine ; another one said that society was on the brink of a total structural disintegration. The proof he adduced for this imminent catastrophe was that he knew of an archdeacon who had actually had to lay the table while his wife did the cooking !

Sir Charles Hotham was appointed Governor of Victoria at the end of 1853. He had one great advantage to begin with in that he was relieving La Trobe, who was unpopular. Hotham was a naval officer devoid of experience of public administration. He had tried to avoid this posting, knowing the sorts of dangers it might well involve. The welcome he received on his arrival in Melbourne must have made him feel for a time that his forebodings were unfounded. Sixty thousand people had gathered, there were triumphal arches and great shouts of joy, gold and profits were forgotten in favour of loyalty and enthusiasm. He received an equally rousing reception when he toured the goldfields. Hotham congratulated himself on his observation that on the diggings there were 'too,ooo of the finest men in the world' needing only 'that grand element of order ... female society'.* Fortified by such philosophical reflections, he went back down to Melbourne and set to work. The first discovery that awaited him was that the colony's financial affairs were far from sound. The spectre of the Lords of the Treasury appeared to him. Since the revenue from mining licences made up such a significant proportion of public funds, he decided that a good way to increase that revenue was by having licence checks carried out twice a week on the diggings.

This was an act of folly that it would be difficult to surpass. The diggers were already putting up with administrative formalities that they saw as outrageous. Despite a reduction in the licence fee from thirty shillings to £1 in 1853, this was still a very considerable sum for men who more often than not were devoid of means and who might have to wait weeks for a lucky break. As well as which, harassment and brutality by the police were all too common. The fee-collectors were not exactly polite – one of their officers described them as the finest gang of drunkards he had ever set eyes on. The diggers were expected to be able to produce on demand the receipt for their duly paid licence fee. As Professor Blainey says, 'the hardships of the licensing system were vexing on the shallow diggings but they were infuriating on the deep leads of Ballarat. † As early as February 1853, there had almost been a revolt on the New South Wales fields, which was only stopped by the threat of military intervention. All of which means that when the well-meaning but inexperienced Hotham took his ill-fated decision a year later, he was adding fuel to a smouldering fire. The atmosphere in Ballarat was particularly explosive, for here, as elsewhere, there was a political grievance to add to the financial ones : diggers did not have the vote, and treatment as second-class citizens outraged these men who were aware of the contribution their work made to the common wealth.

* Quoted by Serle, G., *The Golden Age*, Melbourne University Press, 1963, p. 157.

† Blainey, G., *The Rush that Never Ended*, Melbourne University Press, 1963, p. 50.

The fire was sparked off by a small incident on 6 October 1854. There was a brawl at the Eureka Hotel between the publican and two diggers, one of whom was killed. This publican, despite his already nasty reputation, was subsequently acquitted on a charge of murder. The first protest rally took place on 17 October. Several thousand demonstrators demanded that the murderer be found guilty. They stoned some troopers, then set fire to the Eureka Hotel. The authorities blundered on. The active protesters, most of whom were Irish, were particularly incensed when a semi-invalid, who happened to work for one of their priests, was fined £5 on the ridiculous charge of having obstructed the police. A committee under the name of the Ballarat Reform League was set up, with a truly international flavour: a Welshman, an Englishman, a German, an Italian and two Irishmen. Its demands were the abolition of the licensing system, reforms in the administration of the goldfields and, on a wider scale, manhood suffrage with secret ballot. Hotham received a deputation of three diggers on 27 November. Their mistake was to talk of their 'demands', which was hardly a word to endear them to a former navy man. The Governor made a show of being conciliatory, but simultaneously ordered reinforcements to Ballarat. The arrival there of the troopers was greeted with a hail of miscellaneous projectiles. The following day, at the behest of one of the stump-orators, a great many miners made a bonfire of their licences. The commissioner in charge of that area responded to this act of rebellion by ordering an immediate licence-check. As soon as the police tried to act on this order, shooting broke out.

The goldfields were now in a state of open revolt. The rebels chose as their leader a young man of twenty-seven, Peter Lalor, an Irishman of course. His elder brother back at home was active in a youth movement against 'the foreign tyrant' (Queen Victoria, no less). Lalor designed a blue flag bearing the five stars of the Southern Cross to represent the five Australian colonies. Then he gathered the volunteers, who were arriving by the hundred. This was on 30 November, a day of searing summer heat. There was a certain grandeur in the scene. Lalor made them kneel down – 'and with heads uncovered, and hands raised to Heaven, they solemnly swore at all hazards to defend their rights and liberties.'* Words gave way to actions. They chose a knoll on which to build a strongpoint, a

---

* Blainey, G., *The Rush that Never Ended*, p. 55.

rough stockade made of ropes, overturned carts and interworked logs which was supposed to act as a rampart. Then they set about collecting arms. Friday 1 December passed without incident, despite a vague tense expectancy in the air. Some of them drew up a Declaration of Independence. A column of diggers arrived, led by a band playing the *Marseillaise*, which raised the spirits of the defenders in the stockade. But when they learned that rifles were not to be had, the new arrivals dispersed. A feeling of uncertainty grew as the hours passed. During the night of 1–2 December, most of the defenders left the stockade, which was now occupied by only about 150 diggers. As Serle points out, if the authorities had taken no action, 'it seems certain that the movement would have broken up.'[*]

But the officers decided to act. At about 4 a.m., 400 men stormed the stockade. Within a few minutes the flag was knocked down and the tents set on fire. The whole affair lasted no more than a quarter of an hour. Casualties among the troops were five killed, including an officer, and twelve wounded. On the side of the rebels, there were about thirty killed and a hundred-odd taken prisoner.

Lalor managed to escape. Thirteen prisoners were acquitted two months later. The government then set about redressing the miners' grievances : the licensing system was abolished and replaced by an annual mining right of £1, and an export duty was put on gold. Parliamentary government came to Victoria in 1855, and under the new dispensation the possession of a miner's right qualified one for the vote. It was coincidence that brought about these reforms that year ; but for a long time the Eureka affair was credited with having led to reforms which had in fact been decided on well before it.

The name of Eureka has become part of a legend. Even at that time it gave rise to quite extravagant comment. Karl Marx, in one of his customary errors of judgement, saw in Eureka the sign of a Victorian workers' revolutionary movement. But the facts are these : it is well known that, by the time of Eureka, the alluvial gold in Ballarat had all been mined and men were having to go deeper and deeper underground, and that because of this a co-operative type of mining was already becoming the rule. That is to say that Lalor (who, by the way, was to end his days very peacefully, after having

[*] Serle, G., *op. cit.*, p. 168.

been Speaker in the Victorian Legislative Assembly) and his companions were nearly all small property-holders. It is therefore rather difficult to see them as forerunners of the Paris Commune. They suffered from specific injustices, and it was that state of affairs that they wanted to put an end to. If they could see what a halo has been created for them by posterity, they would be the first to be surprised at it. Even Mark Twain (who was not without a sense of humour, of course) said forty years later, ' I think it may be called the finest thing in Australasian history.'* Some historians and politicians have gone farther than that, some of them calling it ' the most spectacular event in Australian history ' ; another one says, 'Australian democracy was born at Eureka.'† In 1884, when a monument was erected on the site where the stockade had stood, one speaker roused the assembled throngs by stating, 'the glorious constitution now enjoyed was cradled in the Eureka Stockade.'‡ Even the Communists got on the bandwagon during the centenary year of 1954, by giving the name of Eureka to their youth movement.

One must conclude that Australia is indeed a ' lucky country', since it has experienced only one Eureka. What other Western nation could say the same ? Eureka also gives a striking demonstration of the old truth that the history of a country thrives on symbols as well as on facts. On 14 July 1789, Louis XVI did not even bother to note in his diary that the Bastille had fallen, yet nobody would deny the far-reaching significance of this minor incident. It may be that 2 December 1854 fulfils the same subconscious function for Australians as does Bastille Day for the French.

The fact remains that there is a fundamental difference between the two events. July 1789 was the first act of a bloody revolution ; December 1854 was the prelude to a series of peaceful transformations of society, some of them immediate, others less so.

After the Eureka skirmish, the goldfields were calm again. It was the end of the era of individualism, the beginning of the era of companies. The mining of a seam became less of an adventure and more of a skill. In order to get at the precious metal, machines were

---

* Twain, M., *Mark Twain in Australia and New Zealand* [Volume One of *Following the Equator*, first published in New York in 1897], Penguin Books, Melbourne, 1973, p. 233.

† H.V. Evatt, quoted by Serle, G., *op. cit.*, p. 185.

‡ *ibid.*, p. 186.

indispensable for cutting through rock and boring shafts, and if machines were required this meant that capital was also required. And it was in this way, less picturesque no doubt, but more efficient, that gold was to go on increasing the wealth of Victoria. The growth of Melbourne's population, in particular, was astounding, rising from 39,000 in 1851 to 140,000 ten years later. It is a pity that Georgiana McCrae has nothing to say about this metamorphosis. But there were other witnesses. Visitors in the late 1850s and early 1860s remembered how it had been in 1845 and could not believe their eyes. Some claimed to remember kangaroos browsing in Bourke Street only twenty years before. A sense of modernity, of being in the van of progress, tinged the Victorian outlook. 'The Melbourne of 1852,' claimed Archibald Michie in 1860, 'then but a very inferior English town, unpaved, unlighted, muddy, miserable, dangerous, has become transformed into a great city, as comfortable, as elegant, as luxurious (it is hardly an exaggeration to say it), as any place out of London or Paris '.* People's appearance had undergone a similar transformation. One Frenchman wondered, 'Where are the blue and khaki shirts, the muddy trousers and the long cavalry boots ? They have been supplanted by black suits, collars and ties and top-hats.' It was not only the look of things that was different. By 1860, the callow Melbourne of pre-1851 days and the uneasy Melbourne of the 1852 gold-rush had given way to a self-confident Melbourne, a place full of pride at having become the first city in the continent and looking down on its elder, Sydney, which, although fifty-two years Melbourne's senior, was now the smaller of the two towns by 45,000 people.†

This rapid influence of gold on Melbourne's development was not typical of the rest of the country. The fact remains, however, that the discovery of gold is one of the most significant stages in Australian history. The country's population doubled in ten years ; Victoria grew from 70,000 to 540,000 in the same period. The economy, which up until then had been geared solely to wool, now began to diversify. Above all, Australia all of a sudden got over its origins, which had been something of a drawback until then, and became fashionable overnight. It is significant, considering for the

---

* Serle, G., *op. cit.*, p. 369.

† Sydney took refuge in snobbery. A young French visitor said, 'Sydney is the capital of "high life".'

moment only French sources, that two members of the Orléans family,* the Duc de Penthièvre, son of the Prince de Joinville, and the Prince de Condé, the son of the Duc d'Aumale, both of them in their early twenties, travelled to Australia during these years. In fact, the Prince de Condé died in Sydney. The accounts of Australian conditions left by their companions are full of an infectious enthusiasm. They may perhaps be looked on as youngsters' exaggerations. But another Frenchman, Paul Leroy-Beaulieu, an economist who was to become famous, has this to say at that same period : 'In all of history, it would be impossible to find anything resembling the rapid and continuous development of the Australian colonies.' He adds : 'The colonization of Australia is, quite without doubt, England's greatest achievement.' These lines could not possibly have been written before 1851. Since then, the arrival of many thousands of bold, determined men, often men of real quality, had injected a vital intensity into the life of Australia. Most of these men were from Britain and they took pride in having made a new England on the other side of the world. But can one not see that, beneath the misleading appearances, it was really a new Australia that they were building ?

* The Orléans family were cousins to the last few Bourbon kings, deriving from a brother of Louis XIV (*translator's note*).

Chapter Thirteen

A new Australia?

Thirty years of calm prosperity – attempt at farming fails – slow industrialization – the eight-hour day – sugar-cane as a new source of wealth – discovery of important mineral resources – the transport revolution – foreign investment – property speculation – political system – instability of governments – protectionism in Victoria, free trade in New South Wales – religious controversies – non-denominational schooling – lack of an ideal – the legend of the bush – bushrangers – Ned Kelly – some personalities – optimism and petty aspirations

Australia as it is today took shape in those forty years that followed the discovery of gold. It is easy to define the importance of that time, but to describe it is more difficult. Experts on the period believe that insufficient groundwork has been done on it ; it would really require six different accounts instead of one, so great were the differences in the evolution of the six different colonies. What follows in this chapter is therefore only a general survey, so as to avoid becoming lost in too much contentious detail. The convict days were gone for ever, the doings of the squatters were a fading memory and gold-mining had become a part of everyday life. There were no wars, and skirmishes with groups of wretched natives were few and far between. Strikes were, however, not unknown, some of them even leading to violence.

Between 1860 and 1890, an impression of solid, growing prosperity was created by the beginnings of industrialization, an attempt at the parallel development of agriculture and wool-growing, the exploitation of new sources of wealth, a public works programme financed by an inflow of capital and a boom in property speculation. But this was only an illusion of prosperity. The country's economic base was so precarious that it all but collapsed during a subsequent slump (see Chapter 15). Furthermore, the extreme instability of the political system, especially in the more advanced colonies, and the desire that each of them had to maintain its own independence from the others, showed that the country was still going through a period of elementary development and had not yet achieved a state of social equilibrium.

Against this rather grey backdrop, there stand out the surviving passions from the previous periods, and certain figures full of interest.

The goldfields, after a few years, turned out to be not as rich as had been hoped. Also, the increasing use of machines reduced the need for manpower on the fields. By 1858 another exodus was under way, this time in the opposite direction, as discouraged miners drifted back to the coastal towns. There they were received with some misgivings. For one thing, what work was there for them to do ? For another, the echoes of those shots at Eureka still rang in Sydney and in Melbourne. These men had strength aplenty, but most of them were unqualified for any other sort of work. Space, the greatest natural resource of new countries, seemed to be the answer to the problem. The fact that the squatters had by now a de facto monopoly of the available land was coming to be seen as less and less tolerable in a country that was becoming more and more egalitarian. It was beginning to be asked whether agriculture might not be permitted to develop alongside sheep-farming in such a vast continent. Was Australia to have no other future but the shearing of an ever increasing flock of sheep ?

New South Wales was the first to try an experiment that many looked on as revolutionary. It will be remembered that the price of land had been fixed at £1 per acre in 1842. This, of course, was a considerable sum in those days and most wool-growers could not afford it. The authorities had therefore taken to granting leases of variable duration with an ill-defined possibility of buying option. This was essentially a compromise, but it had been looked on as the once-for-all solution by those whom it benefited. It was replaced by a new system in 1861. Under this new arrangement, by depositing only twenty-five per cent of the official price, and contracting to pay off the balance (without interest) inside three years, anyone at all could take immediate possession of a tract of land, whether it was already settled or not, of at least forty and at most 320 acres (sixteen to 215 hectares). The only condition of these leases was that the land must be used for growing crops. This was the beginning of a new breed of Australian, the so-called 'free selectors'. The expression 'free selectors' gives an apt enough definition of their unlimited rights, since the new law gave them a totally unrestricted choice of any land that took their fancy.

One can imagine the fury of the squatters already there, at finding themselves in exactly the same position into which they had put the original settlers thirty years before ! They already had two traditional enemies, the kangaroo, which ate their sheep's grass, and the dingo, which ate their sheep.* Now they had a third nuisance to contend with as fence-poles sprouted and part of their land was enclosed behind barbed wire. Professor R.M. Crawford says : ' They might hold their lands by lease or licence of limited duration ; but they were theirs by natural justice, they felt, if not by law.'† The squatters put up bitter opposition against these newcomers. 'Cockatoos' was the nickname they gave to them, possibly because of the similarity they saw between them and the other local nuisances, possibly because they were as unexpected and rowdy as the flocks of their namesakes.‡ Not all of these unceremonious invaders were intending farmers. They included many people who had been on the goldfields some years before, trying their luck, and who now saw an opportunity for speculation that was too good to be missed. Much land was bought up with the sole aim of reselling at a profit. And, of course, the more necessary the land was to the graziers, the higher the resale value could be pushed. For instance, buying up land that blocked off access to a river or to sheep's drinking water was an excellent way of making a large profit.§ The squatters themselves knew a thing or two about this sort of sharp practice and they set about covertly buying land. The new profession of the ' dummy ' arose – these were people who made a business of buying for somebody else at land sales ; they made £1 per day. The authorities soon got to know them and tried to outwit them by changing the venue of sales at the last moment. But the dummies were up to every dodge and seemed to have inside information.

---

* The catastrophe of the rabbits did not come about until a little later.
† Crawford, R.M., *Australia*, 3rd rev. ed., Hutchinson, 1970, p. 114.
‡ See Roberts, S.H., *The Squatting Age in Australia, 1835–1847*, p. 223.
§ This was expressed in another bird metaphor, 'peacocking', presumably to suggest the brazenness and self-conceit of the selectors.

The example of New South Wales was followed by the other five colonies. On the whole the experiment turned out an utter failure. Over a ten-year period the sheep population rose from five million to fourteen million while the area under wheat grew from 49,000 to a mere 61,000 hectares. In some places, such as the district known as 'Australia felix', results were well above average. But it was only in South Australia that any real success was achieved. There, after twenty years of the system, the area under crops was approximately 3.04 hectares per inhabitant, as against 0.7 in Victoria and 0.3 in New South Wales. This disparity may be explained by more favourable climatic conditions, better quality flat, open country and the fact that in South Australia the wool-growers were less entrenched.

By about 1860, agriculture was still something of a poor relation. The supremacy of wool was still unchallenged, and those who grew it were more and more strongly convinced of their divine right to the land. Eight million acres were grazed by ninety-six sheep-farmers. A.G.L. Shaw has neatly highlighted one of the main reasons for their success, the problem with land legislation being 'to discover how land could be made easily accessible to the poor, without at the same time being made even more easily accessible to the rich'.* It would probably even be true to say that the position of the less well-off had actually got worse. The gradual advent of barbed wire and mechanization of shearing methods had made manpower less necessary and capital more necessary. The sedentary shepherds of the early days had been replaced by boundary-riders, and shearers were being replaced by machinery. These two developments were profitable to the wealthier graziers. How could the selectors, most of whom were living at subsistence level, hope to compete? Ways of increasing the yield of cereal crops had not yet been discovered (see page 267). And in periods of drought the harvests could show disconcerting fluctuations.† In New South Wales at least, such conditions gave rise to a class of poverty-stricken agricultural workers, slaving, as Manning Clark says, 'amid squalor, filth, ignorance and superstition'.‡ and with a strange

---

* Shaw, A.G.L., *The Story of Australia*, Faber, 2nd ed., 1962, p. 139.

† The wheat figures from the late 1860s speak for themselves: 1866, 235,000 cubic metres; 1867, 95,000; 1868, 185,000; 1869, 110,000; 1870, 250,000.

‡ Clark, C.M.H., *A Short History of Australia*, p. 136.

resemblance to the American hillbillies of the pre-Civil War period.

One thing that was lacking was a true Dickensian working-class. Industry had begun to develop after the discovery of gold, but it was on a small scale and almost totally confined to Victoria. Such industrial enterprises as existed were limited to the processing of imported materials. They were continually hampered by shortages of labour, especially of skilled workers, a situation which had two consequences, one economic and one political. From the outset, salaries were high: in 1860 a carpenter was probably worth about ten shillings a day, and a shepherd could earn between £25 and £40 per annum, all found.* Such relative affluence did not favour the growth of any revolutionary political movements. Material things were seen as more important than political considerations. Building workers had managed to organize by 1850. Their programme soon became popular: 'Eight hours' work, eight hours' recreation, eight hours' rest and eight shillings a day'. This ideal had become a reality within five years: it was in 1855, in Melbourne, that stone-masons, plasterers, carpenters, slaters, plumbers and painters achieved the eight-hour day. The following year Sydney followed suit, but there the reform extended only to the masons. This triumph was celebrated in 1856 by a mass demonstration that included a workers' picnic and a pageant depicting the capture of Malakov and the bombardment of Sebastopol, a detail which shows how the workers' movements identified with the established order of things. The trade unions, which achieved definitive recognition after 1870, remained faithful to the traditional attitude of their English counter-parts by keeping politics out of their activities. A workers' party did not arise until the darker years of 1890-4, which was a period of strikes and social unrest. In the meantime, achieving higher wages and improvements in working conditions remained the central preoccupations of the trade union movement. One outcome of this was systematic opposition to all immigration and a latent racism which vented itself against the Chinese on the goldfields† and the 'kanakas' on sugar plantations.

It can be seen that it was not any progress in agriculture or success

* Minus his laundry bill, presumably!

† At one point there were close on 50,000 Chinese working on the goldfields. The last of them were expelled in 1901.

in industry that underlay the potent optimism which was shared by Australians during this period. It was commonly said that what America had done, Australia could (and should) do too. After the discovery of gold, other potential sources of wealth had become apparent which certainly seemed to suggest that in the future Australia would be comparable with the United States. Sugar-cane, in particular, opened up unexpected possibilities. The north-eastern part of the continent had remained undeveloped for a long time. After the establishment of the penal colony at Moreton Bay in 1842,* the region had been settled extremely slowly. Thirty-five years later there were still fewer than 25,000 inhabitants. As had happened in Melbourne some ten years before, it came to seem absurd for these people to be administered from Sydney, more than 800 kilometres away, and at their request, Whitehall agreed to the creation of a sixth colony in 1859. The name 'Queensland' is said to have been a suggestion by Queen Victoria herself. The name, or something, acted like magic and 50,000 new immigrants settled there over the next ten years. The colonization of Queensland followed the usual pattern : to begin with, wool-growing almost exclusively, then an attempt at agriculture, which was as unsuccessful here as elsewhere.

All this changed when it was realized that the northern coastal regions, with their abundant rainfall, offered ideal conditions for the cultivation of sugar-cane. The first experiments in growing cane were begun about 1860. Within twenty years the Colonial Sugar Refining Company, which was to become one of Australia's industrial giants, was exporting sugar worth almost £300,000. The success of Queensland sugar came close to having far-reaching social and political consequences. The planters maintained that white labour was unsuited to this sort of work and imported several thousand Melanesians. The mortality rate among these so-called 'kanakas' turned out to be five times greater than the average of the population, a fact cited as proof that they were maltreated. The great majority of Australians were determined that the history of the Negro slaves in America should not be repeated. A succession of petitions were drawn up demanding that the importation of kanakas should be stopped, the constant reply to which by the Queensland cane-growers was a threatened declaration of inde-

* The site where present-day Brisbane was to develop. See page 190.

pendence. The achievement of a totally 'white' Australia only came
with federation at the turn of the century.

Over this same thirty-year period after Eureka, there was a series
of discoveries of phenomenal mineral resources, new coalfields in
New South Wales, copper in South Australia, a virtual hill of solid
silver, lead and zinc at Broken Hill,* gold, gold and even more gold
in New South Wales, Tasmania, Western Australia† and especially
in Queensland, where it was thought for some months in 1882 that
a gold-rush of Californian proportions was about to take place.

These discoveries and developments were exciting and promising
enough. But what contributed more than anything else to the
transformation of Australia was the revolution in transport and
communications.

Sydney was linked to Melbourne by telegraph in 1858, to
Brisbane in 1861 and to Adelaide in 1867. Cable communication
with London was established in 1872. The Suez Canal had been
opened three years earlier, shortening the distance to and from
Europe by 8,000 kilometres and cutting by half the length of time
that the voyage took. The railway fever that came over Australia
was even more remarkable. Until mid-century, transportation of
goods was by slow, heavy bullock-dray; passengers were carried
in stage-coaches (supposedly light and speedy, but they have been
described as real instruments of torture), run by the famous firm of
Cobb & Co., a local form of the equally famous Wells Fargo in
America.

The building of the railways did not really get under way until
after 1870. At that date there were less than 2,000 kilometres of
track and no railway line went farther than 300 kilometres from the
coast. There was as yet no sizeable town in the interior of the
country; all the large towns were on the coast and the easiest way
of going from one to the other was by sea. There was a strong
temptation to link Melbourne to Ballarat by rail, and Sydney to
Ophir. But the output from the goldfields was subject to extreme
fluctuations, high one day and low the next, and made them an

---

* B.H.P. was founded in 1885. Today it is the largest Australian company.

† Sceptically is how one should treat the advice of technical experts – it had been
the sage opinion of Hargraves, the original discoverer of gold in 1851, that the
geology of Western Australia made it certain that there was no gold there!

unreliable source of business for railways. However, in the long run the advantages of transport by rail could not be denied. Even the best horses in the world could not have enabled Cobb & Co. to compete indefinitely with steam power. The railways had one great thing in their favour : whereas horse-drawn drays were at the mercy of the weather and could be bogged down in mud for weeks or months on end, the locomotives could keep going, rain, hail or shine.

Once they had been started, railways became all the rage and the length of track was increased tenfold over a period of twenty years. Only five private companies managed to survive the acute competition. Most of the construction of the different lines, as well as the use they were put to, was government-sponsored. Needless to say the politicians were active – everyone wanted to have a railway line. The whole enterprise was one of great confusion. Several lines were laid down, going more or less nowhere. One finds references to one railway line which was supposed to lead to a racecourse ; but the racecourse itself was never built and so the line was used only once, for a religious meeting. There was no such thing as an overall plan, and free enterprise, as practised by the powers-that-be, produced some odd results. For example, the colonies could not even agree on a common gauge for their railway systems. When the Sydney-Melbourne rail link was inaugurated on 14 June 1883, the train stopped at the border not only for the ceremony,* but to let the passengers change trains. By the time the whole continent was linked up by rail, a passenger could change trains five times on a trip from North Queensland to Perth. Complaints about this were said to be extremely common ; but one wonders – after all, as Professor Blainey says,† as long as there were no dining-cars on the trains and people had to go through Customs at each border, the necessity of getting off the train was quite a welcome diversion for passengers. And, in any case, train travel was still much more comfortable than those coaches.

To have built almost 16,000 kilometres of track between 1870 and

---

* A small detail, but one which may say something about the difference between Sydney and Melbourne : the Victorian representatives in their morning coats were less formal than their counterparts from New South Wales, who wore tails.

† Blainey, G., *The Tyranny of Distance*, p. 251.

1890 was a technological achievement. It was made possible by a non-stop flow of capital from outside Australia. Great Britain was beginning to favour the offspring which she had hitherto somewhat neglected. It has been estimated that during those twenty years London invested some £250 million in Australia. Professor N.G. Butlin gives a most revealing breakdown of British investments in Australia's development (figures in millions of pounds) :*

Decade	Private Institutions	Government and Other Borrowing	Total British Investment
1861–70	3.4	20.0	23.4
1871–80	12.4	39.6	52.0
1881–90	71.5	103.5	175.0
Total	87.3	163.1	250.4

Not that Britain was the only source of capital – the French banking-house Comptoir National d'Escompte de Paris opened a branch in Melbourne in 1880.

This flood of capital not only led to an easy monetary situation favourable to public works, but also created conditions in which the private speculator could thrive. The land and property boom in Victoria after 1880 is reminiscent of John Law's financial collapse in Paris in 1720. There were exactly the same publicity prospectuses, the same network of non-existent companies set up, the same brief period of high profits, and the same almighty crash at the end. This Victorian flurry gave rise to the word 'land-boomers'. One Frenchman noted in amazement : 'The price of building land has now reached a figure 1,000 times higher than the valuation sixty years ago.' But this comparison does not really mean very much, as there could be a great change in values overnight. According to Michael Cannon, land sales took place in a carnival atmosphere.† A

* Butlin, N.G., *Australian Domestic Product, Investment and Foreign Borrowing 1861–1938/9*, Cambridge University Press, 1962, p. 424.

† See Cannon, M., *The Land Boomers*, Melbourne University Press, 1966.

good land-boomer took a pride in being able to palm off on his victim a piece of land that he had never owned and that he never could own. Sumptuously appointed offices were a necessary part of the stage-management. Melbourne was full of admiration for the Association and Deposit Bank building, the most outstanding of those which had mushroomed out of the land boom, five storeys high and looking as though it were a château transported from the valley of the Loire, columns, pilasters, caryatids and all ! Inside it boasted gas heating and lighting and it even had a lift ! But the most interesting things about the building were the faces of well-known people coming and going ; and the names one heard whispered were often those of highly placed men. For it seems that relations between the master-speculators and the members of the local legislature were closer than might have been wished.

In 1860 all the colonies enjoyed, broadly speaking, the same political structure.* There were two houses in each colony, a lower house, called the Legislative Assembly and modelled on the House of Commons, and an upper house, called the Legislative Council, with functions based on those of the House of Lords. The lower house was elected on universal manhood suffrage, except in Tasmania which did not adopt this system until 1900. The members of the upper house were either appointed by the Governor (as in New South Wales and Queensland) or elected, as in the other colonies, but on a very restrictive property qualification. The executive function was fulfilled by the Governor, who was appointed by the Crown. The Governor also invested the Premier and the members of his cabinet, who represented the majority party, of course, and were at the mercy of votes of no confidence. The independence of M.P.s was supposed to be safeguarded by their stipend, but this was almost invariably insufficient.

This was the design, in theory, at any rate, a close imitation of the British pattern, especially in the consistence that budgetary matters were to be the prerogative of the lower house. However, just because political institutions have been transplanted from one continent to another is no reason to suppose that they will work in exactly the same way. The business of these young legislatures was conducted in a very unWestminsterish fashion. Members often

---

* Except, of course, for Western Australia, which had begun taking in convicts in 1840 and was not to accede to parliamentary government until 1890.

engaged in coarse invective and even came to blows. These activities inside the Chamber were accompanied at times by public demonstrations outside. The French consul in Melbourne gives the following description of the opening of Parliament in 1866 : ' It gave rise to disgraceful scenes. The opposition members were greeted by booing and catcalls from the mob, who cheered the government members to the echo.' This unEnglish and unparliamentary behaviour can be accounted for in various ways. For one thing, the M.P.s had no experience of Parliament ; for another, there was nothing that remotely resembled a political party. Ad hoc groups of M.P.s would join forces, then split up, then form up again in different ranks. These groupings had none of the consistency of party lines, and were attracted together by the magnetism of individuals rather than by common political principles. Add to this the fact that the lower and upper houses were traditionally at loggerheads, one of them trying to create the future and the other to re-create the past, and it will be seen that government instability was bound to be chronic. Between 1861 and 1871, South Australia had eight governments; between 1855 and 1877, Victoria had eighteen governments and New South Wales seventeen. Over a period of forty years there were forty-one governments in South Australia, twenty-nine in New South Wales and twenty-eight in Victoria.

The labels of ' conservatives ' and ' liberals ' were used by political observers, but they had no hard-and-fast meaning, since conviction and principle were as yet secondary to self-interest and expediency. In fact the only issues to rouse the legislatures were economic ones, especially the question of the relative merits of free trade and protectionism. The colony of Victoria plumped for protection in 1880, to safeguard her burgeoning manufacturing industries, a course which was supported by employers and employees alike. New South Wales was still strongly influenced by the graziers and businessmen and remained stoutly faithful to the free-trade principle. * The remaining colonies looked on customs duties as a convenient source of extra revenue. However, those who advocated unification of the country denounced these barriers as absurdities.

---

* This was still a live issue at the turn of the century. But by then discussion of it had reached such a low level that it was impossible to muster serious arguments. Manning Clark tells the story of how George Reid, the Premier of New South

Between 1863 and 1873, six intercolonial conferences tried to reduce some of the differences, but without making an inch of headway. Anthony Trollope, who visited Australia at this time, said, 'At present these colonies all stand towards each other as though they were various nations, with varied interests, and endeavour each to rise on the commercial injuries inflicted on the others by hostile tariffs.'*

These 'varied interests' were largely materialistic. But even in a country which was so taken up with the search for material well-being, there was a religious dimension to people's lives. Until about mid-century, religious thought had dealt mainly with variant interpretations of the Christian faith. This faith itself, however, was called into question when the tremors from the Darwinian upheaval reached Australia. Australian Christians, like their counterparts elsewhere, reacted in a variety of different ways. A small group of Protestants clung to the most literal interpretation of the Bible. Many others evolved towards an imprecise form of deism, which accepted a Creator, but tended to look on Christ as merely an outstanding human being. The Church of England, because of its basic structures, managed to see through the crisis more or less unscathed. As for the Roman Catholics, they reacted by taking a harder line than before. Being nearly all of Irish extraction, they had brought with them to the Antipodes their ancestral belief that they were the true Church, linked to the Divinity by a mysterious contract that was beyond the ken of other believers.

An opportunity arose for them to display their stubbornness. It will be remembered that all forms of Christian worship had been put on an equal footing as far back as 1835. This meant that the Roman Catholics had now as much right as any Protestant group to open schools and receive state aid for them. For the next thirty-odd years, this system muddled along. But in the aftermath of the gold-rush and the profound evolution of the community that it gave rise to, the old system of Church schools soon showed its inability

* Trollope, A., *Australia* (ed. P.D. Edwards & R.B. Joyce), Queensland University Press, Brisbane, 1967, p. 352.

Wales, assured a meeting 'that the superiority of free trade over protection was demonstrated by the fewer lunatics per square mile in Sydney then in Melbourne' (*A Short History of Australia*, p. 168).

to cope with the new social circumstances. In 1880, New South Wales decided that Church schools would no longer receive state aid unless they used the same school textbooks as the government-run schools and made sure that their teaching staffs were as well qualified as those in the state schools. These restrictions were aimed principally at the Roman Catholic schools, which were in the habit of using their own books and relying on clerics to do the teaching.

The reaction of the bishops was immediate and sharp.* One of the most impassioned advocates of their cause, Monsignor Vaughan, saw the problem in black and white terms as a choice between Rome or rationalism, the Catholic church or else no church at all. Those who thought that 'no church at all' was a good idea were in entire agreement with him, of course, and once again there was heard in the land the traditional cry that popery could only thrive by enslaving the minds of men, that the Church of Rome was the guardian of a tradition of plain idolatry. The outcome was the triumph of those who believed in non-religious schooling. And so, just as Australia was the first to adopt the eight-hour day, just as it had brought in manhood suffrage long before the home country, so it was one of the first to establish the principle of free, compulsory and non-denominational schooling ; it was at this very time that France was on the point of trying non-religious schooling as well.† All financial assistance to non-government schools was thereby abolished.

Religious instruction could still be given in state schools, outside class hours. Even so, the bishops were not placated. Monsignor Vaughan, to whom no bread was obviously preferable to half a loaf, saw these new arrangements as being 'symptomatic of a movement

* The first bishop had been appointed to Sydney in 1834. Eight years later he was promoted to archbishop. At that same time, the bishoprics of Hobart and Adelaide were also created ; Perth and Melbourne were established in 1845 and 1847. The British government acquiesced in the setting up of this hierarchy, which as P. O'Farrell points out was 'the first to be erected in a British possession since the Reformation' (*The Catholic Church in Australia*, Nelson, Melbourne, 1968, p. 55).

† Victoria took the lead in 1872 ; South Australia followed suit in 1875, New South Wales in 1880, Tasmania in 1885 and Western Australia in 1895. The French Parliament adopted a similar reform (denounced as 'iniquitous') in 1881.

aimed at "the extinction of the Catholic religion, of the Catholic sacraments, and of the calling of the Catholic clergy"'.* The bishops of New South Wales published a pastoral letter which left no doubt about their feelings. They condemned the secular schools as 'seedplots of immorality' and in the most outspoken terms denounced as 'corrupt, infidel and unjust' the trends in public educational policy.†

This was plain speaking. Such hard words could have been the prelude to further verbal violence. However, just as Eureka had led to nothing further, so before long these religious differences came to nothing. The Roman Catholics set up their own schools at their own expense and went on teaching what they wanted to teach, the only difference being that now they were subject to no outside control. The tension between church and state was further reduced by the appointment to Sydney of a new archbishop, Monsignor Moran,‡ who had learnt the art of compromise during a lengthy stay in Rome.

One does wonder, however, whether the masses took an interest in such problems. In 1877 a Frenchman observed : 'On the religious question, the Australian colonies are among those countries where the spirit of our time has had its most detrimental effects.' One suspects that there may not be much exaggeration in this and that the antagonism between Roman Catholics and Protestants, or Roman Catholics and the civil power, would not have been so sharp if the former had not been Irish in origin and the latter British.

No people can live without an ideal. Ideals could not take root and grow in the economic successes of Australia, in its political life or its religious strife. Australians looked elsewhere for their ideal and created a nostalgic obsession with the bush. One of them wrote·at this time that it was not in the cities that Australians felt an awareness of their nationality, but in the monotonous, boundless countryside. And it is true that there is a strange and intriguing poetry in the ubiquitous unvarying eucalypts, the plains with their stunted bushes and the grazing lands that all look exactly alike. It was this

* Quoted by O'Farrell, P., *op. cit.*, p. 126.

† *ibid.*, p. 127.

‡ The first Australian cardinal. His elevation to the rank of cardinal was welcomed by all and sundry, and was gratifying even to opponents of 'popery' in their growing nationalism.

elusive poetic quality that inspired in some Australians at that period vague qualms of melancholy and a propensity to question their destiny. The early explorers and the first settlers in the bush were seen as men freed of all shackles, men whose only care was to assert their independence, better men than their descendants who were now caught in the vice of an industrial civilization and whose aspirations were reduced to the satisfaction of trite and petty material needs. Although in reality the bushman was already a dying breed, he came to be idealized beyond recognition. It has been said that the Australian myth of the bushman was akin to the myth of the 'noble savage' of the previous century, in that it was just as out of touch with reality.[*]

This unreal myth (which saw the bush as a paradise lost and for ever remembered with regret) was quite compatible with the exploits of real outlaws. For a period, this landscape which was already legendary harboured them and enabled them to carry on their trade. Some of these bushrangers were convicts who had escaped from Tasmania. Others were men who were after adventure and who could not accept the rules and regulations that go with a quiet life. Many of them had been counting on making a fortune on the goldfields and, when that did not happen, they turned their hand to this new way of getting rich quick. Their chosen profession was certainly favoured by the circumstances of the time and place, as settlements in the outback were few and far between, the roads were very bad, and the police were incompetent and oppressive. In fact the police were so universally vilified that, as Russel Ward says, 'it may be doubted whether the police force of any English-speaking country, except Ireland, has ever been more thoroughly unpopular than were those of most Australian colonies in the last century.'[†] The bandits would often enjoy the surreptitious support of shepherds, shearers or free selectors, of anyone in the rural proletariat, which as a class had a covert admiration for any man who dared stand up to the society which oppressed them.

The bushrangers came in all sorts and sizes. There were gentlemanly ones, like Ben Hall, who was so considerate to his victims that he was said to forbid his gang to smoke in the presence of a lady. There were others who were out-and-out cut-throats and arsonists,

---

[*] See Ward, R., *The Australian Legend*, p. 5.
[†] *ibid.*, p. 144.

like Daniel Morgan, who struck fear into Victorians' hearts over a period of years.* Some individuals, such as Frederick Ward, alias Thunderbolt, made a specialty of stage-coach hold-ups in the best manner of the American West. Nearly all of them came to a violent end, of course, being either shot on sight or hanged.

Ned Kelly stands out. His brief destiny is so appalling that one must spend some time on him. At first sight, his is a trite enough adventure. He was of Irish background, born into a poverty-stricken family in Melbourne in 1855. The family lived from hand to mouth by a variety of rarely legal expedients. At the age of ten, Ned was trained as a horse-thief. After some early successes, he got caught, being arrested for the first time at the age of fourteen. There followed a succession of arrests, some of them apparently on trumped-up charges. By the time he was twenty-three he had his own gang, consisting of one of his brothers (who was only seventeen) and two cronies, aged twenty-one and eighteen. Over a period of twenty months, from November 1878 to June 1880, the authorities thought they were within an ace of capturing the gang on no fewer than 129 occasions. But they always made good their escape. This was the basis of Ned's 'Scarlet Pimpernel' reputation. Another element in his reputation was that he only robbed from the rich and never shot to kill except in self-defence – or so he said, having shot three policemen in cold blood. Two of his bank robberies were masterpieces, the police arriving too late and making fools of themselves on each occasion.† Gradually his legend took shape, making him into a latter-day Robin Hood and a protector of the weak.

The circumstances surrounding his eventual capture only added to his glory. In the June of 1880, after a long period lying quiet in a hideout that nobody could locate, the Kelly gang ventured forth and murdered a man who they thought had given them away to the police. They then took over the little town of Glenrowan, taking thirty prisoners whom they robbed and locked in the local hotel.

---

* There is a revealing report from the French consul in Melbourne, dated 24 April 1865: 'On the 10th of this month, the inhabitants of Melbourne were awakened by an unusual commotion. The town-criers were announcing great news; the walls were covered in notices. All faces soon beamed with extraordinary happiness: Morgan, the most notorious of the bushrangers, had been killed.'

† The Kelly gang even staged one hold-up wearing the uniforms they had stolen from the constables.

Having been warned that a trainload of police was on its way from Melbourne, they made an attempt, which failed, to derail the train. The police cornered them and in the ensuing gun-battle Ned's three companions were killed. Ned himself had put on his suit of armour, looking like something out of the Middle Ages, but it did not protect him as he had hoped and he was wounded and taken prisoner. He was hanged on 11 November, after a succession of petitions bearing thousands of signatures had failed to have him pardoned. There is a touch of nobility in his exchange with the judge who read out his sentence. He walked to the scaffold with perfect composure. His last words are supposed to have been : 'Such is life.' His mother, also in prison, had told him the day before his execution that he was to be sure to die like a Kelly. Nowadays, his legend is more alive than ever. It has been said that there is not a single Australian child who does not know his name.

Thus, a quarter of a century after the Eureka affair, fantasy had once again taken over from fact. Heroism finding it hard to thrive in the untroubled atmosphere of Australia, all the latent energies that could not be vented, all the unrequited appetite for admiration, crystallized round the Kelly symbol. And yet there was no lack of notable characters in Australia at that time. One only wonders whether they deserve to figure in a gallery of a nation's great men. The following are chosen almost at random from widely differing backgrounds.

First, Hugh Glass, a squatter, one of the most colourful (possibly too colourful) characters of the time. He was impatient, changeable, generous, warm-hearted and utterly ruthless with anyone who stood in his way. He amassed immense wealth, his house in Melbourne, with its French-style grounds, its artificial lake, its rare birds and exotic fish, being as well known as the Macarthurs' at Camden. He looked on the free selectors as vermin and scum, and fought them by hook and by crook. He was ruined by speculation. In 1865 he got £85,000 out of one of the most reliable banking houses in Melbourne. Four years later he was bankrupt, and two years after that he committed suicide.

It would be difficult to imagine a greater contrast to Glass than William Lane. He has been called a sort of Australian Mahomet. And certainly there was something of the prophet in this Englishman. He came to Queensland in 1843 at the age of twenty-two. He preached socialism like a religion.* But it was a socialism for Australian conditions and was devoid of revolutionary elements. Even so, he would not have been out of place in the 1848 revolution in France. He was full of a utopian altruism and saw solidarity as the solution to all problems. By solidarity he meant 'to be each for all and all for each, to move with a collective strength inspired by collective thought for the collective good'.† Through his newspaper, the *Boomerang*, he exercised a considerable influence on the trade union movement. Eventually, after several years, Lane concluded that the Australians were too slow in designing tomorrow's world. So he set off for Paraguay to found a 'New Australia', but this turned out to be a disappointment as well.

David Syme's genius was of a more practical kind. He was of Scottish extraction and had tried his hand at gold-fossicking in Victoria in the early days of the rush. He soon found out that he was unsuited to this type of work. Before he was thirty he had become a journalist. He ended up owning the paper he worked for, the *Age*, which became a powerful organ of opinion. Through the medium of this newspaper, Syme advocated a body of ideas which one by one became enshrined in legislation : manhood suffrage, free selection of land, non-denominational compulsory schooling. Later he concentrated on economic questions, becoming, in Professor La Nauze's view, 'the one Australian political economist of the 19th century whose work was widely known outside the country of his adoption'.‡ Syme saw protectionism as a cure-all. He was, of course, not the first to advocate protection, but he defended it with greater spirit than anyone else : 'In a few short years hence, if this pre-arranged practice of national industrial abortion is continued amongst us, the people of Australia will be as utter strangers to all scientific skill and practical dexterity in the arts and manufactures

---

* For all his proselytizing, he cannot have lacked a sense of humour. He was in favour of equality of the sexes, but within moderation. On the subject of what is nowadays known as women's 'liberation', his advice to the leaders of the movement was to be careful not to turn narrow-minded, cold and passive women into narrow-minded, cold and aggressive women.

† Quoted by Gollan, R., *Radical and Working Class Politics*, Melbourne University Press, 1960, p. 106.

‡ La Nauze, J.A., *Political Economy in Australia*, Melbourne University Press, 1949, p. 98.

of highly civilized nations as are the Bedouins of Barbary, or the Tartars of Central Asia.'* He could get carried away by the causes he espoused. Eventually, nobody dared contradict him in print and to his envious opponents he was 'King David'.

The *Age* was not only read in Victoria ; nor was Sydney the only place which read the *Bulletin*. Very few readers had noted the appearance of the first number, consisting of eight pages, mainly full of items of local news. But its editor, the self-styled 'Jules François' Archibald,† proved to be a newspaperman of genius. Under him the *Bulletin*, in all its jingoism, its openness to new ideas and what could be called its extremism, soon attracted a team of contributors whose work created great excitement.

It must surely have been read carefully by politicians. One of the latter was Alfred Deakin. He was twenty-four when the *Bulletin* was founded in 1880. He was already well-known, and was to become famous. A year before he had been elected to the Legislative Assembly of Victoria ; the piercing intensity of his eyes and the exceptional fire of his oratory were the basis of his fame. There were surprising sides to his character, his interest in the occult, for example, and his taste for literature in a community which had little time for things of the mind. However, at this stage he was still a novice in politics, unlike another man whose name was almost a household word in Melbourne, Chief Justice George Higinbotham. Deakin said of Higinbotham :

Such a man, rare in the world, seemed rarer still in Australia, where his inflexible purity of life and aim, his irresistible charm and grace, and his transcendent power of convincing and being convinced, left an indelible impression upon so many minds and characters.‡

* Quoted by Gollan, R., *op. cit.*, p. 61.

† According to Vance Palmer, this Frenchifying of Archibald's given names (John Feltham) 'was part of his innate romanticism. For him, France stood for what was light, un-Victorian, incalculable : the colour of the boulevard, chiefly, but, if need be, the barricade' (Palmer, V., *National Portraits*, 3rd ed., Melbourne University Press, 1940, p. 134). At his death in 1919, he left a sum of money to pay for the erection of a memorial in Sydney to the association between France and Australia during the Great War. This aim was realized in 1933 with the inauguration of the admirable fountain in Hyde Park which bears his name.

‡ Quoted by La Nauze, J.A., *Alfred Deakin*, Melbourne University Press, 1965, vol. I, p. 32.

Higinbotham was Irish ; he had arrived in Victoria in 1854 at the age of twenty-eight. A lawyer by training, he had joined the *Argus* for a time as a journalist, before being elected to Parliament. He was appointed Attorney-General in 1863. The parliamentary system was barely ten years old in Victoria and it was Higinbotham's function to interpret the constitution. There could be no question of his loyalty to the Crown ; nevertheless he became the most persuasive advocate of the colonies' right to run their own affairs.

Sydney was as proud of her luminaries as Melbourne was of hers. John Robertson was one of them, Premier of New South Wales five times between 1860 and 1885. A very attractive man, who knew how to use his slightly husky voice to great effect, he was a virtuoso in the art of using the coarsest language, which made him popular both in the House and at public meetings. His great aim was to 'unlock the land', an aim in which he failed, as it happened. However the political consequences of this failure were not too severe for him, a situation that is far from unique to Australia.

Robertson was indisputably outclassed by his rival Henry Parkes, who was even known outside Australia. In 1892, for instance, the Paris periodical *Revue des Deux Mondes* wrote of him : 'He is justly considered to be one of the outstanding figures in the whole British Empire.'* Such a judgement may seem over-indulgent, but it would certainly have been sweet to the ears of Parkes, who saw himself as Australia's Gladstone. According to Deakin, 'He had always in his mind's eye his own portrait as that of a great man, and constantly adjusted himself to it.'† More recently, Parkes has been seen less favourably, as an aloof and at times pompous master of the high-sounding period and the showy platitude. In reality, the man seems to have been extremely complex and it would be superficial to reduce him to mere pride. He was undismayed by his own contradictions – although quite incompetent at managing his own affairs, he saw himself as well qualified to manage public affairs. Despite the sordid deals that he entered into on his climb to power, his behaviour in government was above reproach. He was to play his part in bringing about federation. Even though at times

---

* Not to be outdone, two years later the *Revue de Paris* (jealously contradicting its eminent competitor, perhaps ?) told its readers : 'Butter would not melt in this crafty old diplomat's mouth.'

† Deakin, A., *The Federal Story*, Robertson & Mullens, Melbourne, 1944, p. 25.

he may have abandoned his convictions, there can be no doubt of the sincerity with which he held them. The way in which A.W. Martin sums him up seems the most impartial : ' In his greatest years he was not a maker of events, but a man who moulded himself to events : not a statesman, but a politician.'*

By way of conclusion on this period of 1860–90, one may say, with the benefit of a century's hindsight, that what stands out is the disparity between the marked optimism of the period and the equally marked pettiness of its aspirations. If this state of affairs had lasted much longer Australia might well have settled into the mediocrity of affluence. But instead, it was to suffer from another sudden economic slump which was to rock it to its foundations and demonstrate how precarious that apparent affluence was. And it was only after having weathered this storm that Australia was to take its most decisive steps into the future.

Before looking at this climacteric, a glance at what was happening beyond Australia's shores would be in order.

Martin, A.W., *Henry Parkes*, Oxford University Press, Melbourne, 1964, p. 30.

Chapter Fourteen
Australia looks at the outside world

French settlement of New Caledonia – arrival of the first convicts – the banished communards – Rochefort escapes – French law on recidivists – Australia apprehensive – the New Hebrides affair – Australia attracted by the Pacific – disquiet at German moves – Queensland's occupation of east New Guinea – London's disclaimer – Germany and Great Britain share the territory – birth of Australian imperialism – pro-Americanism during the Spanish-American War – military inadequacy – loyalty to the Crown – the Sudan contingent – Australian support for the Boer War – Australian participation in the war

At the same time as they were approaching a national self-awareness, Australians discovered the outside world. For untold aeons the continent where they lived had been a *terra incognita* ; for the past fifty years, that was the name which they themselves could have given to the rest of the planet. About the middle of the nineteenth century, their loyalty to the British throne gave them their first taste of international problems. Simultaneously, they felt the urge for outward expansion, which was as new an experience for them as the economic transformation they were undergoing.

The French nuisance had faded from view over the previous years. But it turned up again in September 1853 with the French occupation of New Caledonia. Thirteen years before, their rather half-hearted attempt at taking over New Zealand had misfired but only just. Then, in 1843, they had settled for Tahiti. I Sydney some touchy colonials had seen the Tahiti affair as slight on the honour of the British Empire. But this late escapade was much worse – the French had seen fit to hoist the tricolour on an island that Captain Cook had put on the map that was a mere ten days sailing from the Australian coast and that seemed, morally, to be earmarked for British occupation

Feeling ran high in Australia. The French consul in Melbourne reported :

This initiative of ours has upset our old English enemies, who are for ever envious of any French success ... The Wesleyans* especially are screaming with rage ... People are demanding that the British government evict the French and go on to take over Fiji.

However, Whitehall had a better sense of proportion. It was much more important to make sure of Napoleon III as an ally in the Crimean War, which was now imminent, than to pick up another island somewhere in the South Pacific. The atmosphere in Australia was transformed overnight by the signing of the Anglo-French alliance. 'Undying friendship between our two peoples' was the theme of speeches on both sides. The Quai d'Orsay's man in Melbourne had his moment in the limelight. He must have been carried away : having been asked to speak at a dinner (which he did, extempore), he reported to his Minister the following day : 'I should have wished to transmit the text of my speech to Your Excellency, but I have been incapable of rewriting it from memory!'

This honeymoon between France and Australia was short-lived.† It ended abruptly in 1864. In that year it was learnt that the French government had decided to make regular shipments of convicts to New Caledonia.‡ This announcement raised a storm of protest. Australians found it difficult to live down the memory of their own origins and the prospect of having their breed, which they saw as purer with each passing year, sullied by contact with escaped gaol-birds was anathema to them. It must also be pointed out that those Frenchmen who had already settled in Victoria were hardly shining examples of the best that France had to offer. The French consul in

* No doubt referring to missionaries with an interest in the heathens of New Caledonia.
† In Melbourne one can see a gift of books presented in 1861 to the recently established library by Napoleon III.
‡ The first consignment of convicts arrived in New Caledonia on 8 May 1864. An Act of 8 December 1851 had already authorized the transportation of political prisoners to Algeria and Guiana. This category of prisoners was extended to include common criminals in 1854. Up until 1863, Guiana had been the only destination of the transported convicts. One of the main reasons for sending them to New Caledonia was the clemency of the climate compared with that of Devil's Island.

Melbourne described his compatriots as follows in a dispatch dated 23 April 1864 : 'The greater part of the French population here is the scum of the French who went to California ... In no other country that I have visited have I come across so many individuals who bring our country into disrepute.' A year later he talks of 'the frightful French element in this country'. The extreme language makes one wonder whether this gentleman was in his right mind.

Napoleon III's Second Empire was, therefore, not at a peak of popularity among Australians at the outbreak of the Franco-Prussian War in late 1870. This event, however, caused another swing in public opinion, this time in favour of France. The French consul in Sydney noticed it in August 1871 when news arrived of the signing of the peace treaty and the return to order in Paris after the Commune : 'It was the catastrophe at Sedan which brought France back into favour here ; and pro-French feeling is so strong that theatre audiences request the *Marseillaise*.' The Paris Commune and its aftermath once again raised the problem of New Caledonia. The French government had transported some 3,000 prisoners to the island. Nobody in Australia was very sure whether these were common criminals or political prisoners. An escape from the island made them headline news.

It was in March 1874 that the most famous of the political exiles, Rochefort,* landed at Newcastle with five companions. The circumstances surrounding their escape, which was most likely arranged with outside assistance, remain unclarified. Rochefort knew how to make the most of his abundant charm. According to him, 'Newcastle showered us with invitations.' But Newcastle was small beer compared with the reception they got from Sydney : 'Newcastle was agog with excitement over our arrival ; but we almost caused a revolution in Sydney.' No doubt the famous pamphleteer was given to some exaggeration. At any rate he could boast of having landed the French consul in a nasty predicament. In the dispatches of this

---

* Henri Rochefort (1830–1913) was a political journalist of aristocratic origins noted for his opposition to Napoleon III before the Franco-Prussian War and for his part in the Paris Commune of 1871. After the amnesty extended to former *communards* in 1879, he returned to France where he founded an influential radical-socialist newspaper, *l'Intransigeant*. In later life, during the Dreyfus affair he distinguished himself by becoming (against all expectations) one of the more scurrilous of the anti-Dreyfusards (*translator's note*).

hapless official one sees how much Sydney made of its unexpected guests : they were lionized, invited here and there, offered the best seats in the public gallery at Parliament ! The consul felt duty bound to 'put things in a proper perspective' by writing a letter to the press, where it appeared, but alongside ruthless replies from the six *communards*. Rochefort was also a success with the ladies. One barmaid in particular caught his fancy : 'Just imagine that dazzling Australian girl being ushered into a box at the Paris Opera in all the glare of a gala night – there is not one Frenchwoman who would not be put in the shade by her.'

This whole resounding episode gave Australians food for thought. It dawned on them that, if Rochefort could find his way over from New Caledonia, then any unsavoury desperado could presumably do likewise. This became an obsessive preoccupation. One finds it turning up again and again in newspapers of the time as well as in the consuls' dispatches. The apprehension was heightened in 1885 by the passing of an Act in the French Parliament that laid down transportation to Devil's Island or to the Isle of Pines off New Caledonia as the penalty for recidivists. The Australian press, and Australian politicians, stated their opinions on this measure in no uncertain terms. As chance would have it, the Victorian Premier of the day, James Service, was not noted for temperateness. One wishes one could have been present at the dressing-down he gave to the French consul on 20 February 1886. The latter reported him as having said :

When our own mother country attempted to dump her criminals upon our shores, we rose against her, and we shall never stand for your dumping at our very door your rejects and refuse. There are only a million of us, and we are not yet strong enough to go to war with France, but when we are able to do so, we undoubtedly shall, if you go on the way you are going ... And you can tell that to your government !*

Service returned to the same theme four years later, saying that New Caledonia was pouring its moral filth over Australia and reminding the French of the scant respect people have for the man who relegates his refuse to a back corner of his property and lets it overflow on to his neighbour's land.†

* All this, and more, the unfortunate consul glossed, in more circumspect language, in his dispatch to the Quai d'Orsay.

† There does appear to have been an element of demagogy in this righteous

This disagreement over the French recidivists was, of course, unfortunate, adding as it did a touch of venom to relations which were already strained by the New Hebrides question. In this archipelago, the right to spread the peace of the Gospel was being fought over by two groups of missionaries, one of them Protestant (which means British), and the other Roman Catholic (which means French). In the time-honoured manner, traders of both countries were loath to leave everything in the hands of the evangelists. This had brought in the two governments, which in 1878 had reached an unwritten agreement by which they would jointly exploit the islands, an arrangement which had already been denounced by the ever watchful *Argus*. This virtuous sheet had opined in September 1877 that it would be painful to behold a race of industrious, noble, independent natives reduced to slavery, demoralized and oppressed by French convicts, soldiers and gunboats. It is unnecessary to detail the unedifying succession of manoeuvres and underhand deals which this arrangement gave rise to. Suffice it to say that, after many accusations and counter-accusations of intransigence, the outcome was a standard compromise in 1887, under which the precious islands were to be administered jointly by a commission, staffed by equal numbers of British and French naval officers.*

Australia accepted this outcome with resignation, and remained sensitive to French movements in the area, as is shown by a series of incidents which, although insignificant in their own right, still made difficulties for French consular officials in Victoria, where national feelings were always keener than elsewhere. When the French flag was hoisted over the Saint Paul and Amsterdam Islands.† In 1892, the *Argus* saw it as a threat to Australia. Six years later, at the time of the Anglo-French confrontation at Fashoda, the consul in Melbourne reported the publication of 'several violently anti-

---

* This was the first step towards the present condominium, which came into force in 1906.

† In the Indian Ocean to the north-east of the Kerguelen Islands, more than 3,000 kilometres from Australia's western tip.

---

indignation. Thus the French consul in 1887 : 'The alleged invasion of recidivists amounts, according to an official report, to a grand total of forty-seven offenders, some of whom have mended their ways and are leading worthy lives.' Eventually transportation to New Caledonia was officially abolished in 1896, having been informally abandoned several years before.

French articles, advocating an outbreak of hostilities which, the newspapers believe, would present no danger to Australia but might result in federation'. There was a further burst of anti-French feeling in 1899, in an incident that is not without its lighter side. The second court-martial of Dreyfus at Rennes had just pronounced him guilty again. At an official banquet Lord Beauchamp, the Governor of New South Wales, referred to the court's finding as a hideous travesty of justice, adding that he was thankful not to be a Frenchman.* The predictable repercussions occurred – a formal protest from the French colony, bearing sixty-six signatures,† dispatch after dispatch from the consul (who did not hesitate to demand the recall of the Governor), official consultations. The incident blew over. The diplomats smoothed things out and the impetuous Governor wrote a letter of semi-apology, saying he had had no wish to offend the French (but without retracting a word of what he had said).

Presumably this tiff had nothing to do with the fact that no French warship took part in the festivities to celebrate federation at the end of the following year (see page 259). Paris must no doubt be given credit for realizing that France was not the only butt for the bad temper of a young country going through its growing pains.

Australia was irresistibly attracted to the limitless Pacific with its fascinating islands and its untapped wealth. But others were attracted to it too. The Western powers, in their carving-up of the world, cast covetous glances on the whole Pacific area. The Australian colonies tried to steal a march on their rivals. As early as 1858, Henry Parkes seems to have been the first to voice these ambitions. In the high-flown phrases that he was given to, he held forth to the New South Wales Legislative Assembly on the possibility of an

---

* The Governor was twenty-seven years of age. Paul Cambon, the French ambassador in London, was told by Sir Thomas Sanderson of the Foreign Office that when Lord Beauchamp went to call on the Queen before his departure for Australia, Victoria had said : 'What a charming man. But perhaps he should take his tutor with him.' One can imagine the British diplomat adding : 'Naturally, Your Excellency, I am telling you this in strict confidence.'

† From this document one can see that Melbourne already boasted branches of the Comptoir d'Escompte discount bank, the Messageries Maritimes shipping house, the Pasteur Institute and Pleyel Pianos, as well as a great many wool-buying firms.

Australia and New Zealand united to the Pacific islands, where the waves of European civilization were for ever breaking. This poetic vision was soon replaced by harsher realities.

France was not the only fly in the ointment ; there was Germany as well. Germany had, of course, got off to a slow start in the race for colonies. Until about 1880, Bismarck had little interest in imperialism. His second thoughts on the matter were caused by the expansion of the British Empire and the establishment of a new French Empire. But by that time there were few enough places in the sun left for the Iron Chancellor to take. Even so, he made sure of some of those which were still vacant. New Guinea was among them : only the western half of this vast territory was a Dutch possession. A Hamburg-based trading company soon began operations in New Guinea.

The Australians were not inactive. For the past ten years they had been urging the British government to annex the New Guinea archipelago. London had taken the view that it was infinitely more important to consolidate British influence in Egypt than to bother about an island that was practically unknown. Nor did Britain wish to antagonize Bismarck. And so the decision on New Guinea was to hasten slowly. This view was not shared by the colourful business-man who was Premier of Queensland at the time, Sir Thomas McIlwraith. Queensland was badly in need of labour to work the sugar-cane plantations. In 1883, without seeking any permission from the British government, he took it upon himself to annex the eastern half of New Guinea. The French consul in Sydney commented : ‘Queensland seems to be behaving like a young man who has just come into a large inheritance and who is letting it go to his head.’ Unfortunately McIlwraith soon had to change his tune. Lord Derby, the Colonial Secretary, who was renowned for his imperturbable good temper, was not impressed. He sent a chilly message of repudiation and the Queensland politicians had no option but to back down.

They soon had support from the other Australian colonies. There was an intercolonial conference in Sydney at the end of 1883. The Premier of Victoria distinguished himself by referring to those beautiful Pacific islands which were to be ravished by the scum of the French nation.* But the conference decided to broaden the issue.

---

* Meaning the New Hebrides again, of course.

Not content with merely demanding that all transportation of convicts to New Caledonia be stopped, they also drew up a new sort of Monroe Doctrine for their own benefit. They saw the South Pacific as a kind of *mare nostrum* and declared that no flag other than the Union Jack should be allowed to fly there. Lord Derby, as unruffled as ever, said 'stuff and nonsense', and Bismarck acted – within six months the northern half of east New Guinea was declared a German possession. Brisbane seethed, but Melbourne exploded, with indignation. The irrepressible Service telegraphed to the Victorian Agent-General in London : 'England must act promptly and firmly. Latest news Noumea (New Caledonia) shows great danger. Intense indignation here if France is allowed to make New Hebrides cesspool for convicts. Consider this crisis Australian history.'*

This was no doubt something of an overstatement. Nevertheless, Downing Street decided to take steps. The south-eastern part of New Guinea, about a quarter of the island's area, was still unannexed. A British contingent took possession of it in October 1884 in an atmosphere of festive imperialism. The headmen were assembled and treated to a fireworks display and a little speech from the representative of the Crown. The most important of these chiefs, dressed in his short shirt, his red straw hat and his lap-lap, was presented with the insignia of his 'sovereignty' – a walking-stick with a silver ring round it and a florin set in the handle. The celebrations were rounded off by a concert given by a regimental band. Over the following days the officer in command of the detachment visited neighbouring villages, showing the flag. In one of them he came across a tribe that was well known for its indulgence in cannibalism. He tutted and chided them, saying that Queen Victoria did not like her children to pick up that sort of habit.

The relations between the powers still needed to be regularized. This was done by the Anglo-German agreement of April 1885, under which the eastern half of New Guinea was divided into two roughly equal parts. Once again Melbourne saw red and James Service said that Lord Derby's action was 'one of the most melancholy and marvellous illustrations of political imbecility that has ever been recorded in history'.† This time there may have been

* Quoted by Gordon, D.C., *The Australian Frontier in New Guinea, 1870–1885*, Columbia University Press, New York, 1951, p. 185.

† *ibid.*, p. 271.

something in what he said, despite the extreme language in which he couched it. The English historian James Froude visited Victoria not long afterwards. He says : ' In the condition of mind in which I found Melbourne about New Guinea I thought it really fortunate that the Federation was still incomplete '* – his implication being that the federal state could have made it possible for Australia to intervene in New Guinea. As Sir Keith Hancock said half a century later, New Guinea became something of an Alsace for Australians.†

Surprising as it may appear, this feeling of insecurity in Australia that arose from the French presence in New Caledonia and the German presence in New Guinea was induced also by the remote Russian Empire. In Sydney one can still see a cannon of medieval design which was set up during the Crimean War to guard the harbour against the possibility of a Russian assault. During the 1878 war between Turkey and Russia there was a new alarm. It was rumoured that a Russian naval officer had divulged details of a plan to seize a coaling facility at Newcastle and thus hold Sydney to ransom. A few years later a similar sort of rumour circulated concerning a threat to Melbourne, where the French consul reported in 1882 that ' articles are appearing in the press saying that, in the event of war in Europe, Russia would attempt to capture Melbourne.' Again in 1885, when the Russians marched on Afghanistan and looked like threatening India, Australian pessimists pointed out that the Russian Vladivostock fleet was only fourteen days sailing away. The rapprochement between France and Russia was seen as even more disturbing, and in 1893 the story went round that France was going to sell New Caledonia to the Russians.

The possibility of American expansionist ambitions also caused Australia some qualms, despite the thousands of miles of ocean between Sydney and San Francisco. In 1869, when it looked as though America was about to establish a base in Fiji, this was seen in Australia as a sign that the pushing westward of the frontier was about to continue across the Pacific. This problem was only solved in 1874 when Great Britain annexed the Fijian group. Between then and the outbreak of the Spanish-American War in 1898, time and

---

* Froude, J.A., *Oceana, or England and her Colonies*, Longmans, Green, 1886, pp. 98–9.

† Hancock, W.K., *Australia*, p. 207.

the feeling of kinship had gradually done their work, and the six colonies came out passionately against the Spanish cause. They enjoyed witnessing the triumph of an emerging democracy over a waning monarchy.

Australians were very much in favour of imperialism, although they themselves lacked the means to develop it as a policy. The last British garrisons left Australia in 1870. They were replaced by militia which could never have defended the country, let alone undertaken any offensive action. In New South Wales an attempt to create a regular army was abandoned after it had managed to scrape together 300 infantrymen. The New South Wales militia, composed of artillery and a naval contingent, reached 1,200 to 1,400 men. In the other colonies it was the same story. In 1880 the *Australian Sketcher* drew an unfavourable contrast between the apathy in Australia and the initiative shown in Canada where a force 10,000 strong had been created, with the object of fighting overseas as well as at home if the need should arise. It added that when a wealthy community neglected its own defence, it was absurd for it to talk of nationality and to pride itself on any independence. All this was eminently sensible and totally without sequel. The most that was achieved was the agreement reached at the Imperial Conference in 1887, to the effect that the colonies should build certain fortifications and make a contribution to the upkeep of the British naval forces whose protection they enjoyed. This quite evident fact that Australians depended for their survival on Britain partly explains why they were such staunch supporters of the Imperial principle. But it would be a mistake to see their loyalty to the Crown as dictated largely by self-interest. Sentiment played a very great part in it, as was shown by several events in the latter part of the century, the visit of the Duke of Edinburgh in 1867, for example. The Duke was the second son and fourth child of the Queen. The French consul in Melbourne reported : 'These people, despite their deep-seated democratic feelings, are wild with joy.' Then an attempt was made on the Duke's life. The assailant, an Irishman, had to be protected from the fury of the crowd ; a series of demonstrations was held, to protest Australia's attachment to the Crown.* Any occasion was

* This incident offers a prime example of documentary evidence at work. The French consul in Melbourne says of the Duke : 'His manner is unpleasant ; he

good enough to demonstrate by actions rather than by mere words the strength of the emotional bond that linked most Australians to their country of origin.

In 1885, when the Moslem fanatic the Mahdi, believing himself divinely inspired, inflicted a disastrous defeat on the British, New South Wales offered assistance. The Mahdi, having taken over the whole of the Sudan, laid siege to Khartoum. When the beleaguered town fell, he massacred its 11,000 defenders, including the legendary General Gordon. On 3 March, 750 volunteers sailed from Sydney to the aid of the mother country ; their departure had something of the atmosphere of a crusade about it. But by 23 June they were back, with only an insignificant skirmish to their credit.

On the other hand, the Boer War was the first occasion when Australia acted on the international scene. As far back as 1881, when Gladstone had meekly recognized the independence of the Transvaal and the Orange Free State, under the shock of the humiliating setback at Majuba,* a wave of shame and outrage swept over the Australian colonies. They eagerly awaited the chance for revenge. This chance arose, and revenge seemed imminent, on 9 October 1899, when Kruger cut short fruitless negotiations and created a state of war. But it was a shock and not revenge that the British Empire was in for, as over the next two months every battle ended in a defeat for the British. Almost to a man, Australians were aghast at the prospect that these amateurish peasants might get the better of a professional army with a long list of battle honours. There were, admittedly, a few who stood out – one conscientious historian, a handful of trade unionists and 'liberals' – but the majority of Australians sided fervently with Great Britain. So it was that, in January 1900, when Lord Roberts opened the offensive which was calculated to bring the situation back under British control, he was at the head of troops which included sizeable contingents from New

---

* Two hundred Boers had taken an apparently impregnable hill position from the British army. Boer casualties amounted to five wounded and one killed ; the British lost 92 dead (including the general in command) and 134 wounded.

does not speak to a soul, he is never punctual, or else is quite capable of not turning up to functions'; whereas the Sydney consul speaks of him as 'the young prince [he was twenty-three] whose amiable ways have endeared him to all and sundry'. Had he ignored one of them and smiled at the other, perhaps ?

South Wales, Victoria and South Australia. In Roberts' manoeuvres in the veldt, the Australians' bushcraft proved invaluable. The Boers, of course, held out heroically for two more years. By the end of hostilities in 1902, the Australian volunteers numbered 848 officers and 15,327 other ranks. Of these, 518 were killed in action.

At the same time as the Australian troops were fighting in South Africa, another detachment of volunteers, 500 strong, had joined the international force (under a German general) which crushed the Boxer Rebellion in Peking.

Whatever the test, it can be seen that Australian loyalty stood up to it. Nevertheless, by the turn of the century many Australians were beginning to wonder whether their own interests were always going to be those which best served Great Britain. It was this question mark which added force to the arguments of those who advocated federation. And it is to that federation and its origins that we must now turn.

Chapter Fifteen
Crisis and Federation

*Economic difficulties – period of strikes – foundation of a workers' party
– bank failures – appeal of the idea of federation – military problems –
Premiers' meeting – some of the participants – failure of the first Convention – public opinion favours federation – Premiers meet again –
election of delegates to Constitutional Convention – proposed federal
constitution rejected by referendum – a second referendum accepts federation – London's agreement – birth of the Commonwealth of Australia*

Despite Australia's pride in its achievement to date and its confidence in the future, there were abundant signs that a crisis was
coming in the late 1880s. South Australia was the first to feel the
pinch. The agricultural experiment had succeeded better there than
elsewhere (see page 216), and an attempt had even been made to
develop the more arid regions. But, as has been said, ' the plough had
outpaced the rain clouds.'* The price of wheat eventually fell by 40
per cent. Throughout the rest of the country, a similar fate befell the
wool trade : in 1886 prices slumped by 25 per cent. Such phenomena
were customarily put down to local contingencies. Sometimes the
poor returns would be blamed on the rabbits, which were rapidly
becoming a menace ; at other times it was said to be the drought, or
the floods, which were responsible. But the fact is that, if Australia
had not clung to its ' splendid isolation ', it would soon have found
out that the phenomenon was worldwide. Nowadays we are so used
to prices rising that we find it verging on the inconceivable that they
should fall. Yet this is what happened, throughout the Western
world, over a period of some twenty-five years in the late nineteenth
century. The drop of 40 per cent in wheat and 25 per cent in wool
was merely a local manifestation of a general tendency. Economists

* Shaw, A.G.L., *The Story of Australia*, p. 169.

calculate that by 1896 price levels were at only 65 per cent of those of 1856, and explain this reduction by improved productivity, the transportation revolution and a contraction in the money supply caused by the generalized use of gold as the sole standard of value.

As for the squatters, such jargon would have been Greek to them. All they knew was that their profit margins were shrinking and they were ready to try any expedient in the hope of boosting the prosperity which until then they had taken for granted. Their first step, therefore, was to reduce wages. The unions, although still not very strong, resisted and were able to counter this measure to some extent. However, there was no shortage of underprivileged, non-union labour, glad to do any sort of work at any wage. And it was to this labour pool that the employers naturally turned. The only weapon at the unions' command was strike action. Up until then, strikes had had practical, immediate objectives, such as higher wages, shorter hours or better sanitation of workplaces. Now, however, the unions were to engage in a contest of principle, bearing on the right of employers to hire their labour as they pleased, whether it was union labour or not.

The first confrontations took place in August 1890. They began with the Marine Officers' Association, which was forbidden by the employers to affiliate with other union organizations. The movement spread rapidly to the shearers, who had a tradition of great militancy,* and to many areas of the mining industry and the waterfront. By September 50,000 workers had downed tools. There was a whiff of something like revolution in the air. Boatloads of wool were set on fire, 'scabs' were intimidated and forcibly prevented from working, and (according to the French economist, Pierre Leroy-Beaulieu, who was out in Australia some months later) some were even shot dead. The employers, for their part, were resolved not to back down. Repression was savage : in Sydney the Riot Act was read and police made free use of the baton charge ; in Melbourne the officer commanding the troops, a Colonel Price, who had unfortunately seen service in India, told his men that if they should have to open fire on the strikers, they should 'Fire low and lay 'em out !', an order which has become a classic. The shipping strike was defeated in three months. But it was only a prelude to other

---

* Between 1886 and 1889 they are said to have staged 3,000 strikes, successful and unsuccessful.

strikes, for the following year it was the turn of the shearers in Queensland, who raised the Eureka 'Southern Cross' flag and had to be quelled by troops. The year after that, trouble broke out among the miners at Broken Hill. This was dealt with by a lock-out, which reduced them to submission, and their movement was rendered impotent by the jailing of the leaders. In 1894 another attempt at a strike in the wool-growing industry also ended in failure.

As the turn of the century approached the labour movement, after a period of great vitality, seemed to be in retreat. But in fact it had just undergone a change in appearance. Much research has been done to prove (and an equal amount to disprove) that the year 1890 was a turning-point in the evolution of the labour movement. What one can say with certainty is that, since there is no such thing as spontaneous generation in history, the strikes of the early nineties only precipitated a transformation which would have been bound to come about sooner or later. Equally certain is the fact that it was the union leaders' experience of these strikes that made them give thought to the best political path to follow in future. There was a small section of the movement which advocated a total restructuring of society. The great majority, however, took a more moderate line. The ideology that they had lacked was supplied by the theories of the humane and idealistic American economist Henry George, who made a triumphal visit to Australia in 1890. Those who heard him were attracted by his moderate socialism and the appealing simplicity of his single-tax idea, according to which the fiscal problem could be solved by abolishing all taxation except that on land values. Believers in this theory realized that any implementation of it could only be done through legislation, and so the necessity for organized participation in the political arena became apparent. The different labour parties, leagues and federations were born in this way, once again a good ten years and more before a similar evolution took place in Great Britain. In New South Wales, labour candidates won seats at the Legislative Assembly elections in 1891. The labour movement in Victoria followed suit the year after, as did their counterparts in the other colonies over the next ten years or so.

In commenting on these developments, Deakin waxed grandiloquent. He saw the birth of the Labor Party as 'more significant and more cosmic than the Crusades'.* With the benefit of hindsight,

* Quoted by La Nauze, J.A., *Alfred Deakin*, vol. I, p. 144.

one can see such statements as over-simplifications: At the time, however, political circles were intensely interested in the development, upsetting as it did the balance of the status quo. As for the wider public, it was less interested in the birth of a new political force than in the succession of bank failures taking place at this time.

Once again, Australia was just another victim of an international epidemic. In the annals of French finance houses the crash of the Union Générale in 1882 is well remembered. And the collapse of the old, internationally reputable London firm of Baring Brothers in South America was an even more catastrophic event. It also had repercussions in Sydney and especially in Melbourne. There was a sudden loss of confidence and the British made a sharp reduction in investments. As compared with the £175 million which had come into the Australian colonies between 1880 and 1890, only slightly over a quarter of that figure came in over the following decade. As the depression spread, depositors began to withdraw funds. From that point on, the process was the standard predictable one of the closure of a few accounts, followed by the spreading of plausible, not quite unfounded rumours and finally a generalized contagious panic. Things reached such a pass in Victoria that the Premier lost all sense of proportion and stated publicly, 'We are all floundering';* not the sort of thing to inspire confidence. On 1 May 1893 all banks were permitted to close their doors and suspend trading for five days.† Some of them were not to open again for another three years. There were some disturbing instances of politicians being implicated in these bank failures. One of them, James Munro, having been Premier of Victoria for two years, managed to be appointed to the Agent-General's job in London when his bank suspended its operations. Others were less fortunate. The French consul reported from Melbourne on 6 January 1893 : 'Criminal charges have been preferred against the board members of the Mercantile Bank. Among the accused are Sir Matthew Davies, the Speaker of the Legislative Assembly, and a Mr James Bell, a former Minister and member of the Upper House.' In New South Wales, Sir George Dibbs managed to avoid the worst effects of the crisis, but only by the drastic measures of 'authorizing the issue of

* Quoted by Shaw, A.G.L., *op. cit.*, p. 177.

† According to the French consul, only the two British banks (Australasia and Union) did not.

treasury notes and making bank notes temporarily legal tender'.*

This period of strikes and bankruptcies gave Australians food for thought. In the preceding period of prosperity each colony had been confident of its ability to go it alone ; but now, in bad times, they had discovered how interdependent they really were. And of course they were in an absurd situation. Occupying between them a land-mass as extensive as the U.S.A., each of these six separate districts was trying to behave like a sovereign power. They were divided by customs barriers, had different railway gauges, collected quite different taxes, had their own postal systems (which even issued different stamps), operated quite independently of each other in the vital fields of education, social legislation and public works, and even had their own puny and unco-ordinated armed forces. Beside the Canadian provinces which, despite differences in the ethnic origins of their population, in language and religion, none-theless had managed to bring about a form of union as early as 1867, the Australian colonies really did cut a sorry figure.

The idea of a federation of the colonies had in fact been in the air for a long time, and there was always some farsighted person to remind his compatriots of the eventual necessity of some such solution. But the lethargy of established ways had prevailed. The progress of the federation concept had been slow, but it had also been sure, because after all it was a neat solution to the dilemma of the colonies. The problem was brought to a head by outside factors. At the intercolonial convention in Sydney at the end of 1883 (see pages 240–41), qualms about the French presence in New Caledonia and the Germans in New Guinea led to the creation of a Federal Council, which was to concern itself with problems of the Pacific area and the 'influx of criminals', as well as with fisheries, maritime legislation and extradition arrangements with other countries. This Council was a forum for the exchange of views, but it had no executive power delegated to it. In theory, each of the colonies was to send two representatives to it. However New South Wales declined to participate, out of pride in its own pedigree and reluc-tance to have anything to do with the Victorian *nouveaux riches* ; and South Australia, for ever trying to be different, participated in the Council's activities for only two years. This arrangement was

* Shaw, A.G.L., *op. cit.*, p. 178.

approved by Whitehall in 1885 and the Council actually met three times over the next three years.* But its deliberations were quite irrelevant to anybody. This Federal Council, as it was called at the time, may well have been 'the first beat of a national pulse' but, as Professor Pike says, 'each year its pulse beat more faintly and no one mourned when it stopped altogether in 1899.'†

It was in 1889 that the definitive move for federation began. Two years previously, the colonies had been disturbed enough at their lack of military preparedness to request London to send out an expert to examine the question. The War Office dispatched a high-ranking officer, Major-General Sir Bevan Edwards, who probably had great contempt for anyone not trained at Sandhurst. Edwards' report was unequivocal : given the state of affairs in Europe, anything might happen at any moment. In addition, he found the Australian armed forces to be incapable of putting up any resistance against an invasion, unless they were brought under one central command. What this meant, of course, was that federation was the only hope of survival for the colonies. The Edwards report was the subject of one of Parkes' finest speeches. At Tenterfield, in the far north of New South Wales, he made an impassioned plea for the federation that he had been advocating for so many years. An eyewitness describes him, at the age of seventy-four : 'The voice was a little veiled by fatigue and age. The massive shoulders were a little bowed ; but the huge head, with its streaming wave of silver hair and beard, was held as erect as ever.'‡ Parkes' prestige was such that the six colonies (plus New Zealand) decided to send delegates to a conference on federation to be held early the following year.

In 1890 the curtain went up on the first act of the federation drama. Most of the actors were men aged about forty or fifty.§

---

* Hobart was chosen as the venue for the inaugural meeting, perhaps because its summer climate is more clement than that of the other capitals. It may also have been to flatter the sensibilities of the smallest colony - it is interesting to note that the equivalent Canadian discussions leading to Confederation were held on the tiny Prince Edward Island.

† Pike, D., *Australia: the Quiet Continent*, Cambridge University Press, 1970, p. 142.

‡ Quoted by Wise, B.R., *The Making of the Australian Commonwealth*, Longmans, Green, 1913, p. 5.

§ Not all of the men sketched here took part in the same scenes. Nor did all of

Pride of place must go to the New South Welshmen. Parkes, of course, stands head and shoulders above the rest. By this time he enjoyed the reputation of a Grand Old Man and played this part with gusto. People smiled at his vanity, but not to his face. And he was such a fluent and flowery speaker that to argue against him was very difficult. By comparison with Parkes, Edmund Barton (who was to become the first national Prime Minister) seemed lacklustre. Deakin was polite about him : 'A sound lawyer with a judicial dignity of speech, a fine public spirit and a high sense of personal honour'.* But Beatrice Webb wielded a sharper pen, dismissing him as 'an amateur uncertain of the worthwhileness of his hobby ; he is perpetually asking himself whether he wishes to remain in politics.'† Barton may have lacked some colour ; but whatever it was that George Reid lacked, it was certainly not that. He played no part in the federation discussions before 1894, but once he joined them he lost no time in making his mark. His appearance was a boon to him as a politician, crying out to be caricatured. Deakin's description is Reid to a T :

Even caricature has been unable to travesty his extraordinary appearance, his immense, unwieldy, jelly-like stomach always threatening to break his waist-band, his little legs apparently bowed under its weight to the verge of their endurance, his thick neck rising behind his ears rounding to his many-folded chin. His protuberant blue eyes were expressionless until roused or half-hidden in cunning, and a blonde complexion and infantile breadth of baldness gave him an air of insolent juvenility‡ He walked with a staggering roll like that of a sailor ... He never slept in a public gathering more than a moment or two, being quickly awakened by his own snore.'§

He may not have been a great statesman, but there can be no doubt that he was a first-rate politician. Someone who met him at the turn of the century speaks of his 'fighting spirit and sense of humour',

* Deakin, A., *The Federal Story*, p. 32.
† *The Webbs' Australian Diary, 1898* (ed. A.G. Austin), Pitman, Melbourne, 1965, pp. 51–2.
‡ He was fifty-five in 1900.
§ Deakin, A., *op. cit.*, p. 60.

them see out the last act, notably Parkes who died in 1896.

his good temper, acute appreciation of human nature and abundant obstinacy.

The delegates from Melbourne were not going to let themselves be impressed by the men from Sydney. Although their capital was no longer known as 'Marvellous' Melbourne, as it had been about 1880, they were proud of having achieved more in their half century of existence than their New South Wales counterparts in 110 years. Also, they had long believed in federation and were reluctant to let other Johnny-come-latelies have the credit for their initiative. Not only that, but they counted among their number Alfred Deakin – the most 'ardent advocate of federation here and now', says Professor La Nauze* – a man who never lost faith in the federation project and did everything possible to bring it into being. It must be added that Beatrice Webb, uncharitable as ever, saw him as something of a lightweight ('fluent in speech but lacking in force. In political opinions he is a thoughtful pessimist'), although she did say that he had been a disappointment to them, because they were 'expecting much' of him.† Beatrice Webb was just as harsh on Henry Higgins, who was to become famous in the years after federation (see pages 286–9) : she said he was

...anxious to find out the truth and act accordingly. His fault is a curious coldness and perhaps a lack of decision; he hesitates between complete opportunism and rigid adherence to theoretic principles; a hesitation which is emphasized by a slight stammer. ‡

Only one Victorian found favour with Mrs Webb, and that was Isaac Isaacs, whom she saw as

a typical clever young jew: a good lawyer with an acute well-informed mind ... He is the only man we have met in the colonies who has an international mind determined to make use of international experience. And this, in spite of the fact that he has never left Australia ... Like many clever pushing Israelites he presumes too much on the stupidity of the Gentile.§

New South Wales and Victoria were not the only colonies to play a

* La Nauze, J.A., *op. cit.*, vol. I, p. 112.
† *ibid.*, p. 63.
‡ *The Webb's Australian Diary, 1898*, p. 76.
§ *ibid.*, pp. 68–9.

part in the series of deliberations between 1890 and 1900. Tasmania sent its Premier, Edward Braddon, 'the most distinguished looking delegate,' says Deakin, 'with the manner of a diplomat and the face of a mousquetaire'.* There was also Adye Douglas, a former Premier of the same colony. At seventy-five he was one of the oldest of the negotiators, and had thirty-five years of experience of public affairs. Deakin says of him that he was 'the champion of the "stalwarts"', not so much because he was irreconcilable as to the principles at stake, but because he was by disposition and training essentially a fighting man'.†

'Honest Tom' Playford was another who enjoyed a good set-to. He hailed from South Australia and was proud of it. Well over six feet and with a girth to match, he delivered his cut-and-dried arguments in a stentorian voice. Parkes, with his idealism and his complicated procedures, got on his nerves and he did not hesitate to stand up to the old man. His colleague was the massive Charles Kingston, a much more placid man who liked nothing better than hard work ; Barton said of him that the only thing that stopped him was exhaustion.

One must single out three men. John Forrest represented Western Australia which, because it was less advanced than the others and had just struck unexpected riches (see pages 267–8), was extremely reluctant to lose its total autonomy. Forrest had been an explorer, leading one of the expeditions that had searched for Leichhardt, and another trek across the desert from Perth to Adelaide. Deakin says he had a 'bluff Henry-the-eighth appearance'.‡ Then there was the Premier of Queensland, Samuel Griffith, who even won over Beatrice Webb. She saw him as 'a man of mark with a keen subtle intellect' (but she could not resist an implied dig) 'who was, in fact, too fine an instrument for colonial life'.§ Griffith was to play a considerable part in the very first discussions, as Deakin was later to acknowledge : 'His patience, lucidity and thorough grasp of the subject made him a model leader.'‖ Thirdly, there was George Grey. He was in a difficult position, representing New Zealand, which had

* Deakin, A., *op. cit.*, p. 70.
† *ibid.*, p. 42.
‡ *ibid.*, p. 70.
§ *The Webbs' Australian Diary, 1898*, p. 43.
‖ Deakin, A., *op. cit.*, p. 31.

made up its mind from the outset not to join the Federation. But then he had had plenty of experience of difficult situations in a long and varied career as an officer, an explorer, as Governor of South Australia (see page 173), then of New Zealand, then of Cape Province, then of New Zealand again. He was seventy-nine to Parkes' seventy-five – and they could not bear one another. Deakin says of these two :

Each had been so long the 'grand old man' of his own colony, that it was almost with a feeling of affront on each side at an attempted usurpation by an interloper, that they met and from the first moment plainly bristling with hostility to each other [*sic*].*

Although the meeting in Melbourne in February 1890 lasted for only a week, it proved very fruitful. Within a month, on 2 March, an Intercolonial Convention had begun sitting in Sydney.† Its terms of reference were to draw up a draft federal constitution. At its inaugural meeting Parkes, as usual, rose to the occasion and offered a toast to 'one people, one destiny !' Glasses were raised to that high hope and then the delegates got down to the hard task ahead of them.

The atmosphere in which they met was not favourable. The shipping strike had only ended some months before and the material hardships of the moment seemed much more important than the abstract concepts involved in planning a federation. The discussions lasted for five weeks and, helped by the persuasiveness of Parkes and the great practical wisdom of Griffith, ended in the adoption of a document which was not very different from the constitution which was to be eventually endorsed by the Australian people. This document already used the term 'Commonwealth'. The convention dispersed on 9 April and the delegates returned to their home cities, no doubt with mingled satisfaction and misgivings. It was natural that they should take pride in having written a new page in their country's history. But at the same time they were too experienced in the hurly-burly of politics not to realize that there were still many lions in the path. And, sure enough, the proposed constitution bogged down in the Parliament of each colony. The final blow to

---

* Deakin, A., *op. cit.*, p. 34.
† Notice the care taken not to hurt anyone's feelings.

it was when the Parkes government in New South Wales was defeated at the elections.

It looked as though the whole federal concept had miscarried. But ideas can only make their way in a democracy if they have the support of public opinion. Hitherto the problem had been of concern to hardly anyone except the politicians. The social upheavals and the bank failures were to bring it home to the nation as a whole that there was something in Parkes' toast, after all. There were three main positions on the issue. The first was held by a tiny minority and had very little in its favour except the talent of the men who argued it. This view – that Australia should adopt a nationalist republican system, with a dash of socialism – was expounded in brilliant articles in the *Bulletin*. The opposite view was advocated by the traditionalists, who believed that the only future for Australia should be as a member of an imperial federation. This body was seen as an ostensibly co-operative grouping, but Great Britain would obviously have played the leading role in it. The third solution was the one which seemed reasonable and equitable to all those who were not carried away by extreme passions. This was an association between the six colonies which would allow them to control their own destinies while not breaking their ties with the Crown.

Public support gradually grew for the third solution. In 1893 a famous conference was held at Corowa on the Murray. It called on the voters of each colony to appoint representatives to draw up a new draft federal constitution. The aim was to let the people take over the job that their official representatives had failed to complete. What the founding fathers of 1890 thought of this is not recorded. Things continued to move slowly, and it was another eighteen months before the Premiers, meeting once more in Hobart, took two fundamentally important decisions. The first of these endorsed the Corowa resolutions and stipulated that each colony was to elect ten representatives. The second opened up a new possibility by stipulating that the proposed constitution was to be voted on by the whole nation at a referendum.

It may appear surprising that it took fully twenty-six months for these two resolutions to be acted upon. But the fact was that the colonies all had to be talked into signing away their sovereignty and they all tried to postpone that decision in every way possible. The election of the representatives took place on 4 March 1897. New

Zealand had already made it known that she was not interested. Queensland, where the possibility of partial secession again arose (see pages 218–19), also took no part. The ten representatives of each of the five remaining colonies were joined in their discussions by the Premiers and, for various different reasons, by twenty-four other personalities. To these seventy-nine Australians was entrusted the responsibility for the future of the Federation proposal. The sittings of this body lasted for a year, including the time necessary for the members to report back to their constituents. They sat first in Adelaide for six weeks, then for three weeks in September in Sydney, then nearly two months in Melbourne at the beginning of 1898. As had happened in America 110 years previously, in Canada less than forty years before, and as the South Africans were to discover twelve years later, the convention had to settle two fundamental questions : how to prevent the larger colonies dominating the federation, and how to ensure that the machinery of the central government would not encroach on the rights of the local administrations. These problems could only be resolved by compromise (see Chapter 16).

The convention concluded its sittings on 13 March 1898 and the referendum was held on 3 June, without Western Australia's or Queensland's participation. Vehement opposition to federation had appeared in New South Wales, which was much more jealous of its sovereignty than the other colonies, and it was feared that a great many people there would not bother to vote. So that the proposal would not appear to have been adopted by too few people, the colony's government decided that the minimum 'yes' vote in New South Wales should be 80,000. One wonders whether the canny Reid had Norman blood in him * – certainly he expressed his own opinion on the issue of federation in a speech which earned him the nickname of 'Yes-No'.† The count of votes in New South Wales was 71,595 in favour of federation and 68,228 against, showing that once again Reid's instinct to hedge his bets was a sound one. Because the New South Wales 'yes' vote had not reached the 80,000, everything was back at square one, despite the crushing majorities in favour of federation in Tasmania (six to one) and Victoria (five to one), and an honourable outcome of two to one in South Australia.

---

* Normans are proverbially supposed to be incapable of giving a straight answer (*translator's note*).

† See Wise, B.R., *The Making of the Australian Commonwealth*, p. 263.

Altogether, 219,712 voters had favoured federation, while 108,363 had voted against.

This further delay and all the other obstacles that had to be surmounted make one appreciate the force of Deakin's disenchanted observation on the process by which federation was eventually arrived at : 'To those who watched its inner workings, followed its fortunes as if their own, and lived a life of devotion to it day by day, its actual accomplishment must always appear to have been secured by a series of miracles.'* The last of these miracles, the deciding one, happened on 20 June 1899. Since the referendum of twelve months before, the supporters of federation had not been inactive.† A campaign against abstainers managed to get 519,000 voters to the polls at the next referendum, as against the 328,000 of the previous year. This time, only Western Australia held aloof. In two colonies the 'no' vote was insignificant : in Victoria 9,805 as against 152,653 ; in Tasmania 791 as against 13,437. In Queensland it was a close shave, with 38,000 for and 31,000 against. In South Australia the 'yes' majority was doubled and even in New South Wales the 'yes' vote won by 107,000 to 82,000. Over the whole country, federation was approved by more than 70 per cent of those who voted.

The next step was to secure the approval of Her Majesty's government in Westminster. Downing Street invited all the colonies to send delegates to London. None of the colonies declined, Western Australia having decided belatedly to join in too.‡ The Australians arrived in London in March 1900, where they were welcomed by Joseph Chamberlain, courteously enough, of course, but not without a touch of condescension. The outcome of the Boer War was still far from certain and Great Britain was in no position to thwart the wishes of her most loyal overseas subjects. And so the delegates

---

* Deakin, A., *op. cit.*, p. 166.

† One oft quoted Tasmanian orator ingenuously voiced the intimate aspirations of many of his fellow citizens : 'Gentlemen, if you vote for the Bill you will found a great and glorious nation under the bright Southern Cross, and meat will be cheaper ; and you will live to see the Australian race dominate the Southern Seas, and you will have a market for both potatoes and apples ; and your sons shall reap the grand heritage of nationhood' (quoted in Wise, B.R., *op. cit.*, p. 356).

‡ It finally joined the Federation in April, after a referendum in which 45,000 voted for and 28,000 against.

were honoured and fêted and made much of, which was not unpleasant and gave them stories to tell back home. Deakin was unimpressed by it all, seeing London society as 'a Vanity Fair in fact and truth'.* Then the serious business of negotiation began. Out of principle, Britain insisted on several alterations, but in the main the proposed federal constitution came through intact.† The definitive Act which officially brought the Commonwealth of Australia into existence received the Royal Assent on 17 September 1900.

Australia's official birthday had been set for 1 January 1901, and the honour of being chosen as interim capital had fallen on Melbourne (see page 265). Professor La Nauze says that when midnight had rung in the New Year, the city of Sydney burst into an indescribable cacophony of whistles, bells, gongs, accordeons, rattles, kitchen utensils and ships' sirens.‡ At daybreak, it was raining and the weather looked inauspicious. But later the sky cleared and the ceremonies started on a typically hot and humid summer's day. There was a tremendous parade through the city streets, including workers from all the trade unions, the shearers in front, municipal representatives, church dignitaries,§ troops in khaki and lancers roasting in their scarlet tunics, and Lord Hopetoun, in his carriage, pale, bareheaded, gravely saluting the crowds. In Centennial Park, before a vast throng of people,‖ Lord Hopetoun was sworn in as Governor-General of Australia, alongside the Commonwealth's first Prime Minister, Edmund Barton. There followed a banquet for 200 privileged guests.

Australia was no longer only a geographical expression ; it had become a political reality. It only remained for it to become a nation.

---

* Deakin, A., *op. cit.*, p. 162.
† Paul Cambon, the French ambassador, reported to the Quai d'Orsay on the progress of the negotiations. On 10 April 1900 he said : 'The proposal will eventually be agreed to in its entirety. And then Australia will become a most bothersome power for England and for the rest of the world, too.'
‡ La Nauze, J.A., *op. cit.*, vol. I, p. 213.
§ Minus the Roman Catholics. Perhaps their non-participation can be put down to the fact that Cardinal Moran had stood for election as a New South Wales delegate to the 1897 convention, but without success.
‖ Estimates vary, not surprisingly. One newspaper put the numbers as high as 250,000 ; another one says 100,000. The French consul says 60,000.

Part Four
Australia as a Federation
1901-1945

Chapter Sixteen

Australia at the turn of the century

Population – institutions – economic situation – urbanization – the six capital cities – ways of life – intellectual life – the bush mythology – cult of democracy – strong nationalism

By 1900 the era of the epic explorers was past. Over the preceding quarter of a century, a whole series of expeditions had finished off the work of exploration and now, of the original *terra incognita*, nothing was unknown except for some areas in the far north and in the central deserts.

According to the figures of the first census in the twentieth century, Australia now had 3,773,801 inhabitants, which was almost nine times as many as fifty years before. Impressive as this growth is, it is obviously insignificant when compared with the 76,000,000 inhabitants of the U.S.A., a land mass of approximately the same size.* There was a constant rise in the proportion of native-born Australians : by 1871 it had reached 60 per cent ; by 1891 it was 75 per cent ; and ten years later it stood at 85 per cent. This was a factor which made for greater social cohesiveness. Two thirds of the population lived in two States : 1,360,000 in New South Wales and 1,200,000 in Victoria. The rest of the population was mainly in Queensland (493,000) and in South Australia (357,000). The figure of 172,000 for Tasmania's population is relatively high, in view of its habitable area. The vast State of Western Australia, with only 180,000 people, seemed well-nigh uninhabited. Immigration into the colonies had reached a peak fifteen years earlier, with 224,000 new arrivals between 1880 and 1885. Since then, however, the immigration rate had become almost negligible ; on two occasions, in 1892–3 and between 1898 and 1900, the number of departures

---

* Albeit infinitely richer in resources and not nearly so far away from Europe.

actually exceeded the number of arrivals. Over the previous forty years the birth-rate had also declined from 43 per 1,000 to 27 per 1,000. Despite the fact that in these same years the mortality rate had declined from 17 per 1,000 to 12 per 1,000, the overall population growth rate was slowing down. In 1860 the figure had been 25 per 1,000, but by 1900 it had fallen to 15 per 1,000. The annual increase in population was also falling – in 1891 the rate of increase had been 3.51 per cent, whereas by 1901 it was 1.73 per cent. At the same time there were fewer and fewer people in the younger age groups. The first and most important conclusion that can be drawn from these data on population is that in 1900 Australia's demographic outlook was unfavourable.

Against this rather uninspiring population position, there was the fact that the country now had a stable institutional structure. The basis of the new federal institutions was a sound one, as there had been no tampering with the existing territorial divisions. On the map, the colonies (now called States) looked the same as before, and they all kept their own governmental, parliamentary and legal frameworks. Federation had brought little enough change to the integrity of the new States, although all inter-State customs barriers had been abolished and the whole Commonwealth was now a common market in which goods circulated freely. The greatest change was that the States had agreed to cede certain powers to the central authority. The question of which powers were to be delegated was a difficult one to solve. After much discussion, the outcome was a compromise modelled on the American experience. The only powers to be vested in the Commonwealth were to be those expressly set out in the Constitution ; all other powers were to remain with the States, which meant that they retained a substantial range of authority. This included social legislation, education, agricultural and industrial matters, police and control over navigable streams and railways. The three essential attributes of national sovereignty – external affairs, defence and finance – were, of course, vested in the Commonwealth government. In addition, the national government was given the right to regulate inter-State trade, customs, monetary and banking matters, immigration, marriage and divorce, as well as problems of conciliation and arbitration on social issues involving more than one State, a clause which was very soon to be put to the test (see pages 286–9).

This newly born Commonwealth of Australia needed a flag and

a capital city. There was little difficulty with the flag ; it was flying over Melbourne by 3 September 1901. The new emblem symbolized Australia's loyalty to the Crown, with its traditional blue background stamped with the Union Jack, top left ; a white six-pointed star represented the six States and five other stars represented the Southern Cross and indicated the Commonwealth's geographical position. Where the seat of the new national government would be was a more difficult problem. It will be remembered that Melbourne was chosen as the temporary seat of government. New South Wales was determined not to allow this interim state of affairs to become definitive, and managed to have the capital sited on its side of the Murray. The stipulation was made that the new capital must be at least 100 miles (160 kilometres) away from Sydney, as Victoria had considerable misgivings about the influence emanating from the capital of New South Wales.

The institutions of the new Commonwealth were largely based on those of Great Britain, although certain variations, on the American pattern, were built into the Constitution. There was a Governor-General appointed by the Queen as the representative of the Crown.* In him was vested the power to veto legislation or, if he saw fit, to submit to the monarch any Act of Parliament which he declined to approve. He was also given the power to prorogue Parliament (on the condition that no more than twelve months should elapse between two sessions), and in certain circumstances to dissolve it. The Governor-General was empowered to appoint a Prime Minister and the members of his Cabinet ; the members of a government being answerable to the elected Parliament, they must of course be members of the majority. The Governor-General was also to be Commander-in-Chief of the army and navy. As can be seen, such broadly defined powers are, at least in theory, far from insignificant and would appear to allow scope for an authoritarian to misuse them.

The Parliament was to consist of two Houses, the lower being called the House of Representatives and the upper the Senate. Elections for the House of Representatives were to be held every three years, on manhood suffrage. By 1902 women were also given

---

* The first native-born Governor-General was to be Isaac Isaacs in 1931. Beatrice Webb (who had said of him 'He will rise') was proved right (*The Webbs' Australian Diary, 1898*, p. 69).

the vote (which, in colony elections, they had had in South Australia since 1894 and in Western Australia since 1899). The composition of the House of Representatives was to be proportionate to the population of the different States and was to number seventy-five members in all. Like its model, the House of Commons, it was to have sole power of initiating money or taxation bills. No bill could become law unless it passed both Houses. Like the members of the House of Representatives, Senators were also to be elected on universal manhood suffrage, but with the difference that each State was uniformly entitled to six Senators. In this way, as in the U.S.A., it was intended to safeguard the rights of the smaller States against the larger.

The High Court was also set up, empowered to rule on the constitutionality of any law. In the first years of this system, the High Court was to come down invariably on the side of States' rights.

At the turn of the century, neither the nation's finances nor the general economic situation was very promising. The national deficit amounted to almost £200 million, more than half of it accountable to the two largest States. Sixty per cent of the borrowing had been for the construction of railways which often turned out to be un-usable. In March 1901, the French consul reckoned the average of the national debt at 1,340 francs per person, adding that this was 'a figure which is very likely higher than that in any other country in the world'. (One wonders, in passing, how this gentleman could be so sure of his figures.) However, it was definitely a fact that, whatever the figures, the national deficit was extremely high. This was a constant burden on the budget, and it was a situation that took a long time to improve. The figures given by Professor Butlin[*] show the gravity of the position :

Gross national product	1890 : *206.3 m £*	1897 : *153.4 m £*
Industrial production	1890 : *60.0 m £*	1894 : *45.1 m £*

[*] See Butlin, N.G., *Australian Domestic Product, Investment and Foreign Borrowing 1861–1938/9*, pp. 6, 59, 92, 111, 164.

Pastoral production	1885 : *117.4 m £*	1892 : *51.9 m £*
Agricultural produce	1890 : *12.9 m £*	1895 : *5.9 m £*
Woollen products	1890 : *16.3 m £*	1897 : *13.8 m £*

To make matters even more difficult, in 1897 there began a period of drought which, by 1902, had become the most severe for a century.

At the same time there were some grounds for confidence in the future. Despite a brief critical period about 1900 in the pastoral industry,* Australia was still the world's greatest producer of wool and Sydney was already tending to oust London from its position as the most important wool selling market. Sugar-cane was also a source of increasing export revenue and was overtaking wool exports. In 1866, the first cane crop had amounted to two tonnes ; by 1899 the crop had reached almost 200,000 tonnes. It was a period of great change for farming too. Agriculture was being diversified, wine, dried fruits and dairying all being on the increase. Over a period of forty years land under cultivation had grown from a little more than 400,000 to about 3.6 million hectares. In particular, wheat production had risen from 360,000 cubic metres to 980,000. This rate of expansion can be attributed to three main factors : mechanization, superphosphates and new strains of seed developed by William Farrer, an agricultural scientist, to whom the grateful Commonwealth later erected a monument.

In *The Rush that Never Ended* Professor Blainey highlights the constant expectations of mining success held by Australians, expectations that were sometimes to prove unfounded, but were often to be fully justified. In the 1860s, hopes of gold strikes in the north were at first thwarted, but eventually some rich fields were found, including Charters Towers and the Palmer River. On the other hand, the story of the Western Australian gold strikes of the

---

* The sheep population fell from 106 million in 1890 to seventy million in 1900. An official report on this collapse said that rabbits completely cancelled out the benefits of any rainfall by grazing out much of the available pasture as soon as the the grass began to grow.

nineties was Victoria in the fifties all over again. In 1892, two
prospectors found unbelievably rich gold deposits near Coolgardie,
which was then a small village some 600 kilometres east of Perth.
The usual chain reaction was set off, with gold-diggers arriving from
all points of the compass, and before long a whole town had grown
up. Pierre Leroy-Beaulieu, the French economist, visited it in 1897,
by which time it had 5,000 inhabitants and boasted five churches,
one club, one theatre, a cricket club, two newspapers (from which
Leroy-Beaulieu was gratified to learn the details of a Cabinet
reshuffle in France) and bookshops 'with translations of Zola,
Dumas *pere* and even Paul de Kock'. The surrounding regions were
utterly arid but, nothing daunted, the inhabitants had their water
brought in from 500 kilometres away.

The Western Australian gold rush, although a colourful episode,
was actually of little significance. Australia's future was not on the
goldfields, any more than it was in the bush (despite the mystique
that surrounds the word to this day). Australia's real future lay in
the towns, which were increasing in importance every day. The
process of urbanization already mentioned was continuing. In 1850
two out of every five Australians lived in six urban centres ; in 1900
this proportion was little changed : one in three. The fact is that
increasing mechanization in primary industry reduced the need for
manpower ; life on the coast was as attractive as ever ; and as
industry developed it tended to concentrate in areas where facilities
and markets already existed. The population of each of the capital
cities was proportionately greater in relation to its State than thirty
years earlier.*

The largest of the capital cities, in terms of population, was still
Melbourne, with 496,400 inhabitants to Sydney's 481,000. However the population of Sydney was soon to exceed that of Melbourne,
which was losing the position of splendid superiority that a period
of artificial prosperity had conferred on it. A Frenchman who visited
the Victorian capital in 1897 saw it as

* Sydney had grown from 27 per cent to 36 per cent of the New South Wales
population ; Melbourne from 28 per cent to 41 per cent of Victoria's population ;
Adelaide from 23 per cent to 45 per cent of South Australia's ; Brisbane from 13
per cent to 24 per cent of Queensland's. Only in Hobart and Perth did the proportion remain close to constant – 20 per cent instead of 19 per cent in Hobart, and
20 per cent instead of 21 per cent in Perth.

a vulgar upstart, full of its own importance and its rapid prosperity, but which is now feeling the after-effects of its own folly ... Showy façades hastily thrown up, but much shoddy workmanship in evidence ... Shanties and hovels a-plenty and public buildings started, then left unfinished ... fully two-thirds of the fine residences are up to let.

Another Frenchman, some years before, had been impressed by what he calls 'the finest racecourse in the world'. He was also intrigued by the unexpected sight of 'lifesize portraits of General Boulanger* all over the place'. It turned out to be an advertising stunt by a real estate company which was calling its building land 'General Boulanger's Domain'. Mark Twain was in Melbourne in 1897 too. He shared the Frenchman's enthusiasm for the race-track and was lucky enough to be there on Melbourne Cup day, the greatest event of the calendar. He describes the scene as 'a brilliant and wonderful spectacle, a delirium of colour, a vision of beauty. The champagne flows, everybody is vivacious, excited, happy.' There were obviously some squatters who had escaped ruin, for he was told that there were still some whose properties were 'about as large as Rhode Island, to speak in general terms'.† Beatrice Webb, of course, was indefatigable in her search for things intellectual. Her verdict on the Victorians was favourable (wonders will never cease!): 'The men are certainly a better type than the rich men we met at Sydney, superior in intellectual culture and vastly so in public spirit.'‡

On Sydney, though, Mrs Webb was her incorrigible self, seeing it as

a crude chaotic place ... In this city there is neither homeliness nor splendour; only bad taste and cold indifference ... The rich people take no part [in politics] and actually pride themselves on their contempt for public affairs; money-making and racing seem their only concern; such political ideas as they have resolve themselves into a hatred of 'Trade Unions' and a strong desire to escape direct taxation. The working

* Georges Boulanger (1837–91), sabre-rattling, rabble-rousing political general, was very popular in France in the late 1880s. He botched his *coup d'état* in 1889 and fled to Belgium, where he later committed suicide on the grave of his dead mistress (*translator's note*).

† Twain, M., *Mark Twain in Australia and New Zealand*, p. 162.

‡ *The Webbs' Australian Diary, 1898*, p. 71.

men seem also largely non-political ... The most depressing feature of New South Wales is the absence of education among the rich and the bad manners of all classes.

She found no conversation : ' It would be useless to argue or scold them : chaff, chaff, chaff is the only prescription.' *

Can it be that sociologists are more discriminating than historians ? Certainly, a few years previously, James Froude, less cut-and-dried than the Webbs, had had the impression that the climate of Sydney had made the city's inhabitants into southerners. He also thought that it was quite understandable that they should be so unconcerned since, he believed, life in Australia was easier than elsewhere – although one suspects there may have been a touch of irony in his comments. Irony was certainly lacking in the views of French visitors to Australia, which vary between approval and enthusiasm. 'Sydney is more solid, and not as pretentiously elegant as Melbourne. It is also more distinctive a place and does not give one the feeling that it has just recently sprung up out of the ground.' Another Frenchman waxed more lyrical than that : 'There is something more grandiose to Melbourne than there is to Sydney. But Sydney probably has a more homely feel to it, with its almost creole character,† which makes it a pleasanter place.' The harbour brought out their choicest epithets : 'The sail was an unforgettable experience. The setting is fantastic, uncannily spectacular, quite other-worldly. It is a place that makes you feel as though you are dreaming wide awake and fills your imagination with excitement and delight.'

Adelaide (at 162,000 the third largest of the State capitals) also had its particular charm. Pierre Leroy-Beaulieu saw it as ' reminiscent at times of the East, dazzling in the sunlight under the dark blue sky'. Mark Twain too was impressed by ' a modern city, with wide streets, compactly built ; with fine homes everywhere, embowered in foliage and flowers, and with imposing masses of public buildings nobly grouped and architecturally beautiful '. He was also struck by the multiplicity of religions practised, what he calls the ' 64 roads to the other world ' ‡ Perhaps it was this spirituality which accounted for Mrs Webb's unwonted leniency towards Adelaide ;

* *The Webbs' Australian Diary, 1898*, pp. 22, 32, 50.

† Had he read Froude ?

‡ Twain, M., *op. cit.*, p. 181, 183.

she certainly found 'far more amenity' in it than in 'restlessly pretentious Melbourne, crude, chaotic Sydney, or shadily genteel Brisbane'. Her husband thought that Adelaide had 'more chance than any other Australian City of becoming the Weimar or, more precisely, the Stuttgart of the Southern hemisphere'.* In fact, in Adelaide, the Webbs could only find one drawback, and that was the fact that the lower and middle classes were just like those at home – only worse.

Mrs Webb was not very kind to Brisbane either (population 113,000), which she called 'a pretentious little place'. Her husband saw Queensland politics as

a regime of Tory autocracy, kindly but imperative – without either the dignity or large views of English Toryism In Queensland one finds at every turn, a most peculiar reminiscence of the bad manners, sullen insolence, and graspingness of the 'man in possession'.†

The 66,000 inhabitants of Perth and the 34,000 of Hobart were no doubt fortunate to escape a visit from the Webbs. But the conscientious Pierre Leroy-Beaulieu would certainly not have considered his study of Australia complete if he had not paid a visit at least to Perth. He found it to be little more than 'a small, dusty township with short streets and drab houses, although there is a superb town hall'. Perth, of course, was a very new town and could not be expected to have the character of Hobart which was already almost a century old. Mark Twain found Hobart to be

an attractive town ... the neatest town that the sun shines on; and I incline to believe that it is also the cleanest ... In Hobart all the aspects are tidy, and all a comfort to the eye; the modestest cottage looks combed and brushed.‡

As for the people who lived in these cities, and their way of life, it has been estimated that, except in the poorer districts, the one-family detached house accounted for fully two thirds of the build-

---

* *The Webbs' Australian Diary, 1898*, pp. 96, 94. This sort of thinking was prevalent at the time. Two years later the new Governor of South Australia, Lord Tennyson (the son of the poet), called Adelaide 'the young Athens of the South Pole', according to the French consul in Melbourne.

† *ibid.*, pp. 39, 40, 41.

‡ Twain, M., *op. cit.*, p. 182.

ings. This arrangement has been called 'a material triumph and an aesthetic calamity'.* Twenty years earlier the houses had all been of two storeys ; but now they often had only one storey (perhaps an effect of the manpower shortage). During the prosperous years, the fashion had been for the solemn style, of Italian inspiration, for grey facades with artificial ornamentation and false gables. Latterly, builders had been trying for originality and picturesqueness, the staple materials for which were red bricks and orange tiles.

Middle-class women spent the greater part of their day at home, devoting their energies to children, church and kitchen. Better-off women had their clubs or were to be seen at the races, at the theatre or at concerts. But, at all social levels, women were definitely subservient to their husbands. Spinsters were few and far between, as there were still ten per cent more men than women. Votes for women had done nothing to improve their status, the law being, as a Frenchman noted in surprise, ahead of current social practice. In any case the lives led by the two sexes tended to be segregated, wives staying at home and husbands going out to their club or to the local pub. A generation before, Henri Rochefort had praised the beauty of Australian women. Not so Beatrice Webb, needless to say. In fact she reserves some of her most potent venom for Australian women. 'The quintessence of vulgarity' is how she describes the wife of Sydney's Lord Mayor. She saw Sydney's well-to-do women as 'uncivilized' :

... they are dressy, snobbish and idle, and whilst they are willing enough to companion the men on the race-course, they apparently think it 'unwomanly' to take an active part in public affairs ... The clothes are fresh and flashy : powder and paint ruin complexions and the women age rapidly. The women of Australia are not her finest product.

So much for Sydney-siders ! But Melbourne's ladies fared no better :

The women, alas ! are intolerable, untrained minds, over-dressed bodies, and lacking in the charm of physical vigour or grace of manner ... uncommonly inferior to the men – vapid in talk without public spirit or intellectual sympathies.†

* Boyd, R., *Australia's Home*, Melbourne University Press, 1952, p. ii.
† *The Webbs' Australian Diary, 1898*, pp. 23, 32, 49, 71, 87.

It would have been interesting to eavesdrop on the ladies' comments on Beatrice, after she left the room.

Daily life in the smaller towns was monotonous. According to one French visitor, eating and drinking were among the most important pastimes : 'At seven a.m. a cup of tea with milk. At half-past eight, a dish of cold meat, a cutlet or a steak, eggs and bacon and tea. At eleven a.m. beer and biscuits. At one p.m. they have lunch (with more tea). Tea again at three p.m. Dinner (and tea) at six. Bread and cheese at nine or ten at night.' No doubt this timetable was more flexible in the capital cities, where at least there was no lack of entertainment. The same observer states that 'Australians have a mania for enjoyment.' He was invited to the Governor's Ball in Melbourne, where he describes the smiling faces, the gusto of the dancing and the non-stop hubbub of conversation, presumably about horses, for betting on horse-races was 'an obsession, a compulsion ; the whole population goes in for it.' It was at the races that Beatrice Webb saw the ladies in outfits that irritated her so much. The men could be seen, even at 40°C in the shade, wearing black coats and top hats. Apart from racing, the other favourite sports were cricket, rowing and football.

Both Melbourne and Sydney could boast famous theatres – in 1891 even Sarah Bernhardt condescended to appear in them. The *Sydney Morning Herald* saw her visit as a sign that in foreign parts people were becoming aware of the fact that Australia had an intellectual life. The divine Sarah was welcomed by a considerable crowd as 'the hotel servants endeavoured to secure in safety Mme. Bernhardt's hundred and one parcels, wraps, and animals and cages'.[*] To tumultuous receptions, she gave 28 performances in Melbourne, 7 in Adelaide and 32 in Sydney.

One may be sure that there was no performance on a Sunday. For on the Lord's Day there were no games or races, and not a theatre was open. Even the public transport stopped running ; there were not even any trains. The only thing to do was to go for a walk.

Australian intellectual life at this period was dominated by three main streams. One of these was strongly tinged with nostalgia, the second was nourished by hope as well as by memory, and the third saw itself as looking to the future.

---

[*] Quoted in Birch, A. & Macmillan, D.S., *The Sydney Scene 1788–1960*, Melbourne University Press, 1962, p. 215.

The bush mystique still had its adherents. It may even be that the further the country grew away from its origins, the more numerous these adherents became. Compared with the monotonous collective life that industrialized society imposed on people, the figure of the bushman took on heroic dimensions. He was seen as a self-reliant individualist, sticking to his mate through thick and thin. Men like Henry Lawson and 'Banjo' Paterson popularized this myth in stories, poetry and songs that soon became classics. Francis Adams even said that the bushman figure was 'the one powerful and unique national type yet produced in the new land'.* The nostalgia for this legendary lifestyle was still strong enough in the tame, urbanized generations of the early twentieth century for Joseph Furphy and Bernard O'Dowd to define its specifically Australian virtues. The semi-factual, semi-fictional bush hero was said to be the origin of the 'larrikin', although this type can be seen to be a mere caricature of the model. The term 'larrikin' seems to have been coined about 1870 and quickly entered common Australian usage. Whether the larrikins were plain hooligans or possibly forerunners of the hippie phenomenon, their distinguishing feature was that they were in revolt against society.† Their hero was Ned Kelly. Always dressed in black, with huge black hats and high-heeled boots, they were the bane of respectable citizens' lives. Pessimists were given to seeing them as symptoms of decadence ; others held that they were the inheritors of the spirit of independence and adventure that had created the country.

Intellectuals, and readers of the *Bulletin*, might take a passionate interest in such talking-points, but to the great mass of Australians they meant little. What *was* important to them as an intellectual force, one based solidly on their own experience and vitalized by the future they believed in, was their common faith in democracy. Compared with this passion for 'constructing a new democracy' (as Vance Palmer calls it)‡, their religious faith and constitutional controversies seem of tepid interest. In any case, religious strife was a thing of the past. By the turn of the century there was very little

---

* Quoted by Ward, R., *The Australian Legend*, p. 238.

† Their opposite number was, of course, the wowser, the diehard defender of traditional puritan values.

‡ Palmer, V., *The Legend of the Nineties*, Melbourne University Press, 1954, p. 17.

sectarian exclusiveness. There were still a handful of Protestant fanatics, but the echoes woken by their cry of 'No popery!' were even weaker than in the U.S.A. Even the political arena gave this same impression of peacefulness, Beatrice Webb expressing surprise at the odd sort of tolerance which seemed to her typical of the Australian colonies. It was not tolerance, however, so much as equality which had become one of the local articles of faith. An indelible prejudice was now attached to the notion of an elite or an aristocracy. This may well be the reason why Australia has never managed to produce a truly conservative political party on the lines of the one which had such an intelligent contribution to make to the greatness of England. This universal praise of equality may also explain why real inequalities in wealth were tolerated with very little bad feeling. For it would be a great mistake to imagine that Australia in 1900 was anything like the Marxist vision of the classless society. There were, in fact, great wealth and abject poverty side by side. Although the proletarian and the knight were both subjects of Her Majesty, there was as marked a disparity between their situations as there was anywhere else in the world. However, this disparity was more readily accepted in Australia because, despite differences in ways of living, people at all points on the social scale shared the same awareness of their common humanity. And it was this, in fact, that formed the basis of the series of measures which were to put Australia in the forefront of social progress in the twentieth century (see Chapter 17).

The third vital strain in Australia's intellectual life at the turn of the century was nationalism. The slogan 'Australia for Australians' was dinned into people so much at the time and became so ingrained in the national consciousness that it reminds one of Maurras.* This strain had a double origin. Firstly, it developed in reaction against the snobbish Anglomania that was prevalent in tradition-bound squatters' circles, where it had become fashionable to decry anything Australian. It was said that when these upper-class Australians gave a dinner, their boast was that there was nothing 'colonial' on their table. 'Colonial' wine was acid ; 'colonial' beer was watery ;

* Charles Maurras (1868–1952), a brilliant, vituperative, right-wing nationalist ideologue and anti-democratic royalist, whose virulent patriotism did not exclude collaboration with his nation's enemy. He was sentenced to life imprisonment in 1945 (*translator's note*).

'colonial' cheese was rancid ; 'colonial' fruit was too soft ; 'colonial' servants were clumsy ; the 'colonial' sun was unhealthy and the 'colonial' skies were a comical travesty of those in the old country. For too many years, it was said, Australians had been taught that it would be a denial of their glorious British heritage and the system of English law they had inherited if Australian courts had Australian judges. But by the 1890s this was changing with the awakening of Australian patriotic feeling. Instead of running down local products, Australians began to take pride in them. At public dinners, for instance, an effort was being made to use only home-grown produce. And almost all top public positions (except in the railways and the armed services) were occupied by men who had either been born or brought up in Australia. This nationalist spirit was, however, still quite compatible with a lasting attachment to England. As one orator put it : 'Our love of England is still almost as strong as it was when Batman first stepped ashore at Hobson's Bay.'

The other origin of the 'Australia for the Australians' syndrome was perhaps more pragmatic. If Australia *was* to belong to Australians, then it went almost without saying that it must not belong to coloured people. One of the very first acts of the newly established Commonwealth in 1901 was to put into practice the principle of a 'White Australia'. The simplest of tactics sufficed : any would-be immigrant who could not write down, at the dictation of an immigration officer, fifty words in a European language, would be refused admittance to Australia. In theory this test was not used against Europeans ; in practice the aim was to restrict immigration almost exclusively to people from Great Britain. 'White Australia' was seen as good, but 'British Australia' was seen as even better.

In 1897 Pierre Leroy-Beaulieu said of Australia : 'This country is stagnating.' From the economic point of view, this was all too true. But the birth of Federation four years later was certain proof of political vitality. And beneath the surface appearances there were powerful forces at work which were soon to transform Australia into a new nation.

Chapter Seventeen

Experiments and expectations

The three parties – Labor's influence – 'socialism without doctrines' –
a succession of governments – Labor and Liberals sole eventual sur-
vivors – development of social reforms – compulsory arbitration system
– a 'fair and reasonable' wage – the 'New Protection' – old-age and
invalid pensions – the founding of a national bank – defence problems
– acceptance in principle of the concept of an Australian navy – com-
pulsory military service limited to national defence – economic expan-
sion – rapid agricultural development – slower progress in industry –
continuing urbanization – Canberra chosen as national capital

The short period between the establishment of Federation and the
outbreak of the Great War is characterized by a marked instability
in government, the growth of reforming social legislation and a
burgeoning desire for independence. These were thirteen years of
initial uncertainty and growing self-confidence.

Lord Hopetoun had been appointed as first Governor-General.
It was a worthy choice, Hopetoun having made a very favourable
impression during his six years as Governor of Victoria. And yet,
despite this valuable experience, his first official act was a blunder
which still puzzles students of the period. Having reached Melbourne on 15 December 1900, he took only four days to choose as
Australia's first Prime Minister William Lyne, Premier of New
South Wales. The trouble was that Lyne was widely known as one
of the most diehard opponents of the whole idea of federation. One
wonders whether Hopetoun was given bad advice. Or perhaps he
saw this as a way of honouring the oldest of the States. Whatever
the reason, it was a *faux pas* and the resulting furore is easy to
imagine, as one after another the most influential politicians refused
to work with Lyne. Hopetoun had to accept the inevitable (which he
did graciously) and Lyne tendered his resignation. Hopetoun's next

choice was Edmund Barton, whose part in the negotiations leading to Federation over the previous few years was well known. He managed to obtain the support of the Premiers of the other five colonies, notably that of Deakin who was to be unstinting in his assistance to the new Prime Minister.

The new Cabinet was called 'a team of captains'.* But if they were captains, they were not only at odds with one another but also far from commanding unanimous support, as was shown by the first elections for the House of Representatives and the Senate in the spring of 1901, when more than half of the voters did not bother to go to the polls. Admittedly, there was nothing very exciting in the issues before them. The two major parties were still supposed to differ over the relative merits of protectionism as against free trade. Supporters of protection saw themselves as protecting Australia's young and vulnerable industries from foreign competition and could thus count on the support of employers and employees alike. To add to their appeal, they called themselves 'Liberals'. This was the group whose leader was Barton. Their opponents, the free-traders, styling themselves rather daringly 'Conservatives', had the support of wool-merchants, businessmen and financiers. Reid was their chosen leader, as colourful a character as ever, if somewhat lacking in the prestige that wins elections. At the declaration of the polls, the voters were seen to be of two minds, the Liberals having thirty-four seats in the Representatives to the Conservatives' twenty-five ; while in the Senate the latter group had won seventeen as against the Liberals' eleven. Between them, therefore, these two groups had won only fifty-nine of the seventy-five seats in the House of Representatives, and twenty-eight of the thirty-six Senate seats. Both Liberals and Conservatives were thus in need of the support of Labor which, with sixteen seats in the House of Representatives and eight in the Senate, could congratulate itself on having made a very promising start in Federal politics.

The reasons for this success by Labor have been clearly stated by Deakin. A year after the first elections he wrote :

The Labour Party dominates Australian politics ... Its influence is everywhere ... What makes [the workers'] authority paramount is that they alone have a political creed which inspires a religious fervour in its

---

* Quoted by Fitzhardinge, L.F., *William Morris Hughes*, vol. I, Angus & Robertson, Sydney, 1964, p. 123.

devotees, while their loyalty and discipline are exemplary ... The lax, timid, divided, and spiritless operations of the orthodox 'parties' make them an easy prey to this phalanx of earnest and dauntless propagandists.*

Two years later he added :

The secret of the Labour representatives' strength is to be found in the almost religious fervour, often fired to fanaticism, pervading their ranks, making doubt of their doctrine a sinful infidelity and its contradiction unpardonable heresy ... The Labour platform pictures of a vague and vast social regeneration ... are often made of humanitarian hues ... What is against the Labour section ? Apparently everything except faith and unity. Numbers, knowledge, ability, and wealth are all opposed to its domination ... The unfortunate thing is that these are not united ... The prosperous prefer their pleasures, and what are considered the middle class have their business.†

Some years later another Liberal had hard words to add to Deakin's diagnoses, saying that Liberals managed to agree with each other only by eliminating anything that could possibly offend the sensibilities of anyone. In the dish that they offered the electorate, he said, there were no bones, only a sort of pap fit for babies and invalids, which could not appeal to even the most delicate appetites.

This new Labor Party which provoked such embittered heart-searching in its opponents had made its appearance in 1891 in New South Wales and in the other colonies shortly afterwards (see pages 283–4). At Federation the party achieved a national stature. In its early days Labor had stuck to generalities. There is a revealing article which was published in one of its organs, the *Worker*, just before the 1901 elections, dealing with 'democracy', but in such vague terms that it would have been difficult for anyone to disagree with it. However, the party learned quickly, and by the time it had won nine Representatives seats and six Senate seats at the 1903 elections, what Labor stood for had become clearer. Its platform had nine main planks : (1) the maintenance of the White Australia policy ; (2) the nationalization of monopolies ; (3) old-age pensions ; (4) a referendum on import tariffs ; (5) a progressive tax on appreciation of land values ; (6) restriction of public borrowing ; (7) navigation laws ; (8) the principle of the Citizen Defence Force ; and (9)

* Deakin, A., *Federated Australia*, Melbourne University Press, 1968, p. 89.
† *ibid*., p. 137.

alterations to the arbitration system. There was nothing very diabolical about any of this, of course, but at the time it caused an uproar. The bogyman of 'socialism' was trotted out by Labor's opponents. W.A. Holman* took the opportunity to clarify his colleagues' position, saying that if Labor's platform was socialism, then Labor was certainly socialist, but that if socialism meant anything else then Labor was not socialist.

Whether Holman achieved his stated aim of clarification is unclear. Certainly a European socialist like, say, Jean Jaurès could well have been very surprised to be put in the same category as his comrades in the southern hemisphere. The fact is that they had, so to speak, Australianized the European socialist theories. The existing Australian social system was called 'socialism without doctrines' by a Frenchman in a book published in 1901† – meaning that, like Monsieur Jourdain with his prose,‡ Australia had had socialism for years without realizing it. However another opinion seems preferable, that of an acute French consul who spoke from twelve years' experience of life in Sydney :

Their socialism is not without doctrines . . . but it is without bombast . . . It is exclusive, preferring to be free of outside influences and to try its social experiment in its own way . . . Its leaders see themselves as the people's men of affairs.

There is always something rash about summing up in a few adjectives a complex movement of ideas. Despite the risk of being thought presumptuous, if one wished to clarify Labor policies of seventy years ago, one could do them fair justice by saying they were essentially pragmatic. H.B. Higgins said in his down-to-earth manner that tomorrow's breakfast was more important than a golden age in some undefined future, a sentiment that was very close to the philosophy of W.M. Hughes. Hughes said that modern socialism must be carefully distinguished from Utopian socialism or communism :

As I understand it, it is neither more nor less than the substitution of

---

* Already famous for his opposition to Australian involvement in the Boer War.

† See Métin, A., *Le Socialisme sans Doctrines*, Alcan, Paris, 1901.

‡ A character in Moliere's comedy *Le Bourgeois Gentilhomme* (1670), who was flabbergasted to discover that he had been speaking prose for forty years without realizing it (*translator's note*).

national co-operation for the present competitive system, in the industrial sphere. Under Socialism the State would own and control the means of production, distribution and exchange. Private property in all other forms of wealth would remain, and other institutions, social and political, would not be affected by the change. Socialism thus involves an economic change, but not necessarily a political or social one.*

In London, Hughes (who was to be an eminent statesman during the coming war) met Bernard Shaw, Ramsay Macdonald and H.G. Wells. He wrote of them later, ' They were men of parts – Shaw and Wells among the greatest in our age – but I should be very sorry to go into a strike with any of them – or to entrust the govt. of Britain to them.'†

The important thing was to keep one's feet on the ground and not get lost in the clouds. One notices a similar pragmatism in King O'Malley (although he was to have the vision to promote the idea of the Commonwealth Bank, the first state bank of the Federation), who stoutly declared his belief in state-aided private enterprise. He saw himself as Australia's Hamilton (whom he thought the greatest financier ever) and wanted the proposed Commonwealth Bank to be out of the control of politicians, and preferably to be run by a despotic Scotsman, because, he believed, the Scots were the only people in the world who could make money without having any to begin with.

One must also be clear about the ultimate objective of Australian socialism. Whether 'without doctrines' or 'without bombast', it did not aim at the overthrow of capitalist society. It believed in doing things slowly and gradually. 'Australian socialism is patient and persevering' was a comment in 1906 in the Paris periodical *Revue des Deux Mondes*, which looked on the Australian experiment as significant enough to warrant three articles of about thirty pages each. And, of course, not for a moment would any member of the Labor Party have entertained the use of violence. One is struck by the gulf between the French revolutionaries of 1848 or the Paris *communards* of 1871 on their barricades, ready to die to the last man for an idea, and these petty bourgeois whose chief concern was to win material benefits by non-violent means. Lenin had harsh words for them :

---

* Quoted by Fitzhardinge, L.F., *op. cit.*, p. 208.
† *ibid.*, p. 193.

In Australia the Labour Party is purely representative of the *non-socialist* workers of the trade unions. The leaders of the Australian Labour Party are trade union officials, an element which is everywhere most moderate and 'capital-serving', and in Australia is altogether peaceful and purely liberal. *

Peaceableness and liberalism – how could any red-blooded socialist live down such damning epithets? But there is worse to come! Most of the members of the Labor Party, especially the Roman Catholics responding to the encyclical *Rerum novarum*, were in fact sincerely religious men. They were not attracted in the slightest by the international socialist movement and went on being loyal subjects of the British Crown. They were also among the most dedicated supporters of the White Australia policy. Not only that, but, so as to avoid having to share with anyone else the perquisites of their already high standard of living, they were in favour of ending immigration and putting up protective import tariffs.

Whether it deserves the name of 'socialism' or not, this home-grown political ideology was to play a determining role in Australian life between 1901 and 1914. Space makes it impossible to go into the political jockeyings of that period in any great depth. One notices an odd similarity between Australian politics at the time and those of the Third Republic in France. In the space of those thirteen years there were five general elections; only two Parliaments sat out their full term;† there were dissolved; and there were in all nine different governments. Here some detail is called for: there were only six Prime Ministers in that time, Deakin holding the job three times and Fisher, his Labor opposite number, also three times. Two of the Cabinets lasted for less than a year, one of them collapsing after only four months, the other after ten. Quite clearly, the Australian federal parliamentary system was going through its teething troubles. The debates in the two Houses were interminable ('a torrent of words', was one contemporary's opinion), and very often dealt with trivia. The only way some dignity could be preserved in these

* Quoted in Ebbels, R.N., *The Australian Labor Movement*, Cheshire – Lansdowne, Melbourne, 1965, p. 244.

† Laid down as three years by the Constitution. All seats in the Lower House come up for election simultaneously, as opposed to the Senate where only half the seats fall vacant every three years.

un-Westminsterish proceedings was by the Speaker exercising his authority. Absenteeism was rife and it was at times hard to scrape together a quorum. This may well have been an effect of the great comfort which parliamentarians enjoyed, for in 1905 the French consul-general in Sydney mentioned that M.P.s had at their disposal a reading-room, a bar, a billiards room, chess tables, a tennis court, a cricket pitch and a bowling green. This *dolce vita* was especially apparent on occasions when there were all-night sittings and the people's representatives tried to make themselves as comfortable as possible. The Speaker is actually said to have issued orders banning the use of cots in the House.

None the less the Parliaments of this period did put through a body of legislation of remarkable scope and variety. The business of Parliament was made significantly easier in 1910. Until then, none of the three parties had managed to win an absolute majority, and this had resulted in a series of short-lived governments of different persuasions. To begin with, from January 1901 to April 1904 there had been two Liberal ministries, supported by Labor ('Lib-Lab' was the nickname for this combination). A Labor administration had then lasted for several weeks before a Conservative Cabinet (thinking they might as well have a go too) took over for the next eleven months. In July 1905 the Lib-Labs were back, to stay in power for more than three years. Then Labor got another turn, for seven months, and after that it was Deakin's third and last term, from June 1909 to April 1910. This time Deakin had the support of the Conservative free-traders, the two non-Labor groups having united to form the Liberal Party.*

This game of parliamentary musical chairs came to an end with the elections of 1910. Two parties now faced each other. Labor was the sole force on the left, with forty-one of the seventy-five Representatives seats and twenty-two Senators out of a total of thirty-six. The opposition was the so-called Liberal party, which really meant conservative. The Labor Cabinet which took office in 1910 remained in government for the next three years. At the general election of 1913 the Liberals won a one-seat majority in the House of Representatives. The outbreak of war in August 1914 came just after the dissolution of Parliament on 30 July by the Governor-General, Sir Ronald Munro-Ferguson. At the election in 1914 Labor came back

---

* Deakin's erstwhile allies jeered him in the House as a Judas.

A Concise History of Australia

on to the government benches where it was to stay until 1917.

Among the Labor leaders there were many men of calibre. Almost to a man they had risen from beginnings as manual workers and, knowing from personal experience what industrial existence was like, they did not go in for highfalutin phrases. J.C. Watson, for one, who was Prime Minister for those few months in 1904, had begun life as a compositor. He has been described as 'full of tact and ... restrained by a streak of common-sense from advocating the principles of a revolutionary Socialism, for which various Labour platforms were loudly contending.'* Watson's poor health was to shorten his career. Andrew Fisher, for his part, was robust enough, and was Prime Minister three times. He had arrived from Scotland in 1885 at the age of twenty-three to work as a miner in Queensland. His intelligence got him a job as a trade union official and he was later elected to the Queensland Legislative Assembly. He came into the first House of Representatives in 1901. He was known for his willpower, moderation and dignity, although he was not without a touch of craftiness. His opinions were expressed with palpable sincerity in a strong, even voice that people found pleasant to listen to, the Scottish accent that he never lost lending colour to his speech. William Holman was another Labor stalwart who had only been in the country ten years or so at the time of Federation. He had been a cabinet-maker by trade, had risen rapidly in the Labour movement and spread the good word from town to town. His rise to the Premiership of New South Wales was interrupted on one occasion when, after the failure of a newspaper that he was running, he was imprisoned (wrongfully, as it appears) for two months.

Last, but far from least, W.M. Hughes, the most outstanding of them all. He had come out from Wales, where he had been a school-master, landing in Brisbane in 1884 at the age of twenty-two. Declining to continue in the profession for which he had been trained, he became a stonebreaker, a boundary-rider, a drover and even went to sea as a deckhand or cook on a coastal vessel. He settled in Sydney where he worked as a pantryman, acted in Shakespeare, mended umbrellas and opened a bookshop. It was at Hughes' bookshop that the trade union leaders would gather. His

* Turner, H.G., *The First Decade of the Australian Commonwealth*, Mason, Firth & McCutcheon, Melbourne, 1911, p. 85.

284

moment came with the big strikes of the early nineties, although he came to believe more and more that political action would be more effective than trade unionism. And when he did embark on a political career, it was to be a highly successful one. Having been elected to the first national Parliament in 1901, he was Minister for External Affairs by 1904 and twice held the portfolio of Attorney-General (in 1908 and 1910) before becoming Prime Minister in 1915. He was the sort of man about whom legends are created. His undersized, almost dwarfish frame made him a perfect subject for political cartoonists, but he had a devastating capacity for the cut-and-thrust of political controversy, as well as a phenomenal appetite for activity. A dyed-in-the-wool autocrat with a decidedly prickly personality, he was bound to make his mark. And make it he did, as will be seen, during the war and later at the Versailles Conference.

Government instability is often taken to be a sign of a lack of political continuity. The example of France in the nineteenth and twentieth centuries should show how faulty such reasoning is. For France tried one sort of political system after another and the list of her successive governments would be endless. For all that, France still managed to achieve great things which cannot be put down to mere chance. As has often been pointed out, French administrative structures were resilient enough to allow the nation to pull through the succession of crises. What must be added, though, is that these structures served more as a brake on change than as an accelerator of it. The fact is that when a country reaches a certain level of maturity and cohesion, the deficiencies of government are made up for by the national instinct, which is essentially a creative force. Seventy-five years ago, Australia was of course very young and it would be pointless to compare her with a much older country. Even so, Australia had by then reached a stage in her development where, having acquired a certain consistency of political life, the country at large could remain unaffected by spasms at the centre of government. What Australia really wanted in 1900 was to become a model of egalitarian democracy and to reconcile her new responsibility for her own actions with her old ties of loyalty to the mother country. These two constant objectives can be glimpsed through the gradual movement towards a more humane society and through the first attempts at an Australian foreign policy. In these two respects, it was of little importance whether the governments were Liberal,

Labor or Lib-Lab. Only the individuals were different; the aims were the same.

The early Federal Parliaments, working with all the zeal of novices, got through very heavy programmes of legislation. Here there is only room to mention the most important measures. The eight-hour day was already half a century old; to begin with, it had only been observed in some trades, but had gradually spread to all of them. In 1885 Victoria had also been the first to introduce strict regulations on industrial labour. The other colonies had followed suit, albeit some of them with no great eagerness. By 1901 this attitude to industry and labour was so advanced that Métin (the coiner of the phrase about 'socialism without doctrines') could say: 'Australia has not gone in much for social philosophizing, but in concrete achievements has gone much, much farther than any other country.'*

This movement was to be speeded up after the advent of Federation. In 1904 the principle of compulsory arbitration was established, meaning that neither party to an industrial dispute could proceed to use the lockout or strike action until a judge of the Commonwealth Court of Conciliation and Arbitration had pronounced on the point at issue. The only restriction was that, under the Constitution, these provisions could only apply to industrial disputes involving workers in more than one State.† If the parties to a dispute wished, the president of the Court could be assisted by two assessors, one representing the employers and the other the employees. The first incumbent of the new position of president was Henry Higgins, who had been Attorney-General in the first Labor ministry (although not a member of any party). Higgins had had the rare courage and single-mindedness to state publicly that the Boer War was neither necessary nor just. He was a most conscientious judge, exercising his functions with uncommon authoritativeness.‡ He saw the arbitration system as the most effective

---

* Métin, A., *op. cit.*, p. 256.

† See page 264. The new arbitration provisions did not prevent local stoppages, as can be seen from the reports from the French consul-general in Sydney, for example, on 14 April 1908: 'For the last three years, not a month, not a week has passed without talk of strikes'; or on 30 April 1913: 'Since last year, strikes, which were supposed to diminish, have actually increased in number, and disputes between employers and workers are more heated than ever.'

means of promoting industrial and social harmony. The title of his book, *A New Province for Law and Order*, is significant, the 'new province' being 'that of the relations between employers and employees'.*

Higgins had an early opportunity to state his ideas. He had hardly been appointed in 1906 when he had the task of pronouncing on an issue that had been in the air for ten years at least: the concept of the 'fair and reasonable' wage. In 1896 Victoria had adopted the principle that no wages should fall below those paid by 'respectable employers' – but the meaning of 'respectable' had been left undefined. A Victorian judge had attempted to define it by saying that every worker, however menial, should be paid enough to be able to lead a worthy life, to marry, have children and keep his family in a basic minimum of comfort. But once again, what a 'basic minimum' was, was not spelled out.

Higgins was not the sort of man to settle for these approximations. His judgement in the Sunshine Harvester case in 1907 was a milestone. He took as his point of departure the idea that a fair and reasonable wage would be one which would satisfy 'the normal needs of the average employee, regarded as a human being living in a civilized community'.† He declared that it was out of the question to play with human life as though it were a ball and, on a more practical note, that no fair and reasonable wage would ever be arrived at through bargaining. He solved the problem of how to define that elusive concept of fairness by reckoning up the cost of housing and essential commodities for a theoretical family of married couple plus three children, adding in something extra for entertainment and leisure, and working it all out at a figure of seven shillings a day as the minimum wage. Oddly enough, the same minimum was to apply to unmarried workers as to workers without children, an anomaly that Higgins defended by saying that, like Walt Whitman, he was only concerned with the 'divine average'.‡

* Higgins, H.B., *A New Province for Law and Order*, W.E.A., Sydney, 1922, p. 1.
† *ibid.*, p. 3.
‡ *ibid.*, p. 6.

‡ He could boast that, until 1916, none of his judgments was ever contested and that, until 1920, he heard all cases by himself without the assistance of assessors.

This seven shillings a day was to be 'the basic wage' – 'sufficient for the essentials of human existence'.* He added that the employer 'need not concern himself with his employee's domestic affairs'. He ruled that this basic wage was to apply only to unskilled workers and that the existing difference between them and skilled workers should be maintained. This difference Higgins fixed at three shillings. After which, presumably, he considered the problem settled once for all. Happy days, when money was so stable that one could build such illusions on it.

It has been calculated that these decisions, which were revolutionary in their day, amounted to a 25 per cent rise in wages. Which means, of course, that a great many businesses had difficulty in abiding by them. This in turn gave a new fillip to protectionism. In 1902 Parliament had set up the first import tariffs, which had to be stiff, since the Federal government drew all of its fiscal resources from customs duties and indirect taxation.† The government had also begun subsidizing certain enterprises that it wished to protect, such as the wool industry, and others whose development it wished to encourage, such as the iron and steel industry. In 1908 it went further. Not only were tariffs increased, but a novel concept of 'New Protection' emerged. To Deakin,

Old Protection was protection of the local manufacturer by means of tariffs on imported goods. 'New Protection' sought to impose upon employers who were aided by tariffs a legal obligation to provide 'fair and reasonable' wages and working conditions for their employees.‡

In practice it meant that indirect taxation concessions would be granted to industries in which wage levels were judged by the Court to be 'fair and reasonable'.

The High Court soon declared that this legislation was unconstitutional, on the grounds that the Federal fiscal machinery could not be used for such a purpose. From then on, most Australians began to feel that their country was going rather too hastily along

---

* Higgins, H.B., *op. cit.* He stuck to his guns in 1908 by refusing the powerful B.H.P. Company's request for a reduction in wages from seven to six shillings a day.

† As well as which, three quarters of its revenue had to be distributed to the States.

‡ La Nauze, J.A., *Alfred Deakin*, vol. II, p. 410.

the road to state control of the economy. Between 1910 and 1913, three successive referendums rejected proposed amendments to the Constitution which would have had the effect of increasing the national government's powers in the field of social legislation.* This slowed the Federal government's progress but did not stop it. In 1908 the principle of the right to old-age and invalid pensions was established. In 1910 the Land Tax Act was passed, providing for taxation on a sliding scale of estates over £5,000 and the Commonwealth Bank was established, with the object of providing competition for the private banks. Finally, in 1912, Parliament introduced a system of child endowment, £5 being the sum to be paid on the birth of each child.

All this had been brought about without bloodshed, in the Australian way.

It will be remembered how apprehensively Australians had reacted to conflicts on the other side of the world (see page 242). Up to the turn of the century, of course, the echoes of European troubles had been weak and muffled by the time they reached the Antipodes. When the newly founded Federation set up the first Department of External Affairs, it was more a gesture of independence† than a genuine effort to end the country's isolation from the rest of the world. At the beginning of 1901, the French consul-general in Sydney wrote : ' It is curious how little importance is attached to the outside world by political men here.' The shield which made Australia feel protected was still the British fleet. But, as the urge to speak for themselves grew in Australians, so too it became imperative that they should have their own means of defence. An opportunity to raise this issue came in 1902, during one of those colonial conferences in London at which the British enjoyed treating their erstwhile dependencies with politeness and a touch of condescension. Barton was there for Australia, cutting rather a small figure beside the Canadian Prime Minister, Laurier, who was being made much of. However, Barton made a point of urging the creation of an Australian navy, a suggestion which found no favour in the

---

* The abstention rates in these referendums were, respectively, 38 per cent, 48 per cent and 26 per cent.

† It is significant that the first two Prime Ministers, Barton and Deakin, both took on this portfolio.

eyes of Chamberlain, convinced as he was that the force of History (and probably the grace of God, too) made England the natural protector of the Empire. Barton did not press the point and accepted an arrangement under which the Admiralty was to station a permanent squadron in the western Pacific. Great Britain was to bear half the costs of this arrangement, the rest being met by Australia (at the rate of five twelfths of the total) and by New Zealand (at the rate of one twelfth).

This was by its nature only a temporary solution, and events were soon to demonstrate the inadequacy of it. Over the next three years the whole balance of naval power underwent a far-reaching change. In the same year as the London colonial conference, an Anglo-Japanese alliance had been signed, an event which roused mixed feelings in Australians. The pessimistic view was that Great Britain was becoming more and more concerned with purely European problems and trying to get rid of some of its east-of-Suez obligations. But a more optimistic interpretation was that it amounted to a guarantee of safety for Australia. Certainly, anti-Russian feeling was still so strong in the country that most Australians saw the Japanese defeat of Russia in 1905 as a favourable outcome of the war.

The Russo-Japanese war was the first conflict of any importance to have taken place in Australia's half of the world. The Commonwealth's reaction to the hostilities was to urge more strongly than before the need for Australia to have its own fleet. In 1907 another Imperial Conference was held in London at which Australia was represented by Deakin. He outshone the other delegates. Professor La Nauze speaks of the 'daily round of dinners, speeches, and receptions, the pomp and circumstance of ceremonies in historic settings, the weekends at great houses ... For six weeks Deakin spent no more than four or five hours in bed each night.'* In Britain the Liberal party had just formed a government. Now that Chamberlain was no longer in command in London, none of the time that previous conferences had wasted was spent on his obsessive concern for the setting up of an Imperial customs union. Political problems were now of more importance than economic ones. An Imperial General Staff was created, but after having accepted this concession to Empire unity, the Dominions made sure that their affairs would henceforth be looked after by a special department in the Colonial

* La Nauze, J.A., *op. cit.*, vol. II, pp. 496, 510.

Office. The other important outcome was the agreement that Australia could now have her own way.

This step towards independence was soon to be followed by a symbolic gesture. In 1908, the Federal government on its own initiative invited the American fleet to visit Sydney. This may have been an attempt to impress the Japanese or even an indication to the British that, if need be, Australia might one day choose new friends. At all events, the visit was a resounding success. Australia had never seen such a display of naval power – a convoy of sixteen warships, 'silent and stately', steaming into one of the most magnificent anchorages in the world. The city was lit up and gay with bunting and fireworks displays ; the ships' officers and men were wined and dined. Deakin comments that no terms would be 'too glowing to express the indefinite but very positive exultation called forth by the presence of our kindred '.* London, however, was somewhat less than enthusiastic about the visit. Australia tried to make amends for its indiscretion by asking for a British fleet to visit Sydney immediately. But the Colonial Office frowned on the idea, saying that if such a suggestion was really desirable, it should have been thought of before the invitation was issued to the Americans. However, London did think it would be a good thing if a Japanese squadron showed its flag in Australian waters.

This tiff was of no consequence. Australia had already made its choice between its distant cousins from across the Pacific and its mother country, as was to be seen when the dreadnought scare blew up in 1909. This was when Germany's plans for naval expansion looked like jeopardizing British supremacy at sea. London, in some apprehension, decided to lay down immediately eight new battle-ships, and Australia was glad to be able to make a present of one dreadnought to the home country. It was obvious that war was becoming more of a possibility. That same year, the Federal government introduced compulsory military training, but with the strict stipulation that it was solely for service inside Australia. Kitchener came out to inspect the land forces, which do not seem to have impressed him. He was reputedly a man of few words, but Deakin found him 'unexpectedly talkative and even gossipy'.† However, the French consul-general says that his attitude 'was a

---

* Deakin, A., *op. cit.*, p. 240.

† La Nauze, J.A., *op. cit.*, p. 586.

clear disappointment to the people who had welcomed him so warmly'.

The last pre-war Imperial Conference was held in London in the summer of 1911. Australia, Canada and South Africa were represented by Fisher, Laurier and Botha respectively. The festivities were even more lavish than usual, coinciding as they did with the coronation of George V. The three Dominions vied with each other in displays of loyalty, but Laurier was careful to spell out their position, stressing his interpretation of an Imperial unity founded on local autonomy. As Sir Keith Hancock has said: 'Imperial patriotism became an extension of ... nationalism.'* For the first time Downing Street decided to reveal to the leaders of the Dominions some of Great Britain's political secrets, a job that fell to the Foreign Secretary, Sir Edward Grey. Grey's overseas colleagues were flattered by this, but also disturbed by what he had to tell them about the situation in Europe. When Fisher got back to Australia, he was more than ever convinced of the urgency of finding a solution to the problem of national defence.

Australia had come a long way in thirteen brief years. From a position of total military unpreparedness in 1901, the country had by 1914 a nucleus of military forces which would enable it to play an active combat role at short notice.

The thirteen-year period had also proved valuable in the economic field. Federation had happened at a time of great difficulty, when the aftermath of the depression of the 1890s looked like lasting for ever. Then, almost as soon as it had come into being, the Commonwealth had had to meet threats of secession, first from Queensland, which had taken umbrage at the cutting off of its 'kanaka' labour supply, and then from Western Australia, which was upset at the delays in building the promised transcontinental railway link. Such impulses were quieted by the economic recovery which showed its first signs in 1905 and rapidly got under way. The wool industry responded to a rise in world prices and government assistance by making good progress: the seventy-two million sheep giving 247 million kilograms of wool in 1901 had grown to ninety-three million sheep and a wool clip of 330 million kilos ten years later. Industry took longer to recover. Apart from B.H.P., which

* Hancock, W.K., *Australia*, p. 51.

was already a giant, industrial development was confined to medium-sized enterprises. There were, however, a great many more of these, employing a much greater workforce than before. At the turn of the century, in Victoria and New South Wales respectively, there were 3,249 and 3,050 of these medium-sized manufacturing companies, employing 66,500 and 66,108 people. By about 1910, these figures had risen to 5,216 and 5,039 firms, employing 117,900 and 108,708 workers. The population had also begun to grow again, partly under the stimulus of a new influx of immigrants. Between 1911 and 1914 there were 207,000 new arrivals, and by the outbreak of the war the population of Australia had risen to 4.94 million, which represented an increase of a million over the figure for 1900. Nearly three quarters of this population figure was accounted for by Victoria and New South Wales. In the whole of the vast Northern Territory, ceded to the Federal government by South Australia in 1910, there were only one thousand-odd inhabitants. Not only was the population of the country increasing, it was also becoming more homogeneous, with little more than three per cent being of non-British stock. The cities continued to be powerful centres of attraction, their share of the total population being increased by 4 per cent. In addition the nation now had, at least on paper, a capital city, as the site of Canberra had been chosen in 1911 after long and involved discussions of the question.

Australia had come through a period of rapid change, but by 1914 the country was itself again, stable, untroubled and quite unaware that the time had now come for its young men, all unprepared as they seemed to be, to show their mettle.

Chapter Eighteen
The First World War

*Australia's total support for Great Britain – flood of volunteers – first
Australian troops arrive in Egypt – Anzacs land in the Dardanelles –
fierce fighting and evacuation – Palestine campaign and occupation of
Jerusalem, Damascus and Aleppo – Turkish capitulation – the
Somme – Ypres – recruitment crisis – –conscription rejected at two
referendums – Villers-Bretonneux – Monash commands Australian
forces – Anzac participation in the final offensive – Australians as
soldiers – the peace conference – Hughes and Clemenceau – mandates
and reparations – Versailles Treaty signing – implications of victory
for Australia*

Even before Great Britain declared war on Germany on 4 August
1914, Australia had already made a fervent pledge of assistance. On
31 July Fisher, the then leader of the opposition,* had declared in
a famous speech at Colac that Australia would stand beside the
mother-country and 'defend her to our last man and our last
shilling'.† Three days later the Prime Minister, Cook, specified the
terms of Australia's contribution. Her naval forces amounted to one
battleship, six cruisers, six destroyers, two submarines and one
torpedo-boat. These vessels were put at the disposal of the Admiralty.‡ Cook also decided to send over an expeditionary force of

* He became Prime Minister on 17 September, after Labor's success at the
general election.

† Quoted by Robson, L.L., *Australia and the Great War 1914–1918*, Macmillan,
Melbourne, 1969, p. 31.

‡ Churchill would have been glad to transfer the ships to the defence of Great
Britain herself, maintaining that two or three Australian or New Zealand battle-
ships being brought to bear in the decisive theatre of operations could tip the
scales and make victory not only certain but also total; whereas the same ships

20,000 men. This force was to be composed entirely of volunteers, since conscripts could not be sent to fight overseas. Recruiting was no problem ; nor was there any difficulty in finding enough officers, as many of those who had fought in the Boer War re-enlisted. The first contingent, including troops from New Zealand, sailed from Albany on 1 November, in a convoy that was escorted by ships from the Australian, British and Japanese navies. A German raider, the *Emden*, was known to be lurking somewhere in the Indian Ocean. Eight days out, off the Cocos Islands, she turned up and the Australian cruiser *Sydney* was given the honour of engaging her. After a brief duel, *Emden* was sunk and her crew taken prisoner. This battle honour has been especially remembered since it was almost the only one that fell to the Australian ships. For the rest of the war they were to be mainly on patrol and escort duty, a role which brought them more danger than glory.

This was not to be the case with the land forces. The destination of the expeditionary force was changed twice. Originally, they had been bound for South Africa where there had been a mutiny among Boer officers. But the crisis there having been dealt with, the ships set course for England. Then it was realized that there were no facilities in England able to cope with these extra troops. And so they were to be landed in Egypt, where they would be well placed to take part in an eastern Mediterranean offensive that was already being mooted.

On 3 December, after thirty-two days at sea, the Australians and New Zealanders (already being called Anzacs, after the initials of the Australian and New Zealand Army Corps), set up camp in the desert outside Cairo. The pyramids and the Egyptians were not the only surprises in store for them. Tall and well-built as they mostly were, they found their British comrades-in-arms quite undersized. They also discovered that the language they spoke was not the only link between them, for it came home to them that they all belonged to the same Empire and this was a source of shared pride. The Anzacs got on well with their British commanding officer, General Birdwood. They began a period of intensive training : reveille at 5 a.m. and six hours of drill in the blazing sun and soft sand. Then,

---

left in Australian waters would be useless, Churchill said, after a British defeat in home waters. This attitude is similar to Churchill's refusal to throw the R.A.F. totally into the Battle of France in June 1940.

out of the blue, on April Fool's Day 1915, all leave was cancelled
and the order was given to stand by to embark.

For the past two months the British and French fleets had been
trying to force the Dardanelles.* This operation, a brainchild of
Winston Churchill, First Lord of the Admiralty, had come close to
succeeding. But the losses suffered in the last attack on 18 March
had been so severe that the British and French governments had
agreed to try another strategy. This involved the use of land troops.
And the Anzacs, already fit for action, were an obvious choice for
the force which was to do the job. This force, mostly British but with
a French contingent, and under the command of Sir Ian Hamilton,
had as its objective to open the way through to Constantinople.
The invading force gathered at the island of Lemnos.

The date was 25 April 1915. The scene has been described
hundreds of times. The main assault was supposed to be at the tip
of the peninsula, at Cape Helles, and was to be launched by the
British and French.† Another landing, by the Anzacs, twenty kilometres to the north near Gaba Tepe, was designed to distract the
enemy. The night was without stars as the landing craft moved
slowly shorewards. At about 4 a.m. the first troops landed. When
day broke, what they saw bore no resemblance to what they had
been told to expect – the craft had been pushed too far by the current
and had landed them a kilometre north of the chosen spot. They had
been told that they would have to establish a bridgehead on open
beaches surrounded by gentle slopes. But here they were up against
an almost sheer cliff, with stony soil and a thick cover of bushes.
The Turks poured down a withering fire. But there they were and
there they had to stay. Amid the general confusion, the self-reliance
of these amateur soldiers was a constant source of wonder. They
advanced, were halted and dug in, having gained about a kilometre
by the end of the first day. That was as far as they would ever go.

A month later the Turks counter-attacked. Their courage won
admiration from the Australians, who knew a thing or two about
courage themselves. But the outcome of this fighting was the same
as before, with a few metres of scrub being won or lost. The general

* The Allies had declared war on Turkey on 3 November 1914 because the Turks
had harboured two German warships, *Göben* and *Breslau*.

† The French general staff had unsuccessfully tried to persuade HQ that by
landing on the Asian side they would stand a much better chance.

staffs were impatient and in August they decided to try another, more daring plan. Going on the time-honoured strategy of attacking at the most difficult point, their idea was to surprise the Turks. The most dangerous position in this attack was given to the Anzacs, supported by some Indian troops. They landed on one of the northern beaches of Suvla Bay, an area littered with obstacles. Their mission was to capture heights of about 1,000 metres and thus cut the peninsula in two, while to the south British troops were to create a diversion. There followed four days of bloody and unavailing battles, from 6 to 10 August ; after ten days' rest they launched another assault which lasted a week, from 21 to 28 August. They gained some ground but it was quite without tactical advantage.

The autumn passed in a state of tense inactivity. The troops were by now suffering from disease, poor diet and the impossible conditions. Winter was coming on, that ghastly Turkish winter so well described by Pierre Loti, with its downpours and icy north winds. Germany had just overrun Serbia and thrown her army into the sea. Paris (which had looked fairly sceptically on the Dardanelles venture from the beginning) was urging that a thrust should be made up through the Balkans with a landing at Salonika. London eventually accepted that the Gallipoli venture had failed. But the British have an unparalleled capacity for taking pride in humiliation.* Kitchener, who had come to Gallipoli to inspect the situation for himself, ordered the evacuation, which was carried out in December 1915 in such an exemplary fashion that Sir Ian Hamilton's last order of the day reads as though it were in celebration of a victory.

For the Australians it had been neither a victory nor a defeat, but a severe ordeal which had brought out in them the most astonishing military qualities. A quarter of the Gallipoli casualties were Australians : 8,587 killed out of a total of 33,532 and 19,367 wounded out of 78,578. The experience had not only been the Australians' baptism of fire but had also given them an awareness of their own identity. It has been repeated many times that the first Anzac Day was the day on which Australia became a nation, an over-simplification of a complex evolution which had been happening for a long time. But certainly, at the Gallipoli bridgehead, the Anzacs had

---

* For example, their escape from Napoleon at Corunna in 1808 or the Dunkirk withdrawal in 1940.

shown their singular merit for the first time ; and this was to be confirmed. For one thing, everyone admired their physical appearance. John Masefield said they were 'the finest body of young men ever brought together in modern times' ;* Compton Mackenzie, who had also set eyes on them, went one better : 'There was not one of those glorious young men ... who might not himself have been Ajax, ... Hector or Achilles.' He mentions also 'their almost complete nudity, their tallness and majestic simplicity of line, their rose-brown flesh burnt by the sun'.† The most striking thing about them as an army was the atmosphere among them, strangely different from that of other armies. Birdwood speaks of their nonchalant manner, their astonishing virtuosity in the most colourful slang and their liking for wearing as few clothes as possible. The typical Anzac was called 'Wallaby Joe' and has been described as a bushman, tall, lean and strong, an excellent horseman and a crack shot. He usually let his beard grow until a discreet remark from an officer made him have a shave, but he would let it grow again straight away. He was a man of few words, and with an awesome capacity for beer. However, he rarely got drunk because he thought it was beneath him. Usually shy with the fair sex, in everything else the Anzac could be counted on to use his initiative.

What was to be done with 'Wallaby Joe' and his mates ? They were shipped back to Egypt, from where they were split up, the infantry being sent to France and the light cavalry to Palestine where a campaign was soon to be launched.

These latter-day crusaders were to be in the Holy Land for almost the next three years. In 1916 they withstood Turkish assaults, then went on to the offensive and by the end of the year had fought their way through to the border of Palestine. In 1917 Allenby was put in command. He was confronted by two Turkish armies holding an apparently impregnable fortified front about fifty kilometres long, between Gaza and Beersheba, to the south-west of the Dead Sea. Despite the risks a frontal assault was launched, which would have had no chance of succeeding if it had not been for an exploit as famous as (and much more successful than) the Charge of the Light

---

* Quoted by Ward, R., *The Australian Legend*, p. 212.

† Quoted by Serle, G., 'The Digger Tradition and Australian Nationalism', in *Meanjin*, vol. xxiv, 2, 1965, p. 152.

Brigade or the Reichshoffen charge.* On 31 October an Australian cavalry brigade was ordered to turn the enemy's east flank. Their charge has been described in the following fictionalized manner:

The men of the 4th and 12th Regiments mounted. They were learned in desert warfare ... In such a moment the minds and hearts of men rise to a condition in which mean things cannot touch them. A condition such as is known to attacking infantry when the moment comes to leave their trenches ... The pace, at first, was a smart trot, with an eye to the careful alignment of the ranks. ... They had no swords, but rode with rifle and fixed bayonet balanced across the thigh ; others with rifle slung across the back ; bare bayonet gripped in the hand ...

They had to cover more than three kilometres, over unknown ground that might contain any number of obstacles. At a range of 1,000 metres, the guns opened fire on them, soon to be followed by rifles and machine-guns : 'The troopers could now see the men who were firing at them ... They poured across the plain like a living flood, leaving a wide track littered with their fallen.' Fortunately, there was no barbed wire. Some of the Turks ran for their lives ; others fought hand-to-hand with Australians among the trenches. By nightfall, the battle was won :

The smell of water, cold and sweet, was released on the dusty air ... Throughout the night the streets of the town were loud with the clatter of hooves walking. Brigade after brigade, the horses were led in, light horse and gunner, to drink with slackened girths and bitless mouths at the wells of Beersheba.†

This daring manoeuvre caused a general Turkish withdrawal. On 8 December Jerusalem was occupied, and by the beginning of 1918 the Australians had reached Jericho and the valley of the Jordan. After months of endless waiting in the blazing heat and clouds of sand, the decisive attack was launched on 19 September against the Germans who had reinforced their Turkish allies. It was all over in a month, Damascus falling on 11 October. By the 23rd Allenby was

---

* At the Battle of Froeschwiller on 6 August 1870, under Marshal MacMahon, the French cavalry, though greatly outnumbered, made a pointless, heroic charge against the Prussians (who, it is said, cheered in admiration) (*translator's note*).

† Davison, F.D., *The Wells of Beersheba*, rev. ed., Angus & Robertson, Sydney, 1947, pp. 56–65.

at Aleppo, and on the 30th the Turks signed the Armistice. Hughes, unabashed by the overstatement, was to boast that Allenby had succeeded where Richard the Lionheart and Napoleon had failed. There had never, Hughes stated, been a greater victory in the history of the world than the Australians' victory in Palestine.

By the time their comrades had won in Palestine, the Anzacs in France had been out of the firing-line for almost four weeks. But they had paid dearly and had been through many a bloodbath over the previous two and a half years.

The Australian divisions had disembarked at Marseilles in mid-March 1916 and been sent immediately to the north of France. They took up position near Armentières, which though a relatively calm sector was a nasty place to be, where they fought in deep mud for negligible results. The epic battle for Verdun had begun a month before. So as to relieve the pressure on the French army, the Allied command had decided to launch an offensive in the Somme region, in which the British were to play the main part. This offensive was opened on 1 July. Its ups and downs need no retelling. The Australians fought between Albert and Bapaume from the end of July until September, leaving undying memories of themselves at places like Posières, Mouquet and Thiepval. Their casualties were horrifying – 23,000 in only a few weeks.

These casualty figures raised the question of reinforcements. Until the autumn of 1915 there had been no shortage of volunteers in Australia. Over a seven-month period 100,000 men had joined up, including a record figure of 36,000 in July in response to the Gallipoli tragedy. But then enthusiasm had waned. By the summer of 1916 only 6,000 to 7,000 recruits were signing up each month. Hughes (who had taken over as Prime Minister from Fisher in October 1915) had gone to London at the beginning of 1916 at the invitation of Asquith. Later Hughes was to write that the British government was 'a little at a loss to know what to do' with him. The government tried to play on his vanity by inviting him to sit in now and again on Cabinet meetings, Hughes noting with pride that he was given the best place. But such symbolic gestures were not enough for him ; he was not the sort of man to let himself be overlooked. Asquith he found unimpressive, 'temperamentally unfitted to lead the Empire in war. He looked upon action as a kind of disease to be avoided . . . He was perhaps too perfectly civilized.'* He was 'too much Cicero and too little Caesar' for Hughes.†

Hughes sided with another Welshman, Lloyd George (who was very impatient to succeed Asquith) and with those politicians who were in favour of more energetic action. He stumped up and down the country, making a great many speeches,* urging 'Wake up, England !' and ridiculing the old-style Liberals like Asquith and Grey. Hughes' pro-war ardour was further increased by a visit to the western front, where he was nicknamed 'The Little Digger' by the troops.

He returned to Australia on 31 July, about the same time as the news of the slaughter on the Somme reached there. The Imperial General Staff had told him that more than 16,000 new Australian recruits were now needed each month, a figure far in excess of the actual numbers volunteering. Hughes was now convinced that conscription was the only solution, an unpopular idea in the Labor Party which had always been hostile to it. However, *salus patriae suprema lex* ; and anyway 'The Little Digger' liked nothing better than a good fight. He was afraid that his proposal would be defeated in Parliament, at least in the Senate where Labor had a clear majority. Despite the unpromising precedents (see pages 288–9) he chose to try a referendum and threw himself into the campaign with his customary zest. At the last census, in 1915, there had been 600,000 men of conscriptable age, to persuade whom Hughes invoked Lincoln and Jaurès.† One of his supporters went further ; according to a report in the *Argus* on 23 October :

Yesterday morning, the vicar, the Rev. A. Law, preached a remarkable sermon. During the service four children were baptized, and Mr Law, in his sermon, referred to them as conscripts of the Church. He said he did not propose to tell the congregation how to vote on Saturday, but . . .

---

* These speeches brought on a bad case of professional compulsion in an Australian professor, who compared them with those of Demosthenes and even translated some of them into Greek. Not, one might think, the best way of publicizing them (see Garran, R.R., *op. cit.*, p. 228).

† Jean Jaurès (1859–1914), brilliant French socialist leader, assassinated on the outbreak of war on 31 July 1914, just after his party (opposed, *pace* Hughes, to an extension of conscription) had won the elections (*translator's note*).

---

* Hughes, W.M., *The Splendid Adventure*, Benn, 1929, p. 42.

† Garran, R.R., *Prosper the Commonwealth*, Angus & Robertson, Sydney, 1958, p. 227.

Divine love said : Are we to leave the world to destruction ? And Christ submitted Himself to the conscription of Heaven. It was a very real conscription.*

The opponents of conscription were not short of arguments either. They were motivated by complex feelings. Dr Mannix, the new Roman Catholic Coadjutor Bishop of Melbourne, became the mouthpiece of the Irish-Australians, whose latent anti-British feeling had just been roused by the repression of the Easter rising in Dublin. Dr Mannix was the darling of his fellow Catholics. According to Professor Alexander,

The tall, erect Daniel Mannix had, in fact, exactly the right combination of princely presence, dignity and softness of speech and a passionate love of Ireland to assure him the warmest welcome from the almost wholly Irish or Irish-descended Catholics who were to be his charge.†

He was also not a man to mince his words, maintaining that Australia had already acquitted herself better than could be expected, and that there was no reason why her youth should be sacrificed in a sordid ' trade war '.‡ Strong as Mannix's language and influence were, they did not persuade Victoria to vote ' No '. It was one of the three States (Tasmania and Western Australia being the other two) which voted ' Yes '. South Australia, Queensland and especially New South Wales (where the majority was very large) voted ' No '. The first conscription proposal was put on 28 October 1916 and was lost by 1,087,557 to 1,160,037. The abstention rate was lower than 18 per cent. Of the result, it has been said : ' It seems reasonable to suggest that the adverse vote was as much a negative protest against the authoritarian proclivities of the government as a considered rejection of the moral and national implications of compulsory overseas service.'§

The consequences of this move for Hughes came quickly – he and his supporters left the Labor Party.‖ For the next two months

* Robson, L.L., *op. cit.*, p. 72.

† Alexander, F., *Australia Since Federation*, Nelson, Melbourne, 1967, p. 299.

‡ See Smith, F.B., *The Conscription Plebiscites in Australia 1916–1917*, Victorian Historical Association, Melbourne, 1965, p. 10.

§ *ibid.*, p. 12.

‖ One witness said : 'We left the meeting before we were kicked out' (quoted by Garran, R.R., *op. cit.*, p. 231).

the Prime Minister remained in power with the support of his former opponents. Then, on 17 February 1917, definitively forsaking his old comrades, he took over the leadership of a National government, comprising Liberals as well as his former supporters, standing for democracy, victory and a White Australia.

The times were difficult. Over the next few months there was a succession of serious strikes. At one point almost 100,000 workers downed tools. And not only did the recruiting figures not improve, they actually declined. News from abroad was equally dispiriting. The only moment of hope had come on 6 April 1917 with the entry of the U.S.A., into the war, although it was realized that it would be some time before these new allies could make much impression on the fighting, and people feared that the Allies might not manage to hold out until then. In February the Germans had started their all-out submarine offensive. March saw the first Russian Revolution. In the following month the French offensive along the Chemin-des-Dames failed and was followed by mutiny in the French army. In October the Italians were crushed at Caporetto. In December the Bolsheviks withdrew from the coalition and signed a separate peace with the Germans.

The year 1917 was no doubt the most hopeless year of the war, and during it Australian blood had continued to be shed, round Arras in the spring, in the Ypres region between July and October. The efforts of the troops were heroic, but their gains minimal, and in three months they had suffered casualties of 38,000 dead and wounded.

There are many things one can say against Hughes, but not that he was lacking in determination. There was a general election in June that year, which gave him a majority in the House of Representatives of thirty-one and in the Senate of twelve. As a result of this triumph, he decided to try the dubious expedient of another referendum. This time the campaign was even more heated than the previous year. Dr Mannix called the Prime Minister 'a little Czar', in return for which Hughes threatened to have him deported.[*] Since the previous referendum, the 'Yes' case had been strengthened by the adoption of conscription in three allied countries: in New Zealand in November 1916; in the U.S.A. from the start of mo-

---

[*] Clark, C.M.H., *A Short History of Australia*, p. 197.

bilization ; and even more recently in Canada, despite the opposition of Laurier. Australia and South Africa were now the only countries who relied on volunteers, a similarity which did not impress the voters. The question put to the people on 20 December 1917 was ambiguously phrased : 'Are you in favour of the proposal of the Commonwealth Government for reinforcing the Australian Imperial Forces overseas ?' This time the result was even clearer than before : 1,181,457 voted 'No', against 1,015,159 who voted 'Yes', a majority of 186,588, which was 94,112 more than in 1916. At this second referendum only two States, Tasmania and Western Australia, had a majority in favour. Even the troops (who retained their voting rights at the front) did not give any overwhelming support to the proposal : 103,443 voted 'Yes' as against 93,794 who voted 'No'. The abstention rate was 18 per cent.

Despite this second defeat of the conscription proposal, the Anzacs' great year was 1918. The five Australian divisions were now grouped into a separate Army Corps. They also had the satisfaction of being put under the command of one of their compatriots, General Monash. John Monash, at 53, was an outstanding individual. He was the son of a Polish Jew who had come to Melbourne at the time of the gold strikes of the early 1850s, but who had gone into trade. He must have been very proud of this son of his who became a civil engineer. But engineering did not take up all of this young man's time. He was interested in many different activities, especially music, in which he achieved a high standard of competence. The military life attracted him. In the years before the war, the State of Victoria was establishing a militia, the Victorian Rifles. It was in the Militia Garrison Artillery, however, that Monash acquired his commission ; by the outbreak of hostilities he was already a brigade commander, while continuing with his profession as an engineer. He was thus still only a reserve officer when he sailed for Egypt. His rise to fame was rapid. By 1916 he was already a divisional commander, and when Birdwood was put in command of an army, in May 1918, the General Staff had no hesitation in entrusting to a 'civilian' the command of the Australian forces. Within a few months he had almost 200,000 men under him. The British military writer Liddell Hart said that if the war had lasted another year, he could quite easily have become Commander-in-Chief. * Lloyd

* Quoted by Palmer, V., *National Portraits*, p. 223.

George looked on him as 'the most resourceful general in the whole of the British Army' *

Perhaps the thing that accounts for such praise, and Monash's greatest feat, was that he managed to reduce the casualty rate among his troops at a time when they were enduring their harshest experiences of the whole war. He can be put alongside Marshal Pétain in his concern to save lives and the methodical way he set about planning every operation. And, like Pétain, he was rewarded by enjoying the total trust of the men under him. Not that his subordinates found him an easy man to deal with. Vance Palmer says that there was 'a touch of aloofness in his manner, a lack of either the breezy egalitarianism of the "Digger" officers or the graceful condescension of the English '.† The strictest discipline was what he demanded of everyone (he even advocated the introduction of the death penalty, which was unheard of in Australian military regulations) but, again like Petain, he believed that success depended on exact order. He likened the 'perfected modern battle plan' to

a score for an orchestral composition, where the various arms and units are the instruments, and the tasks they perform are their respective musical phrases. Every individual unit must make its entry precisely at the proper moment and play its phrase in the general harmony.

He believed that battles should be won 'before the barrage opens '.‡

Monash had ample opportunity to put his principles into practice. On 21 March 1918 the British Army, north and south of the Somme, was routed by a German offensive. Monash's divisions co-operated with the French reinforcements, which were hastily thrown in to protect the British retreat. Did these troops really save Amiens and Paris from falling to the Germans? Certainly, it has often been stated that they did. No doubt, if one comes from so far away to fight and die in a foreign country, one may be excused a touch of patriotic exaggeration. Be that as it may, the Anzacs lived up to their reputation. On 4 April they broke the German assault on Villers-Bretonneux, and after the Germans managed to take the town, the Anzacs recaptured it on 24 April in a night battle which

---

* Quoted by Hetherington, J., *John Monash*, Oxford University Press, Melbourne, 1970, p. 24.

† Palmer, V., *op. cit.*, p. 218.

‡ *ibid.*, pp. 220–21, 217.

has been called perhaps their finest achievement. By now, of course, the time of great decisions was nearing. From July onwards the Germans were in constant retreat, under ceaseless attack. Monash, as an uncompromising supporter of the offensive policy, appreciated to the full the grandiose strategy of Foch. The Australians took part in the attack along the Somme on 8 August – what Ludendorff was later to call Germany's blackest day in the whole war. They were delayed by the Hindenburg line, where the Germans hoped for a moment's respite. Then, with the help of two American divisions, the Anzacs broke through at the end of September, north of Saint-Quentin. By 5 October the Australian troops were exhausted; through lack of reinforcements* the brigades were reduced from four to three battalions. They were relieved from the front line, having taken proportionately twice as many prisoners as the rest of the British Army, and having captured twice as many guns. After the Armistice, the Australians were garrisoned for some months near Charleroi.

In all, 418,809 men had volunteered to fight. Of these, 330,000 actually saw active service on the western front or in Palestine, and 59,258 officers and men were killed. The relative force of such figures can only be seen in comparison with the rest of the British Empire:

Country	Losses as a percentage of fighting troops	Fighting troops as a percentage of population
Australia	64.8	11.2
New Zealand	58.6	6.8
Canada	49.7	8.9
U.K.	47.1	5.0
South Africa	13.6	2.0
India	9.1	0.4

The Anzac tag had by now become legendary. It meant, first and foremost, outstanding valour. Not that the Anzacs were the only

---

* Monthly recruiting figures had dropped below 5,000 in 1918.

force to fight with courage ; other élite corps in the other armies also had a fine record. But the fact remains that some of their features were so unique that they won themselves an incomparable reputation. Monash called them ' the flower of the youth of the continent '.* They were, he said, full of a sense of duty and comradeship, but at the same time they were inveterate, enterprising individualists, given to criticizing orders and accepting discipline only as a rational expedient. Monash also praises their great practicality, their capacity for picking up the use of new weapons overnight, and their unmatched ability to light a fire, cook a meal or build a shelter out of pieces of corrugated iron.†

Such men were the despair of British officers. They had no liking for saluting superiors, and saying ' Yes, sir ' to anyone came hard to them. It was well nigh impossible to recruit batmen or orderlies from them. In any case the officers ate with their men and shared the same food, at least in the line. Only a handful of these officers had been through Duntroon.‡ The rest had risen from the ranks and, once they were promoted, the usual arrangement was that they went back to their old units in command of their erstwhile comrades. None of them was ever actually elected by the troops, but they were all definitely subject to the tacit approval and disapproval of their men. A British general has seen clearly that one of the consequences of this sort of military tradition is that the Australian officer may be torn between the wish to execute an order properly and the hope of being well thought of by the men under his command. It can be seen that the spirit of egalitarianism that was so powerful in Australian civil life was an equally strong force among her military men.

Hughes had gone back to London for a conference of the Allies in July 1918. He arrived in Paris at the beginning of 1919 : in his party were the former Prime Minister Joseph Cook and the Commonwealth Solicitor-General, Robert Garran.

The French consul-general in Sydney had written in April 1917 :

In the earlier stages of the war, there was little sympathy for the French

---

* Monash, J., *The Australian Victories in France in 1918*, Hutchinson, London, 1920, p. 314.

† *ibid.*, p. 315.

‡ The Australian military college, just outside Canberra, had been established in 1911 at the suggestion of Kitchener.

cause among a great many Australians. Newspapers deliberately suppressed news of French successes and a regular reader would have had the impression that the British were the only ones actually doing anything.'

This was all changed by the battles at Verdun. By 1916 Hughes was speaking in glowing terms of how France was standing straight and firm, covered in glory amid the bones of her dead sons that littered her soil like seashells on the shore, and ready to fight to the last man.* Hughes had been to the front by that time. He had visited it again in 1918, and when he got back to Australia the following year he gave a moving account of his impressions in a speech to the House of Representatives, saying that it would be impossible to express the horrors of the war as the French had experienced it, but maintaining that the 'soul of France' had not been killed. Hughes described Foch as one of the greatest soldiers ever. Garran, too, when he arrived in Paris in January 1919, was greatly affected by what he saw: 'Almost every third woman in the street is in black. Poor France, she has suffered!'†

This meant that the Australian delegation to the peace conference was predisposed to support the French point of view. Hughes and Clemenceau took to each other straight away. The old 'Tiger' has left a vivid picture of the Australian. After having described with his sharp pen the delegates of the great powers, he adds: 'I should have mentioned among the very first Mr Hughes, the noble delegate of Australia, with whom one communicated through an acoustic box which emitted much harmonious good sense.'‡ The two men had various things in common: their intense patriotism, their shared taste for firm authority, the same gift for quick repartee, a realistic view of life not far removed from cynicism and an inability to suffer fools gladly. Both of them were greatly irritated by the moralizing of President Wilson, and no doubt Clemenceau was delighted to see the Australian standing up to the President of the U.S.A. A British general said of Hughes: 'This strange man had the knack, possessed by none other, of knocking the President completely off his balance.'§

* Admittedly, he had his own purposes and used France as an argument in favour of his conscription policy.

† Garran, R.R., *op. cit.*, p. 257.

‡ Hughes was slightly deaf, a defect that he could use to good advantage.

Hughes had his liveliest clashes over the matter of New Guinea. Australia, of course, still attached as much importance to this question as before (see Chapter 14). The British government had handed its part of the island over to the Federation in 1906. Australia had quickly taken up the offer, given the territory the new name of Papua and two years later entrusted the administration of it to a lawyer who knew the region well, Hubert Murray. This choice turned out to be a wise one. The name of the new Governor has become legendary; he kept the position for thirty-two years, a successful practitioner of the methods of enlightened despotism and a technique he called 'peaceful penetration', aimed at a gradual winning over of the hearts and minds of the indigenous people.

During the early years of Murray's proconsulate, the northern half of eastern New Guinea, as well as the neighbouring Islands, had of course remained under German dominion. With the outbreak of the war in August 1914, an opportunity arose for Australia to put an end to the sharing arrangement that she had disliked from the start, and in September she took over the territories, with little opposition from the German token force which guarded them. The Australian government would have been quite prepared to extend its conquests to the Carolinas and the Marshall Islands as well as the Marianas, all of which were German dependencies at the time. But this scheme met with a veto from London, as all German possessions north of the Equator had already been promised to the Japanese.

By the time the peace talks opened, the Commonwealth government was determined to hang on to what it had taken. To Hughes' mind, the only fair solution was a straightforward annexation. But both the word and the thought were anathema to Woodrow Wilson. The Australian Prime Minister actually went so far as to remind the American President that Australia, with a population of about four million had suffered 60,000 killed, whereas the U.S.A., with twenty-five times the population, had only twice the number of casualties, but this reasoning did not impress Wilson. Hughes also distinguished himself by declaring that in certain circumstances, Australia would not hesitate to defy the opinion of the whole civilized world,* an eventuality that did nothing to advance the negotiations. Wilson stood firm in his resolve to impose on New Guinea a League of

---

* Hancock, W.K., *Australia*, p. 205.

§ Quoted by Garran, R., *op. cit.*, p. 261.

Nations mandate ; and Hughes was equally adamant that he was not going to agree to any such thing. The situation was saved by a British diplomat and it was agreed that the mandate would stand, but that it would be tantamount to Australian sovereignty over the area. Article 22 of the League of Nations Covenant was unambiguous :

There are territories such as South-West Africa or certain Pacific islands which, because of the sparseness of their population or their small dimensions, or because of their nearness to the mandate power, or for other reasons, may be more suitably administered if the laws of the mandate power apply to them as though they belong to that power's territory, with the condition that the safeguards for the protection of the native population be respected.

This restricting condition was no impediment to Australia, which was unlikely to turn into an oppressor of the Papua-New Guineans. In fact, apart from this one small compromise, Hughes had won a complete victory, since the League's acceptance of the principle of White Australia would also serve to keep the Japanese out of New Guinea. Hughes described the arrangement as 'a 999-years' lease in lieu of a freehold'.*

'The Little Digger' was less successful on the matter of reparations, despite being appointed Vice-President of the Commission dealing with it. Keynes' ideas cut no ice with him. As far as he was concerned, Germany was the guilty party and should be wrung for every penny that could be got out of her. He wanted the Germans to pay the whole amount that the war had cost Australia (£364 million) plus an indemnity of £100 million. The total Australian bill was first cut back to £100 million. Finally, the constant shrinkage that cost France more than any other country reduced Australia's share to a mere £5.5 million.

The Versailles Treaty was signed on 28 June 1919. Hughes was back in Australia at the end of August and Parliament had ratified the treaty by September.

Rounding off one of the rousing speeches that he delivered so well, the Prime Minister asked what Australia had got out of this war. His reply was simple : national safety, White Australia and freedom from communism. But perhaps he could have added

---

* Garran, R.R., *op. cit.*, p. 265.

something else. For a long time, Australia had been seeking for a legend. Eureka and Ned Kelly had been magnified by this more or less unconscious yearning ; the mythology of the bush and the mateship tradition were even more direct results of it. But these folk myths were all rather artificial and the element of imagination in them was too strong. The 1914–18 war, on the other hand, brought the whole nation hard up against the most undeniable reality. And in the trenches at Gallipoli, in the mire of the Somme and among the sands of Palestine, Australia discovered the splendour and misery that accompany heroism and the free acceptance of collective sacrifice. To her history was now added a new and enriching store of legend.

Chapter Nineteen
Between the two wars

Consequences of the First World War – Australia in 1919 – artificial prosperity – the depth of the Depression – gradual recovery – growing stability in government – the Country Party – the Bruce-Page ministry – Labor in power – failure of the Scullin government – return of the conservatives under Lyons, then Menzies – Imperial Conferences – Washington treaties – the Balfour Declaration – the Statute of Westminster – the growing threat from Japan – appeasement – belated rearmament – Australia on the eve of the Second World War – progress of industrialization – the Commonwealth achieves full sovereignty

The twenty years which followed the Versailles Treaty were characterized in Australia by a period of artificial prosperity, a sudden slump and then a return to a state of equilibrium. During these rapid changes of fortune on the economic front, there was a bitter political struggle between the forces of conservatism and Labor, with the victory almost always going to the former. Foreign problems also came to loom larger as the country approached full sovereignty.

Australia in 1919 was appreciably different from Australia in 1914. The country had gone into the war in good economic condition: a fortnight before the declaration of war, Cook had declared that Australia's financial situation had never been better. Admittedly, these were the words of a Prime Minister during an election campaign (see page 284). In any case, justified or not, this optimism soon waned. Remote through she was from the battlefields, it would have been unlikely that Australia could escape the consequences of the great efforts that, like all the other belligerents, she had to make.

One could perhaps maintain that, considering things solely from the economic point of view, the advantages of the war actually outweighed the disadvantages. For instance, the development of an

Australian iron and steel industry was greatly hastened by the needs
of the armed services. When the first blast-furnaces were lit at
Broken Hill in 1915, it was obvious that the supremacy that had
hitherto been enjoyed by wool-growing and agriculture would one
day be challenged by this new, fast-growing industry.

A wiser financial policy might possibly have minimized the
economic ill-effects which were bound to result from the war.
Unfortunately Australia, although the most disciplined of the
Dominions, did not follow the lead of the home country in taxation
policy. Taxes were only increased in Australia by 50 per cent,
whereas in Britain they increased fourfold. Death duties became
payable by law in 1914, but the Commonwealth government waited
another year before deciding to impose any income tax,* and three
years before taxing war profits. Government revenue thus amounted
to barely 15 per cent of expenditure between 1914 and 1919.
Australian governments were so used to borrowing that they saw
nothing wrong in continuing to do so, even in wartime. When the
City showed reluctance, they had recourse to the national market
and issued seven appeals in five years. But the loan-power soon
flagged. The government, while theoretically disapproving the idea
of forced loans, went so far as to envisage penalties for use against
recalcitrant subscribers. This, of course, was not the best way of
finding money. It was easier to issue Treasury notes, which was
done, in Australia as elsewhere. And, in Australia as elsewhere, the
cost of living rose.

In conditions like these, the outlook for the 'fair and reasonable
wage' promised by Mr Justice Higgins, the latter-day Saint
Thomas, was decidedly unfavourable. Arbitration having proved to
be unworkable, constraint was used instead. In 1916 the Commonwealth government took its first step along the attractive but
disappointing road to price control. Bureaucrats flattered themselves on their knowledgeability, employers cried tyranny and
employees believed that at last a panacea for their ills had been
found. Despite which, the results of this experiment were incon-
clusive: by 1918 wholesale prices had risen by 68.5 per cent, while
retail prices had gone up by 46.6 per cent.

There has never been a war in which those in power have not

---

* New South Wales and Victoria had had recourse to an income tax during the
1893 depression.

used the war itself as an excuse to expand their powers. In October 1914, the Commonwealth government had passed two Acts which gave it almost dictatorial rights over most aspects of Australian life. The first was the War Precautions Act; the second was the Act which established price control.* These two measures hastened the tendency to centralization of power in Australia that the founding fathers had hoped to avoid by entrusting to the Federal government only certain well-defined functions.

The war had other consequences, no less important. The two referenda on conscription had aroused strong feelings in the Australian community. These feelings embittered the rivalry between the political parties and injected into the proceedings of Parliament a spirit that departed more and more from that of Westminster. This polarization engendered an atmosphere in which extremism was bound to thrive. The trade unions, which had been traditionally moderate, now felt the influence of the I.W.W. (Industrial Workers of the World), the revolutionary organization founded in Chicago in 1905 with the aim of uniting workers of all countries. Hughes had met this threat with his usual vigour, imprisoning twelve of the leaders of the movement. However, after the Russian Revolution, even the energy of the 'Little Digger' could not prevent the establishment in Australia of a section of the Communist International in 1922. This was nothing but a toehold, and little came of it. As Manning Clark says : ' It was as difficult for the Communists in Australia to convert people to the overthrow of the existing society as it was for the missionaries in Tahiti to convince the natives of original sin.'† Slight as it was, this burgeoning radicalism made the parties of the right look for a weapon to use against it. This weapon they thought they had discovered in nationalism, which up till then had been seen as the prerogative of of the left.

At the beginning of the post-war period, five million Australians,‡ proud of the military prowess of their compatriots and still seeking

---

* The High Court, having defined the term 'defence' in the widest possible sense, concluded that it was a proper part of the war effort to prevent a rise in the price of bread.

† Clark, C.M.H., *A Short History of Australia*, p. 207.

‡ 5,030,479 at the 1918 census, a rise of 100,000 over the 1914 figure.

an identity, looked to an uncertain future. Over the next twenty years, confidence and anxiety were the poles between which Australia was to oscillate.

With the coming of peace, there was a burst of economic activity. It turned out to be only a flash in the pan, the inevitable acceleration that always happens in such circumstances when a backlog of work orders can at last be met. Within two years, people were beginning to think they were in for a period of stagnation. But this was also short-lived. After all, Australia gravitated within the orbit of the Western world and she naturally followed the trajectory of Europe and the U.S.A., which for the time being was an ascending trajectory. In one of those sudden fits of optimism that seem to come over Australia from time to time, and which make such an odd contrast to what one could call her phases of lethargy, the nation devoted all its energies to the pursuit of the new prosperity. The obvious model to copy was the U.S.A. Australia was not the only nation to dream of rivalling America. One British statesman said at this time that if the U.S.A. could grow in a century from five million to 100 million, there was no reason why over the next 100 years the white population of the Empire should not reach 200 or 300 million. His Australian counterparts also waxed eloquent on their country's 'inexhaustible wealth', its 'unlimited capacity for absorption' and its natural resources which if fully exploited 'would probably solve most of today's economic problems'.

There was no shortage of slogans, then as now. One of them, appealing in its alliteration, was heard all the time : 'Men, money, markets'. These three ingredients were the secret of Australia's future success, it was argued ; and it was these three things that Australia lacked more than anything else. The Commonwealth gave them highest priority. Between 1911 and 1914, 207,000 immigrants had arrived ; since 1914, of course, there had been no more. Great Britain, as had happened after the Napoleonic Wars, was now in favour of an exodus of her excess population towards the Dominions. But the big drawback with emigration from Britain to Australia was the same as it had always been : the immense distance. The two governments reached an agreement on the joint financing of emigration from the U.K. The results of this agreement were substantial, Australia gaining 300,000 immigrants over the next ten years, two thirds of them on assisted passages. But this result still fell far short of the great tidal wave of emigrants which had swept from Europe to America. As for the second of the three desiderata, money, the City was in favour of a new lending programme, and between 1922 and 1926 it is estimated that London lent to Australia some £100 million. With more men and more money, Australia still needed to find the markets. One foreign observer says this involved 'an orgy of expenditure'. In the sharing out of this manna, the returned soldiers were not forgotten – they received almost £50 million.* The State governments also joined in, indulging in the same uninhibited public works expenditure as forty years before. Six thousand more kilometres of railways were laid down, and a great many irrigation and hydro-electric schemes were begun.

There are enough figures on the period to gladden the heart of any statistician. In less than ten years the income from wool grew from £85 million to £116 million ; agricultural produce from £72 million to £89 million. Mining development had been slower, growing from £20 million to £23 million. Nevertheless the country was becoming more and more industrialized, as is shown by the figures for income from manufactured goods, £420 million instead of £290 million. On only one score was the comparison unfavourable : exports in 1928–9 were slightly lower than they had been in 1919–20, £143.1 million as against £143.9 million, which proved conclusively that the third element of the 'Men, money, markets' formula was still lacking. Or perhaps more precisely that, since productivity had not managed to keep pace with production, the higher prices of Australian goods made them uncompetitive in foreign markets.

This should have given food for thought. Certainly, by 1928, there was a voice or two crying in the wilderness that something was not quite right. These rare harbingers of misfortune were to be proved all too true in the next few months. As Professor Blainey writes, 'a depression was drifting across like a fog from the old world.'† The east wind was blowing no good either. The stock market collapse of October 1929 showed how precarious American prosperity was. In Australia, older men thought it was their youth all over again. As had happened in 1890, the prices of wool and wheat collapsed and, as in 1890, if not more suddenly, the City cut off all loans. Within a few months the country was deprived of the

---

* Half of which was apparently never recovered.

† Blainey, G., *Gold and Paper*, Georgian House, Melbourne, 1958, p. 327.

£20 million that it had got into the habit of borrowing every year.

Half measures were tried first. Despite the fact that exports of raw materials had stayed at the same level, the value of them had been reduced by half in less than two years. In an attempt to balance the trade figures, import tariffs were raised on some items, prohibitions and quotas were introduced on others, gold was offered for sale. Long-term operations being out of the question, short-term Treasury notes were issued on the London money market. None of these standard palliatives was of any effect. It seemed desirable to have the opinion of an expert. The man chosen was Sir Otto Niemeyer of the Bank of England. In international financial circles Niemeyer was well known and listened to with respect. As a consultant specialist, he was devoid of any inferiority complex. He came, he saw, he judged. The report that he submitted to the Commonwealth government is remarkable for its tone of condescension, in which one could easily detect a note of veiled scorn. He was categorical – the situation was serious :

... costs must come down. ... In recent years Australian standards have been pushed too high relatively to Australian productivity and to general world conditions and tendencies ... Australia has to adjust herself to a world economic situation more disadvantageous to herself than in the last decade ... Australia is off Budget equilibrium, off exchange equilibrium and faced by considerable unfunded and maturing debts, both internally and externally, in addition to which she has on her hands a very large programme of Loan works for which no financial provision has been made. *

Sir Otto saw one ray of hope : by an extraordinary stroke of luck, no debts were to fall due in 1930 or 1931. He concluded that Australia had thus at most two years to put her house in order. The methods that Niemeyer recommended were the most effective, but the most inhuman : deflation. One eyewitness who met Sir Otto Niemeyer did not like the look of him at all, saying he had an expression like a frozen fish. An uncharitable description, no doubt, but according to those who knew the man, not inaccurate.

Feelings ran high. The Treasurer, Edward Theodore, who was no fool, said the only solution was to issue fiduciary notes ; since the

* Quoted by Louis, L.J. & Turner, I., *The Depression of the 1930's*, Cassell, Melbourne, 1968, pp. 49, 76.

demand for payment exceeded supply, all that was required was to increase the supply. Other suggestions were a little more subtle. Many people believed in Social Credit, a doctrine that had been evolved some years before by a Scot, Clifford Hugh Douglas. This theory had made production into an equation, $A+B=C$. 'A' was the variable costs of any undertaking (wages and dividends); 'B' was the invariable costs (interest, taxes, etc.); and 'C', being the sum of $A+B$, equalled the cost of production. The idea was that, since it is always easier to reduce 'A' than 'B', and since wages are the part of the variable costs that are more usually subject to reduction, it is perfectly possible to bring about a restriction of purchasing power while at the same time maintaining the same level of production. This is what brings about simultaneous poverty and abundance of goods. To remedy this situation, it was argued, the 'people' must be given control of money, all merchandise must be put at a 'fair price' and above all there must be a 'social credit' in the form of a 'national dividend' which was fixed, for some reason, at £25 a month.* These arguments seemed too theoretical to the Premier of New South Wales, John T. Lang, an earthy, forthright, larger-than-life character. According to Lang, the only possible solution was outright repudiation of the debts. One can imagine the imprecations of the bankers who, with greater good fortune than their predecessors in 1893, had managed to keep their firms in a state of solvency.

A compromise was bound to be the eventual result. Economists recommended common-sense solutions. To begin with, of course, it behoved the Premiers to reject them on principle, but they soon came round. It was decided to lower wages by 10 per cent and to make up for this loss of revenue by imposing a tax on interest. The Premiers made the virtuous resolution to balance their budgets within three years. A 25 per cent devaluation, with a stricter control on foreign exchange dealings, gave a boost to exports. Great hopes were held of the growth of an Imperial market, enthusiastically adopted in principle at the Ottawa Conference in 1932. By 1933 the 'fog' from the west and the east was beginning to clear, and Australia began to benefit from the general upturn in activity that became apparent. Australia had come through, but only just, for at the darkest moments of the Depression fully one third of the work-

* This notion is an obvious forerunner of the idea of the guaranteed income that one hears of nowadays.

ing population had been unemployed.

Once the recovery started, it quickly got under way. By the outbreak of the war in 1939, Australia's national income had grown over the preceding five years from £528 million to £814 million. However it was still only about six per cent higher than it had been in the years of prosperity. This improved profitability was unevenly distributed. In twenty years the pastoral industry had improved by only ten per cent and agriculture by not quite five per cent. It was in mining and industry that the best results had been achieved, income from mining having doubled and manufacturing production having increased by more than two thirds.

Political life was of course not immune from these rapid economic changes. One possibly unexpected feature was that the instability that had characterized the early governments of the Federation tended to disappear. Over the twenty-year period there were seven different ministries, as against nine in the previous thirteen years. Of these seven administrations, only one was Labor.

Hughes was in power in 1919 and had no inclination to step down. The first post-war elections had given him a sound majority in Parliament and he stayed at the head of the government for four more years, ruling the country with a rod of iron. Hard-liners were overjoyed when he used one of the special wartime powers – passed in 1914 and never repealed – to break a strike. This won him the praise of the returned soldiers, but the Labor Party was outraged and many people wondered if the Prime Minister had not perhaps lost his sense of proportion through rubbing shoulders with the great.

If authority goes to one's head, this is no doubt incompatible with clear judgement. It is remarkable that Hughes does not seem to have realized that the emergence of a new political force in 1920 was a symptom of at least a period of political uncertainty. Since 1910 (see page 283) it had been thought that a two-party system had evolved in Australia, with Labor and conservatives (under another name). But over those years, wool-growers and farmers had been becoming more aware of the fact that, though they continued to create wealth, the progress of urbanization was turning them into an ever smaller minority. From this realization grew the feeling that they were entitled to a more important place in the system than the one they occupied. They were to some extent influenced by events in the U.S.A., where every now and then the discontent of farmers erupted in fleeting attempts at political unity, and by the knowledge that a similar situation existed in Canada. The outcome was the formation of a new independent party, which came to be called the Country Party. One of those who have studied this phenomenon has acutely analysed the confused motives of its founders, largely an imprecise bush nostalgia, and an equally vague aspiration towards a better life. These founders spoke of the exploitation of the country by the cities, the worthiness of the country life as a source of virtue and manhood, and the nobility of a life spent close to nature. Their political programme was a highly respectable one which attracted supporters from assorted backgrounds, including small farmers, wool-growers, people with semi-socialist notions derived from Henry George, large landowners and out-and-out conservatives. What they all had in common was their desire to make their voice heard and to use their votes to obtain material benefits.

In 1919 they won six seats in the Federal Parliament ; in the 1922 elections they increased their representation to ten. The important element in their success was not their numbers, however. It was the state of the other parties in Parliament which enabled them to hold the balance of power. At the time, Hughes had twenty-eight seats, Labor held thirty and there were three independents. This meant that by themselves Hughes' Nationalists could not have a working majority. On this point the views of Earle Page, the leader of the Country Party, were clear and simple : he was prepared to co-operate in the business of government, but without Hughes. Hughes, who had been Prime Minister for seven years, could not believe his ears. But he had to accept the inevitable.

The new team that took over was led by two men who were so mutually dependent that their administration has come to be known by their two names – Bruce-Page. Bruce, as well as being Prime Minister, held the External Affairs portfolio ; Page was in charge of the Treasury.

The like of Stanley Melbourne Bruce had never been seen as Prime Minister of Australia. Born in 1883, in Toorak, Melbourne's smartest suburb, he was of Scottish origin. He came from a very wealthy family, which owed its fortune to the warehousing company founded by his father. At nineteen he went to Cambridge. In all he was to spend some fifteen years in England, during which time he took part in the landing at Gallipoli, where he was wounded and earned a decoration. In England he had become a lawyer, and would presumably have practised this profession until retirement if the death of one of his brothers had not led him to return to Victoria to take over the family business. Back at home, he felt the attraction of politics and by 1918 was a member of the House of Representatives, one of Hughes' Nationalists, needless to say. By the time of Hughes' resignation, five years later, Bruce had made such a name for himself that he was the obvious choice as the Prime Minister's successor. He was only forty, and had little experience of politics behind him.

A biographer has sub-titled his life of Bruce : 'How to succeed in politics without apparently trying'.* This may well be the secret of his rapid success. Whether Bruce had actively sought eminence so soon or not, he took to it as to the manner born. Everything in his formative years, his family background, his wealth, his time at Cambridge, gave him a quiet self-confidence that was the envy of his friends and an annoyance to his opponents. The *Bulletin* called him

Something of an exquisite ... the most highly-veneered politician we have yet produced. He wears immaculate clothes, has the stunning profile and the air of a *Lady's Journal* hero. Mrs B. is among Toorak's most tastefully-dressed matrons. Her mother was a Manifold. There are no little Bs, but a well-manicured fox terrier does his best to keep the pair from feeling lonely.†

A Labor opponent, Frank Anstey, saw him as

urbanity personified. Nothing was permitted to ruffle the calm of his superiority. No insult could draw from him the slightest protest – only a gaze of curiosity, such as an entomologist might give to a bug ... All the tricks of the Parliamentary game and the arts of mob deception were as natural to him as the ocean to the porpoise ... He delighted the masses with his unlimited promises, and the wealthy by the fact that he never fulfilled them. He said what he meant, but it was never what his dupes thought he meant.‡

This may seem a harsh verdict on the man. But no doubt the

---

* Edwards, C., *Bruce of Melbourne*, Heinemann, 1963.
† *ibid.*, p. 84.
‡ *ibid.*, p. 192.

average Australian found something a little too English in Bruce, with his Rolls-Royce, his spats, his golf and tennis, the horses he rode.* He was actually known to have a valet, something that would have been inconceivable in his predecessors.

Bruce may have revealed his true self in a remark he made to Mrs Lyons (whose husband was to become Prime Minister in 1932) : 'For this job a man really needs three things, or some of them anyhow ; a hide like a rhinoceros, an overpowering ambition, and a mighty good conceit of himself. And your husband has none of them.'†

Earle Page was a man of more common stamp. Lord Beaverbrook once dubbed him 'Abraham Lincoln',‡ a charitable comparison that may be explained by the man's colourful personality. He was born in a small country town in northern New South Wales and was a practising local doctor. However politics had always fascinated him. He was full of ideas and could become incoherent with the effort of matching words to the flow of those ideas. Bruce judged him with severe condescension : 'He had new brainwaves every day. They were nearly always half-baked. He was bursting with energy ; he was full of ideas, and to most of them you had to say : "My dear Page, for God's sake go away and have your head read." '§

The Bruce-Page government consisted of six Nationalist and five Country Party ministers. The Country Party well knew that they could effectively oppose any move with which they might disagree. Bruce called the government 'a new broom', which may seem a trifle excessive in view of the fact that his policies were almost identical to those of Hughes, the three main planks being anti-communism, White Australia and an improvement in the standard of living. Ministers' decisions were greatly facilitated by prosperity, and notably by the solution reached in 1927 to the problem of tax revenue distribution, which had bedevilled relations between the Commonwealth government and the States ever since the inception of the federal system in 1901.

That same year, 1927, deserves a special mention in any history

---

* What is more, he never fell off, unlike 'The Little Digger' whose falls added to his legend.

† Lyons, E., *So We Take Comfort*, Heinemann, 1965, p. 193.

‡ Page, E., *Truant Surgeon*, Angus & Robertson, Sydney, 1963, p. 357.

§ Quoted by Edwards, C., *op. cit.*, p. 82.

of Australia, as it was then that Canberra really became the nation's capital. After the site of the future city had been chosen in 1911, an architect from Chicago, Walter Burley Griffin, was appointed to design the city. Planning had, of course, been interrupted during the war years. In 1920 the Prince of Wales had laid the foundation stone of a non-existent building. In 1924, as a symbolic gesture, Bruce and Page decided to hold a Cabinet meeting at the spot where the future of Australia was going to be formed. The *Age* told its readers that this decision was ' colossal folly ', for it must be remembered that the nation's capital was at this time a tract of sheep country 600 metres above sea level, among hills and mountains, where it was freezing cold in winter and extremely hot and fly-infested in summer. Yet, as has been said (and as anyone who has been there can confirm), it had ' a strange charm, a picture-book placidity of almost treeless plain and timbered hills that turned blue in twilight.'* Three years later sufficient progress had been made for the government to invite the Duke of York (the future George VI) to open the first Parliament in Canberra on 9 May. Manning Clark describes the occasion as follows :

On that day thirty to forty thousand people† gathered outside Parliament House in that small city of undulating plain and open sky to watch the arrival of the Duke and Duchess. As they stood on the steps of the new white building, Dame Nellie Melba sang 'God Save the King' A solitary aboriginal demanded to see the 'whole plurry show', but as he was deemed to be inadequately clad for the occasion, a policeman led him away. From the steps the Duke urged the people to listen to the voices of the noble army of the dead and march in step with them towards a glorious destiny. At the official lunch to celebrate the occasion only one toast was drunk – to His Majesty – and that in fruit cup. No intoxicants were served, and speeches were taboo.‡

One eyewitness says that the whole place was deep in mud.

With all its incongrous elements of the sublime and the ridiculous, that day was an Imperial enough occasion to bolster Bruce's natural optimism. His majority in the House of Representatives had been

---

* Quoted by Edwards, C., *op. cit.*, pp. 88–9.

† A remarkable turnout, given that the two nearest railway stations were 50 and 100 kilometres away, and the roads into Canberra were in only fairish condition.

‡ Clark, C.M.H., *A Short History of Australia*, p. 205.

increased by seven seats after the 1925 elections.* This may have exaggerated his self-confidence. Or perhaps he suffered from that erosion of judgement that sometimes afflicts statesmen. Whatever the facts of the matter, he made a series of blunders which turned popular opinion against him. He had two trade union leaders charged with revolutionary activity and tried to have them deported, but the High Court overruled him. As well as which, as a result of the war, the Commonwealth now found itself responsible for a multitude of different activities: sheep-farming, butchers' shops, fisheries, canning factories, coking plants, smelters, coal mines and even a hotel. The Commonwealth Bank, too, had taken on the role of a savings bank in addition to its original functions. In 1916 Hughes had created a state shipping line, and now the Commonwealth government was responsible for fifty-four ships and for the ever increasing deficit that they incurred. In 1927 Bruce decided to liquidate this shipping line, thus giving 'The Little Digger' an opportunity for getting his own back.

The satisfaction that had come from the early years of the compulsory conciliation and arbitration system had been short-lived. Bruce felt, in view of rising prices and the continuing disputes over jurisdiction between Federal and State tribunals, that the time had come for a review of the workings of the system. Most Australians took pride in the knowledge that their country had been the first to adopt such a system of arbitration, and for them it was an inviolable principle. At the 1928 general election Bruce was returned, but with a reduced majority. Eleven months later he saw fit to bring down the Maritime Industries Bill which in effect abandoned the field of industrial regulation to the States (except in maritime disputes). Hughes judged the time was ripe for revenge and managed to have the government defeated by one vote. Bruce, nothing daunted, had Parliament dissolved and confidently went to the country on the issue. The general election of 1929 was a landslide, the government parties being reduced to twenty-four seats against Labor's fifty-one. Bruce lost his seat, at which Hughes was 'as delighted as a schoolboy home for the holidays'.† But Hughes' own triumph was of brief

---

* Compulsory voting had existed in Queensland since 1915. It was introduced in Federal elections in 1925.

† Whyte, W.F., *William Morris Hughes*, Angus & Robertson, Sydney, 1957, p. 466.

duration, too, and Bruce could console himself with the thought that the architect of his downfall achieved nothing from his coup, for the Labor leaders were unforgiving and had no intention of joining forces with the man whom they still saw as having betrayed his party in 1917.

The Scullin government of 1929 was the first Labor ministry for fourteen years. It had the misfortune to be an undistinguished team matched with a moment of unprecedented crisis. One may be forgiven for thinking that one of Bruce's endowments from his fairy godmothers must have been luck. For it was a stroke of luck to be able to leave office just at the time when the economic crisis had blown up, especially for a man who enjoyed enough personal wealth to weather the storm. Those who took over from him soon found themselves in dire straits. In opposition, all they had had to do was criticize ; now they had to take action, and the tension was increasing every day.

Scullin, the Prime Minister, at fifty-three had no experience of government at all. In fact, his whole experience was of trade union activity and of seven years in opposition as a Victorian member of the House of Representatives. He was a man of Irish Catholic background, simple, sincere and not without competence. In less trying times he could well have made a success of government. Something of the difficulties he met can be gauged from the number of changes among his colleagues : over a period of twenty-six months he had two Deputy Prime Ministers, two different Ministers of Health, Trade and Works, two Postmasters-General and three Ministers of Defence. Scullin led a Cabinet of mediocrities, only three of whom are remembered (and all of these three were of questionable competence in some respect). Frank Anstey was called a remarkable man by John Curtin, the future Prime Minister, but has also been dismissed as an old-style agitator. Edward Theodore was a former Premier of Queensland and was universally regarded as the best man in the team. He was born of a Romanian father and an Irish mother. He was a courageous, brilliant man, who could be brutal when he felt it was called for, and had an undoubted financial ability, as well as an unfortunate tendency to overestimate the power of credit. In 1930 he was implicated in a scandal, and Scullin had to do without his services for six months at a time when he needed him greatly. Thirdly, there was Joseph Lyons, from the same staunch

Irish Catholic background as Scullin himself. He shared the Prime Minister's reliability and honesty, but was a man of much greater subtlety.

Scullin was certainly not the man to meet a crisis of such magnitude, listen to Niemeyer's moralizing, convince his Cabinet colleagues of the accuracy of Niemeyer's diagnosis and suggested remedies, and persuade the State governments to take the sort of steps that might be agreeable to trade unionists as well as to bankers. It has been said that the ordeal of the crisis and the Depression turned Scullin's hair white inside two years. Sir George Pearce, the leader of the opposition in the Senate, said of Scullin :

Trained as he had been to look upon the party as the ultimate expression of all wisdom, he found it difficult when the party went wild to exert his authority as Prime Minister of the Commonwealth ; and the party as such showed him neither mercy nor consideration. Again and again they humiliated him until, when the end came, I think no one was more relieved than he.*

It was his own comrade, Lyons, who ousted Scullin. In 1931, using as his excuse the return of the dubious Theodore to the Treasury, Lyons deserted Labor. Then, like Hughes before him, he offered his services to the Nationalists, forming with them the new right-of-centre United Australia Party, a name designed to reassure in a time of division. At the elections at the end of 1931, Lyons and the U.A.P. won a landslide victory, with fifty-four of the seventy-five Representatives seats and twenty-six of the thirty-six in the Senate.

Joseph Lyons now became Prime Minister. Feelings were still running high. Although defeated in the Federal sphere and in elections for most of the State legislatures, Labor was still in power in New South Wales. The State Labor leader, J.T. Lang, was a living legend. Professor L.F. Crisp describes him as follows :

. . . a tall, well-built man with a large domed head and jutting jaw. He gave a strong impression of toughness, ability, shrewdness, resource and incorruptibility . . . In public, he could be alternately domineering and ruthless or silent and aloof. Lang had all the sterner qualities and steadily developed the techniques of the 'machine boss'. †

* Pearce, G., *Carpenter to Cabinet*, Hutchinson, 1951, p. 188.
† Crisp, L.F., *Ben Chifley*, Longmans, 1961, p. 68.

To trade unionists he was a hero, because of social reforms that he had put through (such as family allowances and the 44-hour week) and his unfailing opposition to any policy of deflation. Elsewhere, he was seen as a 'Communist', the fashionable period insult, although it would be more accurate to see him as something of a dictator.

The bogy of communism had led to the formation of all sorts of defence organizations, which were of course called 'Fascist', after the usual manner of dealing in labels. D.H. Lawrence, who had spent a few weeks in Australia some years previously, has described in *Kangaroo* the stirrings of a political movement in which he saw the hand of Mussolini. The book is notable for its excellent pictures of the Australian landscape and for the example it gives of how even a fine novelist may be devoid of political instinct. By 1932, however, such a mistake would have been more understandable. The 'All for Australia League' had been founded the previous year, with the aim of uniting citizens of all classes in a spirit of patriotism so as to work for the re-establishment of what it saw as Australia's integrity and prosperity. The League was said to have 200,000 members, proud of their badge, but the movement fizzled out with the return of the conservative government in 1931. The 'Riverina Movement', which was also short-lived, included in its programme a boycott on taxation and a proposal to secede from the Federation. The most successful of these movements was probably the 'New Guard' which, reputedly 100,000 strong and led by former soldiers, was reminiscent of the French *Croix de Feu* of the same period in its para-military organization, its concern for 'law and order' and its respect for 'traditional values'. There was an attempt to turn the New Guard into a political party, but by 1935 it too had faded away. Not before it had had its moment in the limelight, however. Saturday 20 March 1932 was a great day in Sydney, the day when the world-famous harbour bridge was officially opened. It has been estimated that 750,000 spectators were present at the ceremony. The traditional ribbon was supposed to be cut by New South Wales Premier Lang, but the New Guard had sworn not to allow this to happen. At the very last minute, just as the Premier was stepping forward, a young, unobtrusive man in uniform spurred his horse into a gallop, drew his sabre and sliced through the ribbon, declaring that he was acting on behalf of the decent and respectable citizens of New South Wales. The *Bulletin* summed the episode up aptly by saying it was like something out of a Victorian melodrama. The ribbon was stitched together again and the official ceremony could begin.

Many a man has survived being made a fool of, and Lang was no exception. Even so, his days in power were numbered. Two months later he went back on his promises under the Premiers' plan agreed to with the Scullin government in June 1931. When Lang refused to pay the interest due on State loans raised overseas, the Governor of New South Wales, Sir Philip Game, dismissed the Premier for breaking the law, despite the majority he still commanded in Parliament.*

With Lang out of the way, the country could now take the ordered and prudent course that the conservatives wanted it to take. Lyons died early in 1939, to be replaced by Page for a fortnight. Then, on 26 April, the job of Prime Minister fell to man who was soon to become famous, Robert Gordon Menzies. He had been born forty-four years before in Jeparit, a small country town in north-western Victoria. His grandfather had been president of the Victorian miners' union, his father, of radical leanings, had been a member of the State legislature. Menzies was called to the Bar in 1918 and made a successful career of it. In 1928 he was elected to the State Parliament, then in 1934 to the House of Representatives in Canberra. Lyons immediately appointed him Attorney-General, a portfolio which he held until the death of his leader five years later. Menzies says that when he was summoned to form a government after the Page interlude, the Governor-General asked him how long he thought he could last :† ' Six weeks, Your Excellency,' was his reply. The Governor-General smiled and said, ' Well, that will do for a start.'‡ The first Menzies government lasted in fact for two years. One of his colleagues has said he was one of the most entertaining speakers in Parliament. He had a sense of humour that could be pungent and a devastating gift of repartee. Opponents treated him with great respect. He `had the advantage of a mind trained in the law and a natural aptitude for clarity of expression, but

---

* One month later, the electorate overwhelmingly endorsed the Governor's action.

† The Country Party having refused its support, Menzies could only form a minority government.

‡ Menzies, R.G., *Afternoon Light*, Cassell, Melbourne, 1967, pp. 13–14.

would tend to lose patience with those whose minds worked more slowly than his own. According to Manning Clark, the man was motivated by three passions : a strong desire for fame ; a veneration, or superstitious respect, for British institutions ; and an attachment to the past, to 'the grandeur, the pomp, the ceremony, the wit and the urbanity' of the Edwardian age.*

One cannot help being struck by the contrast between the peace and quiet of Australian life in the last years before the outbreak of the second world war and the convulsions that were occurring in the outside world. None the less, these upheavals did have their effect on 'the quiet continent'.

Australia, like Britain's other Dominions, had signed the Versailles Treaty and had become a member of the League of Nations. Some diplomats may have seen these actions as tokens of independence, but one may well wonder whether there was any real desire for independence in Australia and, if so, for what sort of independence. Certainly these were two questions which were to be asked more and more as the inter-war years went on.

In 1921 a foreign diplomat in Australia wrote : 'This country offers no openings for a diplomatic or consular career. Nor does anybody seem to object to Australia's interests being in the hands of Great Britain.' One does not have to look far for proof that he was right. The balance of power in the Pacific had been profoundly changed by the First World War. Russia and Germany were now totally absent from the area. Japan, making much of its role in the war, was more determined than ever not to be overlooked. The U.S.A. was coming to the fore as the power that everyone had to reckon with. As for Great Britain, Australia's traditional source of protection, there could be no doubt about her good intentions. But some misgivings were justified about her ability to be everything that she had hitherto been to Australia. Despite this, at the London conference of 1921 and at the Washington conference that same year, Australia played a secondary role. For instance, although Canada had dared to argue against a renewing of the Anglo-Japanese alliance, and despite Australian distrust of Japanese intentions, the Australian government did not follow Canada's lead. When this two-power arrangement was replaced by an international agree-

* Clark, C.M.H., *A Short History of Australia*, p. 219.

ment,* Australia did not seek from America the guarantees that Great Britain might no longer be able to give her. In any case, the Australian representative at the conferences, Senator Pearce, was only accredited as a member of the British delegation.

Australia's semi-colonial status was further demonstrated the following year. The Turks, under Kemal Pasha (with discreet support from the French), had driven the Greeks (whom the British had rather rashly helped to invade Asia Minor) into the sea at Smyrna. This episode all but resulted in a clash between Turkish troops and the British garrison guarding the Dardanelles at Chanak. An outbreak of hostilities was avoided by diplomatic means. But in the meantime Great Britain had taken the belated precaution of sounding out its satellites on their possible support. The difference in attitude between Canada and South Africa on the one hand, and Australia on the other, is revealing: Ottawa and Pretoria politely but firmly declined to offer support, on the grounds that they could do nothing without the approval of their parliaments, whereas Australia, albeit complaining at having been treated with such scant respect, did agree to support British moves.

This incident left unpleasant memories, even in a place as loyal to the boot-heels as Australia. At the next Imperial Conference in 1923, Bruce supported Mackenzie King in his opposition to any centralizing of Commonwealth policies. Curzon, the redoubtable Foreign Secretary, blustered and complained of the Canadian Prime Minister's obstinacy and stupidity, but he had to accept the decision. From then on, treaties with foreign powers would have to be negotiated and signed by each of the Dominions in its own right. The Australian Prime Minister even managed to have a liaison officer attached to the British Foreign Office, whose function was to keep the Australian government directly in touch. The first incumbent of this position was Richard Casey, and this was to be the first stage of his brilliant diplomatic career.

Australia was thus in the position of gradually approaching full independence, at a rate which suited the other Dominions much more than it suited her. In 1924 she supported the other member

---

* Under this agreement, naval power was to be limited by a pro rata formula for every five British and American vessels, Japan was to have three and France and Italy 1.75 each. The integrity of China was guaranteed by Great Britain, the U.S.A., France, Italy, Holland, Belgium and Portugal.

countries of the Empire in demanding a restrictive interpretation of the famous Article 10 of the League of Nations Covenant.* In 1925, like Canada and South Africa, she refused to share British responsibilities under the Locarno Treaty.†

There was still something rather equivocal in the situation of all three Dominions. When the third post-war Imperial Conference met in London in 1926, the South African Prime Minister Hertzog, a former general, was determined that this pragmatism of the British had gone far enough. South Africa was energetically supported by Mackenzie King (and somewhat more reservedly by Bruce) in its demand that theory and practice should coincide. Hertzog was a fastidious man – one clause in the declaration had to be amended eight times before he was satisfied. The final draft, as approved by Balfour, was unequivocal : the Dominions were recognized to be

autonomous communities within the British Empire, equal in status, in no way subordinate one to another in any respect of their domestic or external affairs, though united by a common allegiance to the Crown and freely associated as members of the British Commonwealth of Nations.‡

There was only one reservation, and that was that the British government would continue to look after most questions of foreign policy for some time to come. This last phrase speaks volumes for the intentions of some of the signatories, as did their subsequent decisions. In 1927 Canada and the U.S.A. exchanged formal diplomatic representation, and by 1929 Canada had agents in London, Paris, Geneva and Tokyo. The South Africans were just as quick, opening legations in Washington, The Hague and Rome in 1929. But the attitude of the Australians was quite different. It

---

This was the article which bound the signatories to come to the assistance of any signatory that was attacked ; it was agreed that the importance of each member country and its geographical position would be taken into account.

† This gesture of independence went completely unnoticed by Australian public opinion. Not one speaker from either the government or the opposition thought it worth while to mention it. This was the agreement by which Great Britain, France, Belgium, Germany and Italy pledged themselves to guarantee the frontiers drawn at Versailles (except for the most controversial ones in eastern Europe).

‡ Quoted by Garran, R.R., *Prosper the Commonwealth*, p. 314.

was not until 1935 that they separated the Department of External Affairs from the Prime Minister's responsibilities. In 1937 they appointed an Australian counsellor to the staff of the British Embassy in Washington. They did not set up a separate legation in the U.S.A. until 1940, when they also opened one in Tokyo.

The 1926 conference had appointed a commission to draw up the legislation to embody the Balfour Declaration. The Statute of Westminster, as it came to be called, was approved by the British Parliament in 1931, 550 members voting 'Aye' and fifty voting 'No'. This Statute immediately came into force in Eire, Canada and South Africa. But Australia was in no such hurry and did not ratify it until 1942, eleven years later.* Churchill was one of the fifty who had voted against the terms of the Statute of Westminster, seeing it as a danger to the well-being of the Empire. Hughes, too, along with a great many other Australians, shared this same feeling. It was obvious that the Commonwealth of Australia still saw its future lying with Great Britain and the British Empire.

In that same year, 1931, Japan showed the danger inherent in her expansionism by invading Manchuria. Over the next few years Japan withdrew from the League of Nations, repudiated the 1921 treaties,† declared the independence of Manchukuo, seized Shanghai and carried the war to Hankow and Canton. Canberra was still 7,000 kilometres away from these Japanese invaders, but all that stood between them was Singapore and the British Far Eastern fleet.

It has been said that in these years Australian policy towards Japan swung anxiously between the desire for close relations and the fear that the growing power of the militarists would encourage them to launch new aggressions. The initiative lay quite clearly with the Japanese. In 1931 Australia was in the throes of the Depression and the necessity for new markets had become imperative. Exports to Japan rose from 8.3 per cent in 1929 to 12.1 per cent in 1932.

---

* Australia's ratification was made retrospective to the beginning of the war. New Zealand turned out to be even more British than Australia and did not ratify the Statute until 1947.

† See page 329. The practical consequence of this was the fortification of the Pacific islands under Japanese occupation, north of the Equator (the Carolinas, the Marshalls and the Marianas).

Australian wool-growers had reached the stage of supplying nine tenths of Japan's wool needs. It was hardly the time to upset such a valuable customer. But once the situation had improved and the tension relaxed, Australia decided to make a gesture of independence. Accordingly, in 1936, the government imposed a severe import duty on Japanese products, with a view to favouring trade with Great Britain. This move has been described as combining the maximum of annoyance with the minimum of benefit.

Coherence of policy was non-existent during this period, but it would be unfair to criticize Australia's chopping and changing at a time when European powers were doing likewise. Berlin and Rome seemed very far away when viewed from Sydney, although Australia by now had reason to be aware of Italy. During Mussolini's Ethiopian venture in 1935–6, Australia had given lukewarm support to sanctions against him. The Italian victory roused a completely new sort of anxiety in Australians: what would happen if Great Britain were ever to lose control of the Mediterranean access to the Suez Canal ? In addition, the way the League of Nations abdicated its responsibilities over Abyssinia lost it any slight remaining prestige in Australian eyes. As for Hitler, he seemed less worrying to Australia. Menzies returned from a visit to Germany in July 1938, observing that the character and the attitudes of Great Britain were a source of perplexity to the Germans, but convinced of the necessity for mutual understanding between what he saw as two of the greatest and most virile nations in the world. The Munich agreement was greeted in Australia with general approval, with the sole exception of the *Sydney Morning Herald*. Lyons, the Prime Minister, even took pride in having helped prepare the agreement. He had assured Neville Chamberlain by cable that his overtures to Hitler were supported by the country at large. When all hope of an agreement at Munich had seemed lost, Lyons said, he had wakened the British Prime Minister at dawn with the proposal to send Bruce to Rome with a personal message to Mussolini. One is always more inclined to give away what one does not own, and, while the Australians had no objection to the dismemberment of Czechoslovakia, they declared almost with the same breath their opposition to any possible future claim that Germany might make to its former colonies in New Guinea. A month after Munich, Hughes, once again a member of Cabinet, declared that Australia had built her mandate on the rock of the Versailles Treaty and that hell itself would not prevail against it. Page added his voice, saying that the League of Nations had entrusted New Guinea to Australia as a sacred pledge and that any talk of giving it up would be cowardly and unjust.

At the beginning of 1939 Great Britain, in an abrupt reversal of its European policy, signed two treaties with Poland and Romania. Australia was not consulted. Perhaps Australia preferred it this way. Indeed, her most constant hope was that a new war could somehow be avoided. Nevertheless, although Australia's leaders had been in favour of the appeasement policy, some of them could see quite clearly the likely consequences of their actions. Hughes said in January 1938 : 'Incalculable forces have been unleashed. . . . It is certain that their effects upon Australia . . . will be profound.'* And by the end of that same year Lyons could see what he called a 'bitter truth' – at any moment over the next few years, Australia might have to face an attack on its own soil. Even so, the country's military situation was parlous. In 1929 compulsory national service had been abolished, and during the Depression the armed forces had been reduced to the barest minimum. Sixteen months before the outbreak of the war, the government set in motion a hurried rearmament programme.† By the time the war started the army was 80,000 strong, with five infantry divisions and two cavalry divisions ; the navy consisted of five cruisers, five destroyers and two sloops ; while the R.A.A.F. had at its command 164 fighting planes, many of them obsolescent.

In September 1939 Australia's population reached seven million, an increase of two million since the outbreak of the previous war. The trend towards urbanization of this population was now even more marked : 47 per cent of Australians lived in the nation's seven capital cities. The birth rate, which had been declining over the previous thirty years, had taken a slight turn upwards. However, even though it now stood at 18.5 per 1,000, this figure still represented a drop from 25 per 1,000 in less than a century. Immigration had come to an almost complete halt, with a mere 3,828 arrivals between

---

* Quoted by Whyte, W.F., *op. cit.*, p. 476.

† Three years earlier, Hughes had published an impassioned book denouncing the country's lack of military preparedness. This brought him into such disfavour that he did not come back into the government until the end of 1937.

1936 and 1940. The demographic conclusion drawn from these statistics was a pessimistic one: that Australia's population graph would soon show a marked downturn. The outback still aroused that same feeling of isolation, caught and expressed so well by Ernestine Hill. Socially, the nation appeared to be marking time; the period of the great social reforms seemed to be over. As A.G.L. Shaw writes, the economic recovery 'seemed to be accompanied by a kind of spiritual malaise, wherein the values and virtues of pioneering society had disappeared, but had not been adequately replaced by those of a maturer form of civilized life.'*

None the less, two profound transformations were already taking place in Australia. The first was the triumph of industrialization: production from the mines and factories was soon to outstrip agriculture and wool-growing. Secondly, and no doubt more importantly, Australia was well on the way to becoming a sovereign power,† albeit in spite of herself.

---

* Shaw, A.G.L., *The Story of Australia*, p. 233.
† The British government was the first to recognize this. In 1937 the Irish Free State protested to the publishers of the French Didot-Bottin directory because it had listed Ireland among the Dominions and colonies of Great Britain. The Foreign Office, answering the publishers' inquiry, replied that it would be preferable to list all the Dominions in the general alphabetical list of independent foreign states. It then spelt out that these Dominions were Canada, the Commonwealth of Australia, the Union of South Africa and the Irish Free State.

Chapter Twenty
The Second World War

The 'phoney' war – Dakar – North African successes – setbacks in Greece and Crete – capture of Syria and Lebanon – Menzies resigns – Curtin becomes Prime Minister – Singapore falls – Darwin bombed – Australia in peril – General MacArthur in Melbourne – Battle of the Coral Sea – Midway – Rommel's successes in North Africa – Australian counter-attack in New Guinea – El Alamein – 'the end of the beginning' – Papua liberated – MacArthur takes the offensive – Australian successes in New Guinea, Timor, New Britain, Dutch East Indies and Borneo – Australia and New Zealand sign co-operation pact – Evatt's important role at San Francisco – death of Curtin – Chifley takes over – Japan surrenders

On 3 September 1939, when Great Britain declared war on Germany for the second time in a quarter of a century, Australia had no need to follow suit. The national Parliament did not need to debate the matter ; nor was any notification sent to Berlin. If the mother country was at war, that was enough for Canberra : it meant that Australia was also at war. These same events caused different reactions in the other Dominions. In South Africa they brought down the Hertzog government, and the imperialists, under Smuts, only just carried the day. In Canada, the nation was much more of one mind. Even so, on a point of principle, the Confederation did not consider itself at war with Germany for another week. But in Australia such qualms and equivocations were out of the question. Menzies had declared some months earlier that the British countries must stand or fall together. And when the time came, he bluntly stated the same view, saying there was no 'disunity among the British people on these matters. Australia stands where it stood twenty-five years ago.'* Over the next two years, because of the way

* Menzies, R.G., *Afternoon Light*, p. 15.

the war developed, Australia was to be of two minds. Loyalty demanded that she send her young men to fight on distant battle-fields. But at the same time she felt vaguely uneasy and wondered whether it might not be wiser to keep them at home in case of emergencies. Another question was also being asked, which would have been inconceivable only a short while before: would it not be politic to look to the growing might of the U.S.A. for protection as well as (if not instead of) to Great Britain? Australian statesmen were beginning to look tentatively towards Washington and away from London.

Australia had begun to do something about her military weakness. Compulsory national service had been revived but, as in 1914, no conscript could be sent overseas to fight. This meant that once more, volunteers had to be called for. They came forward in such numbers that by the beginning of 1940, two divisions could be put at the disposal of the Imperial General Staff. Like their First World War counterparts, they underwent intensive training in Egypt. Back in Australia, the months went by uneventfully, for all the world like normal everyday life. The only indications that the country was on a war footing were the dictatorial powers that the Federal government had adopted, and the transformation of peacetime industries into munitions factories. Before long, Menzies made the intelligent decision to entrust this part of the national war effort to one of Australia's leading industrialists, Essington Lewis of B.H.P.

This calm atmosphere was suddenly shattered by the fall of France in the summer of 1940. The equally sudden reaction of Australian youth is obvious from the enlistment figures: April, 5,400; May, 8,000; June, 48,500. What was to become of New Caledonia was an immediate problem. The situation was complicated by the fact that the French who lived there were themselves divided, just like their compatriots in the home country. Canberra, thinking it wise to make sure of what co-operation it could get from the more tractable among the French, sent a cruiser which helped tip the balance in favour of de Gaulle's supporters. However a second Australian naval venture was less successful. The British government, acting on the information that Dakar would not need much encouragement to abandon its allegiance to Pétain, sent in a squadron of ships, including an Australian cruiser, which were expected to take possession of the area without having to fire a shot. But the ships were met by gunfire and had to withdraw. Churchill, who had given his approval to the raid, later saw it as a fine example of bad planning, muddle and timidity. Canberra was offended by the whole thing, having been consulted neither on the initial plan nor on its abandonment. Menzies saw fit to cable to London: ' It is absolutely wrong that Australian Government should know practically nothing ... ; absence of real official information from Great Britain has frequently proved humiliating.'* This was the first tiff of the war, between a Dominion which was approaching full independence and a mother country that was unmindful of that fact.

Such differences of opinion were forgotten in the comradeship of battle. Australian flight-crews took part in the Battle of Britain and, some months later, Australian naval units helped to defeat the Italian fleet at Cape Matapan.† But it was especially the Australian army that lived up to the Gallipoli tradition. In September 1940 Mussolini, disappointed at the performance of his troops, who three months before had only been able to conquer the suburbs of Menton although faced with a mere remnant of the French army, decided to launch a grandiose offensive in North Africa. It began well and by early December the Italian invaders, starting from Cyrenaica, had pushed more than fifty kilometres inside Egypt. However, the laurels they won soon withered, and a counter-attack, headed by an Australian division supported by a division of the Indian army, took almost 40,000 prisoners in a few days. On 3 January the counter-attack reached Bardia, on 21 January Tobruk was captured, and on 6 February the Australians, two divisions strong by now, marched into Benghazi. Rome Radio explained away the debacle by referring to ' hordes of bloodthirsty Australians'.

In theory these victorious Australian troops were under the command of a fellow-Australian, General Blamey, who had once been on Monash's staff. Like Monash he was as much a civilian as he was a soldier, having been a teacher before donning uniform, and according to Air Vice-Marshal Tedder was reliable if unimaginative. In fact, although Blamey was nominally commander-in-chief, during the recent fighting some of his troops had been put under a British general. But in the coming battles at least Blamey and his men were to have the satisfaction of fighting side by side.

The Italians, having been pushed into the sea in North Africa,

---

* Quoted by Churchill, W.S., *Their Finest Hour*, Cassell, 1949, p. 645.
† At the southern tip of Greece.

had no better luck in Greece, where their invading force was marking time. Hitler soon lost patience with his humiliated ally and sent
in German troops. Greek resistance quickly crumbled, and Athens
appealed to London for help. The only available forces were the
sixth and seventh Australian divisions and the New Zealand
division. These forces landed at Piraeus on 7 March 1941, supported
by two infantry brigades, one British, the other Polish. Chifley
criticized this move ; Blamey himself had been very reluctant ; and
Menzies had given his approval not without misgivings. Their
apprehension was only too well founded. The expeditionary force
was thrown into the sea six weeks later, after having fought heroically, like Leonidas and his Spartans, at Thermopylae. The Allied
forces fell back on Crete. This proved only a temporary refuge, as
the German paratroopers landed there on 20 May, backed up by
infantry in sufficient numbers for the Allies to have to abandon the
island on 31 May. This first incursion on to European soil had cost
Australia nearly 1,600 killed and more than 5,000 prisoners.

A brief campaign in Syria and Lebanon gave the Australians an
opportunity to redeem themselves. The brunt of the fighting here
was borne by an Australian division. The objective was to oust the
French, who had had possession of these two countries under a
League of Nations mandate. They were now, of course, under the
Vichy government and were thus highly unreliable. From the
military point of view the campaign, though costly, was eventually
a success (it began in early June and was all over a month later) ;
but from the political point of view the situation was unsavoury.
The operation had arisen out of a suggestion by General de Gaulle,
who supplied the invading force with a support brigade. So it was
that the descendants of the heroes of the Somme found themselves
taking part in the fratricidal struggles of the French.

At the same moment, the news from North Africa was disquieting. But however serious the problem might be there, at least it was
one which could be faced with a clear conscience, the enemy being
not a former comrade-in-arms from the first war but the same enemy
as before. At the beginning of 1941, the balance of forces in North
Africa had tipped against the Imperial armies, the Germans having
arrived to assist their Italian allies as in Greece. Rommel had been
put in command in March and attacked at once. Benghazi fell, then
Derna, and the spearheads of the Afrika Korps reached the Egyptian
frontier. This was as far as they were ever to advance, most of the

German forces being held down round Tobruk, which they had besieged in April.

For four months of the total period that the heroic siege of Tobruk lasted, Australians made up more than two thirds of the garrison. The beleaguered troops were under the command of the Australian General Morshead, who like Monash and Blamey was another part-time soldier, his real profession being that of businessman. When the Italians had held Tobruk, they had built a vast fortified camp right round the town, which stands on a promontory above the Mediterranean. This camp (with its perimeter of forty-odd kilo-metres) was improved by the British and Australian troops : they established two separate lines of defence, the outer one designed to slow the waves of attackers and the inner one, strewn with minefields and barbed wire, studded with pillboxes and machine-gun emplacements every 500 metres, designed to stop them. The Germans launched attack after attack, to no avail. The attacks were in fact not as dangerous as the boredom, the searing heat, the dust-storms and especially the intolerable onslaughts of flies and fleas. Supply lines were kept open by sea and there was no shortage of provisions left by the former occupants ; severe rationing made the stocks of water last out. However, dysentery was rife among the besieged men and their strength was flagging.

These Australian troops had been in action since the previous September. In July 1941 their government ventured to suggest that they be relieved, a suggestion to which Churchill did not take kindly. In his telegram to Curtin he said : 'If you insist, I shall agree.' Nevertheless, Churchill reminded the Australian Prime Minister, he would be assuming a great responsibility before history by depriving the Australian troops of their rightful share of the honour of holding on to Tobruk. But such talk cut no ice in Canberra. The British Prime Minister was obviously put out and hinted at Britain's right to expect sacrifices from Australia for the sake of the Empire. But Curtin stood his ground and Churchill eventually gave in, with marked reluctance which he made a point of mentioning to Curtin in his final cable on the matter. The Diggers were relieved by Polish and British units, and sure enough it was they who had the honour of seeing out the siege. When Rommel called it off it had lasted for 242 days. The date when it ended is an easy one to remember : 7 December 1941, the day of the Japanese attack on Pearl Harbor.

Japan, during the first months of the war, had been surprisingly inactive, which optimists saw as a sign that the Japanese were too taken up with their Chinese conquests. The more pessimistic view was that they were probably playing a waiting game, until the trend of events was clearer. What neither school of thought could deny was that Australia was woefully vulnerable. The collapse of France in June 1940 came as a great shock and increased Australia's disquiet. The Admiralty had no comfort to offer, being convinced that Britain must maintain sufficient forces in European waters to deal with the German and Italian fleets, which could only be done by not sending a fleet to the Far East. Appeasement of Japan seemed the only possible solution to Australia's dilemma. In August 1940 an Australian legation was opened in Tokyo. As for the handful of Frenchmen who were attempting to break the Japanese stranglehold on Indo-China, Canberra was even less able than London to offer them anything but encouragement to heroism. Menzies, worried by the outlook, visited the Near East and London at the end of November. In London he received the usual sort of lavish, patronizing welcome that the British are so good at. But as for promises of help, he came away empty-handed. Churchill would only agree to helping Australia if the worst came to the worst – if Australia were actually invaded, then, said Churchill, Britain would sacrifice all other interests, except those which concerned the defence and supply of Britain itself. Australia did obtain one concession : Earle Page, the former leader of the Country Party, who was sent some months later as Australia's special envoy to the British government, was invited to participate in the deliberations of the War Cabinet. He had the satisfaction of being able to transmit to his own government the news that one of the finest British warships, *Prince of Wales*, was to be sent to Singapore after all.

It had by now become imperative to look to Washington. The future Lord Casey had been there, representing Australia, since 1940. The choice of Casey could not have been bettered. The new envoy and his wife were soon well-known figures in a country where there was no lack of well-known figures. They preferred to fly when they went anywhere, each of them at the controls of a different aeroplane. These 'flying diplomats', as they came to be known, attended meetings and conferences by the score, bringing their country to the attention of Americans, to whom Australia was a completely unknown quantity. In March 1941 Australia was included among the list of countries to receive Lend Lease. Page's successor as leader of the Country Party, Fadden, somewhat given to hyperbole, declared that this agreement would become 'as vital for us and for our children as the Magna Carta and the Bill of Rights'. * During that same month an American fleet made a goodwill visit to Sydney and Brisbane, arousing immense popular enthusiasm and inspiring Mr Fadden once more to the heights of eloquence : 'Nothing', he asserted, 'in the life of Australia has so stirred, inspired, and thrilled the nation as has this visit of a part of the great United States Navy, synchronising with the wonderful action and works of President Roosevelt.'†

In April, the signing of a non-aggression pact between Japan and the U.S.S.R. did nothing to still the apprehensions of those who would have preferred some more tangible evidence of assistance than goodwill visits. Australia urged London to get a firm guarantee of support from America. Churchill knew F.D.R. too well for that. He once told Page that Roosevelt could meet over-insistence with a wall of silence that could halt all progress for weeks. However, once America had decided to place the embargo on oil, war became inevitable. As a diplomat who was closely involved in the negotiations later said, every lowering of the Japanese oil reservoirs brought the inevitable moment of decision closer. In October, Washington asked Canberra for permission to use Australian airfields (a request, need one add, that was agreed to). On 5 December the United Kingdom was able to advise the governments of the Dominions that the U.S.A. had finally committed itself to taking part in the war, if the Japanese should attack Malaya, Thailand, the Dutch East Indies or any 'British territory'. Two days later came the Japanese attack on Hawaii.

The sequence of events in that December of 1941 was dramatic. On the 8th the Japanese Fifteenth Army invaded Malaya, landing 600 kilometres north of Singapore, while at the same time other units crossed from China into Hong Kong. Two days later two British capital ships, *Prince of Wales* and *Repulse*, which had ventured up the Malayan coast without air cover, were sent to the bottom. On that same day, 10 December, Guam island fell to the

* Quoted by Esthus, R.A., *From Enmity to Alliance*, University of Washington Press, Seattle, 1964, p. 102.
† *ibid.*, p. 103.

Japanese. On the 22nd the bombing of the Philippines began, and on the 23rd Wake Island surrendered. Three days later Hong Kong capitulated and the Borneo oil wells were captured. By the end of the month a mere 400 kilometres lay between Singapore and the advancing peril. Of the four Australian divisions, three were still in the Near East and the fourth had been sent to Malaya. This meant that Australia was practically defenceless. Such troops as remained in the country were competent enough soldiers, but there were shortages of arms and equipment. The greatest deficiency of all was in air power. Australia was fortunate indeed, in such straits, to have men in government who were not the sort to shirk responsibility.

When Menzies had come back from England in May 1941, he had cause to realize that he had been out of mind as well as out of sight, as his position as Prime Minister was now less secure than he had thought while on the Thames Embankment. He had survived the election of 1940, but only just. The result had been a tie between his supporters and Labor, so that the Menzies government now relied on the support of two independents, who were ostensibly reliable but quite possibly fickle. More importantly, his opponents were disinclined to make things easy for him. When Menzies decided that his presence in London was once again indispensable, and tried to win the opposition's support for this, Labor refused to give it. They also turned down Menzies' invitation to them to sink their differences and join him in a national government, in which Labor would have had a majority. Luck had seemed to turn against Menzies since the day in 1940 when three of his best ministers were killed in an air crash just outside Canberra.

On 28 August he tendered his resignation to the Governor-General, accompanying it with declarations which had a certain ring of grandeur. His obvious successor was the leader of the Country Party, Arthur Fadden, an affable, hard-working, popular man, but not the sort of person to lead a government in time of war. Fadden's interregnum lasted less than six weeks.

Labor came back into power for the first time since the Depression on 7 October 1941. The circumstances in which the Labor men took over the country were infinitely more desperate than they had been in the early 1930s. What sort of men were they who now had to cope with a predicament that would have been quite inconceivable to their predecessors?

John Curtin was the new Prime Minister: aged fifty-six, born in a small country town in the Victorian gold country, he was the son of an Irish policeman. He had left school at thirteen to become first a manual labourer, then an office worker. His heredity was soon reinforced by the message of socialism. Before long he had come to occupy an important place in the trade union movement, and during the First World War had been noted for his opposition to conscription. Drinking to excess became his way, for a time, of resolving conflicting impulses. But he was basically too well balanced to lose control of himself. He pulled himself together and eventually stood for Parliament, to which he was elected in 1928. He rose to be leader of the Labor Party in 1935. He took a special interest in financial matters and his experience of international affairs was limited to a conference that he had attended in Geneva in 1924. His strongest feeling was that of belonging to Australia ; he was convinced that his country had an important role to play. There was nothing of the stand-offish political purist about him, as was instanced in 1939 when he accepted Menzies' invitation to join the Advisory War Council, of which he became an influential member. Menzies said : 'Right through the years of our political opposition to each other, we had a regular practice of personal meetings and conversation.'[*] Churchill too spoke warmly of Curtin's authoritativeness, competence and devotion to duty, an impression that was shared by all those who met him.

Ben Chifley was the same age as his chief and came from a similar modest Irish Catholic background, his father being a blacksmith. From this background he derived his instinctive urge to help the underprivileged. He rose, like many another Labor leader, from small beginnings, working at hard and menial jobs. In 1917, at the age of thirty-two, he reached a turning-point in his life. As a train driver he had taken part in a strike, for which he had lost his job ; he was taken back as a fireman. It has been said that it was a 'sense of injustice rather than ambition that had carried him into the political field'.[†] Having, like Curtin, realized the importance that financial problems were going to have after the war, he began a systematic study of them. He entered Parliament for the first time in 1928 (again like Curtin). In the 1931 anti-Labor landslide he lost his seat and found himself unemployed at the age of forty-six. But

[*] Menzies, R.G., *op. cit.*, p. 125.

[†] Palmer, V., *National Portraits*, pp. 207–8.

he was not the sort of man to give up trying. He threw himself back into union affairs, and single-mindedly set himself the task of ridding the New South Wales Labor Party of Jack Lang, whom he looked on as a demagogue. Although he was not much of a speaker, his delivery was so impassioned that his voice ended up permanently hoarse. His aim was achieved in 1939, when Lang was deposed from the leadership of the New South Wales branch of the party. By now Chifley was well-known. Some years before he had been invited to be a member of a Royal Commission on monetary and banking matters,* and at the beginning of the war the government had appointed him to the new Capital Issues Advisory Board. He was an inevitable choice for the Curtin Cabinet in 1941. His portfolio was the Treasury, to which was added later the Department of Post-War Reconstruction, where he enjoyed the collaboration of Dr Coombs and a young and enthusiastic team. His biographer says : ' In the nerve-racking loneliness of making crucial war decisions . . . Curtin had looked increasingly to Chifley not only for advice but for companionship, refreshment and moral support.'† Menzies called him 'the most authentic Labour leader in Australian political history'.‡ To Chifley the aims of socialism were not mere slogans, but real formulas for action – 'the light on the hill', as he himself put it. Manning Clark says : 'His life, personality and tastes seemed to sum up the history and aspirations of radicalism in Australia.'§ There can be no doubt that Chifley was a man of noble stamp, a man who commands admiration.‖

Herbert Vere Evatt was a very different sort of person. He belonged to the category of people whom Chifley, in moments of ill humour, would dismiss as 'those bloody B.A.s !' Evatt's books speak for themselves about the man's intellect. He brought to the government an ability to handle general concepts which may have been somewhat lacking in his colleagues. Evatt, too, believed in the

---

* He submitted a minority report recommending nationalization of the banks. See pages 364–5.

† Crisp, L.F., *Ben Chifley*, p. 214.

‡ Menzies, R.G., *op. cit.*, pp. 128–9.

§ Clark, C.M.H., *A Short History of Australia*, p. 251.

‖ Even the great have their petty points, of course. Chifley's was a show of simplicity – he always refused to wear a dinner jacket, even for a banquet at Buckingham Palace. Enough to make Bruce wince.

ideals of socialism and was convinced they were bound to come true in Australia. Professor Pike describes him as 'an impetuous and forceful intellectual'.* Menzies, in a less charitable verdict, put much of Evatt's activity down to frustrated ambition. Certainly, humility was not his strongest point ; some said that he saw himself as a man of destiny and that he had an extraordinary sense of his own importance. His manner, which was inclined to be abrupt and aggressive, and his careless appearance ('a large, untidy, rumpled man, whose clothes looked as if he had slept in them'),† turned many people against him. But when H.V. Evatt became Minister for External Affairs, the sincerity of his convictions and the warmth with which he advocated them made Australia's name and views widely known.

These were some of the men who had been in office two months to the day when they heard the news of Pearl Harbor. Sir Paul Hasluck says that 'realism' seems to have been one of Curtin's favourite words. And certainly the new Prime Minister coped realistically with the test now confronting him and his country. First of all, when he declared war on Japan on 9 December, he made a point of doing it independently of the British government.‡ Within three weeks he had effected a total reversal of Australian policy, which he announced to the country in a New Year message. Newspaper readers must have found it hard to believe their eyes on reading these lines on 29 December 1941 under the name of their Prime Minister :

Without any inhibitions of any kind, I make it quite clear that Australia looks to America, free of any pangs as to our traditional links or kinship with the United Kingdom. We know the problems that the United Kingdom faces ... But we know, too, that Australia can go and Britain can still hold on. We are, therefore, determined that Australia shall not go, and shall exert all our energies towards the shaping of a plan, with the United States as its keystone, which will give to our country some confidence of being able to hold out until the tide of battle swings against the enemy. §

* Pike, D., *Australia : the Quiet Continent*, p. 203.
† Edwards, C., *Bruce of Melbourne*, p. 337.
‡ The same procedure had been followed the previous day for the declarations of war on Finland, Hungary and Romania, against whom the U.S.S.R. had demanded that the Allies take an official stance.

Churchill was upset, saying that Curtin's statement had produced the 'worst impression' and would be exploited by the enemy.* But then Churchill was presumably unaware that Curtin had already stated in Parliament, as far back as November 1936, that Australia would need a sounder basis for its future policy than the goodwill of British statesmen.

By December 1941, certainly, Australia had no further choice in the matter, and had either to seek a new protector in the U.S.A. or to undergo the horrors of a Japanese occupation. Bad news kept coming in. At the end of January the Japanese invaded New Britain and the Celebes, and tightened their grip on Borneo. But the real source of anxiety for Australia was their irresistible advance down through Malaya. The last available Australian division had been sent there, under an energetic commander, Gordon Bennett by name, who seems to have been more hard-bitten than his British colleagues. Bennett was convinced that the only hope lay in counter-attacking as soon as possible, and begged for reinforcements, especially aircraft. But the problem was where these were to be found. By mid-January the Japanese were only about 200 kilometres away from Singapore. On 8 February the invaders reached the island itself, on which a supposedly impregnable fortress had been built (a sort of Far Eastern Maginot Line) – with all its guns set pointing out to sea! General Wavell made an inspection a few days before the end. He reported in a cautiously but unencouragingly worded telegram: 'Morale of some troops is not good, and none is as high as I should like to see.'† The invaders closed the vice. On 14 February the town was cut off from its water supply and the garrison had supplies left for only a few more days. The following day they had to surrender. Bennett and two of his staff managed to escape. Seventeen thousand Australians were taken prisoner, which amounted to almost one quarter of the country's forces in the region; the conquerors of Singapore also captured 125,000 other Imperial troops. Lord Moran says that Churchill was 'stupefied'

---

* In fact, Nazi radio never missed an opportunity of referring to Australia as 'the orphan in the Pacific'.

† Quoted by Moran, C., *Winston Churchill, the Struggle for Survival 1940–1945*, Constable, 1966, p. 27.

§ Quoted by Watt, A., *The Evolution of Australian Foreign Policy*, Cambridge University Press, 1967, p. 55.

when he received the news, seeing it as the worst disaster and the greatest surrender in British history.* Curtin did not mince words ; he told the nation that ' The fall of Singapore can only be described as Australia's Dunkirk. It will be recalled that the fall of Dunkirk initiated the Battle for Britain. The fall of Singapore opens the Battle for Australia.'†

At this juncture the two Australian divisions which had been fighting in North Africa were being shipped eastwards across the Indian Ocean. The decision to withdraw them from North Africa had been taken in January, not at the request of Australia but on Churchill's instructions, according to Sir Paul Hasluck. They were originally bound for Malaya ; but when the British situation became untenable there, it was decided to send them to Sumatra and Java. The first ships of the convoy reached Colombo just as Singapore fell. Now that the barrier of Malaya was down, the Dutch East Indies looked as though they must be the next to fall. However the Allies still held Burma, which was an essential point on the only route still open to China. Churchill, who was nothing if not decisive, agreed with Roosevelt that the Australian division which had arrived first in Ceylon should be sent to Rangoon and, without asking Canberra's opinion, issued his order accordingly. But he was reckoning without Curtin. The Australian leader reacted sharply :

It appears that you ... treated our approval to this vital diversion as merely a matter of form. By doing so, you have established a physical situation which adds to the dangers of the convoy, and the responsibility for the consequences of such diversion rests upon you.‡

---

* In his book *La Guerre du Pacifique*, Paris, 1968, vol. I, p. 100, Bernard Millot writes : 'Great Britain, uneasy at Japan's tremendous expansion and very worried by the direct threat it posed for Australia, made secret peace overtures to Japan on 16 February 1942. The British government offered to recognize Japanese authority over northern China and to use its influence to persuade the U.S.A. to agree to this also. In exchange for this concession, the British government requested that its sovereignty in Malaya and Singapore be re-established.' The Japanese Prime Minister, Tojo, 'rejected the British peace proposals and gave free rein to his ambitious strategists '.

† Hasluck, P., *The Government and the People 1942–1945*, Australian War Memorial, Canberra, 1970, p. 70.

‡ See Churchill, W.S., *The Hinge of Fate*, Cassell, 1951, p. 144.

The indignation of Churchill can be imagined, if one can judge from his reaction to another of Curtin's telegrams at the beginning of January, as recounted by Lord Moran :

The P.M. is in a belligerent mood. He told us that he had sent a stiff telegram to Curtin, the Prime Minister of Australia ... The P.M. fulminated ... London had not made a fuss when it was bombed. Why should Australia ? At one moment he took the line that Curtin and his Government did not represent the people of Australia. At another that the Australians came from bad stock ... I did not worry about the Australians. I knew that he had been persuaded to tone down the cable before it was sent. Besides, he liked them as men and respected them as fighting soldiers.[*]

The exchanges between Curtin and Churchill which followed were just as tart. Churchill was quite clearly flabbergasted that anyone should actually question his instructions. Sometimes there was a touch of insolence in his comments :

We could not help feeling that when in 1940 we had been exposed to the same fearful danger in a far closer and more probable form we had not lost our sense of proportion or hesitated to add to our risks for the sake of other vital needs.[†]

Or he might invoke the authority and name of Roosevelt : 'We could not contemplate that you would refuse our request, and that of the President of the United States, for the diversion of the leading Australian division to save the situation in Burma.'[‡] Curtin stood his ground again, and the troops were sent back to Australia, arriving in the middle of March.

Curtin's inflexibility is entirely comprehensible. On 8 March Rangoon fell to the enemy, and was the prelude to the evacuation of all of Burma. And on that same day the Japanese landed at Lae and Salamaua on the north coast of New Guinea. Three weeks earlier, Australia itself had been suddenly shocked out of its calm sense of remoteness from it all, when Japanese planes had bombed Darwin twice on the same day, 19 February, leaving 243 people

[*] Moran, Lord, *op. cit.*, p. 21.
[†] Churchill, W.S., *The Hinge of Fate*, p. 138. The reference is to the dispatch of a British division to Egypt in August 1940.
[‡] *ibid.*, p. 143.

dead and sinking six ships. Then on 3 March it had been the turn of Broome, a small pearling port in the north-west, where seventy people were killed. Other attacks in the same region followed. At the same time there was an influx of refugees from Malaya and the Dutch East Indies, many of them panic-stricken. From that top end of the continent, Curtin's statements that the entire territory of Australia would be safeguarded, and that the Japanese would be met with resistance wherever they might invade, seemed more like empty words than a declaration of intent. The capital cities, because of distance, were for the time being safe from the bombers, although Sydney did have its moment of alarm on the evening of 31 May, when four Japanese midget submarines managed to penetrate Sydney Harbour. The episode turned out to be comical rather than serious. Bernard Millot has told the story of what became of these craft – one was caught in an anti-submarine net and was blown up by its crew ; another was blown up by the premature explosion of its own torpedo ; the third 'surfaced at the wrong moment' and was sunk forthwith ; as for the last one, 'it was never seen or heard of again'. Australian casualties were nineteen dead ; a harbour ferry was also damaged.*

By that time the general situation had taken a turn for the better. Brisbane had seen the arrival of the first American troops only a fortnight after Pearl Harbor, and their numbers had been increasing ever since. A great event was the sudden arrival on 17 March of MacArthur. This extraordinary man, probably the greatest American of his day, bore the appropriately imposing title of Supreme Commander of Allied Forces in the South-West Pacific. Four days later he made a triumphal visit to Melbourne, being met at the station by members of the government and opposition, top civil servants and military men as well as a huge crowd. He posed obligingly for photographers. He went to Canberra on 26 March, to be greeted, says Sir Paul Hasluck, with all the awe that was normally reserved for visiting royalty.† Here he made the acquaintance of Curtin ; the two men were to get on famously. At the beginning of April, when a whole American division landed in Australia, it was

---

* Sydney and Newcastle came under shelling from Japanese ships again on 7 June.

† Hasluck, P., *op. cit.*, p. 158.

clear the Supreme Commander was not going to be content with token visits.

That autumn Australian anxieties were somewhat allayed by two naval encounters. At the time these engagements (later known as the Battle of the Coral Sea and the Battle of Midway Island) seemed indecisive ; but they came to be seen as the encounters which marked the end of Japanese expansion. New Guinea, however, was still a danger spot. The Japanese, having landed in March at the north-eastern side of the island, once again looked like achieving the impossible, advancing as they were through the jungle towards Port Moresby along the mountainous and seemingly impassable Kokoda Trail. In August they landed troops at Milne Bay, to the east of Port Moresby, a malarial area of torrential rains, where despite the shortage of flat ground small airfields sometimes only a few hundred yards long had been built. Here Australian troops fought the Japanese for five days and inflicted a defeat on them. This defeat was a minor one, no doubt, but it was the first time anyone had withstood them. Then, in September, they were stopped again, this time only a few kilometres short of Port Moresby.

Eight years after the end of the war, Churchill was asked which time had been the most anxious for him. Without hesitation, he replied : 'September–October 1942'. At this time the fortunes of the Allies seemed at their lowest ebb in North Africa as well as in the Far East. The first six months of that year had been catastrophic. Rommel, sweeping all before him, had recaptured Tobruk and by July had reached a place called El Alamein, less than 100 kilometres from Alexandria. Churchill was irritable, petulantly wondering whether Britain had not at least one general who could win a battle. Montgomery was put in command of the Eighth Army. It contained troops of many different nationalities. British, South Africans, Indians, Australians, Poles and even French units which had distinguished themselves in the defence of Bir-Hakeim. Montgomery immortalized these troops in a striking phrase, saying that every man was as confident as an emperor. Rommel's last attack had failed on 31 August. The Allied Commander-in-Chief decided that it was time to go on the offensive. At the end of October Australian units, on three different occasions, were given the task of wearing down the enemy. Then, on 31 October, the full offensive was launched. By 4 November the Germans were in retreat, and they were not to stop until they surrendered at Tunis, on 12 May

1943, where they were caught between the armies of Eisenhower, Giraud and Montgomery. After the battle of El Alamein the Australians took no further part in the North African campaign. Curtin had been requesting their withdrawal for months. They eventually got back to Australia at the end of February. Churchill sent a telegram of congratulation, praising their energy, courage, initiative and daring.

After a period of rest, these troops were sent to New Guinea. There they found an atmosphere of quiet confidence. At the end of September Blamey had been put in command in New Guinea, at MacArthur's request. Since then a counter-attack, with American support, had been under way. The Australians were soon the equals of the Japanese at fighting on the most unfavourable terrain and using camouflage. They hacked their way forward through dense, stifling greenery, across swampy, miasmic, mosquito-infested valleys, over steep, rain-sodden hills. The 'Diggers' said their march over the Kokoda Trail was 'forward on hands and knees, backward on backsides'. Such acrobatic postures did not stop their advance, and by January 1943 all of Papua had been liberated from Japanese occupation.

1943 began auspiciously. The American victory at Guadalcanal had given the Allies control of the South Pacific ; North Africa had been cleared ; Stalingrad was about to fall. As Churchill put it, it was 'the end of the beginning'. MacArthur reviewed his strategy. His instinct was to do things on the grand scale. To set about the business of reconquering one after another all the territories that Japan had occupied struck him as too long-drawn-out and unenterprising a process. His scheme was to bypass these places and go straight for Tokyo, without worrying too much about the quite considerable Japanese armies which this move would leave in the field. He was sure that, once Tokyo fell, these armies would be forced to surrender. This plan posed a problem for Australia. The Australian army still comprised two different elements : volunteers who had fought in North Africa, like their counterparts who had gone to fight in France and Palestine in the first war, and conscripts, who could not be sent overseas to fight. Americans, who had themselves come from overseas to defend Australians, were bound to have at least mixed feelings for Australians who would not go overseas to defend themselves.* This dual composition of the Australian forces was now acutely embarrassing to the government, since the flow of recruits was not keeping pace with reinforcement requirements. Naturally, straightforward conscription for service overseas was out of the question. On this point Curtin's political instinct was too sound for him to attempt any move like the one which had got Hughes into such hot water twenty-five years before.* His solution to the dilemma was a compromise which by his personal authority he managed to get through Parliament. The conscript army could be sent to fight outside Australia, but only to a well-defined region, known as the South-West Pacific Zone. This zone was bounded to the west by the 110° meridian, to the east by the 159° meridian, and to the north by the Equator. This meant that no conscript could be sent to fight in Sumatra, Malaya, the Philippines or the islands under Japanese mandate, the Marshalls, the Carolinas and the Marianas. However, the zone did include all of New Guinea and Timor. Java being bisected by the 110° meridian, and the Solomons by the 159° meridian, the western and eastern areas respectively of these islands were thus out of bounds to Australian conscript units. The same went for the Moluccas, the Celebes and part of Borneo, all of them lying north of the Equator. This arrangement may have been quaint and unprecedented, but it was probably the only possible one in the circumstances.

Certainly it was a solution which ruled out the possibility of Australia playing an important part in the reconquest of the Pacific. Not that America would probably have wanted her to. The arrival of American troops in Australia so soon after Pearl Harbor meant not only that they were there to help a very apprehensive ally, but also that Australia was the only country where they could establish the bases they needed in the region. Also, as C.H. Grattan points out, 'Australia was undoubtedly perceived by the Americans as a close associate of the United Kingdom, not as an autonomous Pacific power, an ancillary character emphasised by Australia's own insistence upon maintaining the " diplomatic unity of the British

---

* Sir Paul Hasluck writes : 'There was a certain comic dexterity about the way in which both Government and Opposition claimed the merits of conscription and avoided the responsibility for it' (*op. cit*., p. 320).

---

* They nicknamed them 'Chocos' (meaning chocolate soldiers) and 'Koalas', because, like their charming little namesakes, it was forbidden to kill them or export them.

Empire".'* It must be added, too, that as American strength in the region increased,† MacArthur became more and more inclined to look on the glory of victory as belonging by rights to the U.S.A.

London went on speaking highly of its most faithful Dominion and forgetting to ask its opinion on matters which concerned it. The representatives of Australia in London, Page and later Bruce, not only made no secret of what they thought, but often had to shout and insist so as to be sure that they were making themselves heard. Heard they may well have been, but listened to probably not so often. This was brought home unpleasantly to Evatt, then Minister for External Affairs, in November 1943, when Roosevelt, Churchill and Chiang Kai-shek met in Cairo. The agenda included the war in the Pacific and ways and means of bringing about an unconditional Japanese surrender. Australia was not invited to take part and its name was not even mentioned in the final communiqué. There was nothing that Curtin and his government could do about this, except perhaps resent it. Their resentment of such treatment must have been strengthened by the knowledge that they had the support of the greater part of the Australian people, for Labor had won a great victory at the elections the previous August and now held forty-nine of the seventy-five seats in the House of Representatives.

Evatt, excluded by the 'Great Powers' from their global strategy sessions, had to be content with planning a regional agreement and drawing as much attention to it as possible. Australia and New Zealand had exchanged High Commissioners in 1943. Both countries had Labor governments. In January 1944, with the aim of reminding their Allies of their existence, they signed a mutual co-operation pact (known as the A.N.Z.A.A.C. pact), declaring that henceforth no question of relevance to the South Pacific could be settled without their participation. This pact may well have been inspired by the two countries' wish to get their own back, as neither London nor Washington had been notified of it in advance. Indeed,

---

* Grattan, C.H., *The United States and the Southwest Pacific*, Oxford University Press, Melbourne, 1961, p. 172.

† In the spring of 1943 there were 111,000 Americans as against 466,000 Australians; at the end of 1944, 531,000 Americans to 436,000 Australians; by the time Japan surrendered, the numbers were 862,000 Americans and 380,000 Australians. This imbalance was especially marked in the navy and air force.

they were only belatedly informed. Great Britain had no objection ; but America did not look too favourably on what seemed to be a latter-day version of the Monroe Doctrine.

While heads of state and diplomats talked, the soldiers went on fighting. In the last two years of the war the Australians had the thankless but proud task of liberating the rest of New Guinea, Bougainville and New Britain. This they did with American assistance. The conditions in which they fought were frightful. The New Britain campaign has been described by Bernard Millot :

They blundered up to the waist into slimy swamps hidden by impossibly dense vegetation and studded here and there with tiny knolls of firm ground. The Americans, some of whom had even seen action on Guadalcanal, were appalled ; they had never seen anything like this. Everything the troops touched was flabby, moist and sticky ; they lived in a precarious world of rotting vegetable matter . . . Even the most watertight tropical coverings were drenched all the time. Men, weapons and munitions were for ever smeared with the same unrelenting slime. In the tropical heat, it was like some great cesspool giving off the most overpowering stench of decomposition.

When the two atomic bombs were dropped on Hiroshima and Nagasaki, the Australians, under General Morshead, the hero of Tobruk, were in Borneo, mopping up (as the soldiers say).

On 2 September 1945 a ceremony took place on the deck of the U.S.S. *Missouri*, anchored in Tokyo Bay. It has often been described : MacArthur receiving the official Japanese surrender ; beside him, Wainwright, beaten in the Philippines, and Percival, beaten at Singapore. Japan was represented by six officers in battle-dress and five civilians in tails and top hats. The final terms were signed by nine victorious countries : the U.S.A., China, the U.K., the U.S.S.R., Australia, Canada, France, Holland and New Zealand. General Blamey signed on behalf of Australia. During the Allied occupation of Japan, it fell to him to command the British Imperial forces. And in certain sectors of the war zone, in Borneo, New Britain, Timor and in some parts of the Dutch East Indies, the Japanese made their local surrenders to Australians.

Some 550,000 Australians, women as well as men, had been involved in the military operations, representing about eight per cent of the nation. Of these, 21,136 lost their lives, 17,505 of them in the Pacific, 3,631 in North Africa ; in all, this amounted only to one third of Australian casualties in the First World War. There were 31,000 Australians taken prisoner, 8,500 of them by Germany and Italy, 22,500 by the Japanese. More than a third of these prisoners of the Japanese died in captivity. When the survivors were freed, it was like the Nazi concentration camps all over again. Typical of the heartbreaking tales they had to tell, of the privations they had suffered and the indignities inflicted on them, is Rohan Rivett's book.*

And then life went on. Curtin did not live to see the victory that he had done so much to make possible; he died on 5 July 1945. Menzies paid him this tribute:

As an Opposition Leader, I have long admired his political skill, his capacity for securing unity of purpose and direction, his unflagging industry ... his selfless devotion to the Australian people ... [He] sought nothing in politics except the good of all others, as he understood it ; [he] followed his lights with unswerving fidelity ; [he] really believed in justice ; [he] saw politics clearly as a conflict of ideas and not as a sordid battle of personal hostilities and ignoble ambitions.†

On 13 July, Chifley became Prime Minister. Over the previous three months Evatt had represented Australia at the San Francisco Conference where the United Nations Charter was adopted. Evatt had played an important role at the conference, using all his vigour and eloquence as the spokesman of the smaller nations. This time, Australia had no grounds for complaint. For by 1945, with her experience and exploits in two wars behind her, who could have questioned Australia's right to sovereignty ?

---

* Rivett, R., *Behind Bamboo*, Angus & Robertson, Sydney, 1946.
† Quoted by Hasluck, P., *op. cit.*, p. 589.

Part Five

Australia as a Sovereign Power
1945-1973

Chapter Twenty one

The curtain rises (I)

Economic transformations resulting from the war – Communist threat – Chifley's policies – social reforms – continuing strikes – bank nation- alization scheme – Labor's defeat – return of the Liberals – Menzies in power for sixteen years – the secret of Menzies' success – defeat of proposal to outlaw Communist Party – Petrov – Santamaria's influence – D.L.P. founded – repeated Liberal successes – Menzies steps down – Holt, Gorton and McMahon – contrast between appearances and reality

There is a French theatrical tradition known as *les trois coups* – three resounding blows are struck on the stage behind the scenes to tell the audience that the curtain is about to rise on the opening scene of the play. One is reminded of these three blows when looking at the history of Australia since the Second World War. On the surface, nothing seems to have changed, the political lines are more or less the same as those drawn in the previous period, and the country's economic growth, although more rapid since the war, is still subject to periods of sluggishness. But on closer inspection one sees that the country has in fact absorbed three tremendous impacts which are bound to have a profound effect on its future. Firstly, the nation's ethnic composition was greatly altered by post-war immigration ; secondly, the discovery of immense mineral wealth raised problems of unprecedented complexity ; and lastly, Austra- lia's accession to full sovereignty forced her out of her complacency and 'splendid isolation'. These changes are the three blows that announce the raising of the curtain on a new Australia.

The transformations effected in Australia's economy by the war were quite unlike anything the country had ever experienced. Twenty-five years before, everyday life had gone on more or less as usual, largely unaffected by a war which was something like a colonial expedition in reverse. But between 1939 and 1945 the danger had been much nearer and more pressing, and radical measures had been needed to cope with it. In fact, during those years Australia knew something of what totalitarianism means.

The first area to feel the effect of this was industry. During the 1914–18 war, Australian industry had supplied England with small arms, some explosives, and especially clothing. But in the life-or-death six-year struggle that Australia had just come through, no source of supply could be overlooked. It must also be pointed out that, by the outbreak of the war, Australia was sufficiently industrialized to be able to make a much more significant contribution to the common effort. A government department was set up to get the programme of industrial expansion under way, decide priorities, fix production schedules and supervise the distribution of raw materials. In such circumstances the number of Federal public servants doubled in five years, growing from 47,000 in 1939 to 94,000 in 1945. Many of these public servants were businessmen who brought the benefit of their experience to the service of the nation. According to E.R. Walker, private enterprise 'supplied most of the technical skill and almost all the managerial activities involved in the actual processes of production'.* The government and the private industries each looked after different areas of production, in a way which was to become typical of the mixed economy that one finds in contemporary Australia (see page 405). The government was responsible for the building of aeroplanes and the manufacture of munitions. The private sector, under strict government supervision, took on the other responsibilities of the war effort. The magnitude of this industrial achievement can best be gauged from two simple sets of figures : between 1939 and 1945 the number of factory workers rose from 549,000 to 753,000 ; perhaps even more revealing are the figures for the increased contribution of women to the workforce, rising from 171,000 to 286,000.

Agriculture was bound to suffer from such large changes in national work patterns. Almost one fifth of the agricultural workforce left the land, the immediate consequences of which were that there was a drop of one third in the area under cultivation ; wheat

---

* Walker, E.R., *The Australian Economy in War and Reconstruction*, Oxford University Press, New York, 1947, p. 153.

production fell from 5.6 million to 1.9 million cubic metres; and sugar production dropped to 680,000 tonnes from 840,000. This situation was worrying enough, but it was aggravated by the lack of fertilizers* and by prolonged drought during the last two years of the war. Wool managed to see it through better than other primary industries, but only because the United Kingdom, aware of the fundamental importance of the pastoral industry to Australia, agreed to buy the wool clip in its entirety.

One result of this situation, with a downturn in agricultural production, manufacturing industry almost totally geared to military needs, and imports reduced to the barest minimum, was bound to be a scarcity of consumer goods. Price control was also inevitable; it seems to have been applied in a most effective manner, since the retail price index rose by a mere 20 per cent over a five-year period, despite a fivefold increase in the amount of money in circulation. Notwithstanding its effectiveness, price control would have been unable to restrain demand without the added curb of rationing. Petrol was rationed from 1940; later, gas and electricity supplies were also rationed. Finally, in 1942, when a Japanese invasion seemed likely, rationing coupons for food and clothing were issued.

Obviously, in this respect, Australia's fate was shared by most of the other countries involved in the war. But there was one feature of Australia's wartime experience which had a profound and lasting effect on the precarious balance that had been arrived at between the Commonwealth government and the States, and which deserves attention. It has been said that the Second World War cost Australia ten times more than the first war had done. But the fact is that whereas the 1914–18 conflict had been essentially financed by loans, the Curtin government, having learned from that experience, insisted on the prime importance of financial management; with the result that, through prudent taxation measures, the government managed to cover two thirds of its expenditure over the war years. Revenue, as always, was a problem. At the inception of the income tax scheme in 1915, the States, which were already taxing incomes, had been empowered to keep this source of revenue. In this way they kept a small measure of their financial independence, which had been greatly reduced in 1901 by the transfer to the new Com-

---

* Most of Australia's phosphates came from Nauru, which had been occupied by the Japanese.

monwealth of their right to impose customs duties and indirect taxation. In 1942, using the argument of wartime necessity, the Federal government (which had already decided that no loans could be launched except under its own auspices) gave itself a monopoly on income tax. Some government action was now necessary to save local authorities from having to beg. It was decided that every year Canberra would distribute funds to the States. This annual distribution of funds has been called one of the least edifying occasions in Australian political life.

By 1945, therefore, the Federation was already very different from the conceptions of its founding fathers half a century before. Having at its disposal the lion's share of the national revenue and exercising a degree of economic control that was more like authority than supervision, there was little that did not come within its ambit. This, of course, suited the Labor men who by the end of the war had been in government for four years.

These men thought the time was now ripe for making the old socialist dream come true. There was, however, one obstacle to this aspiration, which had somehow escaped the notice of idealists who had been waiting long years for this moment. The Communists had by now risen from a position of insignificance to one where their influence could no longer be ignored. Like their counterparts elsewhere, at the beginning of the war they had been violently opposed to taking any part in the struggle between the 'imperialists'. And, like those counterparts elsewhere, they saw the light as soon as the Nazis invaded Russia. From then on they were paragons of patriotism. The prestige of Soviet Russia during the war boosted the Communist Party's recruitment figures. It has been said (although these figures may be unreliable) that membership of the party rose from 5,000 to 24,000 over a period of five years. In any case it was their methods which were dangerous, rather than their numbers. Knowing everything there is to know about infiltration techniques, they systematically took over the leadership of one union after another, and engineered disruption by calling on their members to down tools.

Chifley was in a difficult position, since the greater part of his power base was among the working class. At the same time he was too aware of the need to temper the demands of social justice with the realistic imperatives of rationality for Communism to be anything but anathema to him. When he said of Communists, 'Their interests are not the same as those of the Labour movement and if [it is suggested] that the Labour Party should in any way co-operate with the Communist Party then I definitely cannot agree,'* nobody could be in any doubt of the sincerity with which he spoke, being after all the leader of a political party that owed much of its inspiration to Roman Catholicism. But when he added : ' While we often disagree entirely with the views held by other people, freedom of speech and freedom of the press are cardinal features in a real democracy and are part of the policy of the Australian Labour Party,'† his conviction was equally intense. When a wave of strikes started in 1945 – the worst since 1917, according to T.R. Reese – Chifley must have made the painful discovery (that so many other Labor-style governments have made) that he and his supporters had two different conceptions of the golden future that awaited them.

Chifley decided that the best way to retain the support of the uncritical enthusiasts who were attracted by the mirage of Communism was to press on with a long overdue programme of social security. Within his first year as Prime Minister he brought in the widows' pension. In 1944, not waiting for the end of the war, the Labor government had tried to introduce a national health service, similar in some respects to the one which was soon to be operating in Britain. But Labor had had to be content with a partial service, the High Court having declared the measure unconstitutional and a subsequent referendum having endorsed this view. Chifley was nothing if not dogged. He took the idea up again two years later and this time managed to have it approved by referendum – but only just, the 'Yes' vote being 54.59 per cent. At the same time he had the satisfaction of seeing his government returned at the general election ; the few seats he lost in the House of Representatives were made up for by a few gains in the Senate.

Despite this, disturbing signs for Labor soon appeared in the States. Between March and May 1947 the results of elections in four States must have worried Labor's campaign planners, showing as they did a marked swing away from Labor's recent performance in the Federal sphere. For the first time since 1933, Labor was defeated in Western Australia ; in New South Wales and Queensland its

* Crisp, L.F., *Ben Chifley*, p. 358.
† *ibid.*, p. 356.

majority was substantially reduced ; and in South Australia the anti-Labor coalition was easily re-elected. Nevertheless, Chifley continued to put into practice the theories which, to him, were close to articles of faith. First he decided to streamline the arbitration procedures, which Australia took pride in having pioneered. Industrial disputes were henceforth to be settled by reference to fifteen arbitration commissioners, a change which was designed to make for speedier settlements than those arrived at by the court. The court was still to be responsible for fixing the minimum wage and hours of work ; and Chifley – after a wait of twenty-two months – also managed to have it approve the 40-hour week.

This was all very well, but it did not prevent price rises or Communist activity. These two forces kept the movement of sporadic strikes going. In 1949 the agitation took on a new dimension, becoming localized among the coal miners. This was a sector of the workforce with a long tradition of militancy behind it. This time the demand was for a 35-hour week. When nothing came of their claim, the miners cut off production throughout the country with the exception of Western Australia. It was mid-winter. In this contingency Chifley showed his statesmanship yet again, asking for emergency powers, using them without hesitation or half-measures, bringing in troops, freezing union funds, fining the coal miners' union and even clapping some strikers in jail. In less than two months the strike movement was broken.*

Chifley knew that his government itself was at stake in this situation, as a general election was due in a few months. No matter how often one comes across the phenomenon, one is for ever surprised at how power can blunt the judgement of those who exercise it. Chifley, in this case, had been in power for four years. And at the very time when signs of discontent were growing all about him, he chose as an election issue one of the most unreliable imaginable – bank nationalization. This idea had been part of Labor's platform since 1919. Should it not have crossed the Prime Minister's mind that here was a sleeping dog that should be let lie ? One must point out, of course, that the project to nationalize the banks was one which was close to Chifley's heart, having originated

---

* One wonders whether Chifley had heard of a similar strike in France the year before, which had been broken just as energetically by another socialist minister, Jules Moch.

in his study of financial matters ; and that he had already mooted it two years previously. The Bill, brought down in August 1947, had roused a storm of protest. L.J. McConnan, chief manager of one of the oldest banking houses in the country, the National Bank of Australasia, came to the fore to lead the opposition to the government's proposal. He has been described as an 'urbane and smooth' man, with a 'deep well of charm and tact' ;* he also knew exactly what he wanted – newspaper advertising space was inundated with propaganda and account holders were bombarded with brochures, while radio stations seemed to talk of nothing else. In November, Parliament, unimpressed by all the rumpus, passed the bill empowering the Commonwealth Bank to be the sole shareholder in the businesses of its privately owned competitors. However, this was only the beginning. The Act had to go before the High Court for an assessment of its constitutionality. The Court's ruling, handed down in August 1948, was that the Act was in fact unconstitutional. Accordingly Chifley, undaunted, took advantage of a clause in the 1901 Constitution that provided for appeals to the Privy Council in London. He may have been hoping that this expedient would win over some of the diehards who were in favour of all and any ties with the Crown. If so, this hope was dashed by the Privy Council which pronounced against him only two months before the country was to go to the polls.

At that point, rather belatedly, Labor began to play down the issue. By then an election campaign of unprecedented bitterness was in full swing, during which Chifley was called everything from Hitler and Mussolini to Judas and Ned Kelly. He appeared in newspaper cartoons under the heading 'National-Socialist leaders of the twentieth century'.† One wonders to what extent such tactics influenced the voters. Perhaps they already thought it was time for a change. Whatever the case may be, on 10 December 1949 only forty-seven Labor members were returned, as against seventy-four belonging to the Liberal and Country parties. There was also one individualist daring enough to style himself 'Independent'.

In 1949, before losing office, Chifley had established two bodies which were to be of great significance to modern Australia. The Snowy Mountains Hydro-Electric Authority had been set up to

* Blainey, G., *Gold and Paper*, p. 345.

† Crisp, L.F., *op. cit.*, p. 340.

supervise one of the most farsighted irrigation and energy schemes in the world. Not long after, in Canberra, he had founded the Australian National University, whose teachers were to make significant contributions in all fields of research. The defeated leader must have drawn some consolation from these two achievements. If he was at all inclined to reminisce, he must also have remembered those dark days late in 1941, when his own leader John Curtin had had the courage to make an abrupt (and, to some, a shocking) change of course in the country's external policies; or those four years when his team had steered the country through times the like of which it had never experienced before. He may also have drawn some comfort from the knowledge that even Churchill, another leader who had done much to make victory possible, had been rewarded by electoral defeat.

Credit for the rout of Labor in 1949 must definitely go to Menzies. Four years before, at the end of the war, his chances of being returned to office were meagre indeed. The anti-Labor parties were ridden by factionalism and there was ill-feeling between the United Australia Party and the Country Party. Both groups, as Manning Clark says, were 'close to public ridicule and disgrace'.* But ambitious men can sometimes draw unsuspected strength from their ambition itself. Menzies had time enough to wait, and he knew the importance of good timing. He was convinced that the first condition of any counter-attack by the non-Labor forces would have to be a regrouping under a new flag. The new party was to be called the 'Liberal' party, a term that was imprecise enough to be safe. Menzies explained, twenty years later, what meaning he saw in the change of name:

When ... we decided to call the new and united party the Liberal Party, we were adopting no analogy to the Liberal Party in the U.K. [which] certainly does not constitute an alternative government ... hoping simply to play off one great party against another ...

We took the name 'Liberal' because we were determined to be a progressive party, willing to make experiments, in no sense reactionary but believing in the individual, his rights, and his enterprise, and rejecting the Socialist panacea ...

Socialism means high costs, inefficiency, the constant intrusion of

* Clark, C.M.H., *A Short History of Australia*, p. 237.

political considerations, the damping down of enterprise, the overlord-
ship of routine . . .

My friends and I recognized the economic responsibilities of the State
to assist in preventing the recurrence of large-scale unemployment by
appropriate economic and monetary measures ; to secure, through social
legislation, a decent and reasonable measure of economic security and
material well-being for all responsible citizens ; and to succeed in both
of these purposes by creating a state of affairs which would encourage
the enterprise, resourcefulness, and efficiency of individuals and lead to
the greatest possible output of the needed goods and services.*

So much for the party's origins. In its practice of government it
took an essentially pragmatic approach. In 1967, after sixteen years
in office, Menzies made no bones about this :

There was . . . nothing doctrinaire about our policies . . . My associates
and I knew perfectly well that, in Australia at any rate, there have been
and are certain elements which, in the very nature of our geography and
history, lend themselves to government management and control . . .
But, looking to the future in a rapidly developing country like Australia,
it seemed eminently desirable to look more to the citizen and less to
government. A great reliance must be made on the creative genius of the
individual, assisted, and sometimes controlled by the government in the
general social interest, but encouraged and rewarded.†

For all their lack of originality, these were the ideas which appealed
to the Australian voter in 1949. 'From 1945 to 1948, a band of
young idealists, supported by the manufacturers, the traders, and
the pastoralists, painted a rosy picture of possibilities should
Australia rid itself of the economic planners and the menace of
Communism.'‡ Menzies, with that uncanny instinct of the professional politician, sensed by 1948 that his time was coming. In the
1946 election he had won seventeen seats. What he lacked at that
stage was a single issue on which to fight. And that was what the
bank nationalization plan gave him. He wrote later : 'I knew that
we were at the crossroads.' And in his policy speech in 1949 he
said : 'This is our great year of decision. Are we for the Socialist

* Menzies, R.G., *Afternoon Light*, pp. 286, 289.

† *ibid.*, pp. 282, 283.

‡ Clark, C.M.H., *A Short History of Australia*, p. 237.

State, with its subordination of the individual to the universal officialdom of government, or are we for the ancient British faith that governments are the servants of the people ?'* Menzies, with a touch of pomposity, called on the voters to win the 'second Battle of Australia'.

The result of the vote has already been mentioned. But the events of the next few years were to be even more amazing. Menzies, having become Prime Minister in 1949, remained in office until 1966, winning eight successive general elections, ending up with an increased anti-Labor majority despite almost seventeen years in power† and enabling his party to retain government for six years after he stepped down – which he did of his own volition. This striking record of survival continues to intrigue students of history and politics. No doubt Menzies the man has much to do with it. He was the target of harsh criticism at the time, and it may well be that history will also judge him severely ; it may even be said that his mind and the policies it evolved looked back rather than forward. Yet nobody can deny that he had sound political sense and a brilliant legal mind, or that he was a fine speaker and, perhaps most importantly, an unbeatable opponent in the cut-and-thrust of political infighting. The man could certainly dazzle his opponents, and perhaps took too much malicious pleasure in doing so, in displaying his superiority and silencing an interjector with an unanswerable fact or a well aimed witticism at his expense.

On the Labor side there was only one member who was a match for Menzies. This was the colourful and redoubtable Eddie Ward, who held the seat of East Sydney for thirty-two years, from 1931 to 1962. He had turned his hand to all trades before taking up politics. His enemies saw him as the lowest sort of demagogue (appropriately, he had been one of Lang's supporters) ; but his admirers maintained he was the most sincere person imaginable. He had been a member of the Curtin government. In the House he took endless pleasure in interjecting, for the purpose of upsetting whoever was speaking ; he took pride in the number of times he was called to order or named by the Speaker. Menzies he found irritating (a fact he did little to hide) especially since he could rarely have the last word with him, and over a period of thirty years they crossed

---

* Menzies, R.G., *op. cit.*, p. 295.

† In 1949 they had seventy-four seats ; in 1966, eighty-two seats.

swords on countless occasions. When Ward died, his old foe paid him the sort of tribute that he would have appreciated : 'He accepted no compromise, gave no quarter, and expected none.'*

All human success must be the product of an individual coinciding with a set of circumstances. If Menzies had been born thirty years earlier or later, it is quite probable that nothing would have been heard of him. But in 1949 there can be no doubt that he embodied the aspirations of most Australians. This post-war generation of Australians is reminiscent of America about 1920, both nations having just come through an experience that they had never imagined they would have to go through and wanting above all else to get back to their pre-war lifestyle. Menzies may never have used the 'Back to normalcy' slogan that got Harding elected, but the Liberals' programme could certainly have been summed up in those words. Chifley was no more endowed than Curtin had been with the air of sound traditionalism that came to be associated with Menzies and thus reinforced the Liberals' 'normalcy' image. The country's greatest desires, after a time of trials, seemed to be peace and quiet, and a rightful share of the world's prosperity. The new Prime Minister reaped the full benefit of these two aspirations. Indeed, if one leaves aside for the moment Menzies' foreign policy, one is struck by the disparity between his achievements and the length of time that he stayed in public favour.

One of his first steps on regaining the Treasury benches was bound to be popular : he removed rationing restrictions on petrol, butter and tea a few months after the election. He also sought and received a loan of $100 million from the International Bank for Reconstruction to finance a public works programme. However, all of this was of secondary importance. The move which aroused the greatest passions in the community was Menzies' proposal, in 1950, to ban the Communist Party and prohibit its members from holding any public position. In principle, the measure probably had popular support. But the bill which Menzies brought down omitted to safeguard certain basic freedoms and thus gave its opponents an opportunity which they exploited with great energy. Menzies just managed to have the bill passed ; and then, by a majority of six to one, the High Court declared the Act unconstitutional. Menzies

---

* See Spratt, E., *Eddie Ward, Firebrand of East Sydney*, Rigby, Adelaide, 1965, p. 258.

went to the country on the issue, with the result that he was returned on a slightly reduced majority but with control of the Senate. The difference between an electorate's behaviour at general elections and at a referendum was amply demonstrated by what followed. Six months after Menzies' mandate had been endorsed by the voters, he asked these same voters for the powers that he needed to reverse the High Court's decision. In the three oldest States, where British traditions had struck deeper roots than elsewhere, New South Wales, Victoria and Western Australia, the answer was 'No'. Over the country as a whole the government's proposal won only 49.44 per cent support.

The upshot of these manoeuvres was the Communist Party's survival as a legal entity. As it turned out, it probably became more of an embarrassment to Labor than to the government parties. Labor was going through a bad period. Despite an apparent downturn in business towards the end of 1951, the country recovered so quickly that by 1953 the government was able to reduce taxation, a move that could only take the wind out of Labor's sails. They did, admittedly, have some local successes, having won elections about this time in all States except South Australia. But experience showed that these results had little enough relevance to Federal politics. Then, in June 1951, Labor had suffered a severe blow with the sudden death of Ben Chifley. In place of a man whom all Australians had respected, Labor now had as its leader Dr Evatt, who was anything but universally admired. All his experience on the international scene did not necessarily equip him to lead his party. At all events, he was to display a remarkable lack of elementary tact and political judgement in a tragi-comedy that had all the ingredients of a good spy thriller: the Petrov affair.

On 3 April 1954 a diplomat at the Soviet Embassy in Canberra, Vladimir Petrov, defected. Petrov was a well-known figure in Canberra and elsewhere; in the course of his cultural activities he had made many contacts. Political asylum was granted without difficulty, since Petrov handed over evidence about a Soviet spy ring operating in Australia, produced actual documents, named names. Three days later the plot thickened when it transpired that Mrs Petrov was being confined to the Soviet Embassy, for reasons which it was not too difficult to guess. These reasons became apparent on 19 April when a magnificent black limousine drove up to Mascot Airport. An eyewitness report says :

In the front seat were the driver and Second Secretary Kislitsyn, while in the back a shrouded female figure – presumably Mrs Petrov – sat between two powerful diplomatic couriers – Zharkov and Karpinsky, who whatever their personal qualities, had the appearance of a couple of mobsters from a third-rate gangster film ... Mrs Petrov, confused and bewildered ... was literally dragged up the gangway by the now panic-stricken Russians ... *

There were demonstrators at the airport who tried to prevent her being put aboard. But the plane eventually took off. The who-dunnit was by no means over, however. The plane having touched down at Darwin, the police discovered at 5 a.m. that Mrs Petrov's travelling companions were carrying revolvers. They were disarmed and their charge was asked what she wanted to do. After a telephone conversation with her husband, she also requested asylum. The Soviet Union reacted vehemently, accusing Petrov, predictably, of being a thief, and the Australian government of having trumped up the whole thing. Within four days, diplomatic relations were broken off.

This episode, happening right in the middle of an election campaign, could only redound to the government's advantage. Until then, Menzies had been under strong pressure from Labor electioneering. Now, despite Labor's attractive and moderate policies, Menzies only lost seven seats. But the Petrov affair was still on the boil. Menzies had set up a Royal Commission, composed of Supreme Court judges. Three of Evatt's staff had been named in the documents as sources (albeit unwitting) of some of the diplomat's information. Before the Royal Commission, the Labor leader used such outrageous language, claiming that the documents were patent forgeries concocted to discredit himself and that the whole thing was a McCarthyite witch-hunt, that the Commissioners refused him permission to reappear. They also affirmed the genuineness of the documents and said of Evatt's accusations that they were fantastic and supported by no shred of evidence.

The revelations of Vladimir Petrov† proved merely that the Soviet Union used its diplomatic representatives for purposes of espionage. In so doing, it was of course simply following standard

* Quoted by Birch, A. & Macmillan, D.S., *The Sydney Scene 1788–1960*, pp. 364, 365.

† He and his wife were naturalized in 1956.

practice and using methods that it had not invented. But a more serious result of the whole affair was the knowledge that Australian Communists were implicated in it.

This discovery reinforced the charges that had been made for some time that Communists were using the trade union movement for political purposes. One of the strongest voices making these allegations was that of Mr B.A. Santamaria, an interesting character of Sicilian origin. He was capable of rousing extreme animosity in his opponents, presumably because they could not question the man's sincerity. And also because nothing annoys men of the left so much as seeing men of the right using the same tactics as themselves. Just as the Communists had had great success with infiltrating the unions, so Santamaria decided to do likewise. In 1936, at the age of twenty, he founded the *Catholic Worker*, which drew its inspiration from papal encyclicals. Later he came to the head of the Catholic Action movement and set about the formation of cells, based on the parishes and aimed at countering Communist influence in all walks of life. To begin with they worked secretly ; but word of their activities was bound to leak out before long. In October 1954 Evatt, in the throes of the Petrov Royal Commission, made a public attack on a small group of party members, mainly in Victoria, who he said were becoming increasingly disloyal to the Labor movement and its leaders. This time Evatt was right. Within months a split had appeared in the Victorian branch and this example was soon followed in other states. In 1957 the new anti-Communist groups merged to form the Democratic Labor Party, thus effectively splitting the Labor party on the national scene. Any judgement of the significance of the D.L.P. is fraught with complications, as it was surrounded by controversy from its inception. It was called a Catholic party, numbering as it did among its supporters a great many Roman Catholics, including the redoubtable Archbishop Mannix. Nevertheless the Vatican seemed to treat it with some reserve, and there were other prelates who refrained from imitating their colleague from Melbourne. It has also been called a conservative party, despite which it has always supported social reform. It has even been seen as a manifestation of a new kind of nationalism ; and yet it was always in favour of friendly relations with Asian countries.

No doubt F. Alexander is right to conclude that D.L.P. influence is essentially negative. Not that this means negligible, for ever since

1955 the D.L.P. has played an important part on the electoral scene. This it has done not by winning many seats in Parliament,* but by enabling the Liberals to defeat the A.L.P. The period after 1955 has been called the period of Menzies' hegemony, which is not an exaggeration. There is no need here to do more than sketch in the outlines of a period of stable government and growing prosperity, when Menzies had only to contend with a divided and demoralized opposition. Evatt seemed incapable of doing a thing right – he even announced that he had written to the Soviet Ministry of Foreign Affairs, which had solemnly assured him that the Petrov documents were indeed forgeries ! Menzies could not have wished for a better opportunity. He called a general election for December 1955 and increased his majority from seven to twenty-eight.

At the 1958 poll he defeated the A.L.P. even more roundly, despite a brief period of economic sluggishness two months before the election. On this occasion the D.L.P. was definitely a force to be reckoned with, and Archbishop Mannix had spoken out strongly : ' Every Communist and every Communist sympathizer in Australia wants a victory for the Evatt Party.'† This series of defeats had brought the A.L.P. to the conclusion that it must try a new leader. The choice fell on Arthur Calwell, just as fierce an opponent as Evatt of the D.L.P., but a less controversial figure. Calwell's deputy leader was a lawyer of forty-four years of age, E.G. Whitlam, who soon turned out to be one of the best speakers in Parliament. Labor found grounds for optimism in this change of leadership and came within an ace of winning the next election, in 1961, when three of Menzies' ministers lost their seats and the government hung by one vote. However, this proved to be an illusory episode and by 1963 Menzies had again increased his majority, this time to twenty-two seats. At the age of sixty-nine he was at the peak of his career, having just been knighted by the Queen.‡ Sir Robert stayed in office for another three years before retiring in 1966, a legend in his own lifetime.

In retrospect, what can be seen to be the achievements of those

---

* It had two to four Senators from 1960 onwards ; it has never won a seat in the House of Representatives.

† See Murray, R., *The Split*, Cheshire, Melbourne, 1970, p. 348.

‡ He was made a Knight of the Thistle which is one of the oldest orders of knighthood, only sixteen knights being admitted to it at any one time.

seventeen years in power ? A handful of social reforms – an expansion of the child endowment scheme ; provision for medical and hospital benefits, although health insurance continued to be the responsibility of individuals ; a steady rise in wages and the setting up of a new Arbitration Tribunal ; encouragement of scientific research ; the establishment of the Atomic Energy Commission ; the introduction of television ; the passing of legislation favouring foreign investors ; a banking reform, resulting in the setting up of the Reserve Bank. The list seems so short that one wonders if one has omitted something !

The Liberals' task of finding a successor to Sir Robert Menzies was not an easy one. The two principal contenders were the Minister for External Affairs, Paul Hasluck, and Harold Holt, the Treasurer. Despite the risk of unpopularity associated with the man in charge of public finances, the choice fell on Holt. There was nothing about Harold Holt to arouse strong feelings. He is usually described as suave, immaculately dressed, a professional lawyer and an experienced politician. In November 1966 he led his party to a brilliant two-to-one victory over the A.L.P. But he did not live to show his full worth, being drowned at the end of 1967. He was succeeded by a man who was as unlike him as possible, John Gorton. Gorton, who had been seriously wounded in the war, was now fifty-seven ; since 1958 he had held seven different portfolios, and had thus plenty of experience of government to draw on. He was noted for the unorthodoxy of some of his ways and means, and said to be something of a bull in a china shop. J.D. Pringle has this to say of him :

Journalists, politicians and public servants knew him as a forceful, forthright, headstrong personality, but few of them would then have considered him seriously as a contender for the highest office. I had met him several times during my year in Canberra – usually at diplomatic parties at which he was a constant attender – and had come to enjoy our brief conversations. He would stand there, a glass of whisky in one hand, his other arm round the prettiest girl in the room, a cheerful grin on his handsome-ugly face, invincibly Australian, but always amusing, original, and refreshingly forthright after the other politicians and diplomats one had met.*

* Pringle, J.D., *On Second Thoughts*, Angus & Robertson, Melbourne, 1971, p. 23.

Whitlam, who had succeeded Calwell as leader of the A.L.P. that year, was brilliant and aggressive ; the Liberals needed somebody with marked characteristics. Gorton met that requirement and was elected by the Liberals. His three years in office confirmed his reputation without adding to it. He was deposed by a palace revolution in March 1971. William McMahon, Gorton's erstwhile colleague, now took over. Like Gorton, he had held different Cabinet posts over the previous fifteen years, but his experience was much broader than Gorton's and he was no stranger to international monetary conferences. McMahon's accession to the Prime Ministership was hailed especially in New South Wales, as he was the first politician from that State for more than twenty years to break the monopoly that seemed to be held by Victorians.

This chapter has dealt with Australia's internal political affairs after 1945. If one were to consider only those affairs, one would be tempted to say that this was hardly one of the most stimulating periods of Australian history. However, that would be only a superficial impression. The next chapter proposes to look beneath these surface events and inspect the effects of those three great impacts already mentioned.

Chapter Twenty two
The curtain rises (II)

Policy of massive immigration – British immigrants and 'displaced persons' – other Europeans – minerals discovered – richness and variety of mineral resources – a more active foreign policy – Evatt and the United Nations – Australian support for Indonesia – failure to recognize Red China – Menzies' role – Korea – Colombo Plan – A.N.Z.U.S. and S.E.A.T.O. – troops sent to Malaya – the Suez crisis – Menzies' support for Anglo-French intervention – Menzies opposes South Africa's expulsion from the Commonwealth – West Irian handed over to Indonesia – de Gaulle's opposition to Britain's entry to E.E.C. – Vietnam – Australia's present diplomatic representation

Any anthology of Australiana would surely have to contain two documents in particular : firstly, the text of the announcement by Curtin in December 1941 ; and secondly, the speech in the House of Representatives by Arthur Calwell, then Minister for Labour, on 22 November 1946. Both these declarations transformed the future of the nation, the first one because it was a sign of a completely new departure in foreign policy, and the second because it was a sign of an impending radical change in the ethnic composition of the country. What Chifley's colleague said, in sum, was that if Australia wanted to take her proper place in the world and to ensure her future security, then she must considerably increase her population, both by raising the birth-rate and by adopting a programme of planned immigration. The days of isolation were over.

These were significant words to come from the Labor Party. The A.L.P., relying for much of its support on the trade union movement, had been traditionally hostile to the importation of extra labour. But the experience of government gave its leaders a sense of continuity. As early as 1944, Curtin had informed Cabinet that, as soon as the war was over, he intended to launch an immigration programme, and his successor lost no time in putting the idea into practice. The Ministry was set up in July 1945, and then a commission was sent to Europe to explore possibilities. Some such immigration scheme was imperative for Australia. At that time the population of 7.5 million was ridiculously out of proportion to the size of the country and had been a source of anxiety in those dire weeks after Pearl Harbor. From 1870 to 1930 the birth rate had fallen constantly, and if it should start to do so again, there might be an unpleasant future in store for a small, remote white nation whose vulnerability, as had recently been shown, was all too obvious.

The government adopted an ambitious goal: twenty million Australians by the end of the century. Statisticians stated that an annual growth rate of two per cent would enable Australia to reach the target. Experience had shown that, except for very rare periods, immigration had never accounted for more than a quarter of the population growth. The conclusion was that, as a minimum, an effort should be made to attract as many immigrants per year as there were live births. This latter figure being of the order of 70,000, it was decided that at least to begin with the aim should be to find an equal number of Europeans willing to emigrate to the Antipodes – 'Europeans' being, of course, the operative word, since people with yellower skins were less welcome now than before the war with Japan and, as for Americans, it was difficult to imagine many of them uprooting themselves to go to Australia at the very time when their own country was so attractive to others. If the immigrants could all have been British there would have been no problem. Australians still took pride in the fact that the forebears of almost all of them had come out from the British Isles and would have been glad to preserve this homogeneity. To assuage any offended susceptibilities, it was decided that the ratio of non-British to British immigrants should not exceed one in ten. But, as things turned out, this theoretical maximum was soon forgotten.

The 90 per cent British principle was waived first in favour of the 'displaced persons'. There were six million of these wretched victims of the war, crammed into ghastly transit camps all over Europe. Calwell decided to take a chance and sent over immigration selection teams (with the suggestion that priority should go to men and women with blue eyes and fair hair). They must have found enough of them, since by July 1947 an agreement had been reached with the International Refugee Organization, under which the I.R.O. was to cover the transport costs, and Australia was to pay each immigrant an indemnity of £10, provide accommodation and guarantee a job. This arrangement was reasonably successful, netting Australia 170,000 immigrants over a four-year period. One suspects that the blue-eyes-and-fair-hair rule was not very rigidly enforced. At the same time there was an influx of British migrants, some of them being ex-servicemen, who were given free passages with their families at the expense of the British government ; others being subsidized either by London or by Canberra and contributing only £10 each to their passage.

It had soon become apparent that if Australia were to rely only on these two sources of immigrants, the targets would never be reached. And so a series of agreements were reached with Malta, the Netherlands, Italy, Austria, Germany, Belgium, Greece and Spain. The irrelevance of the original specifications for immigrants is shown by the fact that two of the most recent agreements are with Turkey (1968) and Yugoslavia (1970). The preponderance of Mediterranean countries in the list makes it obvious that Australia's ethnic homogeneity is a thing of the past. The figures can speak for the success of the scheme. After a slow start, the flow of immigrants soon quickened : 10,000 in 1947 ; 150,000 in 1949 ; and 152,000 in 1950, giving an annual intake of about double the planners' original estimates. Between 1950 and 1953 the rate of intake slowed down somewhat, in response to improved conditions in Europe, but an energetic publicity campaign soon increased the numbers once more. In the seventeen years between 1947 and 1964, more immigrants came to Australia than in the fifty-four years between 1860 and 1914. The number of people who emigrated to Australia on assisted passages of one sort or another, and settled there between 1947 and 1970, has been estimated at 1,662,000. If one adds to this figure those people who made the voyage at their own expense, it may well be that over a twenty-year period more than two million inhabitants of the Old World abandoned it for Australia. Of these immigrants, it has been calculated that 58 per cent were younger than forty ; women accounted for 43 per cent of the total ; 'British' migrants represented less than 40 per cent ;* the next most sizeable

* Official statistics do not separate the Irish from the others. Specialists estimate that the proportion of Irish immigrants under the 'U.K.' heading amounts to about one third.

groups were the Germans, Greeks, Italians, Turks and, since 1970, Yugoslavs.

Close on two million New Australians, as they were called – one quarter of the 1945 population ; almost one sixth of the present population. In French terms it would be as though the country had taken in eight million immigrants since the end of the war. Immigration on this scale was unprecedented in Australia's history and was to have profound effects on the country.

The second of the three far-reaching changes was the discovery of Australia's mineral resources. In 1930 the era of the great discoveries seemed to have ended. Between the wars the only new finds of any significance were of gold ; but in other branches of mining, disappointment was much more common than success. Geologists had not abandoned hope, because after all they knew the potential resources of Australia's sub-stratum. Even so, the discoveries of the last twenty years would have been inconceivable at that time. Some of them are barely believable even today. Here we intend to touch only on the most important.

First and foremost one must mention Mount Isa, with its zinc, lead, silver, copper, phosphate, uranium and nickel mines. These immense deposits lie some 1,600 kilometres, as the crow flies, to the north-west of Brisbane, and about 500 kilometres from the southern shore of the Gulf of Carpentaria. This region is in the tropics ; rainfall is slight and the sun's heat is merciless. The landscape is austere, relieved only by a touch of pink on the hills at sunset.

In 1857 a veteran of the Crimea, who had failed to strike it rich on the Victorian goldfields, decided to try his luck elsewhere. Having reached Brisbane he set out alone, almost at random, into the bush, covering almost 2,000 kilometres on horseback. His own will, plus pure chance, got him as far as Mount Isa where he thought he struck copper. Even when proved wrong, he did not give up trying, but he made no fortune. Nevertheless his example was followed by numerous other prospectors, opening up the region which until then had been of little interest to anyone. It was not until 1923, however, that the mineral potential of the area was conclusively proved, and even then it was believed that it only contained deposits of iron and lead. Mount Isa was then taken up by a colourful personality by the name of Leslie Urquhart, of Scottish extraction. He had actually been born in Armenia and had been a large mine-owner in Russia until he was dispossessed by the Revolution. He had great plans for Mount Isa, which was already becoming a legend, but the Depression put paid to them. Large-scale mining did not get under way until after the Second World War, and soon reached colossal proportions. Uranium was discovered in 1954. It was rather like the gold-rush days all over again, except that now the prospectors carried Geiger counters instead of picks and pans. Every stone of the place was inspected. It was said that the near-by hills glowed mysteriously at night and that this was because they were radio-active. The prospecting fever only lasted a few years but it led to the discovery of silver and zinc and, especially, copper. Today Mount Isa is the eighth largest producer of silver in the non-Communist world, the tenth largest producer of lead and the fourteenth largest producer of copper.

In thirty years a town mushroomed, growing from 3,000 inhabitants before the war to 20,000 in 1970, and made up of forty different nationalities. The days of corrugated iron shanties are long past ; nowadays the town, with its air-conditioned houses, each one with lawns and fruit trees, looks much like the suburbs of any of the capital cities. The shortage of water was remedied by piping it in from thirty kilometres away. A railway line linked the mines to Townsville, 1,000 kilometres away on the Queensland coast. Air traffic has become so important that the Mount Isa airport is now one of the busiest in Australia. Shafts are still being sunk ; the deepest of them took more than two years to sink and goes down below the 1,000 metre level. It has been said that when shifts are changing, the shafts are as busy as main roads at the rush hour.

The iron ore saga at the other side of the continent, in the Pilbara region of Western Australia, is just as amazing. This is a stony area, with tints of red, brown, blue and mauve in the rock. Towards the end of last century gold had been found in the region, but before long it was all mined. Geologists were sure that iron was also present. This time it was not a man on horseback who proved them right, but a pilot. In 1952 a grazier, Lang Hancock (whose property reportedly covers 650,000 hectares) was flying homewards one day when a storm blew up. To avoid it he turned up an unfamiliar valley, noticing with interest the odd reddish colour of the peaks in the ranges on either side. Later, having come back for a closer look, he took geological samples and had them analysed. It turned out that he owned a 100-kilometre range of almost solid iron ore, his samples being assayed at 64 per cent haematite. Since 1938 there had been a government embargo on haematite, Australia's reserves bring so small. This embargo was not lifted until 1960, and so production could not begin until then. As always, the first problem was transport. A railway line, 3,000 kilometres long, was built to Dampier, a small town on the shores of the Indian Ocean, where modern port facilities were constructed. Another problem was the total lack of drinking water ; this one was solved by desalinating sea water. Air-conditioning was essential to overcome the rigours of the climate, which has been plotted as the hottest and driest in the whole of the continent, the thermometer staying at 40°C in the shade for weeks on end. In the summer of 1923–4, a heat wave of this sort actually lasted for 160 days ! As for the ore itself, the Mount Tom Price deposits alone constitute a solid mountain of iron, containing some 500 million tonnes of ore which is not only high grade (about 60 per cent) but is the cheapest in the world.

These are only two episodes from a veritable mining epic. Let figures tell the rest of the story. Of the traditional ores, only gold production has decreased since 1963. As for iron ore, the Mount Tom Price deposits look small when compared with the country's total known reserves of 20,000 million tonnes, of which about 18,000 million lie in the Pilbara district, notably in the Hamersley Range. In bauxite, too, Australia is a world leader, with the largest known deposit in the world, at Weipa in north Queensland, estimated at more than 3,000 million tonnes ; taking several other lesser deposits into account, the country's total bauxite holdings amount to about 4,000 million tonnes. Nickel was believed to be non-existent in Australia up to 1966 ; now there are known reserves of 27 million tonnes of three per cent grade ore.* Copper is found in many different places, for example in Tasmania, but Mount Isa remains the centre of copper mining in Australia, with 80 million tonnes varying between 0.8 per cent and 3 per cent grade. Mount Isa has its lead and zinc, of course, which are also to be found at Broken Hill, the doyen of Australian mining ventures (see page 219). Oil, coal and tungsten are also plentiful. In fact one wonders if there is any sort of mineral resource that Australia does not possess. The most recent addition to the list is natural gas, found in the Pilbara

* Comparing favourably with Canada's one per cent.

district in quantities which will give a flow of 280 million cubic metres per day.

As for uranium, the burst of speculation that was set off by the discoveries in the 1950s was short-lived. But since 1970 new finds have been made in the Northern Territory, Western Australia and South Australia which suggest that the country is bound to be an important source of nuclear fuels in the future. Even those endless golden beaches that surround the continent are being mined for titanium, zircon and thorium, minerals whose names may sound outlandish to the layman but which are highly prized by the specialists.

Lists of statistics can be bewildering and boring. But the figures given above are necessary to an understanding of the tremendous significance of the recent mineral discoveries for Australia's future development.

The third of the three great changes took place in the field of foreign policy. Up until 1939 Australia's foreign policy at any given moment was more or less copied from whatever British foreign policy was at the time. During the Second World War, Australia gave a hint now and then of taking an independent line, and this tendency towards self-determination in foreign affairs has become more marked since the war. This growth to responsible adulthood of a country which not long ago was content to play a passive role is one of the most exciting aspects of recent Australian history.

One can see two clear stages in this development, the Labor period and the Liberal period. Under the Labor government, Evatt played an all-important part. As a self-appointed spokesman for the smaller nations, he was effective at least in drawing attention to himself. His crowning achievement in these respects was to be elected to the Presidency of the United Nations. However flattering this distinction may have been to Evatt in his personal capacity, his handling of Australian foreign affairs can certainly be questioned. British Commonwealth leaders, meeting one year after the end of the war, had agreed to make Australia responsible for most Pacific matters. This was a sensible decision, based as it was on geographical realities. Chifley accurately defined the purport of this agreement as being a shift from the previous principle of centralization to the idea of regional defence arrangements. What it meant was a recognition of Australia's priority in a region which was of particular relevance to her. Thus, in 1947, it fell to Australia to collaborate with the U.S.A. in drawing up a joint peace treaty with Japan. It happened that Australia hated the Japanese much more than America did, which explains why Canberra's proposals for the terms of the peace treaty were more severe than those eventually drafted. The final decision lay with Washington, of course, which meant that Australia had to back down from its hard line. This episode left a residue of some bitter feelings on both sides. The Director of the Australian Institute of International Affairs concludes: 'The balance of available evidence suggests that Australia lost ground between 1945 and 1949 in her relationships with the United States.'*

Evatt's bustling methods were perhaps not the best vehicle for Australia's views overseas. There is nothing so dangerous as an imbalance between ends and means. The country was in its earliest stages as a sovereign power. Was it really wise to try to do so many things all at once, especially so vehemently? Sir Paul Hasluck comments: 'The only thing that an Australian need regret is not that Australia insisted on its point of view, but that sometimes it thought it necessary to kick a man in the shins in order to impress his mind.'† The trouble with Evatt was that he saw himself as being of the stuff of which international statesmen are made. To be restricted to the scope of the Pacific region was not enough for him. He took the view that peace and stability in the Far East were only conceivable if peace and stability existed in Europe, which was no doubt a quite unexceptionable conclusion. But when he went on to add that the interest of Australia in the European situation was therefore vital and direct, one cannot help wondering by what means and by what military might Australia would have safeguarded that interest in the event of a crisis in Europe. In March 1948, when Australia gave her blessing to a treaty between Great Britain, France and the Benelux countries, no doubt the signatories were gratified at this encouragement. But perhaps there were a few smiles round the table as well.

That same year, Evatt's impetuousness was to land Australia in an embarrassing situation. It was the period when it was becoming fashionable to be anti-colonialist. India and Pakistan had parted company the previous year and were well on the way to full inde-

---

* Watt, A., *The Evolution of Australian Foreign Policy*, p. 105.

† Hasluck, P., *The Government and the People, 1942–1945*, p. 629.

pendence from Britain. Chiang Kai-shek was retreating before Mao Tse-tung. Ho Chi-minh had proclaimed Vietnamese independence, and Indonesia was in full revolt against Dutch rule. The European countries had not yet accepted the necessity of letting their colonial achievements collapse, after all the effort they had put into them. And the Dutch, stubborn by nature, were more determined than anyone else not to accept it. The United Nations condemned the Dutch for their attitude.

Evatt, who was fond of one-upmanship, instructed Australia's representative at the U.N. to move a stiffly worded amendment to the American resolution condemning the Netherlands – the suggestion being that Dutch behaviour in Sumatra and Java was worse than the invasion of the Netherlands by Hitler in 1940. The Melbourne and Sydney waterside workers, in their time-honoured tradition of political action, boycotted all supplies being shipped to the Dutch forces. Then, a few months later, so as to leave no possible doubt about her intentions, Australia took part in a conference of nineteen Asian and Pacific countries. The final communique, predictably, had not a good word to say about colonialism. Menzies took the opportunity to clarify the situation admirably, saying that since Australia had just helped to chase the Dutch from the East Indies, the same process would logically result in the expulsion of the British from Malaya and Australia from Papua New Guinea. Evatt, who was easily carried away, may not have noticed any contradiction in his attitude. The right of a people to self-determination was his reason for supporting the Indonesians against the Dutch. By that same right he should have recognized the Communist regime in China in 1949, given that it was in undisputed command of the mainland. But the fact is that, on China, he was stumped by Washington's veto. The case is a good example of how ineffectual a would-be independent country can be, when it does not have the means of independence at its disposal.

The situation that the Liberals inherited on coming to power in 1949 was not an easy one. It was on the international scene that Menzies was to show his greatness. His achievement was to consolidate the recent sovereignty that had been entrusted to him, but without harming the Imperial traditions that he held dear. He was quite capable of adopting a different stance from the rest of the British Commonwealth, whenever he felt that such action was called for, despite the quasi-religious importance that the old ties had for him. This 'Queen's man', as he liked to call himself, begged to differ at times from the U.S.A. and even from Great Britain itself. But he could see no point in following Evatt's practice of publicizing to all and sundry the points on which he differed from the other two governments.

In June 1950, Communist troops crossed the thirty-eighth parallel in Korea. The United Nations condemned this action as unprovoked aggression, and President Truman immediately announced that he was sending in the American navy and air force in what he called a 'police operation'. The rest is history. Australia was the first nation to follow the American lead, acting with an alacrity which won her new popularity in Washington. Menzies made a visit to the American capital, where Congress acclaimed him, and came back home with a loan of $250 million, to find that his trip had enhanced his reputation. On the whole, the three years that the war lasted were an affluent period for Australia, the prices of raw materials, especially wool, having risen steeply. On the debit side, Australia's casualties in the war were 280 killed or missing and 1,250 wounded.

On two occasions Menzies was to prove that, despite his devotion to the Crown, he did not feel duty bound to toe the Downing Street line. In 1950 he had recognized the government of Chiang Kai-shek on Taiwan as the rightful government of China, just as London was recognizing Peking. The following year Australia and New Zealand, for the first time in their existence, signed a treaty with the U.S.A. in their own right. This pact, known as the A.N.Z.U.S. pact (from the initials of the three signatories) caused some comment. John Foster Dulles had said that henceforth America's and Australia's destinies were united. But Great Britain was not a signatory, and Menzies felt he had to restate his fidelity to his mother country, saying the pact was 'a local manifestation of closer British-American relations'.* But whether he liked it or not, he had in fact taken another step along the way to full independence.

With the fall of Dien Bien Phu and the end of the French war in Indo-China, it became apparent that Australia was going to have a hand in the settling of all problems in South-east Asia. In September 1954 Canberra joined the U.S.A., Great Britain, France, New

---

* See Greenwood, G. & Harper, N. (eds.), *Australia in World Affairs 1961–1965*, Cheshire, Melbourne, 1968, p. 265.

Zealand, Pakistan, the Philippines and Thailand in signing the S.E.A.T.O. agreement, thus confirming that, by restricting her activity to her own immediate area, Australia could play a much more effective role than by trying to have a finger in every pie like Evatt. In 1950 Australia's new Minister for External Affairs, P.C. Spender, had been responsible for the holding of the first Commonwealth Conference in Asia. At this conference, in Colombo, Spender had been instrumental in the establishment of a sub-committee to look into ways and means of raising standards of living in Asia. This committee's answer to its vast terms of reference was to meet in Sydney and eventually put forward the sort of proposal that was to be expected : a six-year plan. Needless to say, nothing much came of the whole exercise, except the realization that Australians and Asians lived very close to one another and could not afford to ignore that fact. The future Lord Casey, who replaced Spender in May 1951, was determined not to ignore it. He became the first Australian statesman to cultivate close relations with a part of the world that people were beginning to see as their 'Near North' rather than as the Far East. Another result of Casey's efforts was the scheme under which Asian students came to complete their tertiary education at Australian universities. This scheme was to continue to grow over the following years.

Menzies was forced by the nature of things to adopt this new policy towards Asia. But one may wonder whether his heart was really in it. It used to be said that Asia to Menzies was a part of the world one flew over on one's way to London. And certainly he must always have been gratified whenever circumstances permitted him to renew personal contact with Great Britain and to reaffirm his undying loyalty to the Crown.

When Menzies, as leader of the opposition, had maintained that Australia's support for the expulsion of the Dutch from Indonesia was bound to result one day in the departure of the British from Malaya, he never spoke a truer word. By 1955 the situation north of Singapore was so disquieting that the Australian government decided to support the British with a detachment of Australian troops. Menzies justified this decision by saying, ' If there is to be war for our existence, it should be carried on by us as far from our own soil as possible.'* He must surely have been pleased at the thought of

* Quoted by Watt, A., *op. cit.*, p. 168.

Australian troops fighting alongside British units once more.

The following year gave Menzies the opportunity to make a gesture of solidarity with Great Britain. On 26 July 1956, Nasser nationalized the Suez Canal. At the time, Menzies had just completed a visit to London. He returned there, then spent some days in Washington before reporting back to the British Cabinet. The British government called a conference of twenty-two countries on 16 August. Australia's Prime Minister was given the flattering but delicate task of presiding over a sub-committee, composed of the U.S.A., Sweden, Iran and Ethiopia, which was given the job of negotiating with Egypt. Menzies invited Nasser to go to Geneva ; the Egyptian dictator refused to meet him anywhere but in Cairo. Menzies accepted this and went to the Egyptian capital. For a while he thought it possible that the talks might result in a compromise solution ; unfortunately, when Eisenhower made a speech ruling out the use of force, Egypt adopted an even more inflexible position and the negotiations ended in total deadlock. Menzies flew back to Canberra at the beginning of September and made a forthright attack on Nasser in a speech to Parliament. The pace of events quickened. At the end of October the French and British governments decided on military intervention, and only withdrew their forces under the combined pressure of the U.S.A. and the Soviet Union. Evatt, of course, rushed in and denounced the Anglo-French policy, comparing it with the Russian invasion of Hungary ! This stung Menzies to retort that it was unseemly and absurd to see Nasser as the victim of unprovoked aggression, Nasser being in his eyes the instigator of all anti-British and anti-Israeli activities in the Near East. Eleven years later, in his memoirs, he had still not changed his mind :

It is clear to me that the United Nations' performance in 1956 built up Nasser's position and prestige, fatally damaged the regional influence of Great Britain and France and made the position of Israel desperately precarious. In brief, it increased the possibilities of aggressive war in one of the World's critical areas.*

It is surely far from certain that history will prove this view to have been misguided.

Whatever the case may be, the Australian Prime Minister cer-

* Menzies, R.G., *Afternoon Light*, p. 185.

tainly needed to be a man of strong character to stand out as he did even against a decision that had American support. But then Menzies was not one to be daunted by finding himself in a minority of one. In September 1960 he made himself unpopular with Nehru at the General Assembly of the U.N., by opposing a motion that had the support of India. And in London some months later he was even more isolated. South Africa had just declared itself a republic. Verwoerd, the Prime Minister, had been unimpressed by Macmillan's point about 'the winds of change' blowing through Africa and had declared that the *apartheid* policy would continue unchanged. It was in this atmosphere that the Commonwealth leaders met in London in March. At the conference, the group of African and Asian leaders, supported incongruously enough by John Diefenbaker, Prime Minister of Canada,* launched an attack on South Africa. The leaders of Ghana and Nigeria were foremost in telling South Africa to put its house in order. Verwoerd, who would have been glad to remain a member of the Commonwealth despite the fact that South Africa no longer recognized the Queen as head of state,† lost patience and withdrew his suggestion on South Africa's continued membership. Nobody tried to dissuade him. But Menzies made no secret of his disagreement with this situation, in a way which must have won him few friends:

[Apartheid] is still a matter of domestic policy in South Africa which South Africa does not seek to apply to any other country. It is as much a matter of domestic policy to South Africa as Australia's migration policy is a matter for us. To have a member of the Commonwealth virtually excluded from the Commonwealth on a matter of domestic policy presents, in my opinion, a rather disagreeable vista of possibilities for the future.‡

In later years Australia was to take similar stands on many issues. One of these was difficult to explain. It will be remembered how vigorously the Chifley government had opposed a continuation of Dutch rule in the East Indies. Once the issue of Indonesian independence had been resolved, the government in Canberra noticed

---

* Where Red Indians were not even recognized as citizens.

† India, Pakistan, Ceylon, Ghana and Nigeria had all become republics and had remained in the Commonwealth without any special conditions.

‡ Quoted by Watt, A., *op. cit.*, p. 282.

somewhat belatedly that the new Republic of Indonesia was New Guinea's next door neighbour. The Liberals took a diametrically opposite view on this question to their Labor predecessors'. The wicked Dutch, who had held on to the western end of New Guinea, overnight became the heroes of the hour. The Indonesians, of course, were determined to wrest this last bastion from them. But the Australian Minister for External Affairs, no doubt remembering the predictions of his leader some years before, objected that if the Indonesian claims were met it would only be a question of time, whatever assurances they might give, until they tried to extend their domination to the territories that the United Nations had mandated to Australia. It is a diplomat's job to be able to explain and justify complete reversals in policy. And there was no shortage of arguments to support this about-face on Evatt's previous policy. the strategical argument that, even in the nuclear age, New Guinea was still Australia's last line of defence; the political argument that Sukarno had included Communists in his government; the humanitarian argument that it would be intolerable to let the poor Papuans fall into such unworthy hands. At one stage Dutch-Australian relations were so close that a co-operation pact was signed with the aim of upholding their authority in New Guinea until such time as the inhabitants were in a position to decide their own destiny. That was in 1957. And then, a mere five years later, The Hague and Canberra agreed to hand over the administration of the former Dutch colony to the United Nations. This was nothing but a face-saving device, and nobody was at all surprised in May 1963 when the U.N. passed on to Indonesia, under the name of West Irian, the responsibility that had been entrusted to it.

This inglorious episode was made up for, that same year, by better news. Menzies must have heaved a sigh of relief on learning of General de Gaulle's veto on British entry into the European Common Market. London's application to join had caused undisguised misgivings in Australia. Experts vainly pointed out that since 1939 Australia's exports to the West had dropped from 71 per cent to 38 per cent, while in the same period sales to Asian and Pacific countries had risen from 24 per cent to 55 per cent. It was argued, against that, that Great Britain still took a considerable share of Australian wool and agricultural produce, a situation which would presumably have to be altered if the British joined Europe. There were other considerations too, sentimental reasons why Britain's decision to join was of relevance to Australia. Despite all Churchill's fine words, was Great Britain really going to turn its back on its old friends ? The very survival of the Commonwealth seemed to be at stake, the Commonwealth to Menzies' mind being 'something in the blood ... a common allegiance, and a great brotherhood ... a special association, with its roots in history'.*

With de Gaulle's veto, the danger was avoided, but perhaps not for long. It became even more important to look to Asia and to rely on the U.S.A. China helped with the first of these, rousing Nehru from his anti-Western pacifism by its takeover in Tibet in 1959 and its aggression on the frontier with India in 1962. Garfield Barwick, Australia's Minister for External Affairs, visited Delhi and four months later an Indian representative came to Canberra. In addition the Malaysian Federation, an independent entity since 1957, formed some sort of counter-force to the unpredictable northern neighbour, Indonesia. However, if trouble should arise, there was no support to be counted on from those quarters, Washington still being the cornerstone of Australian defence policies. In 1963 Australia's ties with America were further tightened by the signing of two agreements. One of these gave the U.S.A. a naval communications base at North-West Cape on the Indian Ocean, and under the other, American support was guaranteed for the defence of Papua New Guinea.

These developments were, of course, reassuring. Unfortunately there was still a marked disparity between Australia's growing activity in the realm of foreign affairs and her military capabilities, which were becoming more and more inadequate. It has been calculated that at that time American defence spending amounted to 11 per cent of the national budget, as against six per cent in Great Britain and three per cent in Australia. Menzies made a very belated effort to remedy this situation.

The war in Vietnam was a particularly embarrassing problem for Australia. If she participated in it, it would jeopardize her attempt at closer relations with Asia, whereas if she kept out of it, she risked upsetting the U.S.A. Australia's course was a prudent copy of her powerful protector's. In 1962 Australia sent thirty-eight military instructors and six aeroplanes to Saigon. In 1965 she committed a whole battalion and from then on, as with American participation,

* Menzies, R.G., *op. cit.*, pp. 187, 228.

Australian involvement constantly increased, rising to a total of 6,300 men by 1967, 60 per cent of whom were regular soldiers. Menzies' successor, Holt, went 'all the way with L.B.J.', a policy which proved popular for a while, as was shown during President Johnson's triumphal visit to Australia. But support for the war did not last long; the last Australian fighting units were withdrawn in 1971 and the remaining instructors in 1972.

In 1968 it was said of the period of the early 1960s: 'Whereas previously Australia had stood largely on the sidelines, encouraging and supporting the Western alliance and occasionally displaying an independent initiative in the United Nations and in Asian affairs, she now found herself an active participant in great events.'* This evolution towards international maturity had begun in 1945. In 1939 Australia's total diplomatic representation amounted to one High Commissioner (in London), one Counsellor (attached to the British Embassy in Washington), and a handful of trade commissioners. By the early 1970s Australia was represented overseas by forty-five ambassadors, eighteen high commissioners, four consuls-general, five consuls, six heads of mission attached to the United Nations and the E.E.C., and no fewer than forty-nine trade commissioners.

The curtain is rising. The play is about to begin.

* Greenwood, G. & Harper, N., *op. cit.*, pp. v–vi.

Chapter Twenty three
Australia today

Labor in office – the Whitlam government – stability of institutions – Federal-State relations – the territories: A.C.T., Northern Territory, Antarctica – Papua New Guinea on the eve of independence – Aboriginal problem – urbanization – general features of Australian society – ways of life – housing – sport – religion – literature, arts and sciences – a crucial moment

The general election of December 1972 is already a landmark in Australian history. After twenty-three years in office the Liberal-Country party coalition was replaced by the A.L.P., which came into office with a majority of nine in the House of Representatives.* The A.L.P. was taking over the government of Australia in much more favourable conditions than it had done on the two previous occasions. In 1929 the country had been on the brink of the Depression; and in 1941 the government had been in power exactly two months when Pearl Harbor happened. But in 1972 the country was prosperous and there was no sign of any threat from abroad. The most urgent priority of the A.L.P. on assuming office seemed to. be to give an impression of change, judging from the flood of different policy initiatives soon after the election. Their determination to get down to the job was shown by their creation of ten new ministries.† The new Prime Minister, Gough Whitlam, was already well known

---

* The state of the parties was: A.L.P. sixty-seven; Liberals thirty-eight; Country Party twenty. The opposition still had a majority in the Senate, thanks to D.L.P. support.

† Making a total of thirty-seven government departments, under twenty-seven ministers. The ministers, in the A.L.P. tradition, are elected by the party Caucus, although the actual apportioning of portfolios remains the Prime Minister's prerogative.

for his energetic ways. The year before, a profile of him had been drawn by two well-informed journalists. Having pointed out that Whitlam's background seemed somewhat out of keeping with the political philosophy he had espoused, they went on :

At Canberra, Whitlam made an immediate impression. His commanding height, fresh, almost boyish looks, confident manner and alert legal mind distinguished him from the ruck of Labor politicians from early in his career.* Old hands in the Labor Party regarded him with suspicion, questioning his reason for aligning himself with Labor, doubting his convictions, or suspecting a lack of conviction, and criticizing him as a barrister holding a brief rather than an evangelist with a mission. There was some evidence to justify their reasoning, if not their doubts. Whitlam's whole manner and conduct were alien to them. He argued lucidly, clearly, logically, but without passion, almost without interest. He was earnest without being concerned, emphatic without being insistent. When he did cease to be disinterested and became personally involved to the extent of giving way to temper or emotion, it was on personal rather than ideological grounds . . . †

What the party was looking for in the sixties was someone with some of the old-time Labor fervour of a Calwell, the dignity of a Curtin, and the photogenic qualities and warmth of a Chifley. Whitlam had none of the first, little of the second and not enough of the third. But, in fairness to him, it should be emphasized that he probably came nearer to the prescription than anyone else in the Parliamentary party.‡

His career certainly bears this out. He became deputy leader of the party after eight years in Parliament, and took over the party leadership in 1967. There was always something confidence-inspiring about his bearing and manner. It has been said that Whitlam's first achievement was to give the A.L.P. the image of respectability and sophistication that the Australian post-war electorate seemed to demand. The name of Whitlam may eventually come to be

---

* He was first elected in 1952, at the age of thirty-six.

† Those who enjoy the minor details of history will be interested to learn, from this same source, that Mr Whitlam once threw a glass of water in the face of the then External Affairs Minister, who later became Governor-General with the title of Sir Paul Hasluck.

‡ Whitington, D. & Chalmers, R., *Inside Canberra*, Rigby, Adelaide, 1971, pp. 285, 286.

associated with great changes ; but one may be certain that whatever he does he will do it after the local manner, with moderation and without using violent methods. For Whitlam has too much of the middle-class radical in him to be a revolutionary.

It follows from this that the basic Australian institutions are not likely to be affected by the A.L.P.'s accession to government. These institutions are standing the test of time. Up to 1972 the Constitution had only been amended on five occasions.* Voting in Parliamentary elections had been made compulsory and there had been an increase in the numbers of members of both Houses, the Representatives having risen from seventy-four to 125 and the Senate from thirty-six to sixty. But essentially the system was exactly the same as before. As often happens in federal arrangements, the question that gives rise to the most delicate problems is the separation of powers between the national government and the States. The pragmatism inherited from the British tradition has so far coped well enough with these matters. Up to now the Commonwealth has managed to adapt to conditions which were unthought of in 1901 by resorting to expedients such as an annual meeting of Premiers with the Prime Minister, consultations with select inter-State bodies and a Loan Council which settles what is at times the most difficult question of all, establishing an order of priority among States' requests for loans. The High Court, in its capacity as custodian of the Constitution, has also helped avoid any malfunctioning of the federal system. Until about the end of the First World War, roughly, the High Court saw its role as the defending of States' rights ; after which time it favoured some extension of Federal powers. Since the advent of the Curtin Labor government at the end of 1941, the Court has practised what Professor Geoffrey Sawer called 'co-operative federalism', relying more on flexibility and compromise than on strictness of interpretation. The Whitlam government can probably be expected to encourage the tendency to centralization of powers.

Canberra's authority is thus limited by the powers of the six States. However, it is uncontested in the administration of the Territories, or in dealing with what is no doubt the greatest problem of them all : the fate of the Aborigines.

On any political map of the continent, one sees two regions of very

* Of the twenty-two referenda, seventeen had been lost.

different dimensions which do not belong to any of the States. There is, firstly, the Australian Capital Territory, a sort of Australian replica of the District of Columbia. The drafters of the Australian Constitution in 1901, like their American predecessors, preferred not to have the national capital built inside the boundaries of any of the old colonies (see page 265). Canberra was therefore founded in a separate Commonwealth-owned district of a little more than 2,000 square kilometres. It is now administered by the Department of the Capital Territory, with some advisory assistance from the local Legislative Assembly, an elected body of eighteen members. The development of Canberra had stagnated over the years until 1957, when Menzies set up the national Capital Development Commission under Sir John Overall. This Commission, which is still at work, has made Canberra a model of contemporary town planning, with its parklands, its lakes and its superb tree-lined avenues.

The Northern Territory is very different. With two and a half times the area of France, and with four-fifths of that area lying inside the Tropic of Capricorn, it had by 1972 some 70,000 inhabitants, most of whom were Aborigines. However, since the mining developments of recent years, more and more Europeans are to be found there, Russians, Greeks, Italians and especially Yugoslavs. Some fishing is carried on round the shores of the Gulf of Carpentaria. The Gulf Country is buffeted by the monsoon during the southern summers and suffers from appalling droughts during the winters; it abounds with wild buffalo and geese. The landscape changes farther south, where the sky is an intense blue and the earth is reddish-brown or golden. There are only three towns to speak of: Darwin, the capital, on the coast; Katherine in the interior; and the most interesting of them, Alice Springs, an oddly attractive town which is already being disfigured by tourism. Distance and dispersal of population over 1.3 million square kilometres have posed problems that modern technology has had to solve. The flying doctor service uses aircraft for home visits to patients and gives surgery consultations by radio. A similar method is used in education, children on isolated homesteads receiving their lessons by wireless.

An Australian public servant who wanted a change could presumably apply for a transfer from the Northern Territory to the Antarctic Territory, another limitless landscape, but full of ice and snow instead of shimmering desert. In 1936 Australia annexed almost half of the continent and now possesses (if that is the right word) an area between 45° E and 160° E, enclosing the French territory of Adelie Land. In 1961 Australia was a signatory to the agreement by which fifteen nations undertook to use the Antarctic regions solely for peaceful purposes. But one is permitted to wonder what would happen if the predictions that one already hears (to the effect that oil or perhaps even gold will be discovered under the 3,000 metres of ice) are ever proved right.

If the Commonwealth of Australia had no jurisdiction over Tasmania and certain other small islands in the Indian Ocean* and the Pacific,† the Australian flag would soon only fly over the mainland. It will be remembered that in 1906 Great Britain transferred her sovereignty over the south-eastern part of New Guinea to Australia, and that in 1919 the League of Nations gave the Australian government a mandate on the north-eastern part. At the end of the Second World War the two areas were amalgamated into one territory called Papua New Guinea, which Australia was to administer as a United Nations trust. The Australian government had thus acquired responsibility for a sizeable country (about four-fifths the size of France). Having had some experience of it over the previous half-century, Australia was quite aware of the difficulties of her task in Papua New Guinea, a country of volcanic mountains, with torrential rains and a climate generally unfavourable to Europeans. Among the two million natives there was little ethnic unity, there being three main groups, one of them of marked Negroid type, another akin to the Australoids and the third group, often much fairer-skinned than the others, of Melanesian type. Throughout the country somewhere between 700 and 1,000 different dialects were spoken by population groups that had very little in common except a few customs of attested savagery. The population also included 40,000 Europeans.

The Australian administrators acquitted themselves remarkably conscientiously of their responsibility. Their brief was to bring the country to independence. They had no illusions on the dangers

---

* Ashmore and Cartier Island, Christmas Island and the Cocos and Keeling group, all to the south of Indonesia ; and Heard and McDonald Islands, north-west of Australia's Antarctic Territory.

† Norfolk Island and Lord Howe Island north of New Zealand. Nauru, the source of precious phosphates, is now independent.

involved in that process. For the first few years they gave a brilliant performance of the art of hastening slowly. In 1951 a Legislative Council was set up as a first step towards representative government, although, of its eighteen members, only three were Papua New Guineans, and they were appointed. Australia quite obviously did not believe in rushing things. Paul Hasluck, then Minister for External Territories, voiced the government's cautious policy : 'In the generations to come, [Papuans] may be required to manage their own affairs to a greater degree.'* By 1961 the number of members of the Legislative Council was doubled and they included indigenous representatives chosen by local councils. But these advances were not rapid enough for the United Nations. The following year a U.N. commission of inquiry predictably reported that the Australian authorities were 'hopelessly out of touch' with reality.† To which Australia replied that nobody had yet discovered any great desire for independence among the indigenous people of Papua New Guinea. One of Hasluck's successors at the Department of External Territories even stated, as late as 1965, that 'independence is not the inevitable or predetermined result of political development as some commentators . . . would assume.'‡

It is always a tricky business to play at being a prophet. There was for a time some talk of making Papua New Guinea into the seventh state of the Commonwealth of Australia. But this was a pipe-dream and nothing came of it. In 1969 Gorton, who was not averse to startling people, took everybody by surprise with the announcement that Papua New Guinea would certainly become independent, although he refrained from setting a definite date. Since then Papua New Guinea's progress towards self-government has been rapid. Before the Australian general election of December 1972 it was stated that the territory would attain self-government by the end of 1973, and Whitlam has more recently announced that in two or three years it will be a completely independent member of the United Nations and of the British Commonwealth.§

* Quoted by Hastings, P., *New Guinea : Problems and Prospects*, Cheshire, Melbourne, 1969, p. 256.

† *ibid.*, p. 154.

‡ *ibid.*, p. 262.

§ Since this was written Papua New Guinea has become fully independent – on 16 September 1975 (*publisher's note*).

Perhaps it was through having had contact with Papua New Guineans over a period of fifty years that Australians suddenly began to take an interest in their own Aborigines. It has been said that just a few decades ago people who were concerned about the Aboriginal problem were looked on as eccentric or even mad. It had become a commonplace to predict the inevitable extinction of the race, and those who cared did what they could to make their last years on earth as gentle as possible. Then, about 1930, things began to change ; it was then, for example, that for the first time a scientific journal was founded to help study them. Much research was done in the fields of archaeology, sociology and politics, showing just how complex the problem was. About this same time, questions were surfacing from the Australian subconscious about the treatment meted out to the first Australians ever since 1788, the land grabs and the genocide.

Over the last twenty-five years there has been a marked improvement in official treatment of the Aborigines. The original solution had been to concentrate them in reserves, based on their old tribal homelands. But the later policy of assimilation was an attempt to break down the isolation that resulted. The aim of this policy, as defined in 1958, was to extend in time to all Aborigines, full-bloods as well as part-Aboriginals, the general Australian lifestyle as well as full citizenship rights and the ability to participate in all social activities. In its political dimension this policy is now a reality. The 1967 referendum which transferred the States' powers over Aborigines to the Federal government showed how liberal the country had become towards the Aboriginal question. This referendum was bound to facilitate the process of assimilation. Nowadays, before the law, the first Australians are as equal as anyone ; social legislation applies to them and they have the vote.

It should not be assumed from the foregoing, however, that the question of their integration into the Australian community has been resolved once for all. Of late a delicate problem has arisen – land rights. As luck would have it, some of the regions where Aborigines live are particularly rich in mineral wealth. This raises the problem of who owns the land. And of course the Aborigines claim possession of it from time immemorial, the sort of claim that it is difficult to dispute. The opposing view, that of the constitutional lawyer, is that it belongs by right of conquest to the Crown. A test case was brought before the High Court in 1971, which pronounced in favour of the foreign-based company which was seeking to exploit the land. Since 1972 the subject has become of immediate importance once more. One of the Labor government's first announcements was that it intended to grant full tribal land rights to Aboriginal groups. The Whitlam government has been somewhat vaguer on the question of mining rights, which suggests that those who enjoy legal wrangles are in for a field day.

Another problem is connected with the use of the term 'Aborigine' itself, which is applied to groups with so little in common that it is difficult to find a solution that suits them all. Some Aborigines, very few in fact, go on living out the wandering desert life of their ancestors. The rest of them, in one way or another, are in contact with contemporary Western civilization. Some of them, especially those of mixed racial origin, have managed to adapt quite well; others, while seeing the advantages of the new way of life, are suspicious and cautious in the knowledge that they are tolerated rather than accepted. Their greatest handicap is the demoralization that comes from cultural uprooting and dispossession. More and more Aborigines are wondering whether they would not be better off to keep to themselves. A sort of *apartheid* in reverse is becoming perceptible.*

The Aboriginal question is fraught with complexity. Dr Coombs, appointed Chairman of the Council of Aboriginal Affairs in 1968, has clearly defined the real problem of the Aborigines : to let them find their social, economic and cultural identity either within their own society or within white Australian society, while making sure that they do not fall between these two stools.

The 1966 census counted 80,000-odd Aborigines, with a slight majority of men over women. It is difficult to judge how many of these would still be full-bloods, as recent statistics do not distinguish the full-bloods from the others. But, judging by previous surveys, it is likely that they would amount to about five eighths of the total, which would give a round figure of 50,000. When one compares this figure with the thirteen million Australians† counted at the 1972

---

* R.M. and C.H. Berndt quote three examples : in Arnhem Land, Aborigines chose to keep the reserve that was allotted to them ; in Alice Springs, a proposal has been made to have a school reserved for Aboriginal children ; and, from time to time, the idea of separate Aboriginal representation in Parliament is mooted.

† In the general Australian population, men outnumber women by one per cent.

census, it can be seen as infinitesimal; the likelihood of any serious problem arising from this group is therefore very remote.

Australia took some seventy years, until 1854, to reach its first million inhabitants. By the outbreak of the second world war the population had just reached seven million. At its present rate of growth (about 1.9 per cent per annum) it would reach twenty million by about the year 2000, which was the original target of the immigration planners in 1945.

In 1972 five cities, Sydney, Melbourne, Brisbane, Adelaide and Perth, contained 7,372,085 inhabitants.* The percentage of Australians living in these capital cities had further increased over the previous five years. The national figure for urban dwellers had risen from 56.04 per cent to 57.92 per cent. Canberra's rate of growth, at 69.36 per cent, was the highest in the country ; next was Darwin at 66.33 per cent, a long way ahead of Perth (which was growing at a rate of 27.86 per cent), Melbourne (13.31 per cent) and Sydney (11.03 per cent). The only worthwhile conclusions that should be drawn from such comparisons is that they do show something about political and economic tendencies. Canberra can be seen to be benefiting from the increasing importance of the Federal government, and the growth of Darwin and Perth is indicative of the mining activity that is bound to have an important effect on the development of the Northern Territory and Western Australia. Apart from that, these figures appear to bear out another feature of Australian life that has been mentioned before – the population is supposedly the most urbanized in the world.

Some might say that there is nothing 'supposed' about it and that it is a fact. However, Australian society should be assessed more cautiously, and has already been the subject of too many stereotyped generalizations. One may perhaps be excused for not adding to these, except to say that the country is obviously going through a period of profound development and that its identity is still largely undefined.

For one thing, is it really true that Australia is the egalitarian country that it is commonly held to be ? There was certainly never any spiritual or philosophical basis in Australia for a theory of

* Sydney 2,717,603 ; Melbourne 2,288,941 ; Brisbane 816,897 ; Adelaide 809,466 ; Perth 639,622.

Two-thirds of the population is under forty.

equality. Religion had little to do with the foundation of the first colony, and even when there came to be a religious element in Australian life, it did not bring people together but set them against each other. Another factor that must be borne in mind is that all the early immigrants came from Great Britain, which had a tradition of freedom but not equality ; and these immigrants gave no more thought than their British forebears had done to drawing up Declarations of Rights on the American or French pattern.* Nature took the place of ideology. Out in the bush, or on the gold-diggings, it soon became apparent that what counted was a man's individual worth rather than who his ancestors were or what his income amounted to. The concept of mateship, invented by a community that had to cope with real dangers and later idealized to meet the needs of mythology, reinforced the ties of solidarity that enabled Australians to see their aspirations as identical. Out of this realization of a basic similarity grew the concept of equality, a myth that took root and grew unhampered by any aristocracy – when Charles Wentworth proposed in 1853 that the New South Wales legislature include a counterpart to the House of Lords, the suggestion was laughed to scorn. In later years the trade unions were able to turn the now universally accepted idea of Australian equality to their own advantage.

If an 'egalitarian' society is one in which a basic similarity in tastes and familiarity in people's treatment of one another tend to cut across class barriers, and in which differences in wealth are less extreme than elsewhere, then in that sense one can say that Australia is an egalitarian society. Statistics shed some light on this question. In 1968–9, there were 5.2 million Australian tax-payers, of whom almost four fifths were in the salary range between \$1,000 and \$4,000. The two extreme groups were much smaller : at the lower end of the scale, some 500,000 declared a taxable income of less than \$1,000 ; at the upper end, something over a million taxpayers earned an income of between \$4,000 and \$30,000. On salaries above \$30,000 there were a total of only 3,601 taxpayers. The conclusion is obvious : poverty is rare, as is great wealth, and the nation as a whole lives in some affluence but certainly not luxury. A survey on class boundaries showed a similar result. 38.5 per cent of respondents considered they belonged to the working class ; 44

---

* Except at the ill-fated Eureka Stockade. See page 209.

per cent considered themselves middle class ; 12 per cent saw themselves as lower middle class and 5.5 per cent as upper middle. None ventured to describe themselves as upper class. Australia, which in the nineteenth century was called 'the workers' paradise', is more like the 'petty bourgeois paradise' nowadays. This is the feature of contemporary Australian life which is most striking. Rather than any supposed equality, the things that are apparent in every suburb, in every street, in every house, are the slight but telltale clues to social success which are in fact the almost imperceptible infrastructure of the hierarchical society that is supposed to be non-existent in Australia.

This continuing rank-system in society is the creation of Australian women rather than of the men ; the home is the only place where the Australian woman reigns supreme. It is a strange fact that in the first country in the world to have given women the vote, they have no influence to speak of. This could be a survival from pioneer days when of necessity men played the dominant part. The principle of equal pay for equal work has only recently been established. The first woman member of the national Parliament was not elected until 1943 ; only two women have ever occupied ministerial positions – and there are no women in the Whitlam Cabinet. Segregation of the sexes was the rule for a long time. Even fifteen years ago an acute observer could still write about Australian women :

In society they are bold, self-confident, but lacking in poise. They are always conscious of themselves and of their sex, in spite of the fact that the men generally seem quite unaware of their existence. At a party the men will invariably crowd together in one corner of the room and leave the women to talk together in another . . . When they marry, the men will leave their wives alone all the weekend while they go fishing or racing, and on any Sunday morning you may see the wives patiently waiting in their cars outside the pubs while their men drink beer together inside.*

It is to be hoped that in this day and age the wiles of Australian women can put an end to such distressing customs.

The very question of Australia's supposed uniformity is one which deserves some attention. One wonders whether it might not be more accurate to see Australia as more than one nation. For there is a

---

* Pringle, J.D., *Australian Accent*, p. 39.

striking range of diversity among the different States and their cities. As Donald Horne puts it :

In Queensland, where small city-ports are strung out along the coast, each with its own area of influence, even the State capital city does not mean much outside its own area. The Northern Territory sees itself as a colony of the rest of Australia. Tasmania nurses its sense of difference from the brash 'mainland'. In Western Australia they distrust 'the East'. In South Australia they also distrust 'the East', but, at least until its present mineral boom, Western Australia distrusted even South Australia. In Victoria they distrust New South Wales. In New South Wales they distrust Sydney. In Canberra, in the Australian Capital Territory, they distrust Australia. As befits the oldest, only Sydney seems to have no attitude to the rest.*

These differences between Australians are epitomized in the old story about the first question they ask you in the various cities – in Sydney, 'How much money have you got ?'; in Melbourne, 'What school did you go to ?'; in Adelaide, 'What church do you belong to ?'; and in Brisbane, 'Would you like a beer ?'

Jokes, of course, over-simplify the truth ; but they do contain an element of it. Certainly, each of the regions makes its own distinct impression on the visitor. In New South Wales, as it approaches its bicentenary, one is struck by the quaint blend of past and present. It is impossible to look out over Sydney's breathtaking harbour without thinking of Captain Phillip and his convicts. Simultaneously, one cannot overlook the fact that Sydney is a city of tomorrow, with its arresting Opera House, its skyscrapers which are identical to those of any American city, its bustling streets and the cosmopolitan air of its people. One can only hope that they will not turn it into another Los Angeles ! Melbourne is another city that sprawls out over an immense area, being built like all Australian towns in a horizontal rather than a perpendicular direction. Nevertheless Melbourne gives a more measured and balanced feeling than Sydney, which may have something to do with its magnificent tree-lined streets and the charm of certain old houses. An Australian has described it as more sophisticated and more strictly hierarchical in its social structures ; another Australian describes it as 'the most English' of Australian cities.

* Horne, D., *The Next Australia*, Angus & Robertson, Sydney, 1970, p. 126.

Adelaide too could no doubt lay some claim to that description. J.D. Pringle sees it as a staid, serious town, dominated by a lingering Protestant middle-class respectability that is dying out everywhere else. This is not very noticeable to the visitor, who is struck by the parks and gardens, the Mediterranean feel of the place, and the increasing industrial fringe. Perth is very different again, giving an impression of having recently 'taken off', of being as yet unfinished and pulsing with expectation. There is still something of the Western frontier town about Perth. Building sites and American-style freeways abound. The difficulties that surrounded the foundation and growth of the Western Australian colony are inconceivable today. The incalculable mineral wealth that has recently been discovered may one day turn the once thankless land into one of the most privileged regions on the surface of the earth. At the other side of the continent, Queensland's future will be based on a wider range of natural resources : wool, sugar, tobacco, fruit, minerals, even oil. Offshore, the Great Barrier Reef is bound to be a continuing great source of tourist revenue. Perhaps it is the sub-tropical atmosphere in Brisbane that muffles the buzz of expectation so perceptible in Perth. Brisbane is more languid or perhaps even listless.

Tasmania, though the smallest of the States, is by no means the least interesting. To fly the 1,000-odd kilometres from Sydney to Hobart is to fly from one world to a completely different one. For in Tasmania there is still a relaxed pace to life. Round city corners one does not come on the inevitable oppressive skyscrapers, but on vestiges of the past. And one has the feeling that the unAustralian greenness of the gentle Tasmanian countryside is never very far away. There is an unforgettable bridge, too, light and sparkling bright in the sun, crossing the Derwent in a single effortless sweep. At night it is a magical thing, a band of light appearing out of nowhere.*

For all their diversity, these capital cities do give a uniform impression of wealth. As has often been mentioned, the Australian standard of living is among the highest in the world. But once again the figures must be accompanied by some interpretation, as by themselves they can be misleading.

Affluence is certainly widespread, but this is not only the result

---

* This was written before the spectacular collapse of the bridge, when the bulk carrier *Lake Illawarra* ran into it on the night of 5 January 1975 (*publisher's note*).

of Australian social legislation. In fact, in this respect, Australia has been living on a reputation that she made for herself (and deserved) seventy-five years ago. But over the intervening years, many Western countries have outstripped Australia in this field. Australian wage-earners now have the benefits, it is true, of maternity allowances, child endowment, unemployment benefits, workers' compensation as well as invalidity, old age and widows' pensions. But health insurance is still considered an individual's private responsibility.* The government's role amounts to partially reimbursing hospital and medical fees to patients who belong to one of the ninety-eight approved private funds ; those who are not privately insured seem to have to rely on charity or their savings. A previous attempt, by Chifley in 1941, to set up a national health service had failed (see page 363). The new Labor government seems determined to revive this moribund idea, by setting up a universal health insurance scheme under which compulsory subscriptions would be proportionate to the income of breadwinners ; some 350,000 families would be exempt from subscriptions. Medical and hospital fees would be paid directly by the government to doctors and hospitals. This proposal, smacking as it does of nationalized medicine, has aroused vociferous opposition, and if it is put to a referendum, there is no guarantee that it will be accepted.

Neither government control nor completely free enterprise has prevailed in Australia. The country is run by a mixture of officialdom † and individual initiative, a state of affairs that may seem somewhat unoriginal. However, what is distinctive to Australia is the pairing of state enterprises and private businesses. This system is apparent in education, in banking and in broadcasting and television. Perhaps the most striking example of it is in the field of civil aviation, where T.A.A., the official government-owned airline, and its privately owned competitor, Ansett Airlines, both fly exactly the same routes and even operate on the same timetables.‡

---

* The introduction of Medibank in 1975 has of course rendered this statement invalid (*publisher's note*).

† The size and scope of the civil service is attested by figures quoted by Professor G. Sawer : Australia has one public servant for every fifty-four inhabitants, as against one for seventy-two in the U.K. and one for eighty-seven in the U.S.A. (see *Australian Government Today*, Melbourne University Press, 1961, p. 85).

‡ The Labor government is in favour of extending this system to insurance and

There is, finally, one aspect of the economy which must be considered if opinion is to be based on hard fact rather than on uninformed generalization. There is a preconception in many people's minds that Australia's growth has been phenomenal, but the facts do not bear this out. It has certainly been rapid, but that is a different thing. Between 1966 and 1970 the gross national product only increased by a little more than 5 per cent per annum, * which is barely half as much as, say, a country like Japan. Many Australians are quite satisfied with such results ; and they may be right to be satisfied with them. No doubt the atmosphere of life in Australia, with the eternal sunshine of its landscapes, the soft golden sand on its beaches and the lithe and delightful young women one sees everywhere, is more conducive to indolence and relaxation than to effort.

The contrasts highlighted in the last few pages (the middle classes within the middle class ; the differences between regions ; the ingredients of control and free enterprise in the economy) show how careful one must be not to generalize. On the other hand, a certain amount of generalization is possible when it comes to describing ways of life, since certain practices are very widespread indeed.

Firstly, housing. The rule is the detached house set in its own small garden ; it usually has five rooms, a veranda and a garage at the side, and is built of red brick. This type of house is perfectly suited to a country where space is limitless and may be seen as the expression of a traditional self-sufficiency. Australians rarely rent houses, the great majority preferring to buy. The sizes of houses vary, of course, depending on the wealth of the owners, but there are extremely few houses built on the scale of castles in the Old World. For one thing, the lack of servants would make them uninhabitable, and in any case such extravagance would be seen as shocking. The place where one lives is still indicative of one's social level. Robin Boyd says that Australians' aspirations are reflected in the different architectural styles : some architects remain faithful to the English tradition ; others have modelled themselves on the Californian bungalow ; there is a third category of Oriental inspira-

* $21,378 million in 1966 as against $27,118 million in 1970, making allowance for higher prices.

---

pharmaceutical goods.

tion and another of more nationalistic spirit which has tried to revive the house of colonial style or the bush hut.

Australians are as a rule fond of the open-air life, and are probably less interested than the French in the cult of the home. A survey of space given to sports news in an issue of the *Sydney Morning Herald* once showed that 15.3 per cent of the newspaper was devoted to sporting activities, which compared with 11.8 per cent for Australian politics and 7.4 per cent for foreign news.* One wonders if there really is something pantheistic, as has been suggested, in this passion for pastimes through which human beings can renew their contact with the natural world. Perhaps it can be explained as a compulsion to use up excess energy not channelled into work or love. Whatever the reason for it, nobody who is indifferent to sport should consider emigrating to Australia :

Sport of all kinds has a long history in Australia. The first recorded cricket match was played in 1826, and football, as 'an amusement of the military', goes back to 1829, while horse racing and rowing contests are reported in Macquarie's time ... The prevalence of public golf courses is exceeded only in Scotland ... [Australia has] a phenomenal record in international sporting contests – tennis, cricket, football, golf and athletics. Australia is one of the very few countries to have competed in every Olympiad since they were revived in 1896. It has won the Davis Cup in tennis twelve times since 1905 ... It has also produced five winners of major golf championships in Britain and America. Its oarsmen have built up a deserved reputation in their international contests, as have its footballers ... But the most famous of Australian sports is still its cricket ... played throughout the land in all social strata.†

To which must be added the records held by Australian swimmers and waterskiers.

It may be that sports grounds have become competitors with the churches. Anglicans in Australia have been estimated at 35 per cent of the population, Roman Catholics at 25 per cent, other Protestant sects at a further 28 per cent (Presbyterians and Methodists making up the greater part of this figure), Jews at slightly over 0.5 per cent. At every census 10 per cent of the population seem to object to

---

* The survey was done in 1962. But it is quite likely that these proportions would be the same nowadays.

† Shaw, A.G.L., *The Story of Australia*, pp. 279, 280.

stating the precise nature of their religious convictions, although only about one per cent bother to state that they have no religion. A survey of church attendance habits in the early 1960s revealed that of the 88 per cent of Australians who called themselves Christians, only 27 per cent* go to church regularly, 48 per cent attend 'sometimes' and 25 per cent never go to church at all, showing that there is a clear distinction in Australian minds between 'belonging' to a church and real practising of one's religion. Still, this is a universal phenomenon throughout the Western world and lends itself to no conclusion of any particularly Australian relevance. Presumably God alone can interpret such statistics.

Australia is less than 200 years old and the conditions of its birth and growth have been largely unfavourable to the cultivation of intellectual things. It is this tradition that makes today's intellectual vitality all the more welcome. Patrick White was considered twice for the Nobel Prize, before winning it in 1974. The soprano Joan Sutherland has been acclaimed in the world's finest opera houses. Every philosopher has read John Passmore; every architect has been excited by the Sydney Opera House.

Some believe it is possible to speak of a specifically Australian literature. After the last war, there was a group of writers, going by the colourful name of the Jindyworobaks, whose work was noted for the extreme nationalism of its inspiration. As usually happens with extremism, it was outdone at its own thing by a rival group, the Angry Penguins, who succeeded in discrediting the movement. Australia has produced many writers who have drawn inspiration from the local Australian scene while being recognizably in the English tradition – novelists such as Katharine Susannah Prichard, for instance, or Morris West, whose works have been so successful in France; poets like Kenneth Slessor, R.D. Fitzgerald, Alec Hope and Judith Wright; and a host of others.

Painting may be the field in which Australia has shown the most creative originality. As early as 1906, a French consul who knew what he was talking about said that Australia's favourite hobby was painting. All the broad movements of modern European art from impressionism to expressionism and surrealism were taken up with gusto in Australia. But in those periods it was imitation that was

---

* The proportion of Roman Catholics was 54 per cent.

more important than innovation, whereas over the last thirty years there has been a profound development in genuine Australian art. Russell Drysdale painted the burning deserts of the inland with tremendous intensity ; William Dobell was a savage caricaturist, one of the very best portraitists ; and Sidney Nolan's talents are so varied that he is equally at home with scenes from the saga of Ned Kelly, Greek mythology or Australian landscape.

Music, which had always flourished in Australia, has now found premises worthy of it in the Sydney Opera House. This building, which is criticized as often as it is admired, is covered in white ceramic tiles, giving a striking impression of sails blowing in the wind or sea-shells set inside one another. Ballet, which is very popular in Australia, will benefit particularly from the Opera House ; under Dame Peggy Van Praagh and Sir Robert Holpmann, the Australian Ballet Company is already world famous. As for orchestral performances, one has only to listen to the A.B.C. symphony orchestras in Melbourne or Sydney to appreciate their quality.

Australia's supreme intellectual contribution has been made by her scientists. For almost forty years this scientific effort has been spearheaded by the C.S.I.R.O., for which much credit must go to the tireless David Rivett. There are so many names deserving of mention that one can only name the very best, such as the three Nobel Prize winners who have given Australian medical science an international reputation : Sir Howard Florey, who was as much the discoverer of penicillin as Fleming ; Sir Macfarlane Burnet, a specialist in the study of the influenza virus and cancer ; and Sir John Eccles, the neuro-physiologist.

Shortly after coming to power, Mr Whitlam declared his conviction that Australia had before her exciting months and years. There is every likelihood that this prediction will be fulfilled, as Australia has now reached a crucial moment in her history.

Chapter Twenty four
The moment of choice

The immigration debate – Whitlam government decides to reduce immigration – Asians as immigrants – wool and mining – wool recovery – moves to control foreign investment – risks of colonial status – importance of home market – need for population growth – Labor's many new approaches in foreign policy – defence – attitude to Britain and U.S.A. – potential importance of European Common Market – France's role – Asia, the fundamental problem – Australia at the crossroads

Population, natural wealth and foreign relations were the three possible sources of problems for Australia in 1973.

Until recently the immigration programme, initiated by Labor and continued by the Liberals, had been the subject of universal agreement. For 1970–71 a record intake of 180,000 had even been planned. But about that date, some reservations about the rate of immigration were beginning to be voiced. To begin with these doubts emanated especially from intellectual circles, but they were soon to spread. It was argued that immigrants cost too much, since not only do they have to be brought to Australia and housed, they have to be provided for in the social security budget and their children have to be educated. All this expenditure, it was argued, could be more usefully channelled into modernization of the country. Immigration also aggravates problems of urban living, since the New Australians, instead of spreading evenly throughout the continent, tend to concentrate in one or other of the few largest cities which are already endangered by high levels of pollution. These arguments were still somewhat theoretical until the slight recession of 1971 brought them home to many more people. In that year the annual increase in the G.N.P. dropped from the 5 per cent level of recent years to 3 per cent; prices rose by 6.1 per cent; and in particular unemployment reached 1.87 per cent of the workforce, a figure which may seem insignificant when compared with other Western countries,* but which was alarming to Australians after ten years of full employment. At the same time there was a growing movement in the A.C.T.U. in favour of a 35-hour week, and the opinion of its President, Mr R.J. Hawke, cannot be overlooked by any Australian political leader.

The problem was : should the immigration programme be continued at the same rate ? Should it be cut back, or even stopped altogether ? The outgoing Liberal-Country Party government had decided to hold an inquiry into Australia's needs and objectives, the integration of immigrants into the community and the possible sources of immigrants in the future. This last point was not without importance, tacitly implying as it did that there would be a review of the hitherto sacrosanct White Australia policy.† This inquiry was to report in 1974, but Mr Whitlam did not wait for that to define Labor's position on the question. The first change was to be a considerable reduction, of the order of 50,000 to 100,000, in the number of immigrants taken in each year. The recruiting method was also to be altered, as it had resulted in an overwhelming majority of European immigrants, which was seen as a cause of ill-feeling among Australia's immediate neighbours. Immigrants were now to be people with friends or family already in Australia, and people who had an essential contribution to make to the country, skilled workers, specialists and the like. Race was no longer to be as important a consideration as knowledge of the language ; an English-speaking Asian was to be preferable to a person of Mediterranean origin who spoke no English. Mr Whitlam added that it was to be expected that the number of Asian immigrants would in fact tend to drop, and that by the end of the 1970s Australia would have signed reciprocal agreements with several governments, including Papua New Guinea and Fiji, under which there would be equal numbers of their citizens and Australians living in each other's countries.

The founding fathers need not turn in their graves ; there is nothing very serious about any of that. Australia has not jettisoned the White Australia policy. In any case, would anybody deny that

---

* The American figure at the time, for example, was more than 5 per cent.

† The fact was that about 10,000 Asians were already being accepted annually as 'special cases'.

thirteen million Australians have the right to seek to preserve the heritage of their ancestors, if they see fit ? Similarly, would it make any difference to the over-population problem in Asia even if Australia were to open its doors to ten, fifteen or twenty million Asian immigrants ? Would anyone take the responsibility of encouraging Australia to do that, in view of the fact that no multiracial society has ever reached a state of lasting equilibrium ? In the light of history, it seems a reasonable and realistic compromise to abolish the exclusion of Asians on principle and to limit their numbers to those people who can be integrated with a minimum of difficulty.

However, that having been said, one does wonder whether there is as much wisdom in the Labor government's plans for cutting back immigration as a whole. It has been argued that the cities are already too large. But against that it must be pointed out that Australia is blessed with a commodity that has become all too scarce in Europe : space. It is surely possible to foresee that at least along the east coast, which has already proved so attractive to settlement, new cities can rise, with a maximum of a million inhabitants each and sufficiently distant from one another to avoid the claustrophobic feeling so noticeable in the crammed suburbs of Sydney and Melbourne. Canberra, after all, is a perfect example of what Australians can do in this respect. It has been argued that water will be short – Dr Coombs is on record as stating that Australia is the poorest continent in water resources and that this may well prove to be the greatest limiting factor on Australia's growth. However, it is argued against this that irrigation and desalination techniques have now opened up perspectives which would have been inconceivable only a short while ago, and that with wise husbandry of its water the continent could easily support eighty million inhabitants.*

How is the non-specialist to judge ? – especially since the problem has implications far beyond these technological arguments. A historian has said that in the twenty years just before the first World War, when immigration had virtually stopped, Australia became a dull, grey sort of place. Another speaks of the New Australians as a 'lively yeast in Australia's Anglo-Saxon dough'.† A sociologist comments most aptly that even illiterate, unskilled and unsophisti-

---

* Some put the figure of potential population as high as 200 million or 300 million.

† Hancock, W.K., 'Then and Now', in *Institute of Public Affairs Review*, vol. 22, no. 3, 1968, p. 93.

cated peasants from southern Europe increase cultural diversity, create a new atmosphere, give Australian life greater meaning and make it more exciting, more varied, more human and, in a word, more bearable. One wonders whether the immigrants who made America were very different. Surely a young country will always need an abundant flow of new, rich and varied blood.

Australia, the argument runs, has no shortage of manpower. This may be true. Even so, it might be desirable for her to have a larger internal consumer market. On this point one must come back to the mineral discoveries.

Donald Horne calls Australia 'the lucky country', admittedly not without tongue in cheek. But Australia can be seen to be fortunate the fabulous mineral discoveries of the last ten years have probably spared her one of the periods of intermittent stagnation that have cropped up in her history from time to time. Nor is this the only stroke of good fortune in recent years. It had seemed for some time that wool was bound to decline in importance as a textile. The sheep population had been rising constantly: from seventy million at the beginning of the century, it had risen to 112 million in 1950 and 180 million in 1970. However, the value of production had begun to drop from $808 million in 1965 to $735 million in 1970. At the same time, internal consumption of wool remained virtually unchanged at a little over twenty million kilos. An even more significant symptom was the decreasing proportion of wool exports: 37.2 per cent in 1967–8, 33.4 per cent in 1969–70.

These were unpromising years when competition from man-made fibres seemed invincible. By October 1971 the decrease in the value of wool production had reached 50 per cent in five years. Then there came a sudden change in the pattern with a rise estimated at 160 per cent in about fifteen months. This abrupt reversal of an unfavourable trend has been explained by several different factors. First and foremost is the fact that Japan now buys about 40 per cent of the Australian wool-clip, a proportion that may well rise as Japanese dress habits conform more and more to Western customs. Another reason was that stockpiles had been exhausted. New techniques had also enabled manufacturers to compete on better terms with artificial fibres.*

* At the opening of the new season in January 1973, the recovery of wool increased by a further 25–30 per cent.

This resurgence of the wool business brings with it a problem for the government: should priority continue to be given to the traditional source of wealth, or to the more recent mineral discoveries? Dr Coombs had this to say in 1970 (and it is unlikely that he would have changed his mind today):

... is it not time to question the present mad rush to develop – i.e. to exploit – every known or suspected mineral resource which we possess? ... Why should we rush to plunder our inheritance when we are not in need ... and when we can find the savings for that exploitation only by disposing of other assets we may desperately need in the future? ... The Barrier Reef is a source of knowledge, of understanding, of mystery and delight ... it could add to the richness of human life for many from all parts of the world. And this while leaving untouched and potentially available the fuel resources reputed to be there ... Major mining and processing developments largely owned by foreign companies ... bear heavily upon Aboriginal communities ... By what calculus can one assess the relative importance of instant profits from the dispersal of wasting assets against the irretrievable destruction of a way of life unique in the world?*

As Dr Coombs says, mining ventures are 'largely owned by foreign companies'. This foreign ownership of Australian resources is an undeniable fact and its implications deserve attention. In 1967–8, mineral exports amounted to some 16.4 per cent of total Australian exports; by 1970 the proportion had risen above 24 per cent; and no doubt the latest trade figures will show another increase. Such rapid development has its reasons, for it is not enough merely to possess natural resources; capital is required so as to exploit them, and buyers are required so as to turn them into profit.

The last Liberal-Country Party Treasurer announced shortly before Labor's victory in the 1972 elections that since the end of the war, the proportion of foreign ownership of Australian companies had risen from 20 per cent to 35 per cent. Some months later the *Bulletin* put it more bluntly – 'Australia for sale'. And there can be no doubt that such figures are of great significance. They show that Australian equity in the motor manufacturing industry stands at a bare 12 per cent; in oil at 21 per cent; in chemicals at 41 per cent;

---

* See Coombs, H.C., *The Fragile Pattern* (The Boyer Lectures, 1970), Australian Broadcasting Commission, Sydney, pp. 24–5.

and in the pharmaceutical industry at 25 per cent. In the mid-1960s another weekly had examined the fifty largest Australian companies* and produced even more startling results : foreign ownership in the motor-vehicle industry then stood at 95 per cent ; in the pharmacy trade at 97 per cent ; in the bauxite industry at 75 per cent ; in iron at 75 per cent ; and so on. It is reliably reported that between 1945 and 1972 almost twelve billion dollars of foreign money were invested in Australia. The two main sources of these funds were Great Britain and the U.S.A. The shift in the relative importance of these two sources is also revealing : in 1948 British investors provided 82 per cent of foreign investments ; by 1968 the British proportion had fallen to 47 per cent. Over the same period American investment had risen from 9 per cent to 33 per cent, being concentrated especially in motor manufacturing, oil, agricultural machinery, and chemical and pharmaceutical goods. British investments are strongest in banking and insurance companies. The contribution of French investments is by no means negligible.

Japanese investment in Australia has so far been more cautious. Japan has been more concerned to buy raw materials than to own Australian companies. It has been said that having had the front door shut in their face in 1942, they are now trying to come in by the back door. Whitlam, in this regard, has proved a reliable prophet. In the late 1960s he warned Australians that whereas their country used to be an English farm, it was now in the process of becoming a Japanese mine. Japan's share of Australian iron ore† is actually greater than its share in the wool market. In Australian mining circles it was thought in December 1972 that the 7.05 per cent revaluation of the dollar would have an adverse effect on the Japanese market ; but in the wool industry the opposite view was held. Any reduction in Japanese purchases would be only temporary, as Japan relies heavily on Australia's resources. There would appear to be no reason why Europe's meat requirements could not be met by Australia, or Russia's and China's need for wheat. The upshot of any such development could be that Australia becomes a seller of raw materials and a buyer of manufactured goods, an arrangement which would put Australia back into the

---

* Of the very largest only two, B.H.P. and C.S.R., are wholly Australian-owned.

† Two million tonnes in 1966 ; Japanese purchases are expected to rise to 25 million tonnes by 1975.

status of a colonial power which it occupied for such a long time. One wonders whether an independent Australia would be satisfied with such a development.

As things stand at present, Australia's only defence seems to be to limit foreign investment. The McMahon government had taken a step in this direction in the autumn of 1972, by applying controls to all companies worth more than a million dollars. According to the then Prime Minister, the inflow of foreign capital had increased at a disturbing rate over the previous two years : $797 million in 1969–70, $1,418 million in 1970–1, and $1,841 million in 1971–2. McMahon saw Australia as a relatively rich country, no longer needing foreign assistance at the same rate as over the previous twenty years. Whitlam was in complete agreement with this, believing that it was time to put an end to foreign control and time for Australians to start the reconquest of Australia.

This sort of slogan was bound to have a ready hearing among Australians, summing up as it does the nation's imprecise urge towards independence. But the fact is that the reconquest of Australia can only be achieved if Australian capital can take the place of foreign capital. The only source of capital is private investment ; the only way to increase private investment is to increase exports and, above all, to change the nature of Australia's exports. At present 78 per cent of Australia's exports is made up of raw materials.* The nub of the problem will not be affected in the slightest by limiting the percentage of foreign investments. It would appear that Australia's most pressing need at the moment is for a greatly expanded home market which would promote the manufacture of goods at prices sufficiently low for them to be able to compete in foreign markets as well. But thirteen million consumers will never constitute a market big enough for that sort of development.

One might also think that a policy of restriction on immigration and reduction of foreign investment would be too negative to be compatible with an energetic foreign policy.

And certainly Whitlam's foreign policy does seem to be energetic. In less than a month he established diplomatic relations with China

---

* A study done in 1968 concluded not only that it was a minority of manufacturers who had ventured into the export market, but also that 70 per cent of those who did actually disposed of less than 10 per cent of their production in this way. The percentages have probably not changed much in the meantime.

and East Germany ; broke off relations with Taiwan ; brought back the last Australians from Vietnam ; announced that he would not replace the troops based in Singapore at the end of their tour of duty ; called the S.E.A.T.O. pact 'moribund' ; declared Australia's intention of taking France to the International Court of Justice over its nuclear explosions in the Pacific ; and, so as to rid Australia of the racist stigma, decided to apply a policy of strict isolation towards Rhodesia and South Africa. Rhodesia was to have its information office in Sydney closed and was to come under an embargo on wheat exports, and South Africa's presence in the former German territory of South West Africa was to be condemned. Australia was to vote in the United Nations in favour of sanctions against *apartheid*, and decided, somewhat controversially, not to accept visits from South African sporting teams selected on grounds of race, or even to let them pass through Australia on their way to some other country.

The new government's activity was so prodigious that many wondered whether it could maintain such a pace. Some of its other decisions have a bearing on this question. Simultaneously with the diplomatic measures described above, the Prime Minister defined Labor defence policy. National Service was to be abolished* and the army limited to 31,000 men, all of whom were to be regulars. The navy was to be reinforced by the purchase of missile-firing patrol ships and the aviation industry was to be encouraged. Provision for this defence programme was not to exceed 3.5 per cent of the gross national product. It is unlikely that the country would be prepared to see this proportion exceeded. However, if he is to disprove the old adage that the effectiveness of a nation's diplomacy is directly related to its military strength, then Whitlam is going to need a very fine diplomatic touch. For his position is not an easy one as leader of a country which aspires to independence of action, yet which cannot do without protectors. Similarly, Australia is admirably placed to play an eminent role in the South Pacific and in South-east Asia, but her immigration policies are of no assistance to her in this.

The Labor government's attitude to the British connection shows the sort of complexes that still bedevil Australia. Mr Whitlam, who

---

* The number conscripted had been fixed at 12,000 per annum ; conscription was by ballot.

is obviously not one to follow well-trodden paths, made two symbolic gestures. He turned down the honour of belonging to the Privy Council ; and he discontinued the award of British honours to Australian citizens, at least in the Federal sphere. At the same time, Elizabeth II is still Queen of Australia and until recently the passports of Australians reminded the bearers that they were also British subjects. Other traces of British protocol and ceremony remain in the former colony. It has been said that the Governor-General seems to wear tails more often than any member of the Royal Family. Despite the semi-circular French or American shape of the House of Representatives chamber, the Westminster tradition is still visible in the white wigs, the red colours of the Senate chamber (based on the colour of the House of Lords) and the green of the Representatives (based on the colour of the House of Commons) ; the mace carried by the Usher was a gift from Westminster ; the Royal arms above the Speaker's chair are supposed to have been cut from a piece of wood dating back to 1399 ; and the arms of the chair are made of wood from Nelson's flagship, *Victory*.

Unfortunately, such glorious reminders of the past probably serve more to divide Australians nowadays than to bring them together. Immigrants see the Crown as nothing but a symbol, and it raises a smile rather than any loyalty. And even Australians who are quite clearly descended from British ancestors, and who may take pride in them, have no desire to be looked on as British. The nickname 'Pommy'* expresses at least a shade of irony, if not more. Australian attitudes towards the British are a complicated compound of admiration, envy and condescension, and are probably becoming more obvious as Australia moves away from the old relationship. It may not be too paradoxical to suggest that Australia might even feel more at ease in her dealings with 'the old country' if she were to become a republic.

In fact, in that difficult search for an identity that the nation is at present going through, it is a constant concern of Australians to mark themselves off from any other nation with which they might

---

* The word dates from about the early 1890s. One hears two explanations of its origin. According to the first theory, the word derives from a corruption of 'pomegranate' and referred originally to the ruddy complexions of British immigrants. The second theory traces it back to a jingle about immigrants from the turn of the century, containing the rhyme 'jimmygrant/pommygrant'.

be compared. They may not want to be thought of as British any more ; but they certainly do not want to be looked on as Americans either. Donald Horne says :

Australia was the first country in the contemporary world to be saved by the Americans. It is one of the few that will admit that it was saved by the Americans. It has even forgiven the Americans for saving it* ... The rhetorical expression of American idealism may sometimes leave Australians cold, suspicious as they are of all idealism. (What's in it for him ?) But Australians have what they would consider to be a hard-headed respect for American material success and expertise.†

This has become a more acute problem since the war in Vietnam. This conflict had originally given Australia the opportunity of proving what a faithful ally she was (or, as the other school of thought put it, the most submissive of American satellites). The fear of Communism was used as the justification for Australia's taking part in the war. The distance on the map between Saigon and Sydney was pointed out, and noises were made about the presence of Russian ships in the Indian Ocean. But this was largely false pretences. Australia really went into the Vietnam war as a quid pro quo. Once into the war, Australia found herself in a position she had not bargained for. The duration of the war and the savagery with which it was fought came to be pressing reasons for Australia to dissociate herself from American 'imperialism'. Australian waterside workers, always eager for any opportunity to stop work, took the bombing of Hanoi as an excuse to impose a boycott on all goods being shipped to or from the U.S.A. The longer-term view, more intelligent than this sort of outburst of bad temper, is that the Americans' misadventure in Vietnam bids fair to be their last attempt to have a bearing on events in Australia's area, and that this must make Australia's own future that much more uncertain. First the British withdrew from the region. Does the aftermath of Vietnam mean that the Americans are about to do likewise ? Canberra could well see the re-opening of Sino-American relations by Nixon as grounds for disquiet as well as expectation.

Officially the A.N.Z.U.S. pact is still the cornerstone of Australian

---

* However it has been pointed out that no statue has ever been erected to honour General MacArthur.

† Horne, D., *The Lucky Country*, Angus & Robertson, Sydney, 1964, pp. 82, 83.

foreign policy. But already Labor men have been heard to say that A.N.Z.U.S. must be 'updated'.

In her desire to stop being subordinate to the U.S.A. and her awareness of the limited means of Great Britain, Australia now finds herself trying to define her own aims and limitations in foreign policy. Because of the past, she cannot ignore Europe; because of the present and future, she must turn more towards Asia.

Up to the present day, Europe (if one leaves aside Great Britain) has taken only a minor part in Australian trade deals. In 1970 Europe took 13 per cent of Australia's exports and supplied 17 per cent of her imports.* In particular, France receives only 2.77 per cent of Australia's exports and supplies 1.8 per cent of her imports. These incongruous figures must surely give cause for concern when one thinks of the likely future importance of France's relations with Australia. Whitlam has recently drawn attention to Australia's need for 'a third force', by which he means Europe. But when one wonders who can speak for Europe, one sees immediately that Germany, with her scant international experience, is out of the question. The same goes for Great Britain, since any British intervention would be in danger of relegating Australia to the Dominion status that she has only recently left behind. This really only leaves France. And France, after all, has long experience of Australia's part of the world, has no political ambitions in that direction and is better qualified than any other country to remind the thirteen million Europeans in Australia of the hereditary ties linking them to their home continent.

However, it does appear that Australia's future destiny will be seen to lie in the Pacific and in South-east Asia. It has been estimated that 70 per cent of investments in Fiji are of Australian origin. Nauru's phosphates are also controlled by Australian-based capital. Australian equity has partly replaced British in Malaysia and Singapore. But Australia's closest economic and cultural relations are actually with Indonesia; it was no accident that Whitlam made his first official visit as Prime Minister to that country. Once peace comes about in the countries of Indo-China, it is highly likely that similar relations will be established between them and Australia. In fact Australia seems perfectly placed to be an essential intermediary between the West and the Far East. The U.K. is too far away and could no longer afford to take on that role; and for a long time to

---

* As against exports of 25 per cent and imports of 11 per cent for Japan alone.

come, any American move will be bound to rouse suspicions. Australia, on the other hand, is almost geographically situated in the area, and it has no colonialist past or imperialist present to live down. In fulfilling this function of linking two great cultural blocs, Australia would not have to deny her own origins but in fact would draw strength from them. Such a role, one would think, should inspire Australian youth and give them the purpose they feel the lack of at present. It would be a grand enough responsibility to bring out the best in the best young Australians. And Australia should be actively encouraging the growth of her young elite to meet that responsibility. A foreign admirer can only hope that she will take it on and thus begin the most stirring episode yet in her history.

The time has come for Australia to make a choice. One way lies a facile solution – Australia could let herself become a southern hemisphere version of Scandinavia, sheltered from the great movements in the wider world, preferring the peace and quiet of the easy life, concerned primarily with material progress and social justice and untrammelled by tradition. She could become a country where present achievements would be more important than future dreams.

But such aspirations are now surely obsolete figments of Australia's past. What Australia needs in the 1970s is to mark herself off by some arresting characteristic. Now that she stands by herself, without the support (or perhaps, more aptly, freed from the support) of her erstwhile protectors, it is surely up to her to demonstrate her maturity, so that people can think of something greater than mere mineral discoveries when Australia's name is mentioned. Australia in the mid-1970s is no longer the country she was in 1940. Whether Australians like it or not, the wealth of their country, her geographical position, even the isolation of her people, all these factors will tend to thrust greatness upon Australia. Some day somebody may write an instructive history of golden opportunities missed. If such a history is ever written, it is to be hoped that it will not deal with the Commonwealth of Australia.

Summary Chronology

c. 25,000 B.C.	Gradual settlement of Australia by Aborigines
13th century	Marco Polo's voyages
16th century	Portuguese and French voyages
1567	Mendaña's first expedition. Discovery of Solomons
1595	Mendana's second expedition, including Quirós. Discovery of Marquesas
1606	Quirós discovers *Austrialia del Espíritu Santo*. Torres sails through straits between Australia and New Guinea. Dutch vessel coasts northern tip of Australia
1616	Hartog reaches Australia's west coast
1629	Wreck of the *Batavia*
1636	Van Diemen appointed Governor-General of Dutch East Indies
1642	Tasman discovers Tasmania and New Zealand
1644	Tasman explores in detail Australia's north coast
1645	Van Diemen dies
1688	Dampier explores Australia's north-west coast
1696	Vlamingh's expedition
1699	Dampier's second voyage
1730	Bouvet de Lozier's expedition
1756	Publication of *Histoire des Navigations aux Terres Australes* by Charles de Brosses

1766	Wallis discovers Tahiti
1766–9	Bougainville reaches the Great Barrier Reef and circumnavigates the globe
1769	Cook's first expedition. *Endeavour* at Tahiti. Cook circumnavigates New Zealand. Surville reaches New Zealand
29 April 1770	Discovery of Botany Bay
11 June 1770	*Endeavour* strikes Barrier Reef
22 August 1770	Cook takes possession of New South Wales
11 October 1770	Cook reaches Batavia
1771	Saint-Allouarn sails along Australia's west coast. Marion du Fresne lands in New Zealand
13 July 1771	Cook's return to England
1772–5	Cook's second voyage
1776–9	Cook's third voyage
1779	Parliament studies problem of transportation
14 February 1779	Cook killed by Hawaiians
1786	Choice of Botany Bay
13 May 1787	First Fleet sets sail under command of Phillip. Mutiny on the *Bounty*
18 January 1788	Arrival at Botany Bay
21 January 1788	Discovery of Sydney Cove
24 January 1788	Meeting with La Pérouse
3 June 1790	Arrival of Second Fleet
1792	Phillip returns to England
1792–5	New South Wales under military rule
1795	Hunter appointed Governor
1798	Bass and Flinders circumnavigate Tasmania
1799	King appointed Governor
1800–03	Baudin's expedition
1801–03	Flinders' voyages and circumnavigation of Australia
1803	Brief settlement at Port Phillip
1803–04	Tasmania settled
1804	Irish convicts revolt
1806	Bligh appointed Governor

1807	First consignment of Australian wool to England
1808	Bligh deposed
1809	Macquarie appointed Governor
1813	Blaxland, Lawson and Wentworth cross the Blue Mountains
1818	Freycinet skirts Australia's west coast
1819	Bigge's inquiry
1821	British East India Company established in Singapore. Macquarie recalled. Brisbane appointed Governor
1823	Creation of New South Wales Legislative Council
1824	Arthur appointed Governor of Tasmania. Australian Agricultural Company founded
1824–9	Settlement of parts of north coast
1825	Hyacinthe de Bougainville arrives in Sydney in command of French naval detachment. Darling appointed Governor. Tasmania becomes independent of New South Wales
1826	Dumont d'Urville in Australia
1826–8	Temporary settlement at Western Port
1826–31	Temporary settlement at King George's Sound
1827	Cunningham reaches the Darling Downs. Hume and Hovell close to site of Melbourne
1828	Sturt's first expedition. He discovers the Darling. Extension of Legislative Council's powers
1829	Sturt's second expedition. He follows the Murray to Lake Alexandrina. Publication of Wakefield's *A Letter from Sydney*. The 'Nineteen counties' drawn up. Western Australia founded
1831	Bourke appointed Governor. Land prices fixed at five shillings per acre
1834	South Australia founded

1835	Melbourne founded
1836	Thomas Mitchell in ' Australia felix '
1837	Commission of inquiry on transportation
1838	Land prices fixed at twelve shillings per acre. Gipps appointed Governor
1840	Strzelecki crosses Australian Alps and climbs Mount Kosciusko. End of transportation to New South Wales
1841	Eyre crosses the Nullarbor Plain
1842	New South Wales adopts principle of representative government
1843	Land prices fixed at £1 per acre
1844	Sturt's third expedition northward from Adelaide. Leichhardt sets out from Brisbane area, reaches Port Essington
1846	FitzRoy appointed Governor
1848	Leichhardt attempts to cross the continent from east to west. He disappears
1849	Transportation begins to Western Australia
February 1851	Gold discovered in New South Wales
September 1851	Gold discovered in Victoria
1853	End of transportation to Tasmania. French occupation of New Caledonia
1854	Eureka Stockade rebellion
1855	Parliamentary government in New South Wales, Victoria, Tasmania and South Australia
1855–6	Eight-hour day in Victoria and New South Wales
1859	Queensland founded
1860	McDouall Stuart reaches the centre of the continent
1860–1	Burke and Wills expedition
1861	New South Wales adopts system of ' free selection '
1862	Stuart crosses Australia from south to north. First sugar plantations in Queensland

1864	Arrival of first convicts in New Caledonia
1867	Visit of Duke of Edinburgh
1869	Opening of Suez Canal
1872	Sydney-London cable link opened
1874	Rochefort and *communards* in Australia
1880	New South Wales adopts principle of compulsory, free, non-denominational schooling
1883	Execution of Ned Kelly. Discovery of minerals at Broken Hill. Queensland's occupation of east New Guinea, repudiated by London. Intercolonial Conference in Sydney
1884	Germany and Great Britain occupy eastern end of New Guinea
1885	French Act on transportation of recidivists. Anglo-German partition agreement on New Guinea. Australian contingent sent to Sudan. Federal Council created
1887	Anglo-French agreement on New Hebrides
1890–94	Series of strikes
1891	Labor parties founded. First Constitutional Convention. New South Wales rejects proposal for federation
1892	Gold discovered at Coolgardie
1893	Bank failure. Corowa conference
1895	Premiers' Conference at Hobart
1897–8	Second Constitutional Convention
1898	Federation proposal rejected by referendum. Spanish-American War
1899	Second referendum approves federation proposal. London assents
1899–1902	Boer War. Australian participation
1900	Boxer Rebellion. Australian participation
1 January 1901	Beginning of federation
1902	Colonial Conference in London. Anglo-Japanese alliance
1904	Establishment of principle of

	compulsory arbitration
1907	Definition of 'fair and reasonable' minimum wage. Imperial Conference in London. Australia's need for a navy recognized
1908	Visit of American fleet
1909	Compulsory military service
1910	Commonwealth acquires Northern Territory. First Labor victory
1911	Tax on unearned increment of land. Foundation of Commonwealth Bank. Site of national capital chosen
4 August 1914	Great Britain declares war on Germany
September 1914	Occupation of New Guinea
December 1914	First Australian troops arrive in Egypt
25 April 1915	Landing at Gallipoli. Anzac Day
October 1915	Hughes becomes Prime Minister
December 1915	Gallipoli evacuated
July 1916	Australians in Battle of Somme
October 1916	Conscription rejected by referendum
December 1916	Palestine frontier reached
February 1917	Hughes forms 'national' government
March–July 1917	Australians in battles at Arras and Ypres
31 October 1917	Turkish front pierced at Beersheba
December 1917	Conscription again rejected by referendum
8 December 1917	Jerusalem occupied
March–April 1918	Fighting round Villers-Bretonneux
May 1918	Monash takes command of Australian forces
8 August 1918	Australians take part in decisive attack
1 October 1918	Damascus occupied
30 October 1918	Turkey capitulates
11 November 1918	Signing of Armistice
28 June 1919	Signing of Versailles Treaty
September 1919	Australian Parliament ratifies Versailles Treaty
1920	Foundation of Country Party
1921	Imperial Conference. Washington Conference

1922	Chanak incident. Bruce-Page government takes office
1923	Imperial Conference
1925	Locarno Treaty
1926	Balfour Declaration
1927	Parliament opened in Canberra
1929	Labor back in government
1930	Visit of Sir Otto Niemeyer
1931	Formation of United Australia Party. Statute of Westminster. Japan invades Manchuria
1932	Scullin government falls. Lyons forms government
1938	Munich agreement
26 April 1939	Menzies forms government
3 September 1939	Great Britain declares war on Germany
November 1939	Menzies leaves for England. Compulsory military service reintroduced
February 1940	Casey represents Australia in Washington
August 1940	Australian legation opens in Tokyo
September 1940	Italian offensive in North Africa
January 1941	Anglo–Australian counter-attack. Benghazi captured
March 1941	Rommel's offensive. Visit of American fleet
March–April 1941	Defeat in Greece
April–December 1941	Siege of Tobruk
May 1941	Defeat in Crete. Menzies returns
June 1941	Syria and Lebanon captured
August 1941	Menzies resigns
October 1941	Labor back in office. Curtin, Prime Minister
7 December 1941	Pearl Harbor
26 December 1941	Hong Kong surrenders
15 February 1942	Singapore falls
19 February 1942	Darwin bombed
March 1942	Two army divisions return from North Africa. Japanese invade New Guinea. MacArthur arrives in Australia

May 1942	Battle of the Coral Sea
June 1942	Battle of Midway
July 1942	Rommel reaches El Alamein
September 1942	Counter-offensive in New Guinea
October 1942	Victory of El Alamein
January 1943	Papua liberated
February 1943	Third army division returns from North Africa. Parliament authorizes sending of conscripts to fight in south-west Pacific zone
November 1943	Australia not included in Cairo conference
January 1944	Australia and New Zealand sign A.N.Z.A.A.C. Pact
1945	Evatt represents Australia at San Francisco conference on U.N. Charter. Death of Curtin. Chifley becomes Prime Minister
2 September 1945	Blamey signs Japanese surrender on behalf of Australia
1946	Inception of massive immigration policy
1947	Bank nationalization Act
1947–9	Australia supports Dutch expulsion from East Indies
1948	High Court invalidates bank nationalization
1949	Miners' strike. Beginning of Snowy Mountains Scheme. Foundation of Australian National University. Chifley defeated at elections. Liberal-Country Party back in government. Menzies again Prime Minister
1950	Australia recognizes Taiwan. Colombo Plan
1950–3	Australian participation in Korean War
1951	Communist Party dissolution rejected by High Court and referendum. Chifley dies. Evatt succeeds as Prime Minister. A.N.Z.U.S. Pact
1954	Petrov affair. S.E.A.T.O. Pact

1955	Australian troops sent to Malaya
1956	Olympic Games in Melbourne. Suez Canal nationalized. Menzies supports Anglo-French intervention
1957	Dutch-Australian agreement on New Guinea. Formation of Democratic Labor Party
1961	South Africa becomes a republic. Menzies opposes South Africa's expulsion from the British Commonwealth
1963	Dutch West New Guinea handed over to Indonesia. De Gaulle vetoes British entry to European Common Market. Indian-Australian *rapprochement*. Australia accepts U.S. naval communications base. American commitment to defence of Papua New Guinea
1965	First Australian troops sent to Vietnam
1966	Menzies resigns after sixteen years in office. Holt succeeds as Prime Minister
1967	Death of Holt. Gorton becomes Prime Minister
1969	Liberal-Country Party coalition wins its eleventh successive general election
1971	McMahon government
December 1972	Labor back in office. Whitlam, Prime Minister. Australia recognizes China. Last Australians withdrawn from Vietnam

Prime Ministers of Australia

Barton, E.   *1901 – 03*
Deakin, A.   *1903 – 04*
Watson, J.C.   *1904*
Reid, G.H.   *1904 – 05*
Deakin, A.   *1905 – 08*
Fisher, A.   *1908 – 09*
Deakin, A.   *1909 – 10*
Fisher, A.   *1910 – 13*
Cook, J.   *1913 – 14*
Fisher, A.   *1914 – 15*
Hughes, W.M.   *1915 – 23*
Bruce, S.M.   *1923 – 9*
Scullin, J.H.   *1929 – 32*

Lyons, J.A.   *1932 – 9*
Page, E.C.G.   *1939*
Menzies, R.G.   *1939 – 41*
Fadden, A.W.   *1941*
Curtin, J.   *1941 – 5*
Forde, F.M.   *1945*
Chifley, J.B.   *1945 – 9*
Menzies, R.G.   *1949 – 66*
Holt, H.E.   *1966 – 7*
McEwen, J.   *1967 – 8*
Gorton, J.G.   *1968 – 71*
McMahon, W.   *1971 – 2*
Whitlam, E.G.   *1972*

Works Consulted

Abbreviations

A.E.H.R.	*Australian Economic History Review*
A.F.M.F.A.	Archives of the French Ministry of Foreign Affairs
F.N.A.	French National Archives
H.S.A.N.Z.	*Historical Studies Australia and New Zealand* (from vol. 13, 1969, published as *Historical Studies*)
J.R.A.H.S.	*Journal of the Royal Australian Historical Society*
R.D.M.	*Revue des Deux Mondes*

General Bibliography

I Australian history

ALEXANDER, F., *Australia Since Federation: A Narrative and Critical Analysis*, Nelson, Melbourne, 1967.

BARNARD, M., *A History of Australia*, Angus & Robertson, Sydney, 1962.

BLAINEY, G., *The Tyranny of Distance : How Distance Shaped Australia's History*, Sun Books, Melbourne, 1966.

The Cambridge History of the British Empire (gen. eds. J.H. Rose, A.P. Newton and E.A. Benians), 8 vols. in 9, vol. vii, pt. 1, *Australia*, Cambridge University Press, London, 1933.

CLARK, C.M.H., *A History of Australia*, vol. 1, *From the Earliest Times to the Age of Macquarie*, Melbourne University Press, Melbourne, 1962.

——, *A Short History of Australia*, Mentor, New York, 1963.

CRAWFORD, R.M., *Australia*, 3rd rev. edn, Hutchinson, London, 1970.

FEEKEN, E.H.J., FEEKEN, G.E.E. and SPATE, O.H.K., *The Discovery and Exploration of Australia*, Nelson, Melbourne, 1970.

FITZPATRICK, B., *The Australian People, 1788–1945*, Melbourne University Press, Melbourne, 1946.

GREENWOOD, G. (ed.), *Australia : A Social and Political History*, Angus & Robertson, Sydney, 1955.

HANCOCK, W.K., *Australia*, Jacaranda Press, Brisbane, 1961.

PALMER, V., *National Portraits*, 3rd edn, Melbourne University Press, Melbourne, 1954.

PIKE, D., *Australia : The Quiet Continent*, Cambridge University Press, London, 1970.

PRINGLE, J.D., *Australian Accent*, Chatto & Windus, London, 1958.

REESE, T.R., *Australia in the Twentieth Century : A Political History*, Cheshire, Melbourne, 1964.

RIENITS, R. and RIENITS, T., *A Pictorial History of Australia*, Hamlyn, Sydney, 1969.

SHAW, A.G.L., *The Story of Australia*, 2nd edn, Faber & Faber, London, 1962.

SPATE, O.H.K. *Australia*, Benn, London, 1968.

II History of the British Empire

CARRINGTON, C.E., *The British Overseas : Exploits of a Nation of Shopkeepers*, Cambridge University Press, London, 1950.

WILLIAMSON, J.A., *A Short History of British Expansion*, 2 vols., vol. 1, *The Old Colonial Empire*, vol. 2, *The Modern Empire and Commonwealth*, 2nd edn, Macmillan, London, 1930.

III Economic history

BUTLIN, S.J., *Foundations of the Australian Monetary System, 1788–1851*, Melbourne University Press, Melbourne, 1953.

FITZPATRICK, B., *The British Empire in Australia : An Economic History, 1834–1939*, 2nd edn, rev. and abr., reissued Macmillan, Melbourne, 1969.

LA NAUZE, J.A., *Political Economy in Australia: Historical Studies*, Melbourne University Press, Melbourne, 1949.

SHANN, E.O.G., *An Economic History of Australia*, Cambridge University Press, London, 1948.

SHAW, A.G.L., *The Economic Development of Australia*, 5th rev. edn, repr. with minor corrections, Longmans, Melbourne, 1969.

IV Collections of documents

CLARK, C.M.H. (ed.), *Sources of Australian History*, Oxford University Press, London, 1957.

CLARK, C.M.H. (ed.), with PRYOR, L.J., *Select Documents in Australian History*, 2 vols., Angus & Robertson, Sydney, 1950–5.

GILCHRIST, J.T. and MURRAY, W.J. (eds.), *Eyewitness: Selected Documents from Australia's Past*, Rigby, Adelaide, 1968.

V Encyclopaedias etc.

CHISHOLM, A.H. (ed.), *The Australian Encyclopaedia*, 10 vols., Grolier Society of Australia, Sydney, 1963.

LEGGE, J.S. (ed.), *Who's Who in Australia*, 19th edn, Herald & Weekly Times, Melbourne, 1968.

PIKE, D. (ed.), *Australian Dictionary of Biography*, vols. 1–3, Melbourne University Press, Melbourne, 1966–9.

SERLE, P., *Dictionary of Australian Biography*, 2 vols., Angus & Robertson, Sydney, 1949.

Bibliography by Chapters

Prologue

On geography:

RECLUS, E., *Nouvelle Géographie Universelle: La Terre et les Hommes*, 20 vols., vol. xiv, *Océan et Terres Océaniques: Iles de l'Océan Indien, Insulinde, Philippines, Micronésie, Nouvelle–Guinée, Melanésie, Nouvelle–Calédonie, Australie, Polynésie*, Hachette, Paris, 1889.

VIDAL de la BLACHE, P. and GALLOIS, L. (eds.), *Géographie Universelle*, 15 vols. in 23, vol. x, *Océanie: Régions Polaires Australes*, Armand Colin, Paris, 1930.

On fauna:

BOURLIÈRE, F., *Vie et Moeurs des Mammifères*, Payot, Paris, 1951.

FISCHER, P.H., *Les Animaux d'Australie: La Faune la plus Curieuse du Monde*, Payot, Paris, 1959.

1 'Terra australis incognita'

BEAGLEHOLE, J.C., *The Exploration of the Pacific*, A. & C. Black, London, 1934.

—— (ed.), *The Journals of Captain James Cook on his Voyages of Discovery*, 4 vols. in 5, vol. 1, *The Voyage of the Endeavour, 1768–1791*, Cambridge University Press for the Hakluyt Society, London, 1955.

CHICOTEAU, M., *Australie Terre Légendaire*, H. Pole & Co., Brisbane, 1965.

DUNMORE, J., *French Explorers in the Pacific*, 2 vols., vol. 1, *The Eighteenth Century*, Clarendon Press, Oxford, 1965.

FEEKEN, E.H.J., FEEKEN, G.E.E. and SPATE, O.H.K., *The Discovery and Exploration of Australia*, Nelson, Melbourne, 1970.

RAINAUD, A., *Le Continent Austral : Hypothèses et Decouvertes*, Armand Colin, Paris, 1893.

SHARP, A., *The Discovery of Australia*, Clarendon Press, Oxford, 1963.

WOOD, G.A., *The Discovery of Australia*, rev. edn by J.C. Beaglehole, Macmillan, Melbourne, 1969.

2 The first discoveries

As for the preceding chapter.

On Bougainville:

BOUGAINVILLE, L.A. de, *Voyage Autour du Monde par la Frégate du Roi la Boudeuse et la Flûte l'Étoile en 1766, 1767, 1768 et 1769*, 2 vols., 2nd edn, Saillant & Nyon, Paris, 1772.

On Dampier:

DAMPIER, W., *Nouveau Voyage Autour du Monde* ... , P. Marret, Amsterdam, 1698.

WILKINSON, C.A., *William Dampier*, John Lane The Bodley Head, London, 1929.

On De Brosses:

BROSSES, C. de, *Histoire des Navigations aux Terres Australes, Contenant ce que l'on Sait des Moeurs et des Productions des Contrées Découvertes Jusqu'à ce Jour* ..., 2 vols., Durand, Paris, 1756.

MAMET, H., *Le Président de Brosses, sa Vie et ses Ouvrages*, thesis, A. Massart, Lille, 1874.

On the explorations in general:

SMITH, B., *European Vision and the South Pacific, 1768–1850 : A Study in the History of Art and Ideas*, Clarendon Press, Oxford, 1960.

3 The voyage of the Endeavour

As for Chapters 1 and 2, and:

HOOKER, J.D. (ed.), *Journal of the Rt Hon. Sir Joseph Banks ... during Captain Cook's First Voyage in H.M.S. Endeavour, in 1768–71* ... , Macmillan, London, 1896.

MOOREHEAD, A., *The Fatal Impact : An Account of the Invasion of the South Pacific, 1767–1840*, Hamish Hamilton, London, 1966.

NEWBOLT, H., 'Captain James Cook and the Sandwich Islands', *Geographical Journal*, vol. 73, February 1929, pp. 97–101, 119–22.

RYSKAMP, C. and POTTLE, F.A. (eds.), *Boswell : The Ominous Years, 1774–1776*, Heinemann, London, 1963.

4 The Aborigines

The Australian Aborigines, Department of Territories, Canberra, 1967.

BERNDT, R.M. and BERNDT, C.H., *The World of the First Australians : An Introduction to the Traditional Life of the Australian Aborigines*, Ure Smith, Sydney, 1964.

ELKIN, A.P., *Les Aborigènes Australiens · Comment les Comprendre, Traduit de l'Anglais* ... , Gallimard, Paris, 1967 (first published Angus & Robertson, Sydney, 1938).

HASLUCK, P., *Black Australians : A Survey of Native Policy in Western Australia, 1829–1897*, 2nd edn, Melbourne University Press, Melbourne, 1970.

LUMHOLTZ, C., 'Chez les Cannibales : Voyage dans le Nord-Est de l'Australie, 1880–1884. Textes et Dessins Inédits', *Le Tour du Monde*, 29e année, 2e semestre, 1888, pp. 161–208, and 30e année, le semestre, 1889, pp. 241–336.

——, *Among Cannibals*, John Murray, London, 1890.

MOUNTFORD, C., *The Dawn of Time : Australian Aboriginal Myths in Paintings by Ainslie Roberts* ..., Rigby, Adelaide, 1969.

MULVANEY, D.J., *The Prehistory of Australia*, Thames & Hudson, London, 1969.

O'BRIEN, E., *The Foundation of Australia*, Sheed & Ward, London, 1937.

SIMPSON, C., *Primitifs d'Australie : Adam d'Ocre Paré, Traduit de l'Anglais* ... , Société Continentale d'éditions Modernes Illustrées, Paris, 1966.

STANNER, W.E.H., *After the Dreaming : Black and White Australians, an Anthropological View* (The Boyer Lectures, 1968), Australian Broadcasting Commission, Sydney, 1968.

5 The first years

BEATTY, W.A., *With Shame Remembered : Early Australia*, Cassell, Melbourne, 1962.

MOOREHEAD, A., *The Fatal Impact : An Account of the Invasion of* the South Pacific, *1767–1840*, Hamish Hamilton, London, 1966.

O'BRIEN, E.M., *The Foundation of Australia, 1786–1800 : A Study in English Criminal Practice and Penal Colonization in the Eighteenth Century*, 2nd edn, Angus & Robertson, Sydney, 1950 (first published Sheed & Ward, London, 1937).

ROBSON, L.L., *The Convict Settlers of Australia*, Melbourne University Press, Melbourne, 1965.

ROE, M., 'Australia's Place in the "Swing to the East"', *H.S.A.N.Z.*, vol. 8, no. 30, 1958, pp. 202–13.

SHAW, A.G.L., *Convicts and the Colonies : A Study of Penal Transportation from Great Britain and Ireland to Australia and Other Parts of the British Empire*, Faber & Faber, London, 1966.

TENCH, W., *A Complete Account of the Settlement at Port Jackson, in New South Wales, including an Accurate Description of the Situation of the Colony ; of the Natives ; and of its Natural Productions* ... , G. Nicol & J. Sewell, London, 1793.

——, *Sydney's First Four Years*, Angus & Robertson, Sydney, 1961.

On British prisons :

WEBB, S. and WEBB, B., *English Prisons under Local Government*, vol. 6 of *English Local Government*, Longmans, Green, London, 1922.

On the choice of Botany Bay :

BLAINEY, G., 'Botany Bay or Gotham City ?', *A.E.H.R.*, vol. viii, no. 2, 1968, pp. 154–63.

BOLTON, G.C., 'The Hollow Conqueror : Flax and the Foundation of Australia', *A.E.H.R.*, vol. viii, no. 1, 1968, pp. 3–16.

——, 'Broken Reeds and Smoking Flax', *A.E.H.R.*, vol. ix, no. 1, 1969, pp. 64–70.

FRY, H.T., '"Cathay and the Way Thither" : The Background to Botany Bay', *H.S.A.N.Z.*, vol. 14, no. 56, 1971, pp. 497–510.

SHAW, A.G.L., 'The Hollow Conqueror or the Tyranny of Distance', *H.S.A.N.Z.*, vol. 13, no. 50, 1968, pp. 195–203; and

BLAINEY, G., 'A Reply : "I came, I shaw ... "', *H.S.A.N.Z.*, vol. 13, no. 50, 1968, pp. 204–6.

On Phillip :

ELDERSHAW, M. BARNARD, *Phillip of Australia : An Account of the Settlement at Sydney Cove, 1788–92*, Harrap, London, 1938.

On La Pérouse :

BELLESSORT, A., *La Pérouse*, Plon-Nourrit, Paris, 1926.

6 Problems of growth

BASSETT, M., *The Governor's Lady, Mrs Philip Gidley King : An Australian Historical Narrative*, Oxford University Press, London 1956.

ELLIS, M.H., *John Macarthur*, Angus & Robertson, Sydney, 1955.

EVATT, H.V., *Rum Rebellion : A Study of the Overthrow of Governor Bligh by John Macarthur and the New South Wales Corps*, Angus & Robertson, Sydney, 1938.

HAINSWORTH, D.R. (ed.), *Builders and Adventurers : The Traders and the Emergence of the Colony, 1788–1821*, Cassell, Melbourne, 1968.

MACKANESS, G., *The Life of Vice-Admiral William Bligh*, 2 vols., new and rev. edn, Angus & Robertson, Sydney, 1951.

NORDHOFF, C.B. and HALL, J.N., *Mutiny on the Bounty*, Keith Jennison Books, New York, 1960.

7 Towards a new destiny

ABBOTT, G.J. and NAIRN, N.B. (eds.), *Economic Growth of Australia, 1788–1821*, Melbourne University Press, Melbourne, 1969, ch. 8, 'Economic Growth', pp. 139–61.

ARAGO, J.E.V., *Promenade Autour du Monde Pendant les Années 1817, 1818, 1819 et 1820, sur les Corvettes du Roi l'Uranie et la Physicienne, Commandées par M. Freycinet* ... , 2 vols., Leblanc, Paris, 1822, vol. 2, pp. 271–2.

BARNARD, M., *Macquarie's World*, Melbourne University Press, Melbourne, 1946.

ELLIS, M.H., *John Macarthur*, Angus & Robertson, Sydney, 1955.
——, *Lachlan Macquarie : His Life, Adventures and Times*, Dymock's Book Arcade, Sydney, 1947.

HAINSWORTH, D.R. (ed.), *Builders and Adventurers : The Traders and the Emergence of the Colony, 1788–1821*, Cassell, Melbourne, 1968.

SHAW, A.G.L., *Convicts and the Colonies*, Faber & Faber, London, 1966.

8 The search for the continent
On the maritime discoveries :

FAIVRE, J.-P., *L'Expansion Française dans le Pacifique de 1800 à 1842*, Nouvelles Éditions Latines, Paris, 1953.

——, ' L'Expedition Baudin aux " Terres Australes " ', *Rue d' Ulm*, no. 1, June–August 1965, pp. 12–19.

HILL, E., *My Love Must Wait : The Story of Matthew Flinders*, Angus & Robertson, Sydney, 1941.

NAPOLÉON, *Correspondance : Publiée par Ordre de l'Empereur Napoléon III*, 32 vols, H. Plon & J. Dumaine, Paris, 1858–70, vol. xx, no. 16544.

PRENTOUT, H., *L'Île de France sous Decaen, 1803–1810, Essai sur la Politique Coloniale du Premier Empire et la Rivalité de la France et de l'Angleterre dans les Indes Orientales*, Hachette, Paris, 1901.

SCOTT, E., *The Life of Captain Matthew Flinders, R.N.*, Angus & Robertson, Sydney, 1914.

——, *Terre Napoléon : A History of French Explorations and Projects in Australia*, Methuen, London, 1910.

TRIEBEL, L.A. and BATT, J.C., *The French Exploration of Australia with special reference to Tasmania*, Tasmanian Government Printer, Hobart, 1957.

On the land discoveries :

CUMPSTON, J.H.L., *The Inland Sea and the Great River : The Story of Australian Exploration*, Angus & Robertson, Sydney, 1964.

FEEKEN, E.H.J., FEEKEN, G.E.E. and SPATE, O.H.K., *The Discovery and Exploration of Australia*, Nelson, Melbourne, 1970.

FITZPATRICK, K. (ed.), *Australian Explorers : A Selection from their Writings, with an Introduction*, Oxford University Press, London, 1958.

LEICHHARDT, L., *Journal of an Overland Expedition from Moreton Bay to Port Essington, a Distance of Upwards of 3000 Miles, during the Years 1844–1845*, T. & W. Boone, London, 1847.

MOOREHEAD, A., *Cooper's Creek*, Hamish Hamilton, London, 1963.

PARSONS, T.G., 'A Note on T. Perry's "Australia's First Frontier " ', *J.R.A.H.S.*, vol. 50, pt. 2, 1964, pp. 144–7.

9 The pastoral age

FITZPATRICK, B., *The British Empire in Australia : An Economic History, 1834–1939*, 2nd edn, Macmillan, Melbourne, 1969.

——, *British Imperialism and Australia, 1783–1833 : An Economic History of Australasia*, Sydney University Press, Sydney, 1971.

ROE, M., *Quest for Authority in Eastern Australia, 1835–1851*,

Melbourne University Press, Melbourne, 1965.
WARD, R., *The Australian Legend*, 2nd edn, Cheshire, Melbourne, 1965.

On the bushrangers :
WHITE, C., *History of Australian Bushranging*, 2 vols. (first published Angus & Robertson, Sydney, 1900–3), repr. Lloyd O'Neil, Melbourne, 1970.

On the squatters :
ROBERTS, S.H., *The Squatting Age in Australia, 1835–1847* (first published 1935), repr. Melbourne University Press, Melbourne, 1970.

On Wakefield :
BLOOMFIELD, P., *Edward Gibbon Wakefield, Builder of the British Commonwealth*, Longmans, London, 1961.
SIEGFRIED, A., *Edward Gibbon Wakefield et sa Doctrine de la Colonisation Systématique*, thesis, Armand Colin, Paris, 1904.

10 **New colonies and political transformations**
On the French expeditions :
FAIVRE, J.-P., *L'Expansion Francaise dans le Pacifique de 1800 à 1842*, Nouvelles Editions Latines, Paris, 1953.

On British policies :
BURROUGHS, P., *Britain and Australia, 1831–1855 : A Study in Imperial Relations and Crown Lands Administration*, Clarendon Press, Oxford, 1967.
SHAW, A.G.L., 'British Attitudes to the Colonies, *ca.* 1820–1850', *Journal of British Studies*, vol. ix, no. 1, 1969, pp. 71–95.
——, 'Orders from Downing Street', *J.R.A.H.S.*, vol. 54, pt. 2, 1968, pp. 113–34.

On Tasmania :
FORSYTH, W.D., *Governor Arthur's Convict System : Van Diemen's Land, 1824–36. A Study in Colonization*, 2nd imp., Sydney University Press, Sydney, 1970.

On Western Australia :
BATTYE, J., *Western Australia : A History from its Discovery to the Inauguration of the Commonwealth*, Clarendon Press, Oxford, 1924.

CROWLEY, F.K., *Australia's Western Third : A History of Western Australia from the First Settlement to Modern Times*, Heinemann, Melbourne, 1970 (first published Macmillan, London, in association with the University of Western Australia, 1960).

HASLUCK, P., *Black Australians : A Survey of Native Policy in Western Australia, 1829–1897*, 2nd edn, Melbourne University Press, Melbourne, 1970.

——, *Unwilling Emigrants : A Study of the Convict Period in Western Australia*, Oxford University Press, Melbourne, 1959.

On the colony of Victoria :

ROBERTS, S.H., *The Squatting Age in Australia, 1835–1847*, repr. Melbourne University Press, Melbourne, 1970.

On South Australia:

PIKE, D., *Paradise of Dissent : South Australia, 1829–1857*, 2nd edn, Melbourne University Press, Melbourne, 1967.

On constitutional evolution :

MELBOURNE, A.C.V., *Early Constitutional Development in Australia : New South Wales, 1788–1856 ;Queensland, 1859–1922*, Oxford University Press, London, 1934.

On Caroline Chisholm :

KIDDLE, M., *Caroline Chisholm* (first published 1950), abr. edn, Melbourne University Press, Melbourne, 1969.

On political prisoners :

MILNE, M.G., 'North American Political Prisoners', B.A. (Hons.) thesis, University of Tasmania, Hobart, n.d.

On emancipists in Ancient Rome :

CARCOPINO, J., *La Vie Quotidienne à Rome à l'Apogée de l'Empire*, Hachette, Paris, 1939.

FUSTEL DE COULANGES, N.D., *La Cité Antique : Étude sur le Culte, le Droit, les Institutions de la Grèce et de Rome*, Hachette, Paris, 1864.

11 Australia in the mid-nineteenth century

AUDIGANNE, A., 'Politique Coloniale d'Angleterre : L'Australie et la Société Australienne', *R.D.M.*, January–March 1847, pp. 638–72.

BOLTON, G., 'The Idea of a Colonial Gentry', *Historical Studies*, vol. 13, no. 51, 1968, *Essays Presented to Sir Keith Hancock*, pp. 307–28.

BOUGAINVILLE, H. de, 'Notes sur son Voyage 1824–1826', F.N.A., —155 AP./2.

DANCOURT, A.S. de, *L'Australie: Esquisses et Tableaux*, no pub., Lille, 1869.

DARWIN, C.R., *Voyage d'un Naturaliste Autour du Monde, fait à bord du Navire le Beagle de 1831 à 1836, Traduit de l'Anglais ...* , C. Reinwald, Paris, 1875.

——, *Diary of the Voyage of H.M.S. 'Beagle'*, (ed. N. Barlow), Cambridge University Press, Cambridge, 1933.

DELESSERT, E., *Souvenirs d'un Voyage à Sydney (Nouvelle-Hollande) fait Pendant l'année 1845*, A. Franck, Paris, 1847.

JACOBS, A., 'Les Européens dans l'Océanie—Nos Antipodes, la Tasmanie et la Nouvelle-Zélande', *R.D.M.*, March–April 1859, pp. 323–49.

ROBERTS, S.H., *The Squatting Age in Australia, 1835–1847*, Melbourne University Press, Melbourne, 1970.

ROY, J.J.E., *L'Australie: Découverte, Colonisation, Civilisation*, A. Mame, Tours, 1855.

On Melbourne :

KIDDLE, M., *Men of Yesterday: A Social History of the Western District of Victoria, 1834–1890*, Melbourne University Press, Melbourne, 1961.

McCRAE, H. (ed.), *Georgiana's Journal: Melbourne, 1841–1865*, 2nd edn, Angus & Robertson, Sydney, 1966.

On the Aborigines :

HASLUCK, P., *Black Australians: A Survey of Native Policy in Western Australia, 1829–1897*, 2nd edn, Melbourne University Press, Melbourne, 1970.

On religion and culture :

CABLE, K.J., 'Religious Controversies in New South Wales in the Mid-Nineteenth Century : I. Aspects of Anglicanism, 1848–1850 ; II. The Dissenting Sects and Education', *J.R.A.H.S.*, vol. 49, pt. 1, 1963, pp. 58–74 and pt. 2, pp. 136–48.

NADEL, G., *Australia's Colonial Culture: Ideas, Men and Institutions in Mid-Nineteenth Century Eastern Australia*, Cheshire, Melbourne, 1957.

ROE, M., *Quest for Authority in Eastern Australia, 1835–1851*, Melbourne University Press, Melbourne, 1965.

On working-class movements:

HUME, L., 'Working Class Movements in Sydney and Melbourne before the Gold Rushes', *H.S.A.N.Z.*, vol. 9, no. 35, 1960, pp. 263–78.

On Federation:

WARD, J.M., *Earl Grey and the Australian Colonies, 1846–1857 : A Study of Self-Government and Self-Interest*, Melbourne University Press, Melbourne, 1958.

12 Gold

BARRETT, C., *Gold in Australia*, Cassell, Melbourne, 1951.

BATESON, C., *Gold Fleet for California : Forty-Niners from Australia and New Zealand*, Ure Smith, Sydney, 1963.

BLAINEY, G., 'Gold and Governors', *H.S.A.N.Z.*, vol. 9, no. 36, 1961, pp. 337–50.

——, *The Rush that Never Ended : A History of Australian Mining*, Melbourne University Press, Melbourne, 1963.

BROUT, C., *Guide des Emigrants aux Mines d'or en Australie*, no pub., Paris, 1855.

CANNON, M., *Who's Master ? Who's Man ?*, vol. 1 of *Australia in the Victorian Age*, Nelson, Melbourne, 1971.

CHABRILLAN, C. de, *Les Voleurs d'Or*, Michel Lévy, Paris, 1857.

COCHUT, A., 'L'Or en 1854 : De l'Influence des Mines d'Or de l'Australie et de la Californie sur le Marché Européen', *R.D.M.*, January–March 1854, pp. 801–29.

CURREY, C.H., *The Irish at Eureka*, Angus & Robertson, Sydney, 1954.

FAUCHER, L., 'De la Production et de la Demonétisation de l'Or : La Demonétisation en Hollande et la Production en Russie, en Amérique et dans l'Australie', *R.D.M.*, July–September 1852, pp. 708–60.

FAUCHERY, A., *Lettres d'un Mineur en Australie*, Poulet-Malassis & De Broise, Paris, 1857.

JACOBS, A., 'Les Européens dans l'Océanie : L'Australie Civilisée et l'Australie Sauvage, les Dernières Découvertes', *R.D.M.*, January–February 1859, pp. 89–119.

SCOTT, E. (ed.), *Lord Robert Cecil's Goldfields Diary*, Melbourne

University Press, Melbourne, 1935.

SERLE, G., *The Golden Age : A History of the Colony of Victoria, 1851–1861*, Melbourne University Press, Melbourne, 1963.

TWAIN, M., *Mark Twain in Australia and New Zealand* (vol. 1 of *Following the Equator*, first published in New York in 1897), Penguin Books, Melbourne, 1973.

13 A new Australia ?

A.F.M.F.A. (unpublished documents) Trade Correspondence, Melbourne, 1864–7.

FITZPATRICK, B., *The British Empire in Australia : An Economic History, 1834–1939*, 2nd abr. edn, Macmillan, Melbourne, 1969.

GILCHRIST, J.T. and MURRAY, W.J. (eds.), *Eyewitness: Selected Documents from Australia's Past*, Rigby, Adelaide, 1968.

GOLLAN, R., *Radical and Working Class Politics : A Study of Eastern Australia, 1850–1910*, Melbourne University Press, in association with the Australian National University, Melbourne, 1960.

GRIFFIN, J. (ed.), *Essays in Economic History of Australia, 1788–1939*, Jacaranda, Brisbane, 1967.

MÉTIN, A., *Le Socialisme sans Doctrines : La Question Agraire et la Question Ouvrière en Australie et Nouvelle-Zélande*, Félix Alcan, Paris, 1901.

MONTÉGUT, E., 'L'Australie d'Après les Récens Voyageurs : I. Le Passé Australien et le Nouveau Régime Représentatif; II. L'Élément Agricole et l'Élément Pastoral – le Travail Australien', *R.D.M.*, July–August 1877, pp. 72–101, 617–43.

PICROCHOLE, P., *Lettres sur l'Australie*, G. Chamerot, Paris, 1880.

TROLLOPE, A., *Australia and New Zealand*, 2 vols. (first published Chapman & Hall, London, 1873), Queensland University Press, St Lucia, 1967, eds. P.D. Edwards and R.B. Joyce.

On foreign investment :

BUTLIN, N.G., *Australian Domestic Product : Investment and Foreign Borrowing, 1861–1938/39*, Cambridge University Press, London, 1962.

CANNON, M., *The Land Boomers*, Melbourne University Press, Melbourne, 1966.

On religion :

O'FARRELL, P.J., *The Catholic Church in Australia : A Short History*, Nelson, Melbourne, 1968.

On Ned Kelly and the bushrangers :

OSBORNE, C., *Ned Kelly*, Blond, London, 1970.

WARD, R., *The Australian Legend*, 2nd edn, Cheshire, Melbourne, 1965.

WHITE, C., *History of Australian Bushranging*, 2 vols., Lloyd O'Neil, Melbourne, 1970, vol. 2.

On individuals of the period :

LA NAUZE, J.A., *Alfred Deakin : A Biography*, 2 vols., Melbourne University Press, Melbourne, 1965.

——, *Political Economy in Australia : Historical Studies*, Melbourne University Press, Melbourne, 1949.

MARIN LA MESLÉE, E., 'État Social et Politique de l'Australasie Britannique—Un Homme d'état Australien : Sir Henry Parkes et la Fédération des Colonies Australiennes', *R.D.M.*, May–June 1892, pp. 381–421.

MARTIN, A.W., *Henry Parkes*, Oxford University Press, Melbourne, 1964.

——, 'Henry Parkes and Electoral Manipulations, 1872–1882', *H.S.A.N.Z. Selected Articles*, Second Series, Melbourne University Press, Melbourne, 1967, pp. 108–25.

PALMER, V., *National Portraits*, 3rd edn, Melbourne University Press, Melbourne, 1940.

14 Australia looks at the outside world

A.F.M.F.A. (unpublished documents)

Great Britain – Various consulates, vol. xxx, 1846–56.

Trade Correspondence, Melbourne, vols. ii, iii, 1864–74.

Great Britain – Sydney, vol. xl, 1863–5.

Great Britain – Sydney, vol. lxv, 1877–87.

Great Britain – Melbourne, vols. lxii, lxiii, lxiv, 1874–86.

Great Britain – Melbourne, vols. lxxxvii, lxxxviii, 1887–91.

Great Britain – Melbourne, vol. xciv, 1892–4.

Australia, N.S., vol. viii, foreign policy, 1896–1915.

Australia, N.S., vol. ix, relations with France, 1896–1918.

FROUDE, J.A., *Oceana, or England and her Colonies*, Longmans, Green, London, 1886.

LA NAUZE, J.A., *Alfred Deakin : A Biography*, 2 vols., Melbourne University Press, Melbourne, 1965, vol. 1.

LANESSAN, J.-L. de, *L'Expansion Coloniale de la France, Étude Économique, Politique et Géographique sur les Établissements*

Française d'Outre-mer, Félix Alcan, Paris, 1886.

MORRELL, W.P., *Britain in the Pacific Islands*, Clarendon Press, Oxford, 1960.

SCHOLEFIELD, G.H., *The Pacific : Its Past and Future and the Policy of the Great Powers from the Eighteenth Century*, John Murray, London, 1919.

SIMONIN, L., 'Le Monde Océanique : les Progrès de l'Australie et la Future Confédération Australasienne', *R.D.M.*, March–April 1885, pp. 398–451.

WARD, J.M., *Empire in the Antipodes : The British in Australasia, 1840–1860*, Edward Arnold, London, 1966.

On the escape of Rochefort :

ROCHEFORT, H., *Les Aventures de ma Vie*, 5 vols., Dupont, Paris, 1896–8, vol. 3.

On New Guinea :

GORDON, D.C., *The Australian Frontier in New Guinea, 1870–1885*, Columbia University Press, New York, 1951.

On the Boer War :

PENNY, B., 'The Australian Debate on the Boer War', *Historical Studies*, vol. 14, no. 56, 1971, pp. 526–45.

On the Spanish-American War :

WELLINGTON, R., 'Australian Attitudes to the Spanish-American War', *J.R.A.H.S.*, vol. 56, pt. 2, 1970, pp. 111–20.

15 Crisis and Federation

A.F.M.F.A. (unpublished documents)
    Australia, N.S., vol. ii, internal policies, 1899–1904.
    Australia, N.S., vol. i, national defence, 1896–1904.
    Australia, N.S., vol. xi, finance, 1896–9.
    Australia, N.S., vol. xiii, demographic and social questions, 1896–1918.
    Australia, N.S., vol. xiv, trade matters, 1896–1906.

AUSTIN, A.G. (ed.), *The Webbs' Australian Diary 1898*, Pitman, Melbourne, 1965.

FITZPATRICK, B., *The British Empire in Australia: An Economic History, 1834–1939*, 2nd abr. edn, Macmillan, Melbourne, 1969.

LEROY-BEAULIEU, P., *Les Nouvelles Sociétés Anglo-Saxonnes : Australie, Nouvelle-Zélande, Afrique Australe*, 2nd edn, Armand

Colin, Paris, 1901.

MÉTIN, A., *Le Socialisme sans Doctrines : La Question Agraire et la Question Ouvrière en Australie et Nouvelle-Zélande*, Félix Alcan, Paris, 1901.

PALMER, V., *The Legend of the Nineties*, 3rd edn, Melbourne University Press, Melbourne, 1954.

On the importance of the year 1890 :

PHILIPP, J., '1890—The Turning Point in Labour History ?', *H.S.A.N.Z. Selected Articles*, Second Series, Melbourne University Press, Melbourne, 1967, pp. 126–36; and

O'CONNOR, J.E., '1890—A Turning Point in Labour History : A Reply to Mrs Philipp', *H.S.A.N.Z. Selected Articles*, Second Series, Melbourne University Press, Melbourne, 1967, pp. 137–49.

On nationalism :

BLACKTON, C.S., 'Australian Nationality and Nationalism : The Imperial Federationist Interlude, 1885–1901', *H.S.A.N.Z. Selected Articles*, Second Series, Melbourne University Press, Melbourne, 1967, pp. 179–98.

On the origins of Federation :

DEAKIN, A., *The Federal Story : The Inner History of the Federal Cause, 1880–1900*, Robertson & Mullens, Melbourne, 1944.

LA NAUZE, J.A., *Alfred Deakin : A Biography*, 2 vols., Melbourne University Press, Melbourne, 1965, vol. 1.

WISE, B.R., *The Making of the Australian Commonwealth, 1889–1900 : A Stage in the Growth of the Empire*, Longmans, Green, London, 1913.

16 Australia at the turn of the century

A.F.M.F.A. (unpublished documents)
Australia, N.S., vols. i, ii, internal policies, 1896–1901.

AUSTIN, A.G. (ed.), *The Webbs' Australian Diary, 1898*, Pitman, Melbourne, 1965.

BIRCH, A. and MACMILLAN, D.S. (eds.), *The Sydney Scene, 1788–1960*, Melbourne University Press, Melbourne, 1962.

COMETTANT, O., *Au Pays des Kangourous et des Mines d'Or : Étude des Moeurs et Coutumes Australiennes, Impressions de Voyage*, Fischbacher, Paris, 1890.

FROUDE, J.A., *Oceana, or England and her Colonies*, Longmans,

Green, London, 1886.

LA NAUZE, J.A., *Alfred Deakin : A Biography*, 2 vols., Melbourne University Press, Melbourne, 1965, vol. 1.

LEROY-BEAULIEU, P., *Les Nouvelles Sociétés Anglo-Saxonnes : Australie, Nouvelle-Zélande, Afrique Australe*, 2nd edn, Armand Colin, Paris, 1901.

O'RELL, M., 'En Australie', *Revue de Paris*, July–August 1894, pp. 60–92.

PALMER, V., *The Legend of the Nineties*, Melbourne University Press, Melbourne, 1954.

TWAIN, M., *Mark Twain in Australia and New Zealand* (vol. 1 of *Following the Equator*, first published in New York in 1897), Penguin Books, Melbourne, 1973.

ZAINU'DDIN, A.G., 'The Early History of the *Bulletin*', *H.S.A.N.Z. Selected Articles*, Second Series, Melbourne University Press, Melbourne, 1967, pp. 199–216.

On urbanization :

GLYNN, S., *Urbanisation in Australian History, 1788–1900*, Nelson, Melbourne, 1970.

On architecture :

BOYD, R., *Australia's Home: Its Origins, Builders and Occupiers*, Melbourne University Press, Melbourne, 1952.

17 Experiments and expectations

A.F.M.F.A. (unpublished documents)
Australia, N.S., vols. ii–vi, viii.

BIARD D'AUNET, G., 'La Société Australienne', *R.D.M.*, September–October 1906, pp. 100–34.

——, 'Le Socialisme en Australie', *R.D.M.*, September–October 1906, pp. 581–611.

——, 'La Constitution Australienne et son Fonctionnement', *R.D.M.*, November–December 1906, pp. 287–322.

DEAKIN, A., *Federated Australia : Selection from Letters to the Morning Post 1900–1910* (ed. J.A. La Nauze), Melbourne University Press, Melbourne, 1968.

FITZPATRICK, B., *The British Empire in Australia : An Economic History, 1834–1939*, 2nd abr. edn, Macmillan, Melbourne, 1969.

GARRAN, R.R., *Prosper the Commonwealth*, Angus & Robertson, Sydney, 1958.

LA NAUZE, J.A., *Alfred Deakin : A Biography*, 2 vols., Melbourne University Press, Melbourne, 1965.

——, *The Hopetoun Blunder : The Appointment of the First Prime Minister of the Commonwealth of Australia, December 1900*, Melbourne University Press, Melbourne, 1957.

MÉTIN, A., *Le Socialisme sans Doctrines : La Question Agraire et la Question Ouvrière en Australie et Nouvelle-Zélande*, Félix Alcan, Paris, 1901.

TURNER, H.G., *The First Decade of the Australian Commonwealth : A Chronicle of Contemporary Politics, 1901–1910*, Mason, Firth & McCutcheon, Melbourne, 1911.

On the Labor Party :

CRISP, L.F., *The Australian Federal Labour Party, 1901–1951*, Longmans, Green, London, 1955.

EBBELS, R.N. (ed.), *The Australian Labor Movement, 1850–1907 : Extracts from Contemporary Documents*, 2nd edn, Cheshire-Lansdowne, in association with the Noel Ebbels Memorial Committee, Melbourne, 1965.

On Higgins :

HIGGINS, H.B., *A New Province for Law and Order, Being a Review, by its Late President for Fourteen Years, of the Australian Court of Conciliation and Arbitration*, Workers' Educational Association of New South Wales, Sydney, 1922.

PALMER, N., *Henry Bournes Higgins : A Memoir*, Harrap, London, 1931.

On Hughes :

FITZHARDINGE, L.F., *William Morris Hughes : A Political Biography*, vol. 1, *That Fiery Particle, 1862–1914*, Angus & Robertson, Sydney, 1964.

On foreign affairs :

HALL, H.L., *Australia and England : A Study in Imperial Relations*, Longmans, Green, London, 1934.

HANCOCK, I.R., 'The 1911 Imperial Conference', *H.S.A.N.Z.*, vol. 12, no. 47, 1966, pp. 356–72.

MEGAW, R., 'Australia and the Great White Fleet, 1908', *J.R.A.H.S.*, vol. 56, pt. 2, 1970, pp. 121–33.

18 The First World War

A.F.M:F.A. (unpublished documents)
Australia, N.S., vols. v, ix.

BEAN, C.E.W., *Anzac to Amiens : A Shorter History of the Australian Fighting Services in the First World War*, Australian War Memorial, Canberra, 1946.

DAVISON, F.D., *The Wells of Beersheba : A Light Horse Legend*, rev. edn, Angus & Robertson, Sydney, 1947.

HALL, H.L., *Australia and England : A Study in Imperial Relations*, Longmans, Green, London, 1934.

MOOREHEAD, A., *Gallipoli*, Hamish Hamilton, London, 1966.

ROBSON, L.L., *Australia and the Great War, 1914–1918*, Macmillan, Melbourne, 1969.

——, *The First A.I.F. : A Study of its Recruitment, 1914–1918*, Melbourne University Press, Melbourne, 1970.

SMITH, F.B., *The Conscription Plebiscites in Australia, 1916–17*, Victorian Historical Association, Melbourne, 1965.

On the Anzacs :

The Anzac Book : Written and Illustrated in Gallipoli by The Men of Anzac, Cassell, London, 1916.

INGLIS, K.S., 'The Anzac Tradition', *Meanjin*, no. 100, vol. xxiv, no. 1, 1965, pp. 25–44.

McLACHLAN, N., 'Nationalism and the Divisive Digger : Three Comments', *Meanjin*, no. 112, vol. xxvii, no. 3, 1968, pp. 302–8.

MONASH, J., *The Australian Victories in France in 1918*, Hutchinson, London, 1920.

ROE, M., 'Comment on the Digger Tradition', *Meanjin*, no. 102, vol. xxiv, no. 3, 1965, pp. 357–8.

SERLE, G., 'The Digger Tradition and Australian Nationalism', *Meanjin*, no. 101, vol. xxiv, no. 2, 1965, pp. 149–58.

STIÉNON, C., 'Les Anzacs : L'Héroïque Odyssée des Néo-Zélandais', *R.D.M.*, November–December 1917, pp. 198–216.

On Monash :

HETHERINGTON, J., *John Monash*, Oxford University Press, Melbourne, 1970 (first published 1962).

PALMER, V., *National Portraits*, Melbourne University Press, Melbourne, 1940.

On the Peace Conference :

CLEMENCEAU, G., *Grandeurs et Misères d'une Victoire*, Plon, Paris, 1929.

GARRAN, R.R., *Prosper the Commonwealth*, Angus & Robertson, Sydney, 1958.

HUGHES, W.M., *The Splendid Adventure : A Review of Empire Relations within and without the Commonwealth of Britannic Nations*, Benn, London, 1929.

19 Between the two wars

On economic developments :

BLAINEY, G., *Gold and Paper : A History of The National Bank of Australasia Limited*, Georgian House, Melbourne, 1958.

BUTLIN, N.G., *Australian Domestic Product : Investment and Foreign Borrowing, 1861–1938/39*, Cambridge University Press, London, 1962.

COPLAND, D.B., *Australia in the World Crisis, 1929–1933*, Cambridge University Press, London, 1934.

FITZPATRICK, B., *The British Empire in Australia : An Economic History, 1834–1939*, 2nd abr. edn, Macmillan, Melbourne, 1969.

LOUIS, L.J. and TURNER, I. (eds.), *The Depression of the 1930s*, Cassell, Melbourne, 1968.

SHANN, E.O.G., and COPLAND, D.B. (eds.), *The Crisis in Australian Finance, 1929 to 1931 : Documents on Budgetary and Economic Policies*, Angus & Robertson, Sydney, 1931.

On political developments :

CAMPBELL, E., *The Rallying Point : My Story of the New Guard*, Melbourne University Press, Melbourne, 1965.

CRISP, L.F., *Ben Chifley*, Longmans, Melbourne, 1961.

EDWARDS, C., *Bruce of Melbourne : Man of Two Worlds,* Heinemann, London, 1963.

GRAHAM, B.D., *The Formation of the Australian Country Parties*, Australian National University Press, Canberra, 1966.

LYONS, E., *So We Take Comfort*, Heinemann, London, 1965.

MENZIES, R.G., *Afternoon Light : Some Memories of Men and Events*, Cassell, Melbourne, 1967.

PAGE, E., *Truant Surgeon : The Inside Story of Forty Years of Australian Political Life*, Angus & Robertson, Sydney, 1963.

PEARCE, G.F., *Carpenter to Cabinet : Thirty-Seven Years of Parliament*, Hutchinson, London, 1951.

WHYTE, W.F., *William Morris Hughes : His Life and Times*, Angus

& Robertson, Sydney, 1957.

On foreign relations :

HANCOCK, W.K., *Survey of British Commonwealth Affairs*, vol. 1, *Problems of Nationality, 1918–1936*, Oxford University Press, issued under the auspices of the Royal Institute of International Affairs, London, 1937.

MANSERGH, N., *Survey of British Commonwealth Affairs : Problems of External Policy, 1931–1939*, Oxford University Press, London, 1952.

POYNTER, J.R., 'The Yo-yo Variations : Initiative and Dependence in Australia's External Relations, 1918–1923', *Historical Studies*, vol. 14, no. 54, 1970, pp. 231–49.

WATT, A., *The Evolution of Australian Foreign Policy, 1938–1965*, Cambridge University Press, London, 1967.

20 The Second World War

CASEY, R.G.C., *Personal Experience, 1939–1946*, Constable, London, 1962.

CHURCHILL, W.S., *The Hinge of Fate*, Cassell, London, 1951.

——, *Their Finest Hour*, Cassell, London, 1949.

CRISP, L.F., *Ben Chifley*, Longmans, Melbourne, 1961.

EDWARDS, C., *Bruce of Melbourne : Man of Two Worlds*, Heinemann, London, 1963.

HASLUCK, P., *The Government and the People, 1939–1941*, Australian War Memorial, Canberra, 1952.

——, *The Government and the People, 1942–1945*, Australian War Memorial, Canberra, 1970. (These two works are vols. 1 & 2 of *Australia in the War of 1939–1945*, Series 4 (Civil).)

MANSERGH, N., *Survey of British Commonwealth Affairs : Problems of Wartime Co-operation and Postwar Change, 1939–1952*, Oxford University Press, London, 1958.

MENZIES, R.G., *Afternoon Light : Some Memories of Men and Events*, Cassell, Melbourne, 1967.

MORAN, C., *Winston Churchill : The Struggle for Survival, 1940–1945* (taken from the diaries of Lord Moran), Constable, London, 1966.

PAGE, E., *Truant Surgeon : The Inside Story of Forty Years of Australian Political Life*, Angus & Robertson, Sydney, 1963.

PALMER, V., *National Portraits*, Melbourne University Press, Melbourne, 1940.

WATT, A., *The Evolution of Australian Foreign Policy, 1938–1965,* Cambridge University Press, London, 1967.

On relations with the U.S.A. :

ESTHUS, R.A., *From Enmity to Alliance: U.S.–Australian Relations, 1931–1941,* University of Washington Press, Seattle, 1964.

On the North African campaigns :

MONTGOMERY OF ALAMEIN, *Avec la VIIIe Armée d'El Alamein à l'Adriatique,* trad. de l'Anglais, Amiot-Dumont, Paris, 1948.

TEDDER, A.W., *With Prejudice : The War Memoirs of Marshal of the Royal Air Force Lord Tedder G.C.B.,* Cassell, London, 1966.

WILMOT, C., *Tobruk 1941 : Capture—Siege—Relief,* Angus & Robertson, Sydney, 1944.

On the war in the Pacific :

GRATTAN, C.H., *The Southwest Pacific Since 1900 : A Modern History. Australia New Zealand The Islands Antarctica,* University of Michigan Press, Ann Arbor, 1963.

——, *The United States and the Southwest Pacific,* Oxford University Press, Melbourne, 1961.

MAIR, L.P., *Australia in New Guinea,* 2nd edn, Melbourne University Press, Melbourne, 1970.

MILLOT, B., *La Guerre du Pacifique,* 2 vols., 1. Le Déferlement Japonais, Déc. 1941—Oct. 1943 ; 2. Le Raz-de-marée Americain (Nov. 1943—Août 1945), Laffont, Paris, 1968.

RIVETT, R.D., *Behind Bamboo : An Inside Story of the Japanese Prison Camps,* Angus & Robertson, Sydney, 1946.

21 The curtain rises (I)

BIRCH, A. and MACMILLAN, D.S. (eds.), *The Sydney Scene, 1788–1960,* Melbourne University Press, Melbourne, 1962.

CRISP, L.F., *Ben Chifley,* Longmans, Melbourne, 1961.

GRATTAN, C.H., *The Southwest Pacific Since 1900 : A Modern History. Australia New Zealand The Islands Antarctica,* University of Michigan Press, Ann Arbor, 1963.

MAYER, H. (ed.), *Australian Politics : A Reader,* Cheshire, Melbourne, 1966.

MENZIES, R.G., *Afternoon Light : Some Memories of Men and Events,* Cassell, Melbourne, 1967.

MURRAY, R., *The Split : Australian Labor in the Fifties,* Cheshire, Melbourne, 1970.

PRINGLE, J.D., *On Second Thoughts : Australian Essays*, Angus & Robertson, Sydney, 1971.

SPRATT, E., *Eddie Ward, Firebrand of East Sydney*, Rigby, Adelaide, 1965.

WALKER, E.R., *The Australian Economy in War and Reconstruction*, Oxford University Press, New York, 1947.

22 The curtain rises (II)
On immigration :

ROBERTS, H. (ed.), *Australia's Immigration Policy* (Papers presented at the 43rd Annual Summer School of the Adult Education and Extension Service of the University of Western Australia), University of Western Australia Press, Nedlands, 1972.

On the mineral discoveries :

BLAINEY, G., *Mines in the Spinifex : The Story of Mount Isa Mines*, rev. edn, Angus & Robertson, Sydney, 1970.

——, *The Rush that Never Ended : A History of Australian Mining*, Melbourne University Press, Melbourne, 1963.

On foreign affairs :

GRATTAN, C.H., *The United States and the Southwest Pacific*, Oxford University Press, Melbourne, 1961.

GREENWOOD, G. and HARPER, N.D. (eds.), *Australia in World Affairs, 1961–1965*, Cheshire, for the Australian Institute of International Affairs, Melbourne, 1968.

MANSERGH, N., *Survey of British Commonwealth Affairs : Problems of Wartime Co-operation and Postwar Change, 1939–1952*, Oxford University Press, London, 1958.

MENZIES, R.G., *Afternoon Light : Some Memories of Men and Events*, Cassell, Melbourne, 1967.

WATT, A., *The Evolution of Australian Foreign Policy, 1938–1965*, Cambridge University Press, London, 1967.

23 Australia today
On political life :

WHITINGTON, D. and CHALMERS, R., *Inside Canberra : A Guide to Australian Federal Politics*, Rigby, Adelaide, 1971.

On institutions :

SAWER, G., *Australian Government Today*, 7th edn, Melbourne University Press, Melbourne, 1961.

On the Aborigines :

HASLUCK, P., *Native Welfare in Australia : Speeches and Addresses*, Paterson Brokensha, Perth, 1953.

On New Guinea :

HASTINGS, P., *New Guinea : Problems and Prospects*, Cheshire, for the Australian Institute of International Affairs, Melbourne, 1969.

On Australian society :

COLEMAN, P. (ed.), *Australian Civilization*, Cheshire, Melbourne, 1962.

COOMBS, H.C., *The Fragile Pattern : Institutions and Man* (The Boyer Lectures, 1970), Australian Broadcasting Commission, Sydney, 1970.

DAVIES, A.F. and ENCEL, S. (eds.), *Australian Society : A Sociological Introduction*, 2nd edn, Cheshire, Melbourne, 1970.

HORNE, D., *The Lucky Country : Australia in the Sixties*, Angus & Robertson, Sydney, 1964.

——, *The Next Australia*, Angus & Robertson, Sydney, 1970.

PRINGLE, J.D., *Australian Accent*, Chatto & Windus, London, 1958.

——, *On Second Thoughts : Australian Essays*, Angus & Robertson, Sydney, 1971.

On Australian housing :

BOYD, R., *Australia's Home : Its Origins, Builders and Occupiers*, Melbourne University Press, Melbourne, 1952.

——, *The Australian Ugliness*, Penguin Books, Ringwood, Vic., 1970 (first published Cheshire, Melbourne, 1960).

24 The moment of choice

ARNDT, H.W., 'Australia and Asia', *Quadrant*, vol. 14, no. 68, 1970, pp. 25–31.

COLEMAN, P. (ed.), *Australian Civilization*, Cheshire, Melbourne, 1962.

COOMBS, H.C., *The Fragile Pattern: Institutions and Man* (The Boyer Lectures, 1970), Australian Broadcasting Commission, Sydney, 1970.

CROCKER, W.R., 'Foreign Policy for Australia', *Institute of Public Affairs Review*, vol. 25, no. 4, 1971, pp. 91–6.

HANCOCK, W.K., 'Then and Now', *Institute of Public Affairs Review*, vol. 22, no. 3, 1968, pp. 90–5.

HORNE, D., *The Lucky Country : Australia in the Sixties*, Angus & Robertson, Sydney, 1964.

——, *The Next Australia*, Angus & Robertson, Sydney, 1970.

LANDRY, L., 'Indonesia and Australia : International Giving—the Road Not Taken', *Quadrant*, vol. 13, no. 61, 1969, pp. 109–16.

MACKIE, J.A.C., 'Indonesia and Australia : The Cultural Agreement—Prospects and Possibilities', *Quadrant*, vol. 13, no. 61, 1969, pp. 117–27.

MAYER, H. (ed.), *Australian Politics : A Reader*, Cheshire, Melbourne, 1966.

PRINGLE, J.D., *Australian Accent*, Chatto & Windus, London, 1958.

——, *On Second Thoughts : Australian Essays*, Angus & Robertson, Sydney, 1971.

ROBERTS, H. (ed.), *Australia's Immigration Policy* (Papers presented at the 43rd Annual Summer School of the Adult Education and Extension Service of the University of Western Australia), University of Western Australia Press, Nedlands, 1972.

Index